Helping Skills

Helping Skills

Facilitating Exploration, Insight, and Action

Fourth Edition

Clara E. Hill

American Psychological Association

Washington, DC

First Printing, January 2014
Second Printing, December 2014
Third Printing, December 2016

Published by
American Psychological Association
750 First Street, NE
Washington, DC 20002
www.apa.org

To order
APA Order Department
P.O. Box 92984
Washington, DC 20090-2984
Tel: (800) 374-2721; Direct: (202) 336-5510
Fax: (202) 336-5502; TDD/TTY: (202) 336-6123
Online: www.apa.org/pubs/books
E-mail: order@apa.org

In the U.K., Europe, Africa, and the Middle East, copies may be ordered from
American Psychological Association
3 Henrietta Street
Covent Garden, London
WC2E 8LU England

Typeset in Meridien by Circle Graphics, Inc., Columbia, MD

Printer: United Book Press, Baltimore, MD
Cover Designer: Minker Design, Sarasota, FL
Cover art: *Breton Girls Dancing, Pont-Aven,* Collection of Mr. and Mrs. Paul Mellon, Photograph Copyright 2001 Board of Trustees, National Gallery of Art, Washington, 1888, oil on canvas, .730 × .927 (28¾ × 36½); framed: .613 × .1.060 × .035 (24⅛ × 41¾ × ⅜). Reprinted with permission.

The opinions and statements published are the responsibility of the authors, and such opinions and statements do not necessarily represent the policies of the American Psychological Association.

Library of Congress Cataloging-in-Publication Data

Hill, Clara E., 1948-
  Helping skills : facilitating exploration, insight, and action / Clara E. Hill. — Fourth edition.
    pages cm
  Includes bibliographical references and index.
  ISBN-13: 978-1-4338-1678-9
  ISBN-10: 1-4338-1678-4
  1. Counseling. 2. Counseling psychology. 3. Helping behavior. I. Title.

  BF636.6.H55 2014
  158.3—dc23
                                    2013033731

British Library Cataloguing-in-Publication Data
A CIP record is available from the British Library.

Printed in the United States of America
Fourth Edition

http://dx.doi.org/10.1037/14345-000

To my husband, Jim Gormally,
my fellow traveler in the process of learning helping skills;
to my children, Kevin and Katie, who have tested my helping skills;
and to my students, who have taught me how to teach helping skills.

Contents

Preface

My interest in training helpers has developed from teaching helping skills classes to undergraduate and graduate students for more than 40 years. When I first taught these courses, I felt frustrated in trying to find the right textbook that would embody my philosophy of helping and address the needs of my students. Few, if any, helping skills texts integrate the importance of affect, cognition, and behavior in the process of change. Some concentrate on feelings while disregarding the role of challenge and action in facilitating critical life changes, whereas others highlight insight at the expense of affective exploration and behavior change. Several popular texts focus solely on a problem-solving approach, which neglects the critical role of affect in helping clients express, understand, and alter that with which they are dissatisfied in their lives. Other books do not provide the crucial theoretical and empirical foundation for the helping skills. To address these limitations, I used the knowledge garnered from my experiences as a student, teacher, counselor, supervisor, and researcher to write a book that teaches helpers to assist clients in exploring their feelings and thoughts, gaining new insights about their problems, and moving toward positive behavior changes.

My Philosophy of Helping

This text introduces an integrated model that is grounded in practice, theory, and research. Grounding the model in practice and theory is important to take advantage of the work of accomplished clinicians and theoreticians who have articulated a rich theoretical knowledge base. Rogers, Freud,

Bowlby, M. Erikson, Mahler, Skinner, Ellis, Beck, and others have provided brilliant insights into the nature of human beings, the mechanisms of change in counseling and therapy, and the techniques for assisting individuals to achieve their potential and accomplish their goals. The three-stage model is grounded in the contributions of these sage theorists, and readers are introduced to the salient aspects of their work.

The model involves three stages: exploration, insight, and action. The exploration stage is based on client-centered theory (e.g., Rogers, 1942, 1951, 1957, 1959). Psychoanalytic and interpersonal theories (e.g., Freud, 1940/1949; Teyber, 2006; Yalom, 1980) form the foundation for the insight stage. The action stage is based on behavioral (e.g., Goldfried & Davison, 1994; Kazdin, 2013; Watson & Tharp, 2006) theories. These major theories are integrated in this three-stage model because all have proven to be effective in helping clients (see Wampold, 2001).

The helping process can be conceptualized as involving moment-by-moment interaction sequences (Hill, 1992). Helpers develop intentions for how they want to help clients. These intentions are based on what they know about clients and what they hope to accomplish with clients at a given time. With these intentions in mind, helpers select verbal and nonverbal skills with which to intervene. In turn, clients react to the interventions in ways that influence how they then choose to behave with helpers. Thus, helping involves not only the overt behaviors but also the cognitive processes of helpers (i.e., intentions) and clients (i.e., reactions). Awareness of intentions assists helpers in selecting effective interventions. In addition, attention to the clients' reactions to the interventions can aid helpers in planning future interventions.

Finally, I sought to write a book that both supports students' development as helpers and provides challenges to facilitate the development of helping skills. Becoming an effective helper is an exciting and challenging process. For some, this undertaking can be life changing. Many students are fascinated by the process of becoming helpers, and they pose thoughtful questions as they struggle to learn the skills and develop confidence in their ability to assist others. Because the focus of this book is on helpers (not clients), I pose many questions that relate to the helpers' development and concomitant feelings and thoughts.

What This Text Does Not Provide

It seems necessary to clarify the focus of this book by also indicating what this text does not provide. It is beyond the scope of this book to provide information about counseling children, families, or clients who have serious emotional or psychological difficulties. Although the helping skills taught in this book are crucial and form the foundation for work with all these groups, helpers will need much more extensive and specialized training before they will be qualified to work with these groups.

Furthermore, I do not address the diagnosis of psychological problems or identify characteristics of psychopathology, which are two important topics that require extensive additional training. I encourage helpers to pursue additional training in assessment and psychopathology after developing a working knowledge of basic helping skills. I believe that all helpers, even those working with healthy populations, should be able to recognize serious psychological disorders. This level of knowledge aids helpers in making appropriate referrals and working only with clients they have been trained to assist.

Goals for This Book

I have several goals for this book. After reading it, students should be able to articulate the principles of the integrated three-stage model of helping as well as the theoretical and research foundations underlying this model. They should demonstrate an understanding of the interactional sequences of helping, including the intentions that helpers have for interventions with clients, the helping skills that are commensurate with these intentions, the possible reactions and behaviors demonstrated by clients, and the means through which helpers evaluate the interventions used. In addition, readers should gain a better understanding of themselves in relation to becoming helpers, including their thoughts about helping as well as their strengths and areas for continued growth. Finally, I hope to instill enthusiasm for the process of learning to help others—an enterprise that is certain to provide countless challenges and rewards throughout a lifetime.

Changes in the Fourth Edition

I continue to modify the model as I teach and do research on helping skills. I have also obtained extensive feedback from students about what they find helpful. The model feels like a living thing because of how I continually find ways to improve it. The fourth edition of this book differs from the first three editions in several ways:

- I have added a separate chapter on self-awareness. Although covered before, I wanted to highlight this topic given its importance for helper growth.

- I have also added a separate chapter on cultural awareness. Students have been hungry for more information about the role of culture in the helping process. Although we are at an early stage in terms of understanding culture, we need to be aware of its role and sensitive to different reactions of clients based on their cultural backgrounds.
- I have added a greater variety of methods that helpers can use to challenge in the chapter on that topic.
- I continue to try to make the action stage clearer and easier to use.
- A summary of a specific research study has been added to each chapter, with highlights about how the results enhance our understanding of the role of helping skills in the helping process.
- There is now a glossary of the key words so that readers can refer to it when confused by some of the jargon. Much of learning any new system involves learning the language, so we want to make this as easy as possible.

Resources

As with the previous editions, this fourth edition of *Helping Skills* offers a Web-based "Instructor and Student Resource Guide" (http://pubs.apa. org/books/supp/hill4), the student portion of which features a dozen Web Forms (in downloadable PDFs) that are referred to throughout this text to assist students in evaluating their helping skills and helper–client sessions. The Web Forms page also includes an Emotion Words Checklist—a downloadable version of this edition's Exhibit 9.2 (see Chapter 9)—that students have found helpful to have handy in a printed format for easy reference during the exploration stage of a helper–client relationship. In addition, the student resources section of the *Helping Skills* Web site includes downloadable versions of the Labs for various chapters, as well as Practice Exercises for each of the skills chapters of the book.

In addition, two DVDs are available to demonstrate the model. *Helping Skills in Practice: A Three-Stage Model* was created to illustrate the three stages of working with a client struggling with concerns related to childhood, eating, and self-esteem. *Dream Work in Practice* was created to illustrate the three stages with a client who had a troubling recurrent dream. Both DVDs are available from the American Psychological Association.

Acknowledgments

I am grateful to the following students who worked with me extensively in researching different aspects of the different editions of this book: Jennifer Dahne, Judith Gerstenblith, Jennifer Jeffery, and Eric Spiegel.

I am also grateful to the many people who have read selected chapters or all of the book and provided valuable feedback on at least one of the editions: Rebecca Adams, Margaret Barott, Kevin Cramer, Elizabeth Doschek, Jessica England, Lisa Flores, Suzanne Friedman, Judy Gerstenblith, Melissa Goates, Julie Goldberg, Jim Gormally, Allison Grolnick, Kelly Hennessey, Beth Haverkamp, Jeff Hayes, Debby Herbenick, Pamela Highlen, Merris Hollingworth, Gloria Huh, Skyler Jackson, Ian Kellems, Kathryn Kline, Sarah Knox, Misty Kolchakian, Jim Lichtenberg, Rayna Markin, John Norcross, Kathy O'Brien, Sheetal Patel, David Petersen, Jennifer Robinson, Missy Roffman, Katherine Ross, Pat Spangler, Jessica Stahl, Nicole Taylor, Barbara Thompson, Linda Tipton, Terry Tracey, Jonathan Walker, Heather Walton, and Elizabeth Nutt Williams. There are also numerous anonymous reviewers who have read and reviewed the book for the American Psychological Association and provided invaluable feedback.

I have profited considerably from the editorial feedback, guidance, and encouragement of Beth Beisel, Dan Brachtesende, Amy Clarke, Beth Hatch, Phuong Huynh, Linda McCarter, Peter Pavilionis, and Susan Reynolds—all from the American Psychological Association Books program—on the various editions of the book.

I am most indebted to the many students in my undergraduate course in helping skills and graduate course in theories and strategies of counseling over the past several years. They have taught me a tremendous amount about how to teach helping skills with their willingness to challenge my ideas, offering thoughtful perspectives on the process of becoming helpers and providing examples for the text. I tried out all the chapters and the lab exercises on many classes before including them in the book. Finally, and with much gratitude, I recognize and acknowledge my therapists, professors, and supervisors, who served as wonderful models for how to use helping skills and provided much encouragement throughout my process of becoming a helper. I particularly want to acknowledge Bill Anthony (who studied with Robert Carkhuff), from whom I first learned helping skills many years ago in graduate school. I clearly recall the heady times of coming to believe that I could help clients if I applied the helping skills.

OVERVIEW

Introduction to Helping

1

Nothing in life is achieved without effort, daring to take risks, and often some suffering.

—*Erich Fromm*

Angeli was a stellar student and athlete. She was president of her high school class and had been accepted into an elite eastern university. By any standard, she was an exceptional and talented individual with much promise. However, after arriving at college, Angeli began to feel sad. Much to the dismay of her family, teachers, and friends, she lost interest in interacting with others, studying for her classes, and attending track practice. Angeli's track coach encouraged her to meet with a helper, who helped Angeli explore her feelings and gain understanding of the issues underlying her sadness and inactivity. Angeli felt supported, cared for, and challenged by her helper. The helping relationship enabled her to express, understand, struggle with, and overcome the feelings of inadequacy, loneliness, and loss that emerged when she left home for college.

A s you read about Angeli and think about what it would be like to be her helper, you may have contradictory thoughts and feelings. You may feel confident that you could help someone like Angeli because you have listened to and advised friends

http://dx.doi.org/10.1037/14345-001

Helping Skills: Facilitating Exploration, Insight, and Action, Fourth Edition, by C. E. Hill

and family members about similar problems. But you may also feel anxiety about knowing how to help her explore her feelings, gain understanding, and work to get back her confidence.

If you are interested in learning more about the skills that would help you work with someone like Angeli, you have come to the right place. The first purpose of this book is to provide you with a theoretical framework that you can use to approach the helping process. The second purpose is to teach you specific skills to use in sessions with clients to help them explore, gain insight, and make changes in their lives. The third purpose is to get you started in the process of coming to think of yourself as a helper.

This chapter provides an introduction to the helping process, defines helping, and reviews facilitative and problematic aspects of helping. I talk about what makes people seek out professional helpers, and that leads naturally to a discussion about the effectiveness of helping. Next, I introduce the idea of becoming a helper, specifically exploring the healthy and unhealthy motivators for helping other people. Finally, I describe the organization of the book and discuss how it can best be used.

Welcome aboard! I hope you enjoy learning and using helping skills as much as I have.

What Is Helping?

Helping is a broad and generic term that includes the assistance provided by a variety of individuals, such as friends, family, counselors, psychotherapists, and human service providers. I use this broad term (rather than the more specific terms *counseling* and *psychotherapy*) because not everyone learning these skills is in a program that offers training and credentialing to become a mental health professional. Of course, these same skills are used by counselors and psychotherapists, but you cannot call yourself a counselor or psychotherapist until you have had further training, practice, and supervision and pass a credentialing examination.

Throughout this book, then, the term *helper* refers to the individual providing assistance, and the term *client* refers to the person receiving support. *Helping* can be defined as one person assisting another in exploring feelings, gaining insight, and making changes in his or her life. Helpers and clients work together to achieve these outcomes, with helpers guiding the process and clients deciding what, when, and how they want to change.

When I talk in this book about trainees who are learning helping skills practicing with each other or with volunteer clients, I refer to the process as *helping*. In contrast, when I talk about clients seeking help from professionals, I use instead the terms *counseling* (or *counselor*) and *psychotherapy* (or *therapist* or *psychotherapist*).

Students often ask about the differences between counseling and psychotherapy. At times, the two are differentiated by length of treatment (counseling may have fewer sessions than does psychotherapy), by clientele (counseling is more often used with relatively "healthy" individuals who have issues with adjustment, whereas psychotherapy serves those who have more serious pathology or unresolved conflicts), by qualifications of the provider (counselors may have master's or doctoral degrees, whereas psychotherapists tend to be doctoral-level practitioners), and by types of problems presented in sessions (counseling may deal with development and life transition issues, whereas psychotherapy may address more serious psychological disturbances). However, in fact, I know of no empirical evidence that counseling and psychotherapy can be distinguished in terms of the processes or outcomes.

Is Psychotherapy Effective?

Investigators have overwhelmingly concluded that psychotherapy is generally helpful. Most clients improve by the end of psychotherapy. Specifically, Wampold (2001), in his review of the literature, found that the average client who was in psychotherapy was psychologically healthier than were 79% of untreated individuals. Wampold concluded that "psychotherapy is remarkably efficacious" (p. 71).

Once researchers established conclusively that psychotherapy in general is indeed helpful, they began to examine the relative effectiveness of different types of therapy. To date, hundreds of studies have compared different types of treatment (e.g., client-centered, psychodynamic, cognitive–behavioral, experiential), but no one type of therapy has been found to be more effective than others (Lambert, 2013; Wampold, 2001; Wampold et al., 1997). Wampold noted, however, that the treatments studied were all sanctioned forms of treatment rather than fringe or quack forms of treatment, so these results may not hold for nonmainstream treatments. Similarly, no differences have been found between individual and group treatments (Piper, 2008; M. L. Smith, Glass, & Miller, 1980). The findings from this area of research have been humorously summarized using the dodo bird verdict from *Alice in Wonderland:* "Everyone has won and all must have prizes" (Carroll, 1865/1962, p. 412).

It is probably hard to understand how therapies that are so different can all lead to the same outcomes. Many different reasons have been proposed for the lack of differences across approaches. The most currently popular explanation is that factors involved in all types of mainstream approaches (i.e., common factors) lead to positive outcomes. Frank and Frank (1991) discussed six factors that are common across psychotherapies: the therapeutic relationship, instillation of hope, new learning experiences, emotional arousal, enhancement of mastery or self-efficacy, and opportunities for practice. Thus, although therapists from different orientations espouse different philosophies and use somewhat different skills, the most important factor may be what therapists do in common.

Another explanation for the lack of differences among psychotherapeutic approaches is that client and therapist factors explain more of the variance than do treatment types (again, see Wampold, 2001). Thus, differences among therapists and clients may be more important than the approach used.

Yet another explanation (and one that I personally prefer) is that our research is still at a rather primitive state and that our tools for examining the process and outcome of therapy are not sophisticated enough to pick up the differences between approaches. It is quite possible that all approaches can be helpful and lead to similar outcomes but do so through different mechanisms. For example, experiential therapy might heal through allowing deep immersion into feelings, which then leads the client to change thoughts and behaviors. By contrast, cognitive–behavioral therapy might begin with changes in thoughts and behaviors, which in turn lead to a change in emotions. Furthermore, different therapists and clients may prefer approaches that fit with their worldviews and personality styles.

Another interesting line of research involves how many psychotherapy sessions are needed to reduce psychological distress and return the client to normal psychological functioning (e.g., Grissom, Lyons, & Lutz, 2002; Howard, Lueger, Maling, & Martinovich, 1993; Kopta, Howard, Lowry, & Beutler, 1994). In their reviews of a large number of studies, these researchers proposed three phases of the psychotherapeutic recovery process. In the first phase, clients change rapidly in terms of feeling subjectively better. In the second, slower phase, there is a remediation of symptoms such as depression and anxiety. In the third and slowest phase, there is rehabilitation of troublesome, maladaptive behaviors that interfere with life functioning in areas such as family and work. Clients with minimal distress improve fairly quickly, whereas clients with chronic characterological problems (i.e., innate, severe, ongoing, and difficult-to-treat disorders) require the greatest number of sessions to return to normal functioning.

In his review, Lambert (2013) found that 50% of clients who were in the dysfunctional range at the beginning of therapy achieved clinically significant change after 20 sessions of therapy. He noted, however, that it takes more than 50 sessions for 75% of initially dysfunctional clients to reach clinically significant change. It is interesting that positive mental health is rarely mentioned in these studies but is an important index of outcome.

Facilitative Aspects of Helping

There are a number of ways in which helping can be facilitative. For people in emotional pain, helping can provide *support and relief.* For example, Jillian and Jesse went to couples counseling because Jillian had been involved in a sexual relationship with a colleague. Both Jillian and Jesse were extremely hurt and felt angry with each other. Positive changes in their relationship came after months of working on communication skills, receiving assistance in exploring feelings, understanding the factors related to the affair, and learning how to work proactively to improve their relationship. After several sessions, Jillian and Jesse were able to communicate their feelings more openly, grieve the loss of trust in their relationship, and move toward rebuilding their lives as a cohesive and caring couple. They felt that their therapist had been supportive, and they felt relief from the problems for which they sought therapy.

Through the process of helping, clients can also *gain insight,* such that they come to understand themselves in new ways. For example, in her book about serving as a psychologist in Iraq, Kraft (2007) described the process of therapy working with a soldier who could not walk even though the medical doctors found no physiological reason for this inability (a condition called *conversion hysteria*). After establishing a good relationship with the soldier, Kraft was able to help the soldier talk about losing a friend who died trying to shield him from danger. Once the soldier gained insight into the reason for his symptom, he was able to walk again. It is interesting to note that many of Freud's first patients similarly had conversion hysteria and were healed through catharsis and insight.

In addition, helping can assist individuals in dealing with *existential concerns* (i.e., who am I, where am I going, and what do I want out of life?). As Socrates said, "The unexamined life is not worth living." Helping can promote proactive involvement in life when these questions are asked, reflected on, and answered. For example, Max was referred for helping because of failing grades, poor peer relationships, and generalized sadness. After several sessions, Max began to address critical questions regarding how he might live his life, the fears he often confronts within himself, and the salience of his relationships with others. Helping provided him with an opportunity to look within himself, discover what was important, and then make decisions about how to change his unhealthy behaviors.

Moreover, clients can *learn skills* needed to live more effectively and reach their potential. These skills may include learning how to communicate with others, practicing ways to resolve conflicts, becoming more assertive, identifying decision-making strategies, studying more effectively, learning to relax, or changing unhealthy habits (e.g., rarely exercising; having unprotected, anonymous sex). Often, these skills can alleviate the powerlessness that individuals feel when they are unable to communicate their emotions directly and can assist clients in engaging more fully in their lives.

Helping can also assist individuals in *making decisions* about the direction of their lives. The most effective helpers have the ability to assist individuals in determining goals that are consistent with their dreams, values, and abilities. For example, Mai Lin came to counseling because she was uncertain about whether she should move far away from her family and end her relationship with her live-in boyfriend. She described her current situation and asked the helper to tell her what the best path for her would be. After dealing with her anger and frustration at the helper for not providing the answers, Mai Lin was able to explore her unwillingness to take responsibility for the direction of her life and her reluctance to address the questions that plagued her. She contemplated her fear of taking action and of making wrong decisions and connected this with feelings of helplessness she had experienced as a child of a battered woman. Further exploration of thoughts, feelings, and behaviors provided her with the desire to make small decisions (with the support and encouragement of her helper). Soon, Mai Lin was able to progress to more challenging decisions (e.g., ending her romantic relationship, moving across the country alone to explore her independence and to understand herself better).

An additional facilitative aspect of helping involves helpers *providing feedback* about how clients appear to others, information that others might hesitate to provide. For example, a client who is having difficulty maintaining relationships may be able to hear (from the helper) that he appears dependent and needy in sessions and may want to examine whether these behaviors are present in other relationships. When phrased in a gentle manner, honest feedback can sometimes be extremely helpful in motivating individuals to change.

Helping also can enable a client to *experience a healthy, nondamaging, intimate relationship with another person.* Sometimes the helping process involves a corrective relational experience (something like reparenting) in that a caring relationship with a helper alleviates some of the hurtful and unhealthy interactions experienced with important figures early in life. For example, Kondja came to helping because she felt depressed and lacked direction in her life. She believed that her mother did not want her as a child, and she cried when she saw mothers and daughters who were connected and loving with one another. Kondja had been in a series of relationships in which she felt ignored, alone, uncared for, and discounted. During the helping process, Kondja experienced the helper as unconditionally accepting, actively listening, and genuinely caring. The development of a supportive relationship with a helper assisted Kondja in healing past wounds, drinking less alcohol to numb her feelings, and developing healthy relationships in which she valued herself enough to ensure that her needs were met.

Finally, effective helping teaches clients to *function on their own*. Similar to the way children grow up and leave their parents, clients also need to leave their helpers after engaging in the helping process. Perhaps some of you have tried to teach another person to skate: You hold the person up, and she or he hangs on while making a first attempt at skating. In time, the person begins to skate alone. The steps that the learner makes on his or her own are rewarding not only for the learner but also for you as the teacher. The same is true with helping: Providing the initial support and teaching the skills are most effective when individuals internalize the messages and take off on their own.

Problematic Aspects of Helping

Although helping is usually beneficial, there are a few potentially problematic aspects. Sometimes helping can provide *just enough relief to enable people to stay in maladaptive situations or relationships.* For example, battered women's shelters provide needed safety and security to abused women and their children. However, some shelter workers have observed that occasionally they provide just enough assistance to enable women to return to the abusive situation. When the workers in one shelter confronted this "enabling" in themselves and discussed these behaviors with the residents, some of the battered women were able to identify their pattern of seeking shelter during the abusive periods and returning home in the "honeymoon" period. Without this insight, helping could have enabled some of the women to continue in a potentially deadly cycle.

Another potential problem is that helping can create *dependency* if clients rely too much on their helpers for support and feel unable to explore feelings or make changes in their lives without assistance from the helper. For example, Kathleen might decline a spontaneous invitation to join her new partner's family on Cape Cod for a week because her helper is on vacation and unavailable for consultation. Helpers sometimes facilitate dependency by providing clients with "the answers" to their problems (e.g., if her helper told Kathleen not to go to Cape Cod). Effective helpers understand that providing the answers does not typically help clients; rather, most clients need to participate actively in a process whereby they uncover new insights and discover which actions feel best for themselves. This strategy works because only clients fully know the situations, experience the associated feelings, and have the best answers to the presenting problems. In addition, advising others may be problematic when the solution does not fit with what they want or think they need. Many of us have made suggestions to family members or friends about how to handle difficult situations, only to find that our advice was not exactly what they wanted to hear. For example, a helper advised a client to stay away from her boyfriend who broke up with her because he was not good enough for her. Although the client was eager at the time to hear about how rotten the boyfriend was, she resented the helper's critical words about her sweetheart when they later got back together.

In addition, *helpers' personal issues sometimes place them at risk for encouraging dependency in those they assist.* For helpers who are lonely and isolated, their clients' dependency may fulfill personal needs that are not being met elsewhere. Helpers who have not developed a network of social support and personal relationships may be at special risk of encouraging their clients to rely extensively on them.

Another problematic aspect of helping emerges when *helpers unduly impose personal or societal values on their clients* (McWhirter, 1994). Although all of us have values that shape who we are, the goal of helping is to encourage clients to explore and choose their own values. Examples of undue influence are when a helping professional attempts to alter the sexual orientation of people who are lesbian, gay, or bisexual (Haldeman, 2002); advises parents to raise their children in a certain religion because the helper believes that problems in families result from children not having a strong religious foundation; or states that women should not work outside the home because they take jobs away from qualified men who have families to raise. These examples all involve the helper attempting to force his or her values on the client.

Values can also be imposed at a more subtle level. In an investigation of Carl Rogers providing therapy, Truax (1966) found that in fact Rogers was more reinforcing of some client behaviors than others. For example, Rogers responded with more empathy and warmth when the client expressed insight, but with less empathy and warmth when the client was ambiguous. In other words, even Rogers, who worked hard to be accepting and empathic, demonstrated that he valued certain client behaviors over others. These results show that it is difficult to leave our biases behind.

It can also be problematic when *helpers work outside their areas of competence* (e.g., working with someone who has substance abuse but not having knowledge about that area). Similarly, helpers sometimes try to force clients to explore difficult topics, such as sexual abuse, without making sure that clients feel safe and have the necessary emotional regulation skills to explore such topics. Finally, it can be difficult when helpers are paired with clients with whom they do not "click." As in friendships, one needs to have a certain "clicking" with one's helper to feel comfortable enough to talk about one's problems. Without that matching, clients can become discouraged and actually feel more distressed because they might feel that no one can understand and help them.

When Do People Seek Help From Others?

Two factors seem to be necessary for people to seek help (Gross & McMullen, 1983). First, a person must become aware that she or he is in pain or is facing a difficult situation and then must perceive her or his feelings or situation as being problematic. Obviously, the perception of pain varies from person to person, such that what is unbearable for one person is easily tolerated or ignored by another person.

Second, the pain must be greater than the perceived barriers to seeking help. Sometimes the barriers involve practical considerations, such as the time or money required to obtain help; but often the obstacles are emotional and can include fears about exploring problems deeply or concerns about the opinions of others regarding people who seek therapy.

Many people hesitate to seek professional help (Gross & McMullen, 1983) because they feel embarrassed or ashamed about asking for assistance or believe that seeking help constitutes emotional weakness or inadequacy (Shapiro, 1984). Many Americans, for example, believe that individuals should rely solely on themselves and that all problems should be solved individually. Given these beliefs, it is not surprising that researchers have found that people seek help first from friends and family members and only last from professionals (Snyder, Hill, & Derksen, 1972; Tinsley, de St. Aubin, & Brown, 1982; Webster & Fretz, 1978).

Some people are concerned about talking with others because they feel that no one else can possibly understand their situation (e.g., Thomas thought that no one could understand his experience growing up in a religious cult). Others fear a punitive response or a value judgment regarding their thoughts, feelings, or actions (e.g., Candace felt that she would be judged for having had two abortions). Furthermore, some people may be concerned that they will be labeled *mentally ill* and thus be subject to the many negative stereotypes and stigma associated with this label (Hill et al., 2012; D. Sue, Sue, & Sue, 1994). Some clients may be hesitant to seek therapy because they rely on their insurance companies to pay for therapy: They may be concerned that the stigma associated with receiving therapy could have negative ramifications for obtaining insurance or employment in the future.

For example, Conchita came to her first session of psychotherapy because she was experiencing multiple stressors: Her mother had committed suicide 3 years earlier, her sister had been diagnosed with depression, she was failing all of her courses (previously, she had been an *A* student), her first serious boyfriend had broken up with her, and she was pregnant. For some time, Conchita had felt that she should handle her problems by herself because she feared what others might think of her if they knew that she needed to see a therapist. Moreover, she was on a limited budget and was reluctant to pay for therapy. However, Conchita had begun to feel that she could no longer cope with her problems by herself. Her brother had gone to a therapist and felt better, so she thought that going to a therapist might work for her. Thus, Conchita sought help because she perceived herself as having problems and she believed that the potential benefits associated with therapy (e.g., emotional support, assistance with coping) outweighed the costs (e.g., financial expense, perceived stigma).

Individuals in considerable pain who are able to admit their need for psychological assistance have made significant progress toward obtaining the help they need. Support from friends and family can provide the encouragement these individuals need to contact trained helpers (Gourash, 1978). For example, Joe was reluctant to seek help after his wife of 40 years died. His friends and children encouraged him to attend a support group for adults who had lost their partners. Although initially reluctant, Joe was so upset about his loss that he agreed to participate in the group sessions if his daughters would accompany him. The support his family and friends provided enabled Joe to access the help that he needed.

Helpers can work to change negative attitudes about seeking professional psychological assistance in our society. We can begin by seeking help ourselves and encouraging others to seek help when needed. We can also work to initiate and support legislation for additional mental health benefits. In addition, we can work to educate the public by publicizing information about mental health treatments. Finally, we can do research to discover more about the process and outcome of helping endeavors and disseminate these research findings to the public.

On Becoming a Helper

The model I promote in this fourth edition of *Helping Skills* describes three components to being a successful helper: helping skills, self-awareness, and a facilitative attitude. See Figure 1.1 for the connections among these three components.

I propose first of all, however, that the "wannabe helper" begins with a natural inclination toward helping. She or he has taken on a helping role in many situations early in life, friends and family find him or her to be helpful, and she or he has emotional intelligence along with a passion for helping others. As a part of helping others, the wannabe helper has naturally learned communication skills that are helpful, although the person may not be aware of how she or he comes across to others and can sharpen the skills.

This natural inclination is augmented by learning and practicing helping skills until they become an integral part of who we are, even when those behaviors initially feel awkward and forced. Many effective helpers have stories about their initial attempts at assisting others. For example, when one person first started studying helping behaviors, her father was undergoing heart surgery. She spoke with him every day and asked him how he was feeling. After weeks of this, he asked her whether she really wanted to know how he was feeling. "Finally!" she thought, "he'll share his innermost feelings with me." Her father

FIGURE 1.1

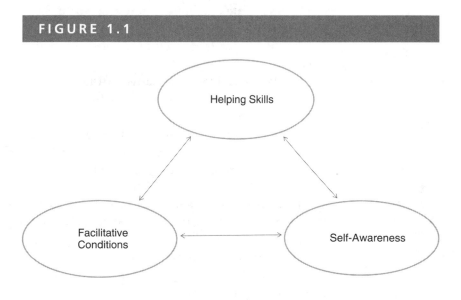

Components needed for effective helping.

said he was feeling as though he liked her a lot more before she began studying helping skills.

Many of your friends and family may have similar reactions as you begin to learn helping skills. This may initially be discouraging, but it may help to know that most effective helpers practice these behaviors for many years before comfortably integrating them into their interactions with clients. In fact, some helpers discover that during the process of becoming a helper, their helping skills and confidence get worse before they get better. This down-and-up pattern makes sense given that trainees learn that not all of their old communication styles work, and they feel temporarily awkward until the new patterns become integrated into their own personal style. Similarly, Goldfried (2012) talked about how, when learning a new behavior, people move from unconscious incompetence (i.e., they are not aware of what they do not know or cannot do) to conscious incompetence (i.e., they become aware that they are not very good at the skills and thus their confidence dips) to conscious competence (i.e., they become skilled but behave in a self-conscious manner) to unconscious competence (i.e., the skills recede into the background, and they have increased self-efficacy).

In addition to the natural inclination and knowledge of skills, helpers must have self-awareness. Chapter 4 describes self-awareness as both a trait (i.e., self-knowledge and self-insight about general personality characteristics or motivations) and a state (i.e., an in-the-moment understanding of what one is feeling and perceiving). Self-awareness is crucial so that helpers know what is going on inside themselves and can then separate out how they are reacting to clients. Otherwise, helpers might act out on impulses and reactions of which they are unaware and harm clients. Hence, self-awareness seems to be a foundation for effective interventions.

Similarly, having a facilitative attitude toward the specific client in the specific moment is a necessary foundation. Facilitative attitudes include empathy, warmth, genuineness, compassion, and nonjudgmentalness. These facilitative conditions are not something that helpers possess generally but rather are something that helpers feel in the moment toward specific people. These facilitative conditions naturally fluctuate across and within clients.

This model suggests that some people are more oriented than others toward becoming helpers. These people then work to gain general self-knowledge about who they are as people and as helpers, and they work to become more skilled as helpers. And then within a specific session with a client, they work to become aware of feelings and perceptions, and they strive to have a facilitative attitude.

In other words, it is not enough just to know the skills, because skills implemented without self-awareness and facilitative attitudes would be noxious and unhelpful. Likewise, having just self-awareness and a facilitative attitude would be nice, but it would not be very helpful, because the person would not know how to communicate and intervene with clients. Thus, helpers need to be self-aware so as not to inappropriately use clients, they need to genuinely care about the client, and they need to know how to use helping skills to help clients.

Overview of This Book

ORGANIZATION

The second chapter in Part I of this book provides an overview of the helping process in terms of the three-stage model and a description of the components of helping. Chapter 3 provides an overview of ethical issues involved in helping. Chapter 4 involves a discussion of self-awareness (including both self-knowledge and in-the-moment awareness). Chapter 5 introduces the important topic of cultural awareness.

Parts II, III, and IV present more description of the exploration, insight, and action stages, respectively. In each part, an overview chapter highlights the theoretical foundation and the goals of the stage. The chapters that follow the overview chapter focus on skills that can be used to accomplish specific goals within the given stage. At the end of each part, a chapter addresses the integration of the skills taught for that stage and presents clinical issues that arise in implementing the stage. Finally, Part V involves integrating the skills into ideas for how to conduct sessions with clients. Issues that arise in helping sessions (e.g., beginning a session, termination) are discussed.

Please note that a lot of examples are used throughout the book to make the points come to life. Some examples are based on real people (names have been changed to protect the identities of those involved); other examples are completely fictitious, created to illustrate a given point.

RESEARCH SUMMARIES

In each of the chapters, there is a special section summarizing the results of an applicable research investigation. Given the importance of an evidence base for helping, some knowledge of research studies is valuable. I encourage readers to study these research summaries carefully and think about the evidence. In addition, given that the establishment of an empirical foundation is in its infancy, I strongly encourage readers to conduct research of their own so that we can have evidence about how to modify psychotherapy and training.

EXPERIENTIAL COMPONENT

Reading about helping skills is important, but reading alone will not make you an effective helper. Many students have said that when they did the reading, the skills sounded easy, but when they tried to actually practice doing the skills, they came to realize how difficult it is to use them and use them effectively.

Acquiring extensive knowledge about helping, although important, is only the first step in your journey toward helping others. Probably the best way for you to learn the skills is first to read and study the text and then try to apply what you have learned by answering questions about the material and by participating in practice helping exercises and lab experiences. The following sections describe the ways in which you can use this book to maximize your growth as a helper.

What Do You Think?

Several questions are provided at the end of each chapter to stimulate your thinking about the text material. I strongly feel that it is important for students to debate the issues raised in this book rather than slavishly accepting everything written here. There are few hard-and-fast "truths" or rules related to helping skills; rather, many of the issues are matters of taste, style, or art, and trainees need to think for themselves about how they want to be as helpers. I encourage you to contemplate each question and discuss your answers with your classmates.

Practice Exercises

Practice exercises provide readers with the opportunity to think about and formulate responses to hypothetical client situations before practicing the skills in the lab setting. You can practice by downloading the PDF of the practice exercise from the student resources area of the *Helping Skills* (4th ed.) website (http://pubs.apa.org/books/supp/hill4), writing down an intervention for each client situation on the Practice Exercise sheet, and then comparing your answers with the suggestions for possible responses (remembering that these are just suggestions).

Laboratories

The companion website for this book (http://pubs.apa.org/books/supp/hill4) contains downloadable lab exercises so that beginning helpers can practice helping skills in dyads or small groups. These labs are ones that I have used over the years in both my undergraduate- and graduate-level helping skills classes, so they have been tested and seem to work (although of course, instructors should feel free to modify these labs to fit their own preferences and situations). You can download the labs from the student resources area of the website.

During labs, helpers are asked to practice the skills with peers who act as clients presenting real or role-played problems. Observers take careful notes and attend to the helper's ability to deliver a particular skill, so that they can provide feedback to the helper. Thus, everyone has an opportunity to experience the roles of helper, client, and observer for each skill. At the end of each lab in the personal reflections section, students are asked to think about their ongoing development as helpers.

Disclosure During Lab Exercises

The success of the lab experiences depends partly on the participants' willingness to reveal information about personal topics. It is preferable for participants to discuss personal topics for two reasons. First, helpers have difficulty learning what is effective when "clients" are not responding genuinely. Second, "clients" often are unable to provide useful feedback to helpers about what is helpful and how the interventions feel if they are not discussing real problems. When role-playing, "clients" are often more involved in trying to think of how the person they are pretending to be might feel or behave than in immersing themselves in the immediate experience.

As clients, however, students should disclose only about easy, safe topics. Students should never disclose about deep topics, even if they are comfortable disclosing, because their classmates will not be comfortable trying to help them, and it takes the focus too much off the helper learning helping skills and on the helper trying to help the client. At times, students might start talking about an issue they think is safe but then become uncomfortable, either because of the depth of the topic or because they do not feel comfortable with the helper. I stress that students always have the right (without jeopardy or prejudice) to indicate that they choose not to explore a particular issue further.

At this point, it may be helpful to note that the "Ethical Principles of Psychologists and Code of Conduct" (American Psychological Association, 2010, Standard 7.04) indicates that

> psychologists do not require students or supervisees to disclose personal information in course- or program-related activities, either orally or in writing, regarding sexual history, history of abuse and neglect, psychological treatment and relationships with parents, peers and spouses or significant others except if (1) the program or training facility has clearly identified this requirement in its admissions and program materials or (2) the

information is necessary to evaluate or obtain assistance for students whose personal problems could reasonably be judged to be preventing them from performing their training- or professionally related activities in a competent manner or posing a threat to the students or others. (p. 9)

This guideline was established to educate people about the perils of requiring disclosure. Thus, although I recommend easy, safe, nondeep disclosure because it typically facilitates the training process, I urge both instructors and students to be alert for possible negative effects.

If students are not willing to disclose personal information, they can role-play a hypothetical client. In such cases, they should not reveal whether the problem is role-played or real—in this way no one ever knows whether the person is actually disclosing or whether the problem is role-played, thus preserving confidentiality.

Exhibit 1.1 provides topics that students have discussed. Although a topic may be "safe" for many people, it may not be comfortable for an individual student, so trainees must think about what they want to discuss. Students may want to refer to this list throughout the semester when a topic is needed for the lab exercises.

Confidentiality During Lab Exercises

Although practice sessions might seem somewhat artificial, the information shared is personal and should be treated in a confidential manner. Helpers should not disclose information shared in practice sessions without the permission of the client. Specifically, helpers should only discuss the material presented in helping sessions with their supervisors and classmates, and then only when it relates to developing their helping skills. When one respects clients, they typically respond by sharing personal information and delving into their thoughts and feelings. Confidentiality of shared information thus provides a foundation for respectful interactions with others (see extended discussion of ethical issues related to confidentiality in Chapter 3).

Benefits of Being a Volunteer Client

The primary focus of the lab experiences is on the helper learning the helping skills. However, students often report that it is beneficial to talk about their concerns when they participate in the client role and that the experience of being a client provided them with firsthand exposure as to how it feels to receive the various helping skills. Moreover, students often develop empathy with their clients after having experienced what is involved in being a client. Being a participant in counseling allows students to experience "the other side" of helping and

EXHIBIT 1.1

Topics for Volunteer Clients to Talk About in the Labs

Ideal Topics
  Anxieties about learning helping skills
  Worries about performance of helping skills
  Academic issues (e.g., studying, test anxiety)
  Career; future plans
  Choosing a major or graduate program
  Pets
  Problems at work
  Public-speaking anxiety
  Roommate issues
  Romantic relationships
  Feelings about technology
  Happy childhood memories
  Hobbies and extracurricular activities
  Problems with health
Relatively Safe Topics Depending on Client
  Minor family issues
  Autonomy–independence struggles
  Minor relationship concerns
  High school experiences
  Personal views on alcohol and drugs
  Existential concerns (e.g., Who am I? What is the meaning of life,
    death?)
  Financial difficulties
  Problems with physical appearance
  Moral dilemmas
Topics to Be Avoided
  Substance abuse
  Fears about going crazy
  Traumas (e.g., sexual or physical abuse, rape, victimization, child abuse,
    serious medical condition)
  Serious problems in romantic relationships
  Shameful feelings
  Serious family disputes
  Sex
  Sexual abuse
  Suicidal thoughts
  Murderous thoughts

to gain respect for the courage clients exhibit when they share their concerns with their helpers. In addition, beginning helpers often report that watching their helpers provide helping skills can teach them about effective (and ineffective) helping techniques.

I stress, though, that being a client in practice helping sessions should not be used as a substitute for seeking counseling or therapy.

Students experiencing personal distress should seek help from a trained and qualified counselor or therapist. University counseling centers or health services often provide counseling services for college students at little or no cost and offer an excellent opportunity for students to learn more about themselves and address salient issues.

Problems Related to Practicing Skills With Friends During the Labs

Another important issue involves the recognition that problems can occur when practicing helping skills with classmates who are friends or acquaintances. During helping sessions with friends, it is a good idea for helpers to pretend that they know nothing about their friend and respond only to what the "client" actually reveals during the helping session. Although it is challenging to discount relevant information, students in my classes have found the lab exercises easier to perform if they consider only information provided in the practice helping session. For example, Nancy was practicing her helping skills with her friend, Katrina, who was bemoaning the fact that her partner had not called her in 2 weeks. Although Nancy knew that Katrina's partner had not called because Katrina had dated someone else, she focused only on Katrina's expressed feelings related to not having contact with her partner. In Chapter 3, I focus more on ethical issues related to using helping skills with friends outside the lab setting.

Providing Feedback to Peers

Providing feedback is an essential component of training. Helpers appreciate positive feedback because learning helping skills is challenging, and they appreciate encouragement when they are on the right track. However, they also need and want feedback that helps them change and improve their helping skills. It is enjoyable to have people tell us that we are doing a terrific job as helpers, but we also need observers to provide concrete recommendations for how we might improve our skills. Students often feel cheated if they consistently receive only positive feedback yet also feel wounded if they receive too many critical comments.

Claiborn, Goodyear, and Horner (2002) recommended providing positive feedback first and then providing only one piece of constructive feedback. It is less overwhelming and more feasible to focus on making one change in a given lab experience rather than trying to fix everything at once. For example, the observer might say,

> You used good attending and listening skills; I particularly liked that you had good steady eye contact, leaned forward while you

were listening, and did not interrupt. One thing I noticed though that you might think about is that you asked a lot of questions in one speaking turn, making it hard for the client to know which one to respond to.

Note that the feedback should be stated in behavioral terms (e.g., "You were looking away a lot and playing with your hair") rather than in broad and nonspecific terms (e.g., "You did not connect with the client"). Having clear, concrete feedback gives the helper specific ideas for how to change.

The best source of feedback is the client who experienced the helper's interventions firsthand and experienced whether or not these interventions were helpful. The next best source of feedback is from observers who have watched the practice session and see from the outside what was happening. It can be beneficial for helpers to hear that different people have different responses to the same intervention, thus emphasizing that there is no one right way to intervene.

DVDs

A new feature of the third edition of the book was an accompanying DVD, *Helping Skills in Practice: A Three-Stage Model*. For this fourth edition, we have also produced a DVD of the helping skills model applied to dream work, *Dream Work in Practice*. These DVDs can be used to illustrate the three stages of the helping-skills model. Modeling has been shown to be an effective training tool (see review by Hill & Lent, 2006), probably because it brings the written word to life. It is important to remember though that the DVDs provide only two examples of how to do the three stages. How you implement the three stages will depend on your style and the needs of the particular client.

Concluding Comments

You are about to embark on an exciting and challenging journey toward becoming a helper. Although learning helping skills takes time, knowledge, and a lot of practice, the rewards for integrating helping skills in your personal and professional repertoire are plentiful. I hope to help you reach your destination of learning helping skills by focusing on the development of these skills while providing a theoretical and research foundation for helping behaviors, as well as by providing exercises to practice these skills.

Effective helping requires practice, and even experienced helpers often return to the basics to review and refresh skills. To become a good helper, you will need to continue practicing after this course. It takes many years to become an expert counselor or therapist (see also Orlinsky & Ronnestad, 2005; Skovholt & Jennings, 2004), so I encourage you to pursue professional training, and practice, practice, practice.

I want to end this section by giving a metaphor that a Korean student used. She likened this book to a Korean bowl of *bibimbap*, a dish of rice with various sautéed and seasoned vegetables and meats that is made by each person as everyone sits around the table. Each person at the table may construct a slightly different bowl of *bibimbap*, but all might be delicious. Similarly, as you go through each chapter of the book, you will throw different skills and ideas into your bowl of *bibimbap*. You may agree more with some skills and ideas than with others, and so you will throw more of these into your bowl (theory). Ingredients that you do not like, you will not throw in, but you might consider them more at some other time when you are again constructing your theory. At the end, you mix all the ingredients together, and you have the beginnings of a cohesive theory of helping.

I hope this book assists you in learning helping skills and exploring your potential for, and interest in, becoming an effective helper. Good luck! And enjoy constructing and sampling your bowl of *bibimbap*.

What Do You Think?

- Think of a time when you felt helped by someone. What did that person do that was helpful to you?
- Now remember a time when you needed help and the person you turned to was not at all helpful. What did she or he do to make this experience unhelpful?
- Describe how society perceives those who seek professional help.
- How could you help decrease the stigma attached to help-seeking in our society?
- Write a brief job description for a helper. Include personal characteristics, required training, and job responsibilities. Now, evaluate yourself in comparison with the description that you developed.
- What would it take for you to seek professional help? Address the benefits and costs you associate with seeking assistance.
- Debate why people want to become helpers.
- Identify several current situations in your life in which helping skills could be used.
- In your opinion, what are the top three characteristics of an effective helper?

RESEARCH SUMMARY

Effects of Helping Skills Training

Citation: Hill, C. E., Roffman, M., Stahl, J., Friedman, S., Hummel, A., & Wallace, C. (2008). Helping skills training for undergraduates: Outcomes and predictors of outcomes. *Journal of Counseling Psychology, 55,* 359–370.

Rationale: We need to know if helping skills training is effective. Do students actually learn the skills? What predicts who benefits most from training?

Method: Undergraduate students from three semester-long helping skills classes (involving weekly 2-hour lecture/skills demonstrations along with weekly 2-hour labs where students practiced skills) participated. Students completed ability measures (self-rated empathy, self-rated perfectionism, and grade-point average) at the beginning of the class so that we could use these as predictors of who would benefit from training. After every weekly lab, students completed measures of their confidence in using the helping skills effectively. At the beginning of the semester and two thirds of the way through the semester, students completed 20-minute helping sessions with classmates and also completed postsession measures assessing the helpfulness of these sessions. At the end of the semester, students reported their current self-efficacy as well as how they felt about their self-efficacy for using helping skills at the beginning of the semester.

Interesting findings:
- Students reported an increase in confidence about using the helping skills across the course of the semester, although there was a dip in confidence during the time they were learning insight skills.
- As helpers in the helping sessions, students used more exploration skills (e.g., restatements, reflections of feelings) and rated the quality better in the second helping session than in the first helping session.
- Similarly, as volunteer clients, students indicated that their helpers used more exploration skills, rated the quality of sessions higher, and rated helpers as more empathic in the second helping session than in the first helping session.
- On the basis of codings of transcripts, helpers used more exploration skills and fewer words in the second session than in the first session.
- At the end of the semester, helpers rated themselves as having higher self-efficacy for using the helping skills than they had at the beginning of the semester.
- Self-rated empathy, self-rated perfectionism, and grade-point average were not associated with outcome of training.

Conclusions:
- Helping skills training appears to be effective in terms of students learning exploration skills, becoming more empathic, talking less in sessions, conducting better sessions, and feeling a sense of self-efficacy for using the skills.
- Insight skills are more challenging to learn than are exploration and action skills.
- We were not able to predict who benefited from training on the basis of the self-report measures used. Performance-based measures (e.g., ratings of how prospective helpers behave in helping-like settings) might be better predictors.

Implications for training:
It seems justified to train students in helping skills.

| BONUS MATERIALS | Practice exercises, labs, and other resources for students and teachers are available on the companion website: http://pubs.apa.org/books/supp/hill4. |

An Overview of the Helping Process

2

We ought to respect the effect we have on others. We
know by our own experience how much others affect
our lives, and we must remember that we in turn must
have the same effect on others.

—*George Eliot*

A theoretical foundation is important for providing an overall picture of the goals of helping. It also enables helpers to
make decisions about how to conduct helping sessions.

We all have theories and philosophies that guide our
behavior, although we are often not aware of these theories
because we have not explicitly examined them. In this chapter, I present the personal philosophy of human development and the helping process that I have developed over the
years. I hope this presentation will help each of you think
through your beliefs and thus help you continue to develop
your personal philosophy.

The theoretical foundation that I propose in this book is
based on an integration of several major approaches. Given
that no differences have been found among the major theoretical orientations in terms of their effects on outcome (see
Wampold, 2001) and because I find value in all the approaches,
I integrate the best of these approaches in a philosophically
consistent way that fits with my personal style and values.
Thus, the three-stage model moves from exploration (based

http://dx.doi.org/10.1037/14345-002
Helping Skills: Facilitating Exploration, Insight, and Action, Fourth Edition, by
C. E. Hill

on client-centered therapy) to insight (based on psychoanalytic therapy) to action (based on behavioral therapy).

Assumptions Underlying the Three-Stage Model

I believe that people are born with varied potential in the psychological, intellectual, physical, temperamental, and interpersonal domains. Thus, some people are genetically more intelligent, attractive, physically strong, active, verbally articulate, and mechanically adept than are other people. In terms of temperament, some people are by nature more active, whereas others are more phlegmatic or slow to warm up. In terms of morality, I do not believe that people are either inherently good (as Carl Rogers postulated) or inherently governed by instinctual urges (as Sigmund Freud postulated) at birth. Instead, once again, I believe that people have certain biological predispositions at birth and have a tendency toward fulfilling these potentials. How they are developed depends largely on the environment, to which I turn next.

The environment can enhance or thwart the innate movement toward survival and development. Healthy environments provide basic biological needs (e.g., food, shelter) and emotional needs (e.g., relationships characterized by acceptance, love, support, encouragement, recognition, and appropriate challenges). No environment is perfect, but the environment needs to be "good enough" to allow children to grow and develop. In contrast, when negative things happen in a child's environment, the child's development is thwarted. A child growing up in the midst of war and terrorist attacks has a different view of life than does a child growing up during peace. Furthermore, either too much gratification or too much deprivation stunts children's growth, but an adequate good-enough amount of support allows children to develop naturally to fulfill their potential. So resiliency, or the ability to adapt, is both biologically and environmentally determined.

Early experiences, particularly in terms of attachment to caregivers, are crucial in laying the foundation for personality. Infants need to be nurtured by caretakers to have a firm foundation for interpersonal relationships and self-esteem. If these attachment needs are not met, children become anxious or avoidant of human contact (Bowlby, 1969, 1988).

People develop defenses to cope with anxiety, particularly during childhood, when they have less control over their personal destinies (e.g., a child might learn to withdraw to defend against dominating parents). A moderate level of defenses is adaptive because one needs strategies to cope with life. These defenses become problematic, however, when the individual cannot discriminate when it is appropriate to use defenses. For example, if a child who was abused avoids all adults, she or he cannot form benevolent relationships with caring people.

Although I strongly believe in the influence of early experiences, I also believe that we look toward the future in determining what we want out of life. Thus, we have existential goals, such as figuring out the meaning of life and determining what we want to accomplish during our lives, that guide our behavior.

I also believe that people have some degree of control over their lives and over their choices about how they behave. Within limits of what is available, one makes choices that alter the course of one's life. For example, although friendliness is influenced by personality (e.g., introversion vs. extroversion) and previous experiences with meeting people, a person still has some range of choices about how she or he acts with others in a new situation. Thus, determinism is balanced by free will. Furthermore, I believe that free will can be enhanced if individuals gain insight into their background, needs, and desires. Understanding enables one to have more control over one's fate. One can never have complete control over fate, but one can have some influence through awareness and conscious effort.

In the United States, there is a strong emphasis on individualism and self-determination, which often works to the detriment of people who have limited control over their lives. In that regard, I cringe to hear the phrase that if people just work hard, they can be successful. From my many years of working in psychology, I know that most people cannot become wealthy, beautiful, and successful because of many factors in their biology, upbringing, and environmental constraints. We can work hard but cannot always achieve everything we want to because of internal and external constraints.

I also propose that emotions, cognitions, and behaviors are all key components of personality that are intertwined and operate in combination with one another. Mind and body cannot be separated. How people think influences how they feel and behave (e.g., if a person thinks that others are out to get him, he will feel afraid and back away when another person approaches). How people feel has an impact on how they think and behave (e.g., if a person feels happy, she is likely to seek out other people and think that they will like her). Finally, how people behave affects how they think about themselves and how they feel (e.g., if a person studies hard and gets good grades, he or she is likely to feel efficacious and have high self-esteem). Thus, any treatment approach must focus on all three aspects of human existence (emotions, cognitions, and behaviors) to help people change.

In summary, I believe that people are influenced by both their biology and their environment, particularly early experiences that contribute to the development of attachment to others and self-esteem. Furthermore, although people are influenced by past experiences, they have some choice and free will and an impetus to make a difference and have meaning in their lives. It is also important to recognize that people develop defenses as strategies for coping with the demands of the world.

I believe that people can change within limits. They cannot discard past learning or biological predispositions, but they can come to understand themselves more, live with themselves, have self-compassion, and accept themselves. They can develop more adaptive behaviors, thoughts, and feelings. People can adjust to their inner potential, make the best of what they have, and make choices about how they want to live their lives within the limits imposed by biology, early experiences, and external circumstances. These assumptions lead to an optimistic, but cautious, view about the possibility of change.

I should emphasize that my philosophy and assumptions are clearly influenced by my culture. I was born and raised in the United States, where there is a strong emphasis on individualism and determinism. Had I been born and raised in another culture, I might well have put more emphasis on harmony and collectivism. Readers from other cultures should be aware of my biases and think carefully about the components of this model that fit for them given their cultural context.

The Three-Stage Model

In this section, I focus on the skills taught in this model. But recall that I outlined in Chapter 1 that the skills must be intertwined with self-awareness and facilitative attitudes to yield a productive helping process.

The helping process involves taking clients "down and into" understanding themselves more and then "up and out" into the world, better able to cope with problems (Carkhuff, 1969; Carkhuff & Anthony, 1979). Thus, as Figure 2.1 illustrates, the helping process involves begin-

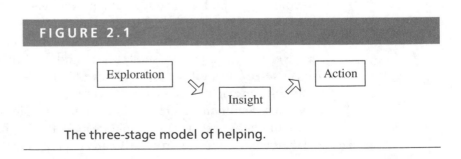

FIGURE 2.1

The three-stage model of helping.

ning with exploration, moving to insight, and then moving to action. In the next section, I list the goals and skills relevant to each stage and then describe what occurs in that stage. See Exhibit 2.1 for an overview of the stages, goals, and skills.

It is important to state early on that the stages are not rigid. Helpers do not need to spend a specific amount of time in each stage, and in fact, in actual helping, the stages often blur together such that it is hard to know what stage a helper is in. For training purposes, however, it is useful to think about the different goals that we have at different times during sessions. Thus, the three-stage model is a useful philosophical framework to use in understanding the goals of the overall process, but one need not strictly adhere to a set structure in using this model.

EXPLORATION STAGE

In the exploration stage, one goal is to attend nonverbally to clients and listen carefully to everything they say. Helpers attend to and listen through nonverbal behaviors (e.g., appropriate eye contact, head nods), minimal encouragers (e.g., "mm-hmm"), paying attention, and not interrupting. Another goal is to encourage clients to explore thoughts, which helpers implement through questions/probes for thoughts and restatements. A third goal is to encourage exploration of feelings, which helpers do through questions/probes for feelings, reflections of feelings, and disclosures of feelings.

Exploration is crucial to give clients an opportunity to express their emotions and to think through the complexity of their problems.

EXHIBIT 2.1

Goals and Skills for the Three Stages

Stage	Goals	Associated skills
Exploration	Attend, observe, listen	Nonverbal behaviors, minimal verbal behaviors
	Explore thoughts	Restatements, open questions/probes for thoughts
	Explore feelings	Reflections of feelings, disclosures of feelings, open questions/probes for feelings
Insight	Foster awareness	Challenges
	Facilitate insight	Open questions/probes for insight, interpretations, disclosures of insight
	Facilitate insight into relationships	Immediacy
Action	Facilitate action	Open questions/probes for action, giving information, process advisement, direct guidance, disclosures of strategies

Having another person act as a sounding board or mirror is often help-ful because it allows clients to open up; it is much easier to examine one's concerns when another person is actively listening. When clients think about issues by themselves, they often become blocked by their defenses and anxieties rather than gaining insight and making changes.

The exploration stage also provides helpers an opportunity to learn more about their clients. Helpers cannot assume that they know clients' feelings or problems, even when they are similar in age, race, gender, religion, or sexual orientation. For example, Jennifer—who was simi-lar in age, race, and gender to her helper—disclosed that she had just become engaged. The helper had just recently gotten married and was very happy in her relationship, so she assumed that Jennifer felt simi-larly and started congratulating her. Jennifer, however, broke down in tears and ran out of the room. Fortunately, the helper realized her mistake, called Jennifer and apologized, and asked her to return for another session. It turned out that Jennifer felt pressured to get engaged and, in fact, felt quite ambivalent about the relationship. When the helper could listen without assumptions, she was able to learn how Jennifer truly felt.

INSIGHT STAGE

The first goal of the insight stage is to foster awareness, which help-ers do primarily through challenges. The second goal is to facilitate insight, which helpers do through questions/probes for insight, inter-pretations, and disclosures of insights. The final goal is to work on the therapeutic relationship, which helpers do through immediacy (talking in the here-and-now about the therapeutic relationship).

In the insight stage, helpers collaborate with clients to help them achieve new understandings about themselves, their thoughts, their feelings, and their behaviors. They also work to help clients attain new awareness of and take responsibility for how they perpetuate their problems. Insight is important because it helps clients see things in a new light and enables them to take appropriate responsibility and con-trol over problems.

In contrast to the purely client-centered stance in the exploration stage, helpers work more actively with clients in the insight stage to construct meaning together. In addition, helpers provide clients with feedback about their behaviors in sessions and assist clients in under-standing how these behaviors have developed and the function they now serve. By understanding how they are perceived by their helpers, clients are often better able to understand how other people react to them. Helpers and clients also sometimes work through problems that arise in the therapeutic relationship, helping clients have a corrective relational experience, modeling how to interact with others more effectively, and working together to attain insight into relationships. Thus, the relationship itself can be a focus of learning in the insight stage.

ACTION STAGE

The overall goal of the action stage is to help clients explore the idea of changing and then implement action plans. The major skills for this stage are open questions/probes for action, giving information, process advisement, direct guidance, and disclosure of strategies. More important, there are four major types of action plans (relaxation, behavior change, behavioral rehearsal, and decision making), each of which is implemented through several steps and several skills.

When clients have some understanding, it is usually easier for them to change. For example, it was easier for Jacques to take a chance on getting involved in another relationship once he understood that he became scared of getting close to others because of his punitive relationship with his mother. Thus, understanding, however imperfect, guides future behavior. Insight may also lead to long-lasting change because it provides clients with a template for making sense out of events and helps them make better choices.

Together, helpers and clients explore the idea of changing, determine whether or not clients want to change, and explore the meaning of change. They also might consider possible changes and help the client make decisions about which changes to pursue. In some cases, helpers teach clients skills needed to make changes. They also might help clients develop strategies for trying new behaviors and asking for feedback from others outside the helping relationship. In addition, helpers and clients continually evaluate the outcome of action plans and make modifications to assist clients in obtaining the desired outcomes. As in the first two stages, the process is collaborative. Helpers continue to ask clients to talk about their feelings related to changing. Again, helpers are not experts but are guides who assist clients in exploring thoughts and feelings about action and about making positive changes in their lives.

Psychoanalytic theorists have often assumed that insight naturally leads to action and thus that helpers do not have to be concerned with encouraging clients to think about making specific changes. For some clients, this may be true. However, clients often do not have the skills to behave differently, have defenses that block them from making changes, and have obstacles in the real world that make it hard to change. Therefore, they may need help to make the changes occur. By putting their new ways of thinking into practice, clients are able to consolidate the changes in their thinking that occurred in the exploration and insight stages. Without action, changes in thinking (insights) are typically short-lived.

RELATIONSHIP AMONG THE THREE STAGES

The exploration stage lays the foundation for clients to understand their motivations and take responsibility for changing. Both helpers and clients need an adequate understanding of the scope and dynamics of the clients' problems before developing an action plan. Unlike radio and television talk show psychologists who listen for three sentences and then advise clients, helpers rely on careful, thoughtful listening and probing to help clients fully explore their problems and gain new insights.

Thus, each of the stages in the model is important in the helping process. Thorough exploration sets the stage for the client to gain insight, and deep insight prepares the path for the client to make good decisions about action. Furthermore, making changes encourages the client to begin exploration of other problems.

It is important to note that all the skills are used in all three stages but to varying degrees. Figure 2.2 shows that exploration skills are used most in the exploration stage but are also used quite frequently in the other two stages. Insight and action skills are used mostly within their own stages but are sometimes used in the other stages.

Although it sounds straightforward to move from the exploration stage to the insight stage and then to the action stage, the process rarely flows so smoothly with real clients, and stages are not always as differentiated and sequential as they seem to be when reading about them (Figure 2.3 shows some of the variations on the basic model). Within sessions, helpers and clients sometimes move back and forth among the stages. For example, helpers often have to return to exploring new facets of a client's problem during the insight and action stages. Furthermore, attaining insight often forces a client to explore newly recognized feelings and thoughts. Realizing that a client is reluctant to change in the action stage might necessitate more exploration and insight about obstacles.

Sometimes action needs to be taken after minimal exploration. For example, a client may be in crisis and need specific help immediately (e.g., discuss plans for the next 24 hours, have the number of a hotline). Or a client who has medical problems caused by anorexia might first need to learn to eat in a healthy manner and only later might be ready and able to explore motives underlying his or her eating disorder. In other cases, clients cannot really explore until they have been taught to relax. Other clients cannot handle insight and are resistant to having anyone "poke around in their heads"; they only want guidance about specific problems. With such clients, helpers may need to move more quickly to the action stage. However, I caution helpers to explore enough

FIGURE 2.2

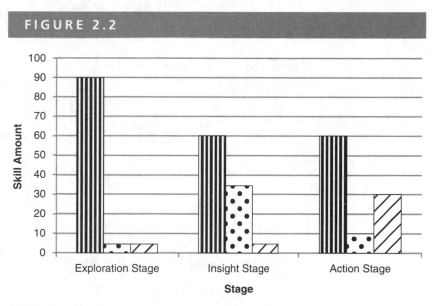

IIIIIII = Exploration skills (restatements, reflections of feelings, disclosures of feelings, open questions about thoughts and feelings)

••• = Insight skills (challenges, interpretations, immediacy, open questions about insight)

ZZ = Action skills (information, direct guidance, process advisement, feedback, open questions about action)

Approximate amount of skills used in each stage of the model.

to make sure they know what is going on, what actions have been tried, and what help is needed, and also make sure it is for the client's needs rather than for the helper's comfort or preference before they rush to generate possible actions.

In summary, the three-stage model provides an overall road map for the helping process, but helpers must attend to individual needs of clients and environmental pressures before determining how to respond at any given moment. This book is not meant to be a simplistic "cook-book" or manual of what to do at every specific moment in helping. That would not be possible, given the infinite number of situations that could arise with different helpers and clients. Instead, helpers need to think about what they are trying to accomplish at each point in the helping process, become skilled at delivering the various possible skills, and then

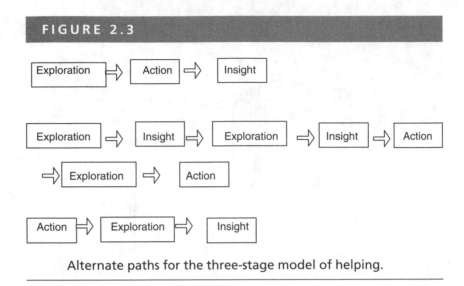

FIGURE 2.3

Alternate paths for the three-stage model of helping.

observe the client's reactions to help devise better interventions for that particular client.

Facilitative Conditions

I postulate that helpers must not only use skills well but must also convey an attitude of empathy, feel compassion, and collaborate with their clients. Empathic collaboration and compassion are major features of all three stages of the model. Because of the importance of these facilitative conditions, I describe each in more detail.

EMPATHY

Helpers need to try to understand their clients as much as possible, while at the same time recognizing that it is never possible to fully understand another person. Empathy involves understanding clients at both a cognitive level (their thoughts and expressions) and an affective level (their feelings; Duan & Hill, 1996). Empathy also includes genuinely caring about the client, nonjudgmentally accepting the client, being able to predict the client's reactions, and communicating one's experience to the client in a sensitive and accurate manner.

Although helpers sometimes feel the same emotions as their clients, empathy requires that they recognize that the pain, anger, frustration, joy, or other emotions belong to the client and not to the helper. Empathy is sometimes confused with a certain way of responding to clients (e.g., using reflections of feelings), but empathy is not a specific response type or skill; rather, it is an attitude or manner of responding with genuine caring and a lack of judgment. Empathy involves a deep respect for clients and for the clients' willingness and courage to explore their problems, gain insights, and make changes. This empathic attitude is experienced and also implemented through a variety of helping skills, depending on what helpers perceive clients as needing at specific times.

As mentioned earlier, we can never fully understand other people. We can try to empathize and imagine how the other person feels, but we can never fully remove ourselves from our own experiences to understand another person completely. Similarly, although we might try to have unconditional positive regard (i.e., caring about, understanding, and appreciating clients for who they are, regardless of how they behave), our regard for clients is usually conditional (e.g., that they allow us to help them, that they talk openly about their problems, that they not get angry at us). Unfortunately, we are not always fully aware of all of our personal issues and the conditions that we place on clients. As helpers, we need to do our best to form positive therapeutic relationships with clients; but when we are not able to establish good relationships, we need to examine our own issues as well as think about how client dynamics might be influencing the interaction.

COMPASSION

Compassion involves feeling aware of and open to suffering without judgment (Vivino, Thompson, Hill, & Ladany, 2009). Compassion goes beyond empathy and understanding by genuinely allowing oneself to feel the pain and suffering and desire to relieve it. Another way to think of compassion is loving kindness, of genuinely caring about the other person because of who they are, not because they deserve it or not. Often, we sit in judgment of ourselves and others, and trying to think about empathy and gaining compassion can help us shift into a more open and caring posture toward self and others. I have found it enormously helpful when supervising student therapists to ask them to try to find their compassion for clients; this exercise allows them to feel into where the client is hurting.

COLLABORATION

Furthermore, the whole helping process is collaborative in that helpers guide or coach clients in working through problems. Helpers are not experts in how clients ought to live their lives, but helpers can be experts at facilitating the process of helping clients explore feelings and values, achieve understanding, and make choices and changes. Rather than giving answers to clients, helpers try to teach clients how to think through problems, make decisions, and implement changes. This whole model is essentially client-centered in that helpers work with clients to choose their solutions to the problems they face. A good metaphor is the parable about teaching a hungry person to fish: Giving someone a fish feeds the person for one meal, whereas teaching her or him to fish enables the person to eat for a lifetime.

BEING EMPATHIC, COMPASSIONATE, AND COLLABORATIVE

Although empathy, compassion, and collaboration are crucial components of the helping process, they are not specific skills that can be taught directly. Rather, they are outcomes of the successful implementation of helping skills and a reflection of an attitude that the helper feels toward the client. As helpers, we can be knowledgeable about our implementation of verbal and nonverbal behaviors, aware of how we come across when using these interventions, aware of our intentions for using different interventions, and aware of client reactions to these interventions. However, we cannot always control the outcome of the helping session. We can strive toward empathy and collaboration, but we cannot always attain these goals because much depends on clients and how well we "match" or "click" with them. Even so, through knowledge, self-awareness, and a genuine desire to understand, respect, and work with another person, empathic collaboration is likely to emerge and to be experienced by clients.

A Model for the Process and Outcome of Helping

Much of what happens in helping situations is so complex that it is often difficult for helpers, especially beginning helpers, to have a full awareness of the process. Furthermore, the helping process occurs at many different levels (e.g., conscious awareness, unconscious processing) and at lightning speed, which does not give helpers much time to give conscious thought to every component and decision that accompanies interactions. Helpers must learn to react quickly because clients constantly present new needs and challenges.

By looking at the individual components of the process and outcome, helpers can begin to understand their reactions and responses in different situations and learn about possible client reactions to interventions. Analyzing each part of the helping process and outcome initially feels uncomfortable and cumbersome because beginning helpers are not used to breaking down their interactions and examining them so carefully. Furthermore, most beginning helpers are not used to thinking about their reasons for doing things and are not used to examining the reactions of others. With continued practice, however, beginning helpers can become more comfortable taking apart and analyzing the process and then putting it all together again to function in sessions. So let's turn to some of the variables that go into the moment-by-moment process.

BACKGROUND VARIABLES

Clients and helpers bring unique ways of viewing the world to the helping process. They contribute their personalities, beliefs, assumptions about the world, values, experiences, and cultural and demographic characteristics.

In addition, helpers bring their theoretical orientation (beliefs about how to help) and their previous experiences in helping (both informal and formal). For example, one could imagine that an introverted, young, European American female helper with a psychodynamic theoretical orientation would have a very different impact on the helping process than would an extroverted, middle-aged, Iranian American male helper with a cognitive–behavioral theoretical orientation. Moreover, helpers have preferences and biases related to clients, which undoubtedly influence their behavior. In Chapter 4, we spend a lot of time talking about the importance of self-awareness and self-care for helpers.

Similarly, client background variables greatly influence the process. A young, bright, attractive college student who is away from home for the first time and is feeling lonely and homesick is very different from a substance-abusing, older man who has been ordered by the court to attend counseling sessions because he batters his wife.

It is also important to be aware that clients are at various stages of readiness for change. Some are reluctant to participate in any form of helping; others are eager to learn more about themselves; and yet others are ready to make changes in their behaviors. Prochaska, Norcross, and DiClemente (1994, 2005) identified five stages of change:

▪ In the *precontemplation stage,* clients are unaware of the need to change or have no desire to change. Precontemplators lack information about their problems, engage in denial about their problems, and often blame other people or society for their problems. Other people are typically more bothered by the precontemplator's behavior than is the precontemplator.

- In the *contemplation stage,* clients are aware of and accept responsibility for their problems. They are beginning to think about changing but have not yet actively decided to change. Fear of failure often keeps clients stuck in this stage. Clients in this stage spend time thinking about the causes of their problems and ponder what it would be like to change.

- In the *preparation stage,* clients have made a commitment to change and are preparing themselves to begin the change process. Some clients make public announcements that they plan to change (e.g., "I plan to lose 30 pounds"). Some clients prepare themselves mentally for how their lives will be different (e.g., "When I lose weight, I will feel healthier and be more attractive, and it will be easier to exercise").

- In the *action stage,* clients actively begin to modify their behaviors and their surroundings. They might stop smoking cigarettes, begin studying at regularly specified times, start taking more time for themselves, or decide to get married. The commitment and preparation accomplished in the contemplation and preparation stages seem to be crucial for success in this stage, in that prepared clients are more aware of what they are striving for and why.

- In the *maintenance stage,* clients have changed and are trying to consolidate their changes and deal with lapses. The process of change does not end, then, with the action stage. It takes several weeks or years for change to become incorporated into one's lifestyle, and people often return to earlier stages in the process of change, suggesting that it is not easy to make lasting changes. This stage is very challenging because permanent change is difficult and often requires major lifestyle alterations.

Clients sometimes go through these stages linearly. But more often clients are at one stage for one problem and at a different stage for other problems (e.g., a client could be in the maintenance stage for stopping smoking but in the precontemplation stage for resolving spiritual issues in his life). Clients might also bounce around among the stages (e.g., on a good day a client may have a lot of insight but then regress to the precontemplation stage when scared).

Working with precontemplative clients can be difficult (but not impossible) because they often come to helping under duress (e.g., court referral) rather than because they genuinely want to change. One can compare working with precontemplative clients to trying to push carts with square wheels: It is more difficult to push a cart with square wheels than to push a cart with round wheels. In contrast, working with clients in the later stages tends to be easier because these clients are more eager to work on themselves. The process works better when clients are interested in, rather than resistant to, change.

THERAPEUTIC RELATIONSHIP

Gelso and Carter (1985) defined the *therapeutic relationship* as "the feelings and attitudes that counseling participants have toward one another, and the manner in which those are expressed" (p. 159). Researchers have consistently found that the therapeutic relationship is a major predictor of the outcome of therapy (Gelso & Carter, 1985, 1994; Horvath & Bedi, 2002). Clients typically report that the most helpful aspect of therapy is feeling understood and supported. For some people, the relationship itself is curative, and they need nothing else from the helper; others need the therapeutic relationship as a foundation for other interventions. We can think of the therapeutic relationship as being made up of three parts: the real relationship, the working alliance, and transference/countertransference (Gelso & Carter, 1985, 1994).

The *real relationship* is the genuine, authentic nondistorted connection between the helper and client. This part of the relationship is similar to relationships you would have with other people in your life.

The *working* (or therapeutic) *alliance* is the part of the relationship focused on the therapeutic work and consists of the bond (i.e., the connection between the helper and client), an agreement on goals (a consensus about changes the client needs to make), and an agreement on tasks (a consensus about what is to take place during the helping process to meet the goals). Interestingly, different types of working alliances may fit better for different types of clients. For example, Bachelor (1995) found that some clients prefer helpers who are warm and supportive, whereas others are put off by too much warmth and prefer helpers who are objective and businesslike.

Transference and countertransference involve distortions based on experiences in previous significant relationships. Transference involves client distortions of the helper, and countertransference involves helper distortions of the client. Transference and countertransference are thus like lenses or filters through which one views the world. For example, a female client may expect that the helper will be bored with her because her parents ignored her (transference). Likewise, the helper may react poorly to client anger because anger was not an acceptable emotion in her or his family (countertransference).

Although most researchers agree that a good therapeutic relationship facilitates the helping process, they are much less clear about how to establish good relationships with clients. I postulate that helpers establish good therapeutic relationships by attending and listening carefully to clients, using the appropriate helping skills at the right times, treating clients according to their individual needs, being aware of feelings and limitations, being aware of clients' reactions to their interventions, being open to feedback from clients, and being willing to change (see also Hill, 2005b).

I propose that the therapeutic relationship works as follows. Clients often come to helpers feeling that no one listens to them or cares about them. Helpers attend to their clients and communicate an understanding of clients' feelings and experiences. Helpers are empathic and non-judgmental and accept clients as they are, which allows the clients to feel safe enough to express deep feelings. Finally, helpers are skilled in their interventions, helping clients explore, gain insight, and make decisions about action and building clients' confidence that they can be helped. Within the context of the helping relationship, clients begin to feel that if their helpers accept them for who they are, they must be okay. It also allows clients to see that not all people are like those with whom they have experienced difficulties. Furthermore, working with helpers facilitates clients in reducing their anxiety and thus increases their capacity for facing interpersonal pain and anxiety. Clients slowly begin to build self-esteem and gain hope that they can change.

Helpers cannot establish relationships with all clients, even though we would all like to think that we can. Some dyads just do not "click." Some clients are not motivated or ready to be helped. For example, an adolescent girl might be forced by her parents to go for helping but not want to be there. Moreover, some clients have been so hurt and their capacity to trust so seriously impaired that they cannot benefit from a facilitative relationship. Clients who have been seriously damaged in relationships often have difficulty attaching to therapists. The problem sometimes lies with the helpers, however. Similarly, all helpers have limitations related to their backgrounds (e.g., dysfunctional families) and personal problems.

Furthermore, some matches between helpers and clients are not ideal and do not result in positive therapeutic relationships. For example, a female client who was raped recently might not be able to talk to a male helper no matter how kind he is because she is terrified of all men. An alcoholic client might not want to see a helper who has never had problems with alcoholism because he fears that such a helper could not understand his struggle to stay sober. Similarly, helpers who have not resolved their own experiences of traumatic sexual or physical abuse might not be able to hear a client's story of abuse without having strong emotional reactions or being distracted by their own pain.

MOMENT-BY-MOMENT INTERACTIONAL SEQUENCE

Figure 2.4 shows a graphical representation of the helping process. Given the background variables and context, helpers formulate intentions and decide on specific helping skills. In turn, clients react to the helpers' interventions, which lead them to reevaluate their needs and

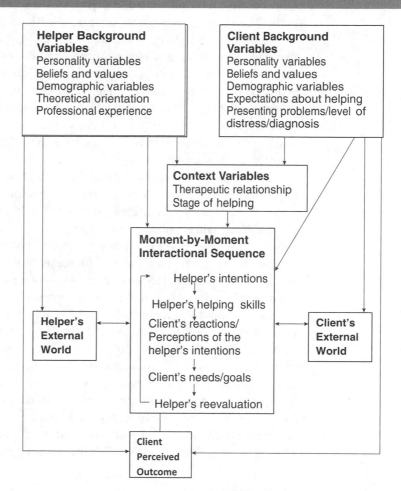

Factors influencing the helping process.

goals and decide how to behave with the helpers. Helpers then assess clients' reactions and reevaluate what to do next. The process thus continues with each person reacting both overtly and covertly, trying to determine the intentions of the other and deciding how to interact. Let's slow down the process and look at each piece.

Helper Intentions

Helpers develop intentions (i.e., goals, plans) by thinking about everything that has previously occurred and what they would like to accomplish next. Through asking therapists about why they did what they did, Hill and O'Grady (1985) developed a list of the intentions. Therapists indicated that they often had intentions to set limits, get information, and give information. In addition, they wanted to provide support, focus, clarify, instill hope, and encourage catharsis. Other goals related to exploration include intent to identify maladaptive cognitions, identify maladaptive behaviors, encourage self-control, and identify and intensify feelings. Related to insight and action, therapists wanted to promote insight, promote change, reinforce change, deal with resistance, challenge, and deal with the therapeutic relationship. Last, one nontherapeutic intention was revealed: to relieve helper's needs. The definitions for these intentions are listed in Web Form D (found at http://pubs.apa.org/books/supp/hill4).

Helpers are not always aware of their intentions at the time of delivery (Fuller & Hill, 1985). For example, helpers sometimes inadvertently self-disclose to make themselves feel better rather than to be helpful to clients. Reviewing audio- or videotapes after sessions (alone or with a supervisor) and thinking about or writing down intentions for each intervention is an excellent way to increase awareness of what one was trying to accomplish. Helpers are typically able to identify intentions pretty easily when they review tapes within 24 hours of the session and recall how they were feeling and reacting at a given moment in the session (rather than indicating how they currently feel about their interventions). By slowing down the process and examining it piece by piece, helpers can discover the different layers of feelings, thoughts, and actions. After gaining experience with examining intentions during videotape replays, helpers are often able to obtain more awareness of intentions while they are in sessions with clients. I encourage beginning helpers to become intentional in their interventions and to think about what they are trying to accomplish during each intervention.

Helper Helping Skills

For each intention, the helper could use a few different helping skills (see the Helping Skills System, Web Form E). For example, to facilitate the client talking about feelings, the helper might reflect feelings, disclose about feelings, or ask open questions/probes about feelings. All of these might be quite appropriate but subtly move the client in different directions.

In addition to matching the skill to the intention, helpers should bear in mind that the same intervention can have a different impact depending on the manner of delivery. If the helper says, "You seem to be feeling anxious" in a supportive, gentle tone, the client will probably have a different reaction than if the helper uses a critical, judgmental tone.

Client's Reactions

A helper intervention is met by one or more client reactions (see the Client Reactions System, Web Form G). When a helper is successful, the client's reactions match the helper's intentions and helping skills. For example, if the helper's intention is to provide emotional support and the helping skill used is an encourager such as "I understand what you're going through," the client's reaction might be to feel understood and supported. However, if the intervention is not successful, the client might feel that the helper did not really hear what was being expressed or that the helper made incorrect assumptions.

Clients are sometimes consciously aware of their reactions, although at other times they might be unaware of their reactions to helpers. In addition, clients sometimes have difficulty admitting to reactions that are not socially acceptable (e.g., feeling angry at a helper's intervention). Admitting negative feelings about helpers can be difficult if clients respect and depend on the helpers or if clients cannot allow themselves to have negative emotions. For example, a client might react negatively to something a helper says because it is similar to something her parents said, but the client might not allow herself to express these negative feelings for fear of hurting the helper. Instead, the client might smile politely but feel somewhat distant and unengaged, not understanding why she withdrew from the interaction. Research suggests that clients often hide negative reactions from their therapists out of fear of retaliation or out of deference to the helper's authority (e.g., Hill, Thompson, Cogar, & Denman, 1993; Hill, Thompson, & Corbett, 1992; Rennie, 1994). For example, clients who feel angry at or misunderstood by their helpers are not likely to reveal those feelings if they feel unsafe in the therapeutic relationship. And even if they feel safe, they might feel uncomfortable expressing negative feelings because of cultural prohibitions against offending others.

A number of factors influence the reactions that clients have to helper interventions. First, clients' reactions are influenced by their needs at the time. For example, clients in severe crisis might tolerate almost any intervention because they are desperately in need of help. In contrast, high-functioning clients might be more demanding that helpers be competent and knowledgeable about how to specifically help them.

Second, client reactions are moderated by the therapeutic relationship. In generally positive relationships, clients might tolerate some mistakes from helpers without an adverse reaction because they feel that helpers are genuinely trying to be helpful. If the relationship is problematic or rocky, however, anything helpers do might elicit negative reactions from disgruntled clients.

Third, clients' reactions seem to be influenced by their impressions of the helper's intentions. For example, if clients think that their helpers were acting out of their own personal needs rather than in the best interest of the clients (regardless of what the helpers' actual intentions were), they might have negative reactions. If clients think that therapists want to extend therapy to make more money rather than because their clients need help, clients might become angry and uncooperative. In contrast, if clients think that their helpers are beginners who are just learning to be helpers, they might feel sympathetic and have positive reactions. Clients' perceptions, then, even though they might not match the "reality" of helpers' intentions, seem to influence clients' reactions.

Clients' Needs or Goals

Clients react according to what they need and want from the interaction with the helper, and determine what is possible to obtain from helpers at a particular time. Thus, rather than being passive recipients of helpers' interventions, clients are actively involved in trying to get what they need from interactions. For example, one client might feel a need to retreat to avoid further confrontation. Another client might decide that he wants to reveal more because his helper is accurate in understanding him and can be trusted with secrets.

Clients also want to have an impact on their helpers. For example, Sam wanted to please his helper and so kept telling her what a good job she was doing. Other clients might decide not to reveal shameful secrets because they do not want to tarnish the helper's opinion of them.

Clients do not typically consciously plot the reactions they want to elicit from their helpers. Rather, they act on the basis of their past experiences in ways that maximize the probability of getting their needs met (e.g., to feel close to or distant from the helper). Some of these client goals are influenced by transference, which occurs when clients project how significant people in their lives (e.g., parents) behaved onto how they expect their helpers to behave (see Gelso & Hayes, 1998; Gelso, Hill, Mohr, Rochlen, & Zack, 1999). For example, if Sue feels that no one listened to her as a child, she might not be able to believe that anyone could possibly want to listen to her now. Hence, even though the helper is attentive, Sue might want the helper to "prove" that he really wants to listen to her, or she will not talk in the session. Rather than being aware that the helper is silent because he is trying to give her space to talk, Sue might perceive the silence as occurring because the helper is bored by her.

Clients' Behaviors

Clients engage in specific behaviors (e.g., resist, agree, make an appropriate request, recount, engage in cognitive–behavioral or affective exploration, come to insight, or discuss therapeutic changes; see Client Behavior System, Web Form H) on the basis of their reactions, feelings about the therapeutic relationship, needs in the interaction, and goals (intentions) for a desired impact. Clients' behaviors are determined not only by the interaction but also by their communication ability, awareness of needs, level of pathology, and personality structure. Hence, one client might be very articulate and insightful about describing the causes of his pain, whereas another client might be unskilled at communicating feelings and be unaware of what she is feeling in the moment.

Helpers' Assessment of Client Reactions and Reevaluation of Goals

Helpers, in turn, try to assess clients' reactions to their interventions. They observe how the client reacted to the intervention (e.g., whether the client felt supported and understood, felt confused and misunderstood, or had no reaction). Unfortunately, helpers are not always accurate in perceiving clients' reactions. In fact, research suggests that helpers are not particularly adept at perceiving negative client reactions to their interventions, but they are more accurate at perceiving positive reactions (Hill et al., 1992). The diminished ability to perceive negative client reactions might occur because, as noted earlier, clients hide negative reactions from helpers. People often learn as young children not to show negative reactions for fear of evoking displeasure or being punished (e.g., imagine what would happen if an elementary school student told her teacher that she did not like what the teacher said). Hence, helpers cannot assume that clients feel positively just because the clients are not displaying negative reactions.

In addition, helpers might be reluctant to recognize when clients have negative reactions. For example, many helpers have a hard time with clients' anger directed at them (Hill, Kellems, et al., 2003). Because they want clients to like them, having clients get angry at them feels scary and upsetting. These helpers worry that clients will drop out. When clients are angry, helpers might misinterpret the anger as a personal rejection. Other helpers might have difficulty allowing clients to become upset and cry because they feel obligated to make everything better and have all clients be happy.

Unfortunately, not all helpers have learned to examine the effects of their interventions on clients, so they use interventions that feel comfortable (e.g., giving advice) rather than ones that match the client's needs in the specific situation (e.g., empathy, listening). In addition, there is a danger that over time, helpers can become insensitive to the influence of their behavior on clients and assume that they know how the clients are reacting internally. Helpers, even when they are experienced, can strive to be aware of the impact of their interventions on clients. Rather than making assumptions, helpers might ask the clients how they are feeling or reacting.

On the basis of their perceptions of the client's reactions (whether accurate or not) and observation of the overt behaviors, helpers reevaluate what they are trying to accomplish and thus come up with new intentions and accompanying skills for the next intervention. If a helper perceives that the last intervention was successful and thinks that a similar intervention would be appropriate, she might continue with the same intention–skill combination. For example, if a reflection resulted in the client talking about sadness, the helper might use another reflection to help the client delve even deeper into these feelings. If a helper perceives that the last intervention was helpful but that something new is needed, he might choose a different intention–skill combination. For example, if a helper had reflected feelings and the client responded by talking in depth about a variety of feelings, the helper might decide to use an open question/probe to shift the focus to other aspects of problems.

If, in contrast, a helper perceives that the last intervention was not received well by the client, the helper would try to determine why the intervention was not successful. If the timing was poor, the helper might decide not to continue that intervention but to go back to a more exploratory intervention to learn more about the problem. If the helper decides that the intentions were on target but the wrong skill was used, the helper might use a different skill to implement the same intention. For example, a beginning helper might try to encourage the client to talk about feelings by asking a closed question, such as "Did you have any feelings about that?" If the client responds, "No," and adds nothing further, the helper might realize that the closed question stopped rather than facilitated exploration. The helper might then use a reflection of feeling (e.g., "Perhaps you feel scared right now") in the next intervention and observe how the client responds. Thus, by paying attention to client reactions, helpers can devise new interventions to fit the immediate need.

Given that the most important criterion for the effectiveness of the helper's intervention is the client's response, helpers need to monitor client reactions to determine whether their interventions are helpful and make adjustments when clients respond negatively. I like to think of helpers as personal scientists, investigating the effects of each intervention, testing what works and what does not work, and then deciding what needs to be done next. Helpers thus have to be very attentive to what works with individual clients. Even if a helper finds that certain helping skills work well with one client, those same skills might not work the next time with the same client and may not work with the next client.

EXTERNAL WORLD

Many external forces influence the helping process. We can look at these forces for both clients and helpers.

Clients' Lives Outside of Helping Sessions

Typically, sessions last only 1 hour per week, whereas clients live another 167 hours outside of the sessions. As helpers, we hope that clients take what they have learned from helping sessions and try to apply it to "real life." In one case of brief psychotherapy presented by Hill (1989), the therapist confronted the client with the fact that the client did not seem to need him or listen to anything he said. The client was very surprised because she had never viewed herself this way. She thought that she was working hard on her issues both within and outside of therapy. She discussed this feedback with her friends, who agreed with the therapist's assessment that she seemed self-possessed and did not appear to need anything from them. Hearing this feedback from both the therapist and her friends forced the client to look at her behavior; she used the feedback from her friends to validate what she was learning in therapy.

In intensive psychotherapy, clients sometimes form images, or what have been called *internal representations,* of their therapists to remind them of their helpers in-between sessions (Farber & Geller, 1994; Geller, Cooley, & Hartley, 1981; Geller & Farber, 1993; Knox, Goldberg, Woodhouse, & Hill, 1999; Orlinsky & Geller, 1993). For example, some clients might think about what their therapist would say and use that for guidance or to comfort themselves between sessions. These internal representations often help clients cope between sessions.

Another important influence in the external world is social support, which has been researched extensively (e.g., Cobb, 1976). Specifically, clients who have social support tend to do better in therapy than do clients who do not have support (Mallinckrodt, 2000). Clients with friends are less likely to become overly dependent on their therapists. They have other people to talk to, and they have enough social skills to form friendships.

However, relationships in the external world can sometimes present obstacles to progress in therapy. Perhaps the clearest example is when a client's changes threaten the status quo of family life, causing family members to undermine the client's progress. For example, a severely overweight man's weight loss may threaten his marital relationship. The wife may fear that the husband is now attractive to other women and that he might lose interest in her. She may begin to cook tasty, fattening desserts to tempt the man to regain the weight and thus stabilize the relationship. These behaviors are not necessarily performed consciously but often are desperate attempts to maintain stability in relationships (see Watzlawick, Weakland, & Fisch, 1974).

Thus, events in the external world can both help and hinder the therapeutic work. Helpers cannot just attend to what goes on in session; rather, they also need to be aware of how external events influence the client and the helping process. They can also encourage clients to talk in the helping setting about issues that come up outside of helping, and they can encourage clients to take responsibility for making changes in their lives.

Helpers' Lives Outside of Helping Sessions

Many of the same forces that influence clients also influence how helpers feel and behave in helping sessions with clients. If helpers have a lot of stress and conflict in their personal lives, it is difficult for them to put these aside (bracket them) so that they can focus on their clients. A particular stress that affects beginning helpers is anxiety: The more anxious helpers are about their ability to perform in helping sessions, the less able they are to focus on and be empathic with clients. Another stressor that many helpers face is burnout or compassion fatigue, when they feel drained from all they have given to clients.

I highly recommend that helpers seek personal therapy to work on their personal issues and seek supervision to work on their professional issues so that they can be as helpful as possible to clients in sessions. In addition, helpers can be attentive to self-care, ensuring that they eat properly, exercise, have a fulfilling personal life, and have adequate social support.

OUTCOMES OF HELPING FOR CLIENTS

All of the variables discussed to this point (helper and client background variables, context variables, moment-by-moment interactional sequences, and the external world) interact to determine the outcome of the helping process for the client. Thus, the outcome is influenced by many factors, and individuals react idiosyncratically to different aspects of the process.

One way to categorize outcomes is in terms of three areas: (a) *remoralization,* or the enhancement of well-being; (b) *remediation,* or the achievement of symptomatic relief; and (c) *rehabilitation,* or the reduction of troublesome, maladaptive behaviors that interfere with functioning in areas such as family relationships and work. Outcome research indicates that remoralization happens first and is the easiest area to change in therapy; remediation follows at a slower pace; and rehabilitation takes the longest time to accomplish (Grissom, Lyons, & Lutz, 2002; Howard, Lueger, Maling, & Martinovich, 1993). Hence, a client may feel more hopeful after a few sessions of therapy, but it may take longer for the client to feel less depressed and anxious, and even longer for the client to make changes in terms of new ways of behaving in relationships and work.

Another way to conceptualize outcome is in terms of *intrapersonal, interpersonal,* and *social role performance* (Hill & Lambert, 2004). Intrapersonal changes refer to outcomes that occur within the client (e.g., decreased symptoms, increased self-esteem, improved problem-solving abilities, more assertiveness, increased subjective well-being). Interpersonal changes take place in the client's intimate relationships (e.g., improved communication, increased marital satisfaction, healthier relationships). Social role performance refers to the client's ability to carry out responsibilities in the community (e.g., improved job performance, increased participation in community activities, greater involvement in school, reduced antisocial behaviors). For example, a female client with good outcomes in all three areas may feel better about herself, have a clearer sense of who she is and the meaning of her life, have an improved relationship with her husband, and have fewer days of absence at work related to illness.

It is important to note that therapy does not result in "cures." In my view, there is no such thing as functioning perfectly because the human condition involves inherent feelings of existential issues such as isolation, fears of responsibility and freedom, and death anxiety. Rather, helpers can expect that clients begin to function more effectively, feel better about themselves, and become more acceptant about their condition in life. Sometimes, however, therapy can actually make clients more anxious as they grapple with existential issues (Yalom, 1980); becoming more anxious is thus not surprising.

Helpers, clients, and clients' significant others often have different perceptions of the outcome of the helping process (see Strupp & Hadley, 1977). For example, a helper might feel pleased with her performance as a helper with Jack and believe that Jack benefited a great deal from the helping because he said he was going to change his major. In contrast, Jack might feel that he only participated in counseling to please his parents and that he listened politely and responded compliantly in the sessions to appease the helper but dismissed all the helper's advice as soon as he left. Jack's parents might feel sad because their son is not choosing the career they want for him and resigned that even helping did not improve their relationship with their son. Thus, the outcomes of helping can be quite different depending on the individual's perspective.

Concluding Comments

The whole helping process undoubtedly seems incredibly complex, especially to the beginning trainee. Similarly, all the components of driving at first seem overwhelming to a person learning to drive, but later, driving becomes so familiar that the driver often does not even need to think about the separate steps (e.g., turning the wheel to make a turn). Another metaphor is that learning to be a helper is like learning to dance: At first, you pay great attention to the steps, but once you learn, you forget the specific steps and respond to your partner. At this point, having a broad overview of the model can provide you with a framework for understanding the individual intentions and skills.

What Do You Think?

- What are your assumptions about human nature and the possibility of change?
- Debate whether all three stages are needed for a complete helping process or whether another model might be better.
- Discuss the role of empathic collaboration in helping.
- Discuss whether empathy is an attitude or a skill.
- The helping process was described as being very complicated. Do you agree? What components were left out of the helping process, and what components were not necessary?
- What parts of the helping process are unconscious (i.e., not open to awareness)?
- Why do you think that helpers and clients experience the same interaction differently?
- How important do you think helping skills are to the therapeutic relationship in terms of leading to client change?
- Debate whether empathy would be different with clients who are of a different race, gender, religion, or sexual orientation than is the helper.
- Would you personally have more difficulty establishing empathy with a person who has different rather than the same demographic characteristics as you?

RESEARCH SUMMARY

Covert Processes

Citation: Hill, C. E., Thompson, B. J., Cogar, M. C., & Denman, D. W. (1993). Beneath the surface of long-term therapy: Therapist and client report of their own and each other's covert processes. *Journal of Counseling Psychology, 40,* 278–287. doi:10.1037/0022-0167.40.3.278

Rationale: In an overt (one that you can observe) exchange, the therapist might ask the client to do homework between sessions, and the client might agree, which would look like a very good interchange. However, even though the therapist intended to be encouraging, the client might feel misunderstood and not do the homework, which is quite a different outcome of the interchange. Given that previous research (Hill, Thompson, & Corbett, 1992; Regan & Hill, 1992; Rennie, 1994; Thompson & Hill, 1991) has shown that clients hid negative reactions and that therapists were not very accurate at detecting such hidden reactions, the authors of the current study wanted to investigate more about these covert processes.

Method: Therapy cases representing a wide range of theoretical orientations and countries were studied. Prior to the session, therapists reviewed the Therapist Intentions List, and clients reviewed the Client Reactions System. Therapists then audiotaped/videotaped a middle session of ongoing therapy. In a review of the audiorecording of the session, therapists rated the helpfulness of each intervention, indicated up to three intentions that they had for the intervention, guessed up to three reactions that they thought the clients had for that intervention, and guessed any client reactions that they thought were hidden during the intervention. At the end of the tape review, therapists indicated what thoughts and feelings they thought clients had but did not share, as well as rated the overall quality of the session. Similarly, clients reviewed the audiorecording and rated the helpfulness of each therapist intervention, indicated up to three reactions that they had to the intervention, indicated any reactions that were hidden during the intervention, and guessed up to three intentions that they thought the therapist had. At the end of the tape, clients also indicated any thoughts or feelings that they had during the sessions that they did not share with their therapist and the reasons why they did not reveal them, as well as rated the overall quality of the session.

A team of judges coded things left unsaid for valence (affective tone) and then judged whether there was a match between clients' and therapists' perceptions of things left unsaid. The judges then developed categories of cited reasons for leaving things unsaid and for secrets and then coded all responses into these categories.

Interesting Findings:
- Therapists matched (accurately guessed) about half of the reactions reported by clients.
- Therapists were more accurate at guessing client reactions related to therapeutic work (e.g., better self-understanding) than other reactions. And when therapists were accurate about these client reactions related to therapeutic work, clients were more likely to rate their next interventions as helpful.
- Clients hid more negative reactions (e.g., feeling stuck or angry) than other types of reactions.
- Most clients (65%) reported that they left at least one thing unsaid during sessions.
- The primary reason for leaving things unsaid during sessions was that the emotions were overwhelming and they wanted to avoid dealing with the topic.
- Similarly, 65% of therapists reported that they thought clients had left something unsaid during sessions, but they were accurate in only 27% of the cases.
- About half of the clients (46%) had not disclosed at least one secret in therapy.

(continued)

- Most of the secrets were about sex (e.g., "unorthodox sexual persuasions," "I am more sexually attracted to my therapist than I have let on," "childhood sexual abuse").
- The most frequent reasons clients gave for not disclosing were feeling shamed or embarrassed.
- Therapists reported that most of their intentions related to assessment (34%), support (19%), exploration (18%), and restructure (16%).
- Clients accurately matched (guessed) on half (50%) of therapist intentions, with the best matches on assessment, support, and restructure intentions.
- Both therapists and clients gave higher helpfulness ratings when clients did not match on assessment intentions than when they did match.
- Both therapists and clients thought it was more helpful when clients were not aware that therapists were intending to assess the client (e.g., get information from the client).
- Therapists thought it was helpful when clients were aware that therapists were intending to help the client explore (e.g., identify and intensify feelings) and restructure (e.g., promote insight).

Conclusions:
- Clients sometimes hide negative reactions, thoughts, and feelings during sessions, often because the feelings are overwhelming or are too difficult to deal with in therapy.
- Many clients have secrets, especially about sexual matters, that they do not reveal because of feelings of shame.
- Therapists are not very aware of clients' reactions, particularly negative reactions.
- It is helpful if clients know that therapists are trying to help them engage in therapeutic work (exploration and restructuring), but not particularly helpful if clients know that therapists are trying to get information from them.

Implications for Therapy:
- Helpers need to be aware that clients do not disclose everything they are thinking or feeling. Far from being able to read clients' minds, therapists are often not aware of what clients are feeling, especially if the feelings are negative. Helpers need to observe clients carefully for nonverbal indications of discomfort, and perhaps more important, ask clients about how they are feeling about the helping process.
- Clients do not need to focus on trying to figure out the intentions helpers have for their interventions. But it is important for clients to tell helpers when they are dissatisfied with something in therapy so that helpers know more what they need and can tailor the treatment to their needs.

BONUS MATERIALS — Practice exercises, labs, and other resources for students and teachers are available on the companion website: http://pubs.apa.org/books/supp/hill4.

Ethical Issues in Helping 3

Intellectual integrity, courage, and kindness are still the
virtues I admire most.
                                                    —*Gerti Cori*

One hopes that we all aspire to provide high-quality services
that are respectful of the rights of the people with whom we
work. But how do we know what the standards are?

Mental health professionals have been very concerned
with issues of ethics because of the potential for harm. Thus,
most helping professions (e.g., counseling, medicine, nursing, psychology, social work) have developed ethical codes
that are intended to protect both the practitioners and the clients. These codes describe the underlying ethical principles to
which professionals aspire in making their decisions, especially
in terms of acting in a responsible manner, ensuring quality
client care, and contributing to society through their work.
Rather than providing "the right answer," the principles provide guidelines to helpers for behaving in a responsible manner and resolving ethical dilemmas. The codes also involve
specific standards of conduct for what professionals should do
(e.g., talk about confidentiality) and should not do (e.g., have
sexual relations with clients). Exhibit 3.1 lists the websites of
the ethical codes for several professional organizations.

http://dx.doi.org/10.1037/14345-003
Helping Skills: Facilitating Exploration, Insight, and Action, Fourth Edition, by
C. E. Hill

EXHIBIT 3.1

List of Professional Organizations and Websites for Ethical Codes

---

- American Association for Marriage and Family Therapy
  http://www.aamft.org/imis15/content/legal_ethics/code_of_ethics.aspx
- American Counseling Association
  http://www.counseling.org/Resources/aca-code-of-ethics.pdf
- American Psychological Association
  http://www.apa.org/ethics/code/index.aspx
- American School Counselor Association
  http://www.schoolcounselor.org/school-counselors-members/legal-ethical
- National Association of Social Workers (1996)
  http://www.socialworkers.org/pubs/code/default.asp

Ethics are principles and standards that ensure that professionals provide quality services and are respectful of the rights of the people with whom they work. Acting in an ethical manner also involves following the laws and rules governing one's profession. Hence, a mental health organization's or association's principles are aspirational guidelines that people in the profession have agreed on by consensus, whereas the profession's standards (its bylaws and rules) are enforceable through sanctions or professional censure as stipulated by the relevant organization or association. Furthermore, principles and standards can be differentiated from personal morality (e.g., being for or against abortion rights).

Although beginning helpers are not yet professionals and as such are not obligated to follow the professional principles and standards, they should aspire to uphold the ethical principles and standards of the profession because it is the right thing to do. They should conduct themselves in a professional, therapeutic manner.

The instructor of the class (or his or her supervisor, if the instructor is a graduate student), in contrast, is a professional, and is therefore responsible for what goes on in the classroom and in required helping sessions. Thus, the instructor has a responsibility to be aware of the ethical issues and educate students about these issues. It is advisable for instructors to have conversations with students early in training as well as throughout training about what topics should be disclosed in helping sessions (see Exhibit 1.1), informed consent (see more detail later in this chapter), confidentiality (see more detail later in this chapter), and other potential ethical issues. In addition, because laws, statutes, and legal decisions vary in different jurisdictions and states, instructors should be aware of and educate students about local requirements.

General Ethical Principles

Many ethical codes stress the importance of six basic ethical principles (Beauchamp & Childress, 1994; Kitchener, 1984; Meara, Schmidt, & Day, 1996):

- *Autonomy* refers to the right (of both the consumer and the provider) to make choices and take actions, provided the results do not adversely affect others. This principle grants individuals the opportunity to determine their actions on the basis of their belief systems. For example, a helper may be working with a client about career decisions, independent of the client's parents' hopes for her to pursue law school. Suddenly, the client announces that she is ending counseling and giving up her scholarship to pursue a career as a country music singer. The helper might encourage the client to consider the pros and cons of life as a country music singer. However, the principle of autonomy allows the client the right to make her own decisions, provided these decisions are not harmful to others. In this example, the helper supported the client's decision to attend college and simultaneously pursue her dream of becoming a musician.
- *Beneficence* refers to the intent "to do good" by helping and promoting growth in others. This principle clearly states that helpers should be committed to the growth and development of their clients. Helpers who strive to provide the most comprehensive, empirically supported services to their clients are embodying the principle of beneficence, whereas helpers who see clients solely to make money violate this important principle.
- *Nonmaleficence* can be described with the phrase "Above all, do no harm." Professionals are asked to ensure that their interventions and actions do not inadvertently harm their clients. Thus, neglect on the part of the helper (even if unintentional) would be problematic. For example, a student in a helping class might be out drinking margaritas with friends and telling them about the practice helping session he had in class that day. Later, he might notice that his practice client is at the table next to him and probably overheard him telling his friends about her issues. Although the helper may not have used the client's name or intended to harm her, he would be responsible for the unintentional harm that resulted from having disclosed confidential information about his practice client.
- *Justice* can be defined as fairness or ensuring equality of opportunities and resources for all people. One could interpret this

principle to mean that helpers have an ethical responsibility to rectify the unequal distribution of helping services by making their services more accessible to those who are unable to pay. For example, helpers can contribute to building a just society by volunteering at not-for-profit agencies (e.g., shelters for battered women, clinics for people with AIDS). An additional method of promoting justice involves attempts to influence public policy or legislation to ensure that mental health services are available to those in need, regardless of their ability to pay, location, language preference, or disability status.

- *Fidelity* refers to keeping promises and being trustworthy in relationships with others. Fidelity is a critical component of the relationship between helpers and clients. Without confidence in the helper's ability to be faithful to the agreements articulated in the helping session, minimal progress can be made. For example, the agreement between helpers and clients typically involves both parties meeting at a certain time for a specified number of sessions. If helpers are consistently 20 minutes late for each session, they are breaking the promise to be available to clients at an arranged time. Violations like these can have a detrimental impact on the development of the helping relationship.

- *Veracity,* which refers to telling the truth, is a powerful and necessary principle in helping settings. Clients often rely on their helpers to provide honest feedback about their interactions in the helping sessions. One example involves a 21-year-old client, Takiesha, who worked with a helper for many months. Takiesha had not made much progress in the last few sessions and asked the helper for some direct feedback about her work in the helping sessions. The helper provided several positive remarks and also indicated that at times, Takiesha appeared to place responsibility for her problems on others instead of empowering herself. Although Takiesha was upset about hearing this feedback, she was grateful to the helper for being honest and was able to understand how her reluctance to take responsibility prevented her from making necessary changes in her life.

Ethical Issues for Beginning Helpers

Professional therapists and counselors deal with many ethical issues. Here are a few of the ethical issues that beginning helpers may encounter.

CONFIDENTIALITY

Beginning students who are learning helping skills may encounter confidentiality issues when they practice with classmates or with volunteer clients who present real problems. It is important that helpers respect a client's confidentiality by not divulging information shared in the helping session, except in limited circumstances (see next paragraph). Sometimes, maintaining confidentiality can be challenging if students interact with clients outside of the sessions or if they have friends in common. However, the success of the helping relationship depends on the client's ability to trust that information shared with the helper will be kept confidential.

There are a few limits to confidentiality (recall as mentioned earlier in this chapter that requirements often vary by jurisdiction or state, and so you need to be aware of local requirements). First, you need to be able to talk about your clients with supervisors so that you can learn from your errors and grow as a helper; supervisors are ethically bound to keep everything confidential and thus discussing a client's situation with a supervisor is not a threat to confidentiality. Second, if the client reveals to you plans to harm self or others, you (and the responsible instructor or supervisor) may be (depending on the situation and local laws) legally obligated to report this threat to the appropriate authorities. Third, if the client reveals the occurrence of abuse of children, elderly persons, or disabled persons, you (and/or the responsible instructor or supervisor) may be legally obligated to report such abuse to the appropriate authorities.

It is important to inform clients about the general principle of confidentiality at the beginning of the first session and then have the client sign an informed-consent form similar to the one shown in Exhibit 3.2. In addition, helpers can deal with issues related to confidentiality as they arise in sessions, by first reminding clients about the limits of confidentiality as they begin to disclose issues related to harm or abuse (e.g., "I need to remind you before you say anything more that I may need to report anything you say related to possible harm to yourself or others or abuse") and second by consulting immediately with supervisors and legal authorities and then carrying out the recommended procedures.

RECOGNIZING LIMITS

It is critical that helpers recognize and practice only within the areas for which they have been trained and are competent. For example, after going through this course, you will probably be able to use the exploration skills (e.g., listening, reflecting feelings) with classmates, but you will not have expertise in such areas as working with children, facilitating personality change, doing crisis intervention, or working

EXHIBIT 3.2

Informed Consent Form

I understand that my helper is a student-in-training.

I understand that my helping session(s) may be audio- or videotaped for training and supervisory purposes; that only my helper and those involved in the course will review any tapes; and that confidentiality will be strictly maintained in accordance with the law. Recordings will be destroyed in a timely manner.

I understand that all information shared in this session will be kept confidential, with a few key exceptions:

a. supervisors may listen to the session or read transcripts of sessions (transcripts will have no identifying information);
b. harm or intention to harm self or others (as required by law);
c. reasonable suspicion of current or previous abuse of children, elderly, or disabled individuals, as required by law;
d. court orders.

With the understanding that I may withdraw my consent to the above conditions at any time, I grant my permission to participate in the session(s) and to be audio/videotaped by the helper whose signature appears below.

Signature of Client: _____ Date: _____

Signature of Helper: _____ Date: _____

with patients with severe mental illness. As an example, a friend who discovers that you are learning helping skills may ask you to speak with her cousin who has been acting in a strange manner and hearing voices that tell him to destroy the psychology building at the university. Appropriate ethical behavior in this case would involve telling your friend that meeting with her cousin is outside of your area of competence. You might, however, offer to speak with your professor to obtain a referral to a competent practitioner who has training and expertise in working with people who hear voices.

In a related vein, as a helper, you need to be honest about your qualifications—that you are a beginning trainee. Helpers who describe themselves as counselors or advertise that they provide psychological interventions that they have not been trained to use are not acting ethically. For example, a practice client may refer to you as his "psychologist." Given that *psychologist* is a legal term associated with having earned a doctoral degree and passing a major national examination, ethical behavior would involve telling the client that you are a trainee learning helping skills and do not have a degree or license to practice psychology.

Furthermore, beginning helpers should consult with supervisors to enable them to best serve their clients. In one helping class, a student met with a client who mentioned that she had considered suicide because of all of the stressors in her life. The student immediately contacted her lab leader who consulted with the instructor, who then intervened with the client to provide the necessary assistance. Furthermore, when one's own issues threaten to interfere with the helping process, helpers need to consult supervisors. For example, at the same time John was struggling with his decision to marry his long-term girlfriend, his client was also considering whether to make a lifelong commitment to his partner. John realized the potential for harm in this situation and discussed with his supervisor how to ensure that his personal issues related to commitment would not have a negative impact on the helping sessions with his client.

EDUCATING CLIENTS ABOUT THE HELPING PROCESS

Clients have a right to understand the nature of the helping relationship. Many clients have never experienced a formal helping relationship and are uncertain about what to expect. If helpers explain their theoretical orientation in simple, clear terms, clients can make an informed decision about whether or not to participate in the process. For example, helpers should provide information about fees, length of the helping relationship, techniques used, whether anyone will be observing or supervising, and whether the sessions will be audio- or videotaped. As was noted previously, beginning helpers must also inform clients about the limits of confidentiality and their status as helpers (e.g., that they are not professionals). Helpers might ask clients to sign an informed consent form that explains the process (see Exhibit 3.2). Similarly, many health care professionals are required by the Health Insurance Portability and Accountability Act (HIPAA) of 1996 to have their patients sign statements related to privacy and security of health care information.

Furthermore, clients have the right to understand what outcomes can be expected. Here it is important not to promise anything that you cannot necessarily deliver. Thus, for example, it is appropriate to say that helping involves an opportunity for clients to explore themselves and that you are optimistic about your work together, but you cannot guarantee that they will be "cured" or even that they will see improvement.

In addition, when providing services to families or couples, helpers must clarify their roles and the relationships that occur during the time of service. For example, a helper was seeing an adolescent client whose parents were divorcing. The mother was struggling during this time and asked whether she could talk privately with the helper to discuss some of her issues related to the divorce. The helper gently reminded her of the importance of having a special relationship with the client (the daughter) and indicated that this relationship might be jeopardized by even one helping session with the mother. The mother was given referrals to other qualified helpers.

DEVELOPING APPROPRIATE BOUNDARIES

Helpers need to think about boundaries, or the ground rules and limits of the helping relationship. Boundaries can be about the structure of helping (e.g., length, fees, policies about touching and violence, confidentiality) or about the interpersonal nature of the interaction (no sexual intimacies, friendships, or business relationships with clients outside of helping). Considerable research has been conducted on the practices of experienced therapists regarding boundaries (see Borys & Pope, 1989; Conte, Plutchik, Picard, & Karasu, 1989; Epstein, Simon, & Kay, 1992; Holroyd & Brodsky, 1977).

Initially, helpers need to clarify the rules about confidentiality, the length of helping, and any fees involved. Helpers typically choose to avoid involvement in social activities with clients outside of sessions because such activities may make it difficult for helpers to be objective and for clients to feel comfortable disclosing in the therapy setting. I encourage beginning helpers to give their work phone number or e-mail address but not their private cell phone number or e-mail address to clients (although I also encourage you to check local regulations, and I also recognize that issues around technology change rapidly). Clients need the work number or e-mail address in case of schedule changes (and need to be given emergency numbers or hotline numbers in case of off-hours emergencies), but giving out private numbers can be problematic because some clients take advantage of beginning helpers who have difficulty setting limits about not talking on the phone at any hour for any reason. I vividly recall one of my first clients in a practicum during graduate school. She called for several nights at midnight because I had not clarified that calling was not appropriate. When I finally told the client that she could not keep calling every night, she felt hurt and abandoned, and the therapeutic relationship was damaged. It would have been better if I had discussed this limit with her initially to clarify the rules and expectations.

Developing appropriate boundaries is often quite difficult. It is probably best for beginning helpers to start out being overly cautious and then relax their boundaries as they gain experience. Consultation with supervisors can be helpful when in doubt about which boundaries are appropriate and how to set them. Furthermore, exploring one's own personal values and issues is important when thinking about establishing boundaries in general. It is even more important for helpers to examine their own issues when they want to violate or adjust boundaries with a particular client, because these urges to violate boundaries often reflect countertransference issues (e.g., need to be loved, need to not have others get angry).

FOCUSING ON THE NEEDS OF THE CLIENT

At times, the needs of the helper may conflict with the needs of the client. For example, Jim (the helper) may be preoccupied during a session because he needs to study for an exam. Jim may have a difficult time focusing on the client (e.g., listening, giving eye contact) and may even hope to end the session early to study. However, it is critical that Jim set aside his own concerns about the exam and focus on listening carefully to the client and being as present as possible in the helping session.

An interesting situation results when the client's unresolved issues result in behaviors that benefit the helper. For example, Himee noticed that her helper often had a soft drink on his desk. Himee then began to give the helper a soft drink at the beginning of each helping session. Although the helper might like being taken care of in this manner, ethical behavior requires that the helper try to understand the meaning of Himee's behavior and act in a manner that places the client's needs first. In this case, the helper might assist Himee in uncovering her desire to please the helper and her fear that the helper might abandon her if she did not bring gifts to the sessions. It might be in the best interest of the client to assist her in viewing herself as valuable in relationships, independent of the gifts she presents to others.

AVOID HARMFUL DUAL RELATIONSHIPS

A potentially harmful dual relationship occurs when someone in power (e.g., a helper, professor, supervisor) adds another role to his or her interaction with a less powerful individual (e.g., a client, student, supervisee) because the dual relationship may lead to the harm or exploitation of the less powerful person. For example, it would not be unusual or necessarily problematic for a supervisor also to be a student's professor and evaluator; however, if the supervisor-professor also took on the role of therapist, the dual relationship could be harmful because confidential information disclosed in therapy could potentially be used against the student. Helpers need to be aware of the power differential when working with others and ensure that clients are not harmed by their interactions. For example, if a beginning helper is assigned a client for whom she or he is also a teaching assistant, harm might occur if the client-student feels that the helper could not fairly and objectively evaluate him or her when grading exams. Hence, helpers should not take on clients with whom they have other relationships that would interfere with the helping process, nor should they develop conflicting relationships with ongoing clients.

Perhaps the most blatant example of harmful dual relationships involves a helper having a sexual relationship with a client. Sexual involvement with clients (and former clients) has been shown to have negative outcomes (Pope, 1994). Thus, many professions have developed explicit rules prohibiting sexual intimacies between helpers and clients. In addition, providing counseling to someone with whom one has been sexually involved in the past can be destructive to the client. Helpers typically cannot be objective and provide quality services to clients with whom they have been intimately involved. For more discussion of sexual attraction (a common feeling for helpers at all levels), see Chapter 19.

Helpers also should avoid getting into the *role* of being a therapist with friends or family members. Although helping skills can certainly be used to communicate effectively in personal relationships and the ultimate goal is for people to turn to friends and family for support, taking on the role of a therapist or helper with friends or family members can be detrimental for several reasons. First, when a person takes on the role of therapist, the primary goal is to help the client, whereas the goal with friends and family is to have a 50–50 relationship. Hence, by taking on the role of therapist with family and friends, it is difficult to get one's own needs met. Second, it is difficult to be objective when listening to the problems of friends or family members. A lack of objectivity could have a negative impact on a helping session because the helper's own needs could interfere with assisting the client to act in her or his best interests. In my own relationships with family and friends, I certainly dispense advice and support, but I make clear that it is not from being in the role of a therapist at this time. Third, the role of helper is powerful and could disturb the power dynamics in the relationship. For example, Alfonso began to rely on his friend to be his helper while he was going through a divorce. In time, Alfonso became dependent on this friend for assistance when problems emerged at work or with his children. His relationship with his friend-turned-helper was harmed because their interactions were always focused on Alfonso's problems. Obviously, the differences between relationships with friends and family members versus a professional therapeutic relationship are complicated and overlapping, so I encourage readers to think through these issues carefully and debate them in class.

BE AWARE OF YOUR VALUES

Empirical literature has shown that helpers' values influence clients (e.g., Beutler & Bergan, 1991), so helpers need to be aware of this influence of values and beliefs in their interactions with clients. For example, a helper who believes that all women should work outside the home in high-status, nontraditional occupations may inadvertently discourage a client from selecting a traditional career that seems to be a good fit for her interests and that would enable her to focus on her family. Beginning helpers, like advanced clinicians, should work to understand their biases. Thus, I encourage helpers to increase their awareness of their values and to ascertain the influence of these values on the helping process. Becoming aware of values is a part of self-awareness that will be covered more in Chapter 4.

The influence of values in helping can be subtle. Helpers can influence the direction of sessions and clients' selection of actions through nonverbal behavior of which they are unaware, such as smiling or nodding their heads at particular moments. Beginning helpers sometimes struggle with inadvertently encouraging clients to talk about situations that are comfortable for or interesting to the helper. For example, a helper might use nonverbal behaviors to indicate great interest when the client is talking about her romantic relationship but seem somewhat less interested when the discussion moves to roommate concerns. Viewing videotapes, talking to supervisors, and self-reflecting can enable helpers to become aware of how their values influence the helping process.

ETHICAL BEHAVIOR RELATED TO CULTURE

Ethical behavior mandates that helpers be mindful of differences among individuals and use basic helping skills that reflect an understanding of the people with whom they are working (see also American Psychological Association, 2003). I spend more time talking about ethics related to culture in Chapter 5.

ACT IN A VIRTUOUS MANNER

Professionals concerned with ethical behaviors have begun to move from a focus on behaving in an ethical manner (i.e., following the guidelines delineated in an ethical code) to behaving in a virtuous manner. Virtues are not as concerned with laws and rules as much as with striving to be a person of positive moral character (Meara et al., 1996). Part of this change results from the reality that ethical codes, in and of themselves, cannot provide exact specifications for behaviors. Helpers need to internalize the six basic ethical principles discussed earlier in this chapter (autonomy, beneficence, nonmaleficence, justice, fidelity, and veracity), practice a comprehensive ethical decision-making model, and monitor themselves and their behaviors to ensure respectful interactions with clients.

For example, a helper had a very successful helping session with a client at the university counseling center. She used her basic helping skills to provide a safe and open environment. The client shared much personal information in the session and struggled with concerns of importance in his life. The following weekend, the helper ran into the client at a party. She was confused about how to deal with this situation because her training had not addressed guidelines for meeting clients in social situations. However, the helper was a sensitive and respectful woman, so she waited for the client to speak to her first and returned his brief greeting as they passed. Her response was consistent with virtuous behavior. It is important to recognize that it is not possible to provide helpers with answers to every ethical situation they might encounter; instead, helpers need to behave with clients in a caring and respectful manner that is consistent with acting in a virtuous manner (which is most likely also ethical).

TAKE CARE OF YOURSELF TO ENSURE THAT YOU CAN CARE FOR OTHERS

One final often-ignored dimension of ethical behavior involves helpers taking care of themselves. Helping can be an exhausting enterprise that requires helpers to give much of themselves to others. The fastest road to burnout involves taking care of others without paying attention to relaxation and caring for one's own needs. It behooves helpers to monitor their health and energy to ensure that they can provide quality services to others. Helpers might regularly evaluate the presence of added stressors, poor health, and exhaustion. Helpers can try to achieve balance by integrating rewarding work, supportive relationships, regular exercise, and healthy eating habits into their lives. Helpers can also seek counseling when they need support or assistance with pressing concerns.

Working Through an Ethical Dilemma

Although beginning helpers may not encounter many ethical dilemmas, learning how to work through these situations can be helpful so that helpers can be prepared. Ethical dilemmas occur when there are competing ethical guidelines (Kitchener, 1984). At times, the actions that helpers could take to uphold one ethical principle would violate another ethical principle. Kitchener (1984) described inherent contradictions that exist in ethical codes (e.g., individual autonomy vs. making decisions for clients; confidentiality vs. protecting others). For example, ethical codes often ensure a client's right to privacy and confidentiality. They also endorse the importance of working to minimize harm to others. These important standards can, at times, conflict with one another. For instance, one helper worked with an adolescent client who was threatening to kill herself but did not want the helper to discuss this with her parents. The adolescent felt that her parents would not take her seriously and might punish her for disclosing these thoughts to her helper. The helper was faced with an ethical dilemma that was not easily resolved by examining the profession's ethical code. In this case, the helper talked with the adolescent about the importance of disclosing this information to her parents to ensure her safety. Then, in the presence of the client and with the client's permission, the helper discussed the client's concerns with her parents.

Helpers can follow the A-B-C-D-E strategy for ethical decision making (Sileo & Kopala, 1993) when they are confronted with an ethical dilemma. To illustrate its application, let us consider a situation in which a client discloses to a helper that she was raped by an acquaintance the previous night. The helper in this case is a beginning helper who feels outraged by the crime and wants to call the police immediately. The client, however, is concerned about her boyfriend finding out and definitely does not want the rape to be reported. The helper realizes that this is not a situation in which he is legally required to break confidentiality and report the rape, but instead is an ethical dilemma between reporting a crime against the client's wishes and maintaining confidentiality. The helper uses the A-B-C-D-E strategy for ethical decision making to work toward resolving how to proceed in this challenging situation.

A: ASSESSMENT

The helper identifies the situation; the client's status and resources; and the helper's values, feelings, and reactions to the situation. In this case, the helper notes that the client is a well-adjusted, bright, and competent young woman who is finishing her 4th year in college, majoring in business administration. She reports having a good relationship with her boyfriend. Two close friends have promised to support her through her recovery from the rape, and she has indicated an interest in attending a rape survivors' group. The helper, however, feels strongly that the rapist should be punished for what he did to the client. When he reflects more on the issue, however, the helper acknowledges that the strength of his emotions may result from his feeling helpless when he discovered that his younger sister had been raped.

B: BENEFIT

The helper evaluates what is most likely to benefit the client, the helping relationship, and the client's significant others. In this case, the helper believes that disclosure of the rape to the police and subsequent prosecution of the rapist could benefit the client, her boyfriend, and possible future victims. However, he also acknowledges that the client believes that she would be helped most by discussing the rape with her helper, her best friends, and a rape survivors' support group and would be harmed by going to the police. As with many ethical dilemmas, different benefits are present for several possible solutions.

C: CONSEQUENCES AND CONSULTATION

Moving on to the ethical, legal, emotional, and therapeutic consequences that could result from possible actions, the helper consults with a supervisor who provides assistance in identifying and working through salient issues. In this case, the supervisor helps the helper identify that his disclosure of the rape to the police would undermine the trust that he had worked to develop with the client. Moreover, the helper would be violating the client's wishes, confidentiality, and right to privacy. His reporting of the rape might reinforce feelings of powerlessness that the client felt after being raped.

D: DUTY AND DOCUMENTATION

The helper next considers to whom a duty exists. In this case, the helper's primary duty or responsibility is to the client rather than to other people in her life (e.g., her boyfriend or other women that the rapist might harm). His job as a helper is to do no harm to his client and to provide services that enhance her growth and potential. The helper is beginning to realize how important it is to abide by the client's wish for nondisclosure, despite his own desire to prosecute the rapist and protect others.

Sometimes, the helper may have a duty to protect someone other than the client (i.e., an identifiable person whom the client is threatening to harm). In situations in which a child is being abused, helpers are mandated by law to report the abuse or to assist the client in reporting the abuse to child protective services (laws vary across states, so it is important to be aware of local laws). Furthermore, in cases in which the client threatens to harm self or others, the helper must ensure the safety of the individuals identified as at risk for harm. For example, if this client told her helper that she planned to murder the rapist and had enlisted the assistance of an assassin to carry out the plan, the helper would have a responsibility to prevent harm to the rapist and report this threat to the police.

The documentation part of this step involves keeping records of what happens. Given that some of these situations involve sticky legal issues, it is important for helpers to document what happened as precisely as possible, remembering that all such documents can be subpoenaed.

E: EDUCATION

The helper reviews his education to determine what he has learned about appropriate actions to take in dealing with similar ethical dilemmas. The helper speaks to his supervisor, refers to his notes from his courses, consults current websites (see Exhibit 3.1), and determines that in this situation the best strategy is to maintain the client's confidence and assist in her recovery from the rape. The helper also decides to go for therapy to address his residual feelings about his sister's rape.

Concluding Comments

Ethical dilemmas can be aptly described by the two Chinese symbols representing *crisis:* danger and opportunity. Ethical dilemmas can be dangerous in that the welfare of the client may be compromised but they also present an opportunity for helpers to reflect on what they have learned and what they value and then to act in a manner consistent with professional and (one hopes) personal values. Ethical dilemmas provide a unique challenge for helpers to confront and resolve important questions and to ensure, to the best of their abilities, that their clients' needs are being served. In my experience when ethical issues arise in classes (and they have a few times), it provides a great opportunity to think through important pedagogical issues and make sure that the best possible educational services are being delivered.

What Do You Think?

- How do you feel about professional groups imposing ethical restrictions on helpers?
- What do you think the consequences should be if someone violates the ethical standards?
- What is your opinion about cultural considerations in ethics? Discuss how your response may be influenced by your cultural background.

- Discuss the possible positive and negative consequences of discussing confidentiality and informed consent and how they influence the therapeutic relationship.
- What are some ways, other than those covered in the chapter, that helpers could inadvertently cause clients harm?
- Do you agree that taking care of oneself as a helper helps to prevent problems in the helping role?

RESEARCH SUMMARY

Ethics

Citation: Kitson, C., & Sperlinger, D. (2007). Dual relationships between clinical psychologists and their clients: A survey of UK clinical psychologists' attitudes. *Psychology and Psychotherapy: Theory, Research, and Practice, 80,* 279–295.

Rationale: Ethical codes indicate that dual relationships (i.e., when the therapist and client have another relationship beyond the professional one) can be problematic. Sexual relationships between therapists and clients are strictly prohibited in most ethical codes, but it is less clear about the appropriateness of nonsexual relationships. Kitson and Sperlinger noted that some nonsexual dual relationships have the potential to upset the dynamics of the therapeutic relationship, particularly because of issues related to power, boundaries, and whose needs are being met. Ethical guidelines related to dual relationships have been developed to minimize loss of objectivity and exploitation by therapists. The authors wanted to replicate past work on attitudes about dual relationships.

Method: Participants (UK clinical psychologists with an average of 14 years of postdoctoral experience) completed a survey about the appropriateness of 38 different scenarios representing dual relationships.

Interesting findings:
- Participants rarely discussed with clients the likelihood of out-of-therapy contact and how they would manage such an encounter. However, this issue was more likely to come up in therapy after there had been a chance encounter outside of therapy.
- Participants unanimously agreed that it is never appropriate to have a sexual relationship with a client being seen currently or in the year after therapy has ended.
- Participants also rated it as inappropriate to provide therapy to a friend, trainee, employee; to develop a business relationship with a former client; or to accept as a referral a partner of a colleague or employee.
- Instances when participants thought that it was sometimes or often appropriate to have dual relationships included continuing to shop at a supermarket where they regularly see current or former clients, accepting a referral for therapy of someone who was referred by a former client, continuing to see a client whom they realize is closely related to a previous client, remaining at a party after accidentally encountering and interacting with a client at that party, attending a party unconnected with their work where they know one of their clients will be, and testifying as a witness in a personal injury case after they have established a therapeutic relationship with the client involved.
- Clinical psychologists who viewed dual relationships as less appropriate were female, younger, less experienced, psychodynamic oriented, worked in an urban area, and did not work and live in the same area as their clients (these findings replicate research in the United States).

Conclusions:
- Clearly, therapists should not be sexually involved with clients.
- Therapists should not engage in dual relationships that will exploit clients or are for their own personal benefit.
- Many other types of dual relationships are ambiguous in terms of appropriateness.

Implications for Therapy:
- When confronted with any potential dual relationship, helpers need to think through the potential problems. It is a good idea to refer to ethical codes and consult with colleagues.

BONUS MATERIALS

Practice exercises, labs, and other resources for students and teachers are available on the companion website: http://pubs.apa.org/books/supp/hill4.

Self-Awareness | 4

Every human has four endowments—self-awareness,
conscience, independent will, and creative imagination.
These give us the ultimate human freedom . . . the power
to choose, to respond, to change.

—*Stephen Covey*

Emma was working with HIV clients who were mandated to come to sessions. When they did not want
to be there or hear anything she had to say or when
they had homophobic attitudes, Emma found herself
not liking these clients and getting angry at them. In
contrast, when other clients listened to her, asked lots
of questions, and were very involved, she found it very
gratifying to be with them and she felt as though she
had really helped them. But she had to ponder whether
she was being unfair to those reluctant clients, who
might actually have really needed her help but did not
know how to accept it.

Self-awareness has been thought of as intrinsically positive,
necessary for ethical practice, and critical for skillful helping (Williams, Hayes, & Fauth, 2008). Most people would
agree that helpers need to be aware of themselves, because
who the helper is influences the process. For example, clients may have a different reaction to a big, imposing ath-
letic man than to a small, unimposing attractive woman.
Furthermore, helpers use their reactions to their clients as

http://dx.doi.org/10.1037/14345-004
Helping Skills: Facilitating Exploration, Insight, and Action, Fourth Edition, by
C. E. Hill

one gauge of how others might react to the client, so the helper needs to be aware of how his or her reactions to the client are influenced by the helper's own issues. For example, the helper might be very sensitive to feeling criticized by an older female client who reminds him of his mother. Finally, the helper's mood (e.g., being hungry or sleepy, being distracted because of having had a fight with a partner) can influence how she or he feels and behaves in the session.

But what is self-awareness? Williams et al. (2008) suggested that self-awareness can be thought of as either a stable characteristic (i.e., self-knowledge or self-insight) or a state of heightened self-focus (i.e., sensitivity in the here-and-now). The first type is "Who am I?" whereas the second type is "What am I feeling in this moment?" Both seem important for anyone who is interested in helping others.

Many aspects of self-awareness are unconscious, but our goal as helpers is to examine ourselves on an ongoing basis and become more conscious. We strive to become as aware as possible of who we are and what we bring to the helping process. At the outset of this chapter, however, I want to stress that self-awareness is an aspiration and something that we all strive for throughout our lives, but not something easily obtained and maintained. I suggest that you read this chapter at the beginning of your training and then come back to it over the years as you grow and change, because you will have different thoughts about self-awareness based on your experiences in providing helping.

Self-Knowledge and Self-Insight

Helpers need to have a general awareness of their own issues, biases, strengths, and weaknesses because these influence how they behave in sessions and how clients perceive them. Given that helpers use themselves (they rely on their own reactions to know how others react to the clients), they need to be aware of who they are and how they come across to others so that they can determine what is coming from them and what is coming from the clients. Furthermore, by being aware of their own painful experiences, helpers can become more attuned to and sensitive to others' experiences.

So as helpers, we need to be aware of who we are and what we bring to the process, and use ourselves to help others. In the next sections, I focus on typical characteristics of helpers, motivations for wanting to be a helper, and potential biases as a helper. As you read each section, think about yourself and how these ideas fit for you.

CHARACTERISTICS OF HELPERS

Helping seems to be a natural tendency of many people who have an innate desire to assist others (Stahl & Hill, 2008). Such individuals may recognize a special talent in themselves for listening and supporting others. Many students in helping skills classes say that friends and family often seek them out.

Helpers tend to have several characteristics in common. They listen carefully and empathically, are nonjudgmental, are open to new experiences and perspectives, are approachable and friendly, and like to listen (Hill et al., 2013). Summers and Barber (2010) added that helpers need to have hope, love, kindness, social intelligence, flexibility, curiosity, creativity, persistence, humility, and humor, all of which contribute to their being able to have a flexible emotional, open, reflective relationship with clients.

There are also some characteristics that make it difficult to attain and maintain self-awareness. Perfectionism and a lack of tolerance for ambiguity can make it hard to deal with the fact that there are rarely "right" answers about what to do in helping. Furthermore, defensiveness and a lack of willingness to explore difficult topics such as sexual attraction, anger, and biases can make it difficult to be open to painful or taboo feelings. Of course, many practicing therapists are perfectionists, have a lack of tolerance for ambiguity, and are defensive, so these characteristics do not imply that such people cannot be helpers. Rather, I mention these as characteristics so that aspiring helpers can look at those qualities in themselves and think about the potential impact on their helping abilities.

MOTIVATIONS FOR WANTING TO HELP

As you start the process of becoming a helper, it is valuable to try to understand what motivates you to want to help others. Most people have a mixture of many motivations, and these motivations change over time. Motivations are difficult to be aware of and understand, but it is important to reflect because these reasons could influence what you do in helping sessions. Recently, Hill et al. (2013), in a study of undergraduate students taking helping skills classes, found that some motivations are other-oriented (i.e., to help others and give back to society), whereas others are more self-oriented (i.e., to feel good and to provide meaning to life).

Other-Oriented Motivations

One reason for aspiring to become a helper is to make a difference in people's lives. For example, helpers might want to provide support to those in need by volunteering to work in a shelter for homeless women or by becoming a buddy to a gerontology patient confined to a nursing home. People who are motivated to use helping skills in situations such as these provide others with supportive relationships in which clients feel listened to, cared for, and understood. Some helpers also choose to make a difference in children's lives by mentoring or tutoring young students, using their foundation of helping skills to develop encouraging relationships. Others hope to make life less painful for those in troubled situations. For example, helpers can provide an important function by assisting teens who think they might be gay or lesbian and fear retribution from family and friends.

Furthermore, some people aspire to be helpers because they experienced therapy themselves as clients when they were struggling with painful issues, and they want to help others so that others do not have to experience as much pain as they have. They might also feel grateful to their therapists for helping them through a difficult situation and want to give back and contribute to society, For example, when Kendra was 12 years old, her mother died, and Kendra had to assume her mother's role with her five siblings. She engaged in her own personal therapy to help her cope with her loss and her new responsibilities. Kendra now aspires to help children who have experienced loss in their lives. Another example involves rape survivors who become crisis counselors after receiving supportive counseling that helped them resolve issues related to the rape. Similarly, some people who overcome substance abuse want to help others both as a way of helping others with similar problems and as a way of helping themselves stay sober.

Finally, people may enter helping fields to work for social change. Helping affords a unique opportunity to make a difference in the lives of individuals and, sometimes, to influence social policies. Helpers who work with adolescents in at-risk environments may provide them with skills, hope, and encouragement to overcome obstacles and graduate from high school and college. Other helpers may draft legislation or testify on behalf of policies that fight discrimination (e.g., sexual harassment) or encourage funding for social services (e.g., child care). Contributions to social change can also occur through research that helpers undertake to evaluate the effectiveness of helping interventions (e.g., studying the efficacy of training undergraduate students to be effective helpers for battered women who have entered the criminal justice system).

Self-Oriented Motivations

Most of us are also motivated to become helpers for more self-oriented reasons. Most of you have probably heard the jokes about how students major in psychology to heal themselves (or their families or friends). Indeed, many people enter helping fields to work through unresolved personal issues or to change situations that they found painful in the past (e.g., an unhappy childhood).

In addition, some people view helping as consistent with their cultural values and thus seek careers that enable them to assist others. These people are often natural helpers and have had role models (e.g., parents, aunts or uncles, cousins) who have dedicated their lives to the service of others (e.g., were counselors, ministers, or social workers).

For many individuals, the helping environment is attractive because it allows them to work with clients who are striving toward actualization of their potential. Furthermore, helpers are often excited by their contribution to the process of change in clients' lives and are energized by their clients' hard work and personal growth. One therapist told me that there was no better job in the world than being able to facilitate and be a witness to the growth of people in the journey to understanding themselves.

Yet another motivation is that it is intellectually challenging to help others. People are endlessly fascinating and unique, and it is intriguing to try to understand them and intervene to help them change. Furthermore, helpers learn a lot about other people through helping. Helpers can vicariously experience other ways of living, similarly to traveling, reading novels, or watching movies. Hearing clients challenge themselves can in turn impel helpers to examine themselves. In this way, being a helper can lead to personal growth. One therapist said that one of her motivations for being a therapist is that she values self-reflection, personal growth, and ongoing learning. Being a therapist keeps her on her toes in terms of her own wellness and mental health. Similarly, a helping career may appeal to many people because of the opportunity to interact with smart, capable colleagues who value personal growth and helping others. They may receive support from their colleagues to actively examine their own issues and improve themselves to ensure their continued success in the helping role.

Some would consider the idea of wanting to make a difference in people's lives to be altruism. According to definitions, however, altruism involves an unselfish concern or devotion for the welfare of others. One dictionary notes that altruism is not necessarily beneficial to oneself and can sometimes even be harmful to oneself (especially if you disregard your own needs). Most people, however, want to be helpers not only to give to others but also because it makes them feel good to help others (Hill et al., 2013). Many students in helping skills classes describe helping as fulfilling and giving them a sense of purpose or meaning in life. They also describe it as rewarding and gratifying to be able to help others and to be able to make a difference in their lives.

Of course, some self-oriented motivations can be less positive or healthy (Bugental, 1965). Some people may want to help others because they are needy themselves and view helping as a way to develop relationships and fulfill their interpersonal needs. These people might have difficulty with intimacy and therefore seek a safe way of getting close to others. In addition, some individuals sometimes envision themselves as saviors for the less fortunate or as wise distributors of knowledge and advice, and want to go into the helping profession as a mission, to save others. Others may use helping as a way to feel better about what they have by comparing themselves with those who are less fortunate. For other people, helping others enables them to feel superior to those whom they are attempting to help. Yet others like the sense of power or authority of being in the counselor role with people who are suffering. Such motivations can be dangerous, especially if the helper is not aware of them and acts out of them in the helping session. For example, when helpers need clients to get better to build their own self-esteem, they often cannot allow clients to explore and make their own choices (e.g., choosing not to change). Clients might even feel worse after being in a session with a helper who is contemptuous, demanding, or seductive.

Finally, some people might aspire to become therapists for achievement, wealth, prominence, fame, prestige, and glory. Such motivations might be unrealistic. Although people in the helping professions are generally well-educated professionals with credibility and good standing within their communities, and a few do become well known because of their scholarly work and a few do become wealthy, therapists generally get their gratification from helping others rather than from wealth or prominence. For those people wanting or needing fame and glory, the therapeutic profession may not be the best choice.

Balance Between Other-Orientation and Self-Orientation

In general, it makes sense to have some balance between other-oriented and self-oriented motives for becoming and being a therapist. Being too altruistic could lead to burnout, and being too self-oriented does not fit with the values of helping others and could lead to harming clients.

AWARENESS OF BIASES

All of us have biases based on stereotypes of other people. It is perhaps a basic, but lamentable, human tendency to have in-groups and out-groups and to believe that people who are not a part of our group are different from us in fundamental ways, making it hard to empathize with them. Indeed, some recent neuroscience research indicates that we may be hardwired to be more attracted to people who are similar to us racially (Ito & Batholow, 2009). I call these biases *hot buttons* for helpers, because they reflect problems that can get triggered or set off in the helping setting. Becoming aware of hot buttons is important so that we do not inadvertently or unconsciously mistreat clients.

Some typical hot buttons are based on cultural factors (see also Chapter 5 on culture), especially if we have had limited contact with people from other cultures. Another common hot button that students in helping skills classes have admitted over the years (and in a recent study; Hill et al., 2013) is thinking about working with clients who have abused, raped, murdered, committed crimes, or are generally unlawful. Trainees worry that they will not be able to be open, nonjudgmental, and empathic with such clients. Because of their anger and rage at such offensive behaviors, they cannot imagine having compassion for the suffering of these people or having curiosity about how these people came to behave in this way. Students also often have difficulty thinking about working with clients who express hostility, anger, disdain, or disrespect toward them as helpers. Because helpers are often very empathic, unaggressive people who want others to like them, it is threatening and scary for them when they think clients do not like them and might even want to harm them.

We all also have biases based on our own personal backgrounds, which might show up as countertransferences. For example, a helper may find that she instinctively dislikes boisterous male clients because they all remind her of her loud, overbearing father. Another helper might get annoyed with dependent clients because she did not get enough nurturing herself as a child. Countertransference is discussed more in Chapter 11.

In general, beginning helpers often have trouble with clients whom they perceive to be different from them on any salient dimension. For example, a beginning helper might have difficulty imagining working with a client who is much older. Helpers also often have problems working with clients who have different values (e.g., on politics, gender equality, stereotyping, racism). Similarly, and understandably, clients have difficulty believing that helpers who are different can understand them.

Also difficult, although less often acknowledged, is that helpers have trouble working with clients who are too similar to them. Helpers often assume that these clients are exactly like them on every dimension and forget to help the clients explore, or they might treat the client as a friend and start chatting and disclosing. An example might be when a female college student client starts talking about roommate problems, the beginning helper (a female college student) might project that the client has trouble being assertive just as she does and might even start disclosing about her own difficulties with roommates. In such a situation, the client might respond by shutting down and not exploring her own distinct feelings further.

STRATEGIES TO INCREASE SELF-KNOWLEDGE/SELF-INSIGHT

It is important that helpers learn about themselves so that their personal issues do not intrude on sessions with clients and so that they can be more helpful with clients. By taking care of ourselves, we are more likely to be helpful to our clients and avoid demanding inappropriate things from clients.

In this section, I discuss two major strategies for increasing self-knowledge. The first involves personal psychotherapy with a good psychotherapist. The second involves self-reflection. These are not mutually exclusive. Personal psychotherapy enhances self-reflection because it can provide an outside perspective and a healing relationship. Likewise, self-reflection can enhance personal psychotherapy because typically, people take more personal responsibility for what they want to discuss in therapy after they have engaged in self-reflection. Later, when you are seeing clients, supervision can be another helpful strategy.

Psychotherapy

The ideal place for beginning helpers to learn about themselves is through their own personal psychotherapy. I heartily recommend that people who want to become helpers seek therapy not only to resolve personal problems but also to learn more about themselves and their motivations for becoming helpers. For an account of my own, very valuable experiences in therapy, see Hill (2005a).

Getting into their own personal therapy can enable helpers to recognize personal issues that could interfere with their ability to help. If they are preoccupied with themselves and their problems or are unaware of negative personal behaviors, helpers rarely have energy left over to focus on clients. Furthermore, therapy can enable helpers to work on their own growth and self-understanding. An occupational hazard (and benefit) of being a helper is that the helping process stirs up personal issues that might otherwise lay dormant. For example, if a client talks about problems with alcoholism and the helper has not resolved similar problems, it might be difficult for the helper to attend to the client's pain instead of focusing on his or her own. Or helpers might minimize the extent of clients' problems because their own problems have been neglected. Although people learn a great deal about themselves through the process of being helpers, personal therapy gives them the opportunity to work on these issues in an appropriate setting.

Moreover, being in therapy themselves as clients can teach helpers about the process of helping. Being a client allows helpers to learn what it is like to be on the receiving end of helping, to see what is and is not helpful, and to experience how difficult it is to open up and reveal painful information about oneself. It is helpful to be a client to empathize with the anxiety, attachment, struggle, and rewards of the process. Being in therapy also provides a model for helpers about how they would (or would not) want to act in sessions with their clients. The firsthand experience of what it is like to be on the receiving end of helping is invaluable.

It is troublesome when helpers-in-need refuse to seek help themselves but are willing to be helpers for others. One worries about the motivations of such persons for wanting to be helpers. Helpers who have the attitude that seeking help is only for weak or defective people may inadvertently communicate that attitude and cause clients to feel ashamed for seeking help.

At this point, you might stop and reflect about what your reaction was when you read this section about personal psychotherapy. Did you say to yourself, "Terrific, I'm going!" or did you say, "No way, I don't need therapy"? What does your reaction say about you and your intentions for wanting to be a helper?

Self-Reflection

Another suggestion is to set aside time for self-reflection. Journaling (i.e., writing about your thoughts and feelings) is one way of doing self-reflection. Likewise, meditation and yoga can be helpful for slowing down and focusing on being present in the moment.

Mindfulness, which involves attending to each aspect of experience as it unfolds in the present moment (Kabat-Zinn, 2003), is also very helpful. Rather than rushing around and multitasking, mindfulness entails focusing attention by nonjudgmentally observing physical perceptions, sensations, emotions, and thoughts. An attitude of warmth, curiosity, and acceptance toward whatever emerges is suggested, whether the experience is positive or negative. For example, mindfulness might involve paying attention when you eat to each taste and sensation without focusing on other things, or sitting outside in the sun and being aware of the various emotions as they emerge without denying them. In this mode, you witness and explore each experience rather than attempting to fix or change the experience in any way. Essentially, a thought or feeling comes into your mind, you observe and experience it, and then you let it go. Practicing mindfulness is good preparation for nonjudgmentally concentrating on and listening to clients, to what they are saying and feeling, while putting aside one's own agenda and preconceptions.

State of Heightened Self-Focus

Visualize yourself in the following situations:

- It's your first session ever seeing a client.
- A client is 25 minutes late to your session.
- You're scheduled to take an exam right after your session.
- You didn't get much sleep last night.
- You sense that your client did not react well to your intervention.
- You think that your intervention was brilliant.
- You had an argument right before the session.

What reactions did you have when you visualized these scenes? Did any of the scenes seem more provocative to you than did others?

When most of us think about helping clients, we think immediately about the type of client. Will we be seeing someone who is depressed or anxious? Is the person male or female, old or young? What we often think less about (other than our initial anxiety and lack of self-efficacy) is how we as helpers feel. What issues get triggered in us when clients talk about various experiences, thoughts, or feelings? What reactions are we having to clients when we sit across from them, and how do these reactions influence how we relate to the client?

Helpers can use their inner experiences as a tool for understanding what is happening in the helping process. By being aware of their reactions, helpers can make better decisions about how to intervene and are less likely to act out their reactions in helping situations (Williams, Hurley, O'Brien, & DeGregorio, 2003). Moreover, helpers' reactions can provide valuable clues as to how other people react to clients. For example, if the helper feels bored when a client talks in a monotone voice, chances are that at least some other people in the client's life also feel bored when the client talks that way. Hence, helpers have some firsthand information about how the client comes across to other people. So, interestingly, if the helper has a reaction, it could be due to the client, or it could be due to the helper. Let us say that the helper gets angry at the client. Is that due to something that the client did verbally or nonverbally, or is it due to the helper's issue? One way of telling is that if you have the same feeling with many clients (or people in your life), it is probably you and not the clients (or other people).

In addition, given that we are all human beings with needs and wishes, our personal issues often unconsciously influence the helping process. In fact, as previously mentioned, it is this human relationship that helps clients change, grow, and reach their full potential. But we want to avoid using the helping process to meet our own needs, which can harm the clients. We also want to model healthy interactions for clients in which they are not being taken advantage of and can feel free to act genuinely in our presence. But it is also important to be genuine. As McCullough et al. (2003) said, it is important to be able to laugh when happy and cry when sad. Helpers are not just statues, but real people with real feelings.

Difficulties obviously arise, however, when helpers genuinely have feelings that are in opposition to those of clients. For example, perhaps Don talks about how he uses illegal drugs and loves them, and you have a strong visceral reaction and have a genuine impulse to tell Don that it is not healthy to use drugs. In such situations, it is always important to have your feelings and reactions, and to think about them, but also to think about your goals and intentions for the helping process. To help Don explore, you might need to back off of your immediate reactions, but keep track of them later to try to understand where they come from.

An experienced colleague said that she has a double track going on in her head during sessions. She both pays attention to what the client is saying and is aware of her own reactions. She noted that it was many years before she was able to do this comfortably, and she actually was not sure how she learned it. But she did notice that if she focuses too much on trying to be aware, she is not able to be aware. When this colleague loses track of her reactions, she does a body scan to sense how she is feeling physiologically (does she have a tense jaw, furrowed brow, crossed or uncrossed legs?). She also noted that she is much more comfortable with silence and less talking on her part, which leads to a slower pace, allowing her clients more space to explore.

This same colleague talked about the necessity of bracketing personal events in order to focus on the client. Experienced therapists generally can bracket their personal issues when they are in session unless they are undergoing a major crisis, in which case they are usually aware that they should not be doing therapy at the time. The most dangerous time is when the therapist is not aware of or minimizes the stress and thus cannot bracket it. For one helper, having a teenage son who was constantly pushing limits caused her to have difficulties with teenage clients who pushed boundaries. Not being able to maintain a sense of her boundaries made it difficult for her to nonjudgmentally empathize with such clients.

TYPES OF IN-THE-MOMENT SELF-AWARENESS

We can think about two types of in-the-moment self-awareness (Williams, Judge, Hill, & Hoffman, 1997). The first involves a facilitative self-awareness (i.e., being able to be mindful and accepting of thoughts and feelings as they emerge). The second involves hindering or interfering self-awareness such as distracting, negative self-talk about personal issues, anxiety about one's skills, anxiety about being taped, and rumination about errors. Not surprisingly, hindering self-awareness has been linked with therapists' negative feelings about their own performance in sessions (Williams et al., 2008). Sometimes beginning helpers are so distracted by interfering thoughts ("What am I going to say next?") that they stop listening to the clients. The goal is to increase facilitative self-awareness (i.e., to be fully present in the moment and emotionally available to the client) and to decrease hindering self-awareness (i.e., to bracket distractions and negative self-talk).

STRATEGIES FOR INCREASING IN-THE-MOMENT FACILITATIVE SELF-AWARENESS AND DECREASING INTERFERING SELF-AWARENESS

It is important that helpers learn about themselves so that personal issues do not intrude on sessions with clients. By taking care of ourselves and having healthy relationships, we are less likely to demand inappropriate things from clients. It is when we feel depleted, have either high or low emotional instability, lack self-compassion, are generally in bad shape that we are more likely to act out or engage in inappropriate or unethical activities with clients. Being aware can help us draw back and figure out ways to take care of ourselves and restabilize into a more optimal state. Practicing these strategies in daily life can make it more likely that you will be able to use them within the helping setting.

Increase Self-Awareness

Make a conscious attempt to become aware. Get in a quiet space and turn off all machines. Focus on your body (e.g., "Is there any tension in your head, neck, stomach?) while breathing deeply. Focus on your breath. Be aware of whatever thoughts come into your mind and then let them go. It can also be useful to practice mindfulness, meditation, and relaxation.

Increase Self-Compassion

It is important to have compassion for yourself, or put another way, to love yourself as you truly are. We all have problems given that it is hard to be a human being, so it is important to be self-aware and make changes in your life but not to be too hard on yourself. Accept yourself as a person who is imperfect and striving, who has both positive and negative feelings, positive and negative motivations, biases, judgments, and aspects you like and dislike. I recommend that you read Neff's (2011) book on self-compassion.

Explore/Gain Insight/Make Action Plans

Try to understand from where the feelings are coming (therapy, of course, can help greatly with this). Particularly, think back to childhood and how you were raised. Also, think about major events in your life, both positive and negative, and how these influenced you. Then think about the last few days and what experiences you are currently encountering. Ask yourself the following:

- When have I felt this way before?
- With whom have I felt this way before?
- What was the situation when I felt this way before?
- Why did I feel this way?

Once you have some understanding of where your feelings come from, you can figure out what to do about them. You are certainly influenced by your past and your current situation, but you have some choices and can make some changes.

In Sessions With Clients

When you are in a session and suddenly become aware of interfering self-awareness (e.g., you feel critical, inept, anxious, blocked, cannot listen, cannot be empathic, or you find yourself fiddling with a pen, holding your breath, leaning back or forward, jittering), you can pause, take a deep breath, focus on your breathing, and give yourself a chance to think without having to respond immediately. You can say "Hmmm" or "I need time to think" to slow down the process. Again, accept that you are not perfect and have a moment of compassion for yourself. Positive self-talk can be helpful here. And then return the focus to the client instead of on self. Often we become so overwhelmed by our own feelings, or we get stuck trying to implement an agenda that is not working. It can be useful at such moments to return the focus to the client, perhaps asking how they feel or reflecting feelings. These suggestions are supported by consistent finding in the research (e.g., Williams et al., 2008) that therapists return to the use of basic techniques as a way of reigning in hindering self-focus and returning their positive attention to the client.

One colleague said that when she has a strong feeling in the session that she does not immediately understand (e.g., she is angry and has lost empathy for the client), she makes a mental note of the feeling and then lets it go and moves on with the session. After the session, she comes back to this feeling and tries to understand it, trying to think about the origin of the feeling. This reflection helps her better plan for subsequent sessions with the client. The important point here is to give yourself time and space without feeling pressure to understand it in the moment. You can also say, "Sorry that I lost focus there for a minute, could you please repeat what you said?"

I also want to highlight the idea of staying in touch with your body, asking, What is your body telling you? If you have a feeling that you cannot identify, do a body scan: Are you feeling tired, does your back hurt, do you feel an urgent need to run out and go to the bathroom? Your body and its physiological reactions can be a valuable source of information regarding your emotional status.

I also want to stress that many of the reactions that helpers feel in sessions may be evoked by clients. In such cases in which the stimulus is interpersonal rather than intrapersonal, the helper will need to conceptualize how to be immediate with the client. Immediacy, or talking directly about the relationship, is covered in Chapter 14.

In addition, as a colleague reminded me, it is important for helpers to consciously plan their days and not see too many clients in a row. Helpers need to take time before each session to prepare themselves mentally and after each session to reflect about what happened and write some process notes. And they need to engage in self-care between sessions to go to the restroom, have a snack, make phone calls, and clear their head.

Supervision

An ideal place to examine these issues is in supervision (i.e., consultation with a trained professional). With the help of an experienced supervisor, helpers can begin to identify which feelings come from personal issues, which are stimulated by clients, and which are due to a combination of personal issues and client behavior. Peer supervision can also be invaluable (of course, remember to be concerned about confidentiality here).

Reviewing Sessions

It can be very helpful to play back sessions and think about your thoughts and feelings at each moment. Thinking about your intentions and the client reactions can also help. Similarly, students have found it helpful to transcribe an occasional session because transcribing helps slow down the process so that you can really try to see and understand what was happening.

Healthy Lifestyle

An important way to prepare yourself for being fully present in your work with clients is to engage in self-care. These suggestions are not going to be surprising to you, as huge amounts of research support them. Most basic is that you need to take care of yourself physiologically. You need to get an adequate amount of sleep (most people need at least 8 hours of sleep per night), have a healthy diet (with a minimum of junk food and lots of fruits and vegetables), exercise (your body is a machine that needs at least 30 minutes of exercise per day), and have good interpersonal relationships (a strong support network is vital). Balance is the keyword. Freud talked about how all of us need both love and work in our lives. It is not good to work too much or play too much.

In conclusion, although self-awareness is hard, there are many strategies for working on it both in and out of sessions. Being fully present in life is not only good for being a helper, it is also a good goal for living.

What Do You Think?

- Is self-care really important?
- What message do you give to clients if you are obviously not caring for yourself (e.g., you come to a session with a cold or look extremely tired)?
- Is self-awareness a trait or can it be developed?
- What interferes with self-awareness?
- Is it possible or desirable for everyone to become more self-aware?
- What impact or role do you think the less-positive motivations for becoming a helper have on the helping process? Is it possible that they could even be helpful?
- Can you have too much self-awareness?
- Do you think that personal psychotherapy and self-reflection are necessary or helpful?
- Can people change? Is there free will?

RESEARCH SUMMARY

Journaling to Enhance Awareness

Citation: Hill, C. E., Sullivan, C., Knox, S., & Schlosser, L. Z. (2007). Becoming psychotherapists: Experiences of novice trainees in a beginning graduate class. *Psychotherapy: Theory, Research, Practice, Training, 44,* 434–449.

Rationale: We need to learn more about how trainees experience training, specifically in terms of what they learn and where they struggle. In a previous study relying on questionnaire data collected immediately after sessions with volunteer clients, Williams, Judge, Hill, and Hoffman (1997) found that beginning graduate trainees were very concerned about their therapeutic skills, performance, ability to connect with clients, anxiety, self-efficacy, role as therapist, similarities to and differences from clients, and problematic reactions to clients. Coping strategies included focusing on the client and positive self-talk. Hill et al. hoped to expand on this study by having students write in journals about their experiences throughout their first semester of training.

Method: In their first semester of graduate training, students (none of whom had any previous training) engaged in helping skills training following the model used in this book, saw volunteer clients for 10 one-hour sessions, read and discussed several books about psychotherapy theory, met weekly with an individual supervisor who also watched their sessions in vivo, wrote a self-examination paper, and transcribed and analyzed the data for one of their sessions. In addition, students wrote two to four typed pages in weekly journal entries about any of the following topics: helping skills, competence, countertransference, anxiety, self-efficacy, supervision, learning about therapy, cultural issues, ethics, the process of becoming a therapist, reactions to class, or anything else that seemed relevant. In a final paper, students reflected on changes they made throughout the semester. The professor and a graduate research assistant who had taken the course the previous year read each entry and sent feedback to the students, typically offering support and encouragement but also challenging discrepancies and asking them to elaborate on important topics. Students typically responded to the feedback in subsequent journal entries. Data from the journals were analyzed via qualitative methods.

Interesting Findings:
- Students reported many challenges. They were self-critical, anxious about beginning to see clients, felt pressured to do the "right" thing, had difficulty being aware of their feelings and fully present during sessions, and were distracted by their thoughts and worries. They worried about their therapeutic abilities and felt some discomfort in the therapist role.
- Students often underidentified (focused on differences) or overidentified (focused on similarities) with their clients. Students were uncomfortable when clients did not conform with expectations of how clients should behave in sessions (e.g., did not want to explore deeply), were too psychologically knowledgeable (e.g., talked about transference), or seemed disturbed. Students often felt pulled to step out of the client-centered role that they were learning and, rather, fix the client, give advice, self-disclose inappropriately, soothe the client, or cry with the client.
- In terms of learning the helping skills, students expressed concerns about how to formulate the exploration skills to get the clients to explore deeply and not being stilted or repetitive with their open questions/probes. Regarding insight skills, they were apprehensive about doing them accurately and appropriately. They found it particularly difficult to master the insight skills. They seldom mentioned any difficulties learning or using action skills or with integrating skills across stages.
- Students mentioned difficulties with managing the logistics of sessions, including client recruitment and figuring out what to do when clients did not show up or cancelled.

RESEARCH SUMMARY *(Continued)*

- Students reported major improvements in becoming therapists as the semester progressed. They became less self-critical, more able to connect with clients, better at using the exploration and insight skills, felt better about themselves in the therapist role, less anxious about seeing clients, more self-efficacious, and better able to connect with clients.
- Students felt that they used supervision to help them cope with anxieties and difficulties. They found it helpful when supervisors provided instruction, took an active directive role, were supportive, facilitated exploration of concerns related to becoming therapists or of personal issues that influenced their work with clients, challenged them, and provided specific feedback about their behavior. All students expressed positive feelings about supervision, but a few students also had neutral or even negative reactions (about lack of clear expectations about supervision and difficulties in the supervision relationship).
- Coping strategies included positive self-talk, focusing on the helping skills to deal with anxiety, and turning the focus back to the client instead of self. Between sessions, students prepared for the logistics of sessions (e.g., practiced their introductions, wrote in their journals) so that things ran more smoothly.

Conclusions:
- Major challenges were self-criticism, managing reactions to clients, learning and using the helping skills, and session management.
- Gains were primarily in the areas of learning and using the helping skills, becoming less self-critical, and connecting with clients.
- Supervision was helpful, although there were occasionally ruptures in the relationships.
- Trainees used both in-session (positive self-talk) and outside-session (preparation for sessions) to cope with anxieties.

Implications for Training:
- Writing in a journal is an excellent way to become aware of anxieties and growth.
- More than one semester is needed for trainees to feel competent in the skills of all three stages. Exploration skills can be learned relatively easily, but insight skills require much more practice.
- Individual supervision is a very helpful addition to helping skills training. Supervision provides individualized instruction as well as a forum for discussing challenges related to being a helper.
- Preparation outside of sessions is helpful to becoming able to deal with challenges raised in working with clients.
- During sessions, it is important to be present and aware of feelings and reactions. When self-awareness hinders the helping process, trainees can return to focusing on the client and using the exploration skills (reflections of feelings, restatements, and open questions/probes).
- Trainers can help trainees become aware of their hot buttons and reactions to clients.

BONUS MATERIALS Practice exercises, labs, and other resources for students and teachers are available on the companion website: http://pubs.apa.org/books/supp/hill4.

Cultural Awareness | 5

If we are to achieve a richer culture, rich in contrasting values, we must recognize the whole gamut of human potentialities, and so weave a less arbitrary social fabric, one in which each diverse human gift will find a fitting place.

—*Margaret Mead*

Ruth, a 24-year-old European American woman, was working with George, a 55-year-old African American man who was a drug addict. Ruth thought she was doing a pretty good job until she read a play that George asked her to read. In George's vivid description of the drug culture, Ruth realized that she really knew very little about George's world. This realization spurred her to do some reading about the African American and drug cultures, which enabled her to ask George better questions about his background life.

One specific aspect of self-awareness that is crucial for helping is cultural awareness. Given that culture pervades everything we think and do, we need to become aware of who we are and who our clients are culturally and what both parties bring to the helping process.

My goal in this chapter is to get you to start thinking about culture. I hope to help you become more aware of your own culture and your worldview, to be more empathic with people

http://dx.doi.org/10.1037/14345-005
Helping Skills: Facilitating Exploration, Insight, and Action, Fourth Edition, by C. E. Hill

from other cultures, to think about the significant role of culture in the helping process, and to think about how your cultural biases would play out in the helping process.

Defining Culture

Culture can be defined as the customs, values, attitudes, beliefs, characteristics, and behaviors shared by a group of people at a particular time in history (Skovholt & Rivers, 2003). In addition, culture can be considered the "shared constraints that limit the behavior repertoire available to members of a certain sociocultural group in a way different from individuals belonging to some other group" (Poortinga, 1990, p. 6). It can also be thought of as "a convenient label for knowledge, skills, and attitudes that are learned and passed on from one generation to the next. Accordingly, this transmission of culture occurs in a physical environment in which certain places, times, and stimuli have acquired special meanings" (Segall, 1979, p. 91). An even broader definition of a cultural group is "any group of people who identify or associate with one another on the basis of some common purpose, need, or similarity of background" (Axelson, 1999, p. 3).

Culture includes race/ethnicity, gender, age, ideology, religion, socioeconomic status, sexual orientation, disability status, occupation, and dietary preferences (Pedersen, 1991, 1997). The acronym ADDRESSING provided by Hays (2001) might be helpful in remembering some of the major components of culture (this list is not all-inclusive but provides a useful acronym):

A = age and generational influence
D/D = developmental or acquired disabilities
R = religion and spiritual orientation
E = ethnicity
S = socioeconomic status
S = sexual orientation
I = indigenous heritage
N = national origin
G = gender

Each of us belongs to many cultures, any one of which may become salient at a particular time depending on the people, place, or situation (Pedersen & Ivey, 1993). Some cultural groups require admission (e.g., one has to attend school and pass tests to become a psychologist), others are biologically determined (e.g., age), and still others are a person's choice, albeit influenced by environmental factors (e.g., religion, vegetarianism). Given that our socializations create a web of complex cultural influences, some cultural identities can carry more weight than others (e.g., religion may be more important than sexual orientation to a particular person).

It is important to learn about the history and general characteristics of a culture to understand the background and worldview (see, e.g., McGoldrick, Giordano, & Garcia-Preto, 2005; Muran, 2007). Inaccurate perceptions of a client's culture can negatively affect the therapeutic relationship by creating more distance between the therapist and client and potential for premature termination. It is also important, however, not to assume that everyone within a given group is the same (e.g., not all Irish are jokers, storytellers, and dreamers) because you might be making assumptions that are not true. In fact, there are generally more differences within groups than there are between groups (D. R. Atkinson, Morten, & Sue, 1998; Pedersen, 1997). For example, you see more differences among women than you generally do between women and men.

Dimensions of Culture

It is important to be aware that race is not biological. At the DNA level, there are no differences between people of different "races." Rather, race is a socially constructed idea, such that we categorize people on the basis of some physical characteristics (e.g., skin color, hair type). Thus, when referring to a person's heritage or background, we often refer to *race/ethnicity.*

Racial identity, or how individuals identify with their racial or ethnic culture (Fouad & Brown, 2000; Helms, 1990; Helms & Cook, 1999), is often more important than race/ethnicity because identity is more indicative of how people define themselves. Of course, people can develop their sense of racial identity over time (Helms & Cook, 1999). In the United States, for example, racial and ethnic minority group members often move from depreciating their own race/ethnicity or culture to a more appreciative perspective. Majority group members, in contrast, hopefully move from a perspective of ignorance and entitlement to understanding the privilege inherent in their status and thus begin to advocate for social justice.

Enculturation and *acculturation* are also key constructs to consider for people who have moved from one culture to another (e.g., when a person emigrates from Vietnam to the United States). Enculturation refers to retaining the norms of one's indigenous culture, whereas acculturation refers to adapting to the norms of the dominant culture

(Kim & Abreu, 2001). Note that this acculturative process can foster a bicultural experience for individuals in which two distinct cultures are seen as salient parts of their identity simultaneously (e.g., Berry & Sam, 1996). However, adults who come to the United States from another country (first generation) often remain closely aligned with the way that their culture of origin was when they left, whereas their children (second generation) quickly acculturate to American ways. This difference in cultural values often causes problems in the family, with parents being upset that their children are not retaining the traditional cultural values and dress but rather are behaving according to different cultural norms. It also can cause strain in the family and upset the lines of authority when children acculturate faster than do the parents and use the new language better than can the parents. Children often have to serve as interpreters with teachers and cannot receive help with their homework, which interferes with traditional familial hierarchies.

Individualism versus collectivism refers to the relative importance placed on the individual versus the group (McLeod & McLeod, 2011). Some cultures (e.g., the United States) focus more on the rights of the individual and tend to see people as independent and autonomous. Other cultures (e.g., Korea) tend to focus more on the family and view people as interdependent. A therapist colleague, for example, told me that he routinely starts sessions with Hispanic clients by asking about the family rather than about the individual because being considered within the context of the family immediately sets these clients at ease.

Egalitarianism refers to how much power and authority is considered, with some cultures valuing everyone equally and others having more of a hierarchical power structure (McLeod & McLeod, 2011). For example, in a helping session, clients from some hierarchical cultural backgrounds might expect the helper to be the authority and tell them what to do, whereas clients from egalitarian cultural backgrounds might want the helper to be more of a consultant or friend.

Rationality–spirituality refers to how much a culture is based on a rational-scientific perspective versus a mystical, spiritual perspective (McLeod & McLeod, 2011). Thus, some clients might want helpers to cite research evidence to back any claims, whereas others might prefer more of a spiritual explanation and approach.

Cultures can also vary in terms of *gender and gender orientation differentiation,* with some cultures having very defined roles to which men and women must adhere, and others being more relaxed in terms of role definitions (McLeod & McLeod, 2011). In Middle Eastern cultures, for example, women's roles are very limited and different from those of men, whereas roles in the United States are more flexible in general.

People internalize these cultural dimensions from early in childhood and are typically unaware of them until confronted with people who have different cultural expectations. When cultural expectations are violated, a client may not be aware of why she or he feels uncomfortable but may feel intensely ill at ease. Likewise, a helper may simply not understand why a client does not share his or her values.

Cultural Issues in the Helping Process

Helpers need to be aware of and sensitive to cultural differences in the helping process. It is important to note that we as counselors will not always get it "right" and are not expected to. The importance is in how we address it once we become aware of cultural issues.

Skovholt and Rivers (2003) suggested that helpers need to consider (a) the general experiences, characteristics, and needs of the client's cultural groups; (b) the client's individual experiences, characteristics, and needs; and (c) basic human needs—those common to all people (e.g., food, shelter, dignity, respect). Hence, knowledge of general cultural characteristics can provide some background information about societal forces impinging on clients, but helpers also need to learn about the individual from the individual. Thus, helpers work to determine which helping skills are most effective with different clients. Similarly, helpers need to be aware of their own cultural values, how these impinge on them and shape the way they view the world, and how they influence the ways in which the helper interacts with others from different cultures.

There are two basic types of problems that can emerge in cross-cultural interactions. The first is that group differences can result in a lack of knowledge. For example, a Latino helper may not understand the cultural background of a Native American client. In addition to group differences, there are often power differences that cause other problems. For example, if a White Christian helper makes assumptions about, dismisses, or discriminates against an Arab Muslim client, the client may not feel comfortable confronting the helper because he or she feels in a lower prestige or power position. The second type of problem is that it can be uncomfortable for a minority helper (e.g., a younger, poor, gay, African American helper) to be paired with a majority client (e.g., an older, wealthy, heterosexual, European American) client because it goes against the cultural stereotypes of the helper being the person in higher social power in the dyad. For example, a colleague told me about an older woman who told her during the first session that she was afraid the therapist would not be able to understand her because she was so much younger. My colleague gently suggested that they work together in the session to see if it would be a good fit. After the first session, the client told my colleague that she thought it would be helpful to her after all.

Ethical Behavior Related to Culture

As is noted in Chapter 3, helpers need to be mindful of differences among individuals and use skills that reflect an understanding of the people with whom they are working (see also American Psychological Association, 2003). Beginning helpers should not assume that helping skills transfer across cultures and individuals. One example is the assumption that maintaining eye contact is a sign of openness, interest, and willingness to participate in the session. In some cultures, however, a lack of eye contact signifies respect for an authority figure and thus should not be interpreted according to societal norms that there should be eye contact in sessions.

At times, helpers who are working with clients from a different culture either neglect or attribute too much significance to the culture of their clients when providing interventions. It is important for helpers to realize that helping in the traditional manner may (or may not) be sufficient for these clients. Thus, heterosexual helpers who are working with lesbian or gay clients should investigate the literature about working with these clients and be aware of the special challenges that may be present for these clients, while also understanding that lesbian and gay clients may share many similarities with heterosexual clients. For example, Shawn was depressed and felt hopeless when he sought help at the university counseling center. His helper assumed that because Shawn was a gay man, his depression ensued from the discrimination that gay men experience on campus. The helper told Shawn that he understood how painful it must be to be a gay man on a predominantly heterosexual college campus. Shawn was stunned and angry at the helper. He had sought assistance because his sister had recently been killed in a car accident and he was having trouble grieving the loss, not because of problems related to his sexual orientation. Thus, it seems critical to be aware of the client's culture as deeply influencing the client, but never to assume that the client's cultural background and related experiences are the primary motivators for seeking assistance.

Furthermore, a helper who is working with a client from a different culture should not assume that the client's goals are to assimilate (or not assimilate) into the majority culture. For example, Mei immigrated to the United States from another country and asked for assistance in selecting a career. She explained to her helper that her parents wanted her to go to medical school, but she was doing poorly in her science courses. The helper incorrectly assumed that Mei did not want to pursue a medical career and directed her to select a different occupation on the basis of her interests, values, and abilities (because making career decisions in terms of individual needs and abilities is a cultural value for many people living in the United States). However, if the helper had listened carefully, he would have discovered that Mei was feeling devastated about her inability to meet her parents' expectations and dreams in part because of her cultural background, which valued familial harmony and parental approval. In another situation, the client may not even feel as though she or he is from a different culture than that of the helper. For example, a Hispanic client who goes to an all-Black school may feel more comfortable with a Black counselor than a Hispanic one because he does not identify with the Hispanic community. Thus, the helper cannot make assumptions based solely on skin color.

Demonstrating interest in clients' cultures is important, but helpers should not expect clients to educate them about culture. For example, an African American client who worked in a battered women's shelter expressed frustration not only with being a member of a group of people who have less power in American society, but also with being asked to train and educate European American helpers about her culture.

Helpers can educate themselves about culture in multiple ways. They can talk with people from different cultures, travel, try food from different places, watch movies, and read novels. Above all, perhaps the best idea is to read relevant professional literature about culture. Several excellent texts provide further information about multicultural counseling and counseling with specific groups (D. R. Atkinson & Hackett, 1998; Helms & Cook, 1999; McGoldrick, 1998; Pedersen, Draguns, Lonner, & Trimble, 2002; D. W. Sue & Sue, 1999). It is always important, however, to remember that much of the description of cultures in the professional literature or popular media perpetuates stereotypes, or generalizations, about groups of people. Although these stereotypes are perhaps accurate in very general terms, they may not apply to individuals within a given culture. Thus, it is important to learn the stereotypes about cultures but also to listen to the individual client for how he or she has been influenced by the many different cultures to which he or she belongs.

All of us need to engage in serious self-examination to discover our cultural values and beliefs as well as our prejudices and biases. Being aware of our cultural beliefs (e.g., valuing independence, autonomy, religion, and family) is important so that we can recognize what we value; but it is also important so that we do not automatically assume these values are right for everyone else. Understanding our prejudices and biases is important so that we do not hurt the therapeutic relationship or accidentally offend clients who are culturally different from us.

All of us have been socialized to have beliefs about what is good and bad, and these beliefs form our worldviews. We have firm roots in these beliefs, and we are often unaware that these beliefs are actually biases and prejudices and that these biases and prejudices surface when we are least aware of them. Self-awareness is key. How we convey our awareness of these biases often informs our clients of whether they can trust and communicate with us.

Sometimes we are so accustomed to these feelings that we do not even question their validity. Think about your "hot buttons," or the reactions you might have to different clients. If you have different reactions to different clients (e.g., to working with a male vs. female client), you might want to step back and try to understand these reactions.

It is also important to think about what biases clients might have toward helpers for various reasons (i.e., personal experiences of discrimination or an awareness of this nation's history of discrimination towards non-White racial groups). For example, an African American client might automatically not trust a White helper. Providing a safe space for clients and being open to explore these biases of clients can be helpful in the strengthening of the therapeutic alliance. On the other hand, the African American client might be very used to being in a White environment and not have an issue with having a White helper. Furthermore, it is important to take the whole person into consideration rather than just one aspect, such as race/ethnicity. An African American person with a middle-class background will likely share many of the values of a White middle-class helper.

In addition, ethical behavior goes beyond having an awareness of individual and cultural differences to embracing a commitment to eliminate bias and discrimination in one's work. This commitment may involve actively examining our biases, confronting colleagues who act in a discriminatory manner, advocating for those with less power, and working for social change. For example, some helpers facilitate support groups for clients who have been marginalized in society. Another helper might use her experience as a counselor, teacher, and researcher to write a book about empowering clients through the process of counseling (McWhirter, 1994).

Becoming a Culturally Competent Helper

D. W. Sue and Sue (1999) asserted that becoming a culturally skilled helper is an active, ongoing process that never reaches an end point. It is something to which helpers aspire and work toward, rather than accepting complacency. The following are characteristics of culturally sensitive helpers (Arredondo et al., 1996; Skovholt & Rivers, 2003; D. W. Sue & Sue, 1999):

- They strive to understand their culture and how it influences their work with clients.
- They strive to understand how their culture influences their beliefs about helping (e.g., style, theoretical orientation, definition of helping).
- They honestly confront their biases, prejudices, and discriminatory behaviors and work to keep them out of the helping process.
- They have a wide range of helping skills and use them flexibly to fit the needs of clients from different cultures.
- They are knowledgeable about the cultures of their clients.
- They understand the extent to which discrimination and oppression influence clients' lives and contribute to their problems.
- They acknowledge and address cultural differences between themselves and their clients while still communicating willingness to help.
- They seek supervision or refer when necessary.

Difficulties Helpers Have Related to Cultural Issues

You might wonder whether it would be better to match clients with helpers on the basis of race/ethnicity, gender, sexual orientation, etc. There is not much evidence that such matching makes a difference. In fact, Hays (2001) suggested that it is more important to match on cultural values (such as those mentioned earlier related to egalitarianism) than on race/ethnicity. That said, it has been my experience that there are some clients for whom matching on demographic variables is extremely important. For example, some female clients refuse to see a male helper, some gay clients are very wary about being paired with a helper who thinks that homosexuality is sinful, and some religious clients are concerned about being misunderstood by secular helpers.

Beginning helpers also often worry that they need to be an expert in all cultures before they can be effective helpers. But it would not be possible to be an expert in all cultures, because each person is an individual and comes from a somewhat different culture. However, you can educate yourself in a variety of cultures, be aware of your own cultural biases, and be open to learning about the culture of your clients. One beginning helper recalled meeting a first-generation client from an Asian country. Because she was aware that she had some hot buttons related to immigrants, she went out and searched the literature about immigration, but then she also asked the client about her experiences. She found looking at the specific cultural issue to be more helpful than generally learning about Eastern cultures.

You might also question whether it is appropriate to apply the three-stage model (and other psychotherapy models) in other cultures. In other words, are our models and theories universal or are they culture-specific? For example, Western theories, particularly client-centered and psychoanalytic theories, have recently been imported to China. Yet in many ways these Western theories conflict with Chinese cultural values. In studies we have conducted in China (Duan et al., 2012; Duan et al., 2013), we have examined the effects of using directives (i.e., giving advice or homework). On the one hand, in the hierarchical Chinese culture, it is quite common for the person in authority (such as a teacher or counselor) to give advice. But client-centered and psychoanalytic theories eschew advice, which puts Chinese helpers trained in Western theories in a conflict given that their clients expect to be given advice.

Beginning helpers might also be concerned about when it is okay to ask clients about their culture and when they should not expect the clients to educate them. I would suggest that it is appropriate to ask clients about themselves personally and what their experiences have been in their families, with peers, and in the world to learn about them and their unique experiences. But it would not be appropriate to expect clients to educate helpers about general characteristics and stereotypes about classes of people.

Most of our true thoughts and feelings about identity and diversity lurk at the unconscious level. Many of us have been raised to be color-blind (e.g., not to notice differences and pretend that everyone is equal). Others of us were raised to be prejudiced; some are deeply ashamed of being prejudiced and worried about having others discover our unconscious feelings; others are not aware of these as prejudices or actively believe them. Because these thoughts and feelings are often unconscious, it is difficult to become aware of them and to sort out realistic feelings (e.g., a specific client may not be very smart or may act inappropriately) from prejudices based on stereotypes.

Recently, I heard Dr. Kumea Shorter-Gooden, the chief diversity officer at the University of Maryland, speak about diversity and inclusion at the university (April 15, 2013). Her point was that in 2013, overt sexism or racism or other "isms" occur less frequently than they did in the past because most people, at least in academic circles, value fairness and equality and want to be nonprejudiced. More problematic are the implicit biases that we are not aware of and that just slip out. She noted the discrepancy between intention and impact, such that a person has a good intention but says something or acts in a way that is biased or prejudiced. When called on it, the person feels incredibly embarrassed and ashamed because she or he sees himself or herself as fair, egalitarian, and unbiased. Her point is that we all are struggling with our biases and need constant retooling to keep in shape.

Finally, most of the examples related to culture assume that the difficulties arise because of differences in group membership between the helper and client (e.g., between gay and heterosexual, between physically disabled and able-bodied). But it is equally important to stress that difficulties can also arise when working within our own cultural groups (e.g., two lesbians, two older people) because the matched identity becomes more salient and can trigger complex emotions (e.g., anger, jealousy, disappointment, pride). For example, if both the helper and client are members of a majority group, the helper might not question a client's assumptions regarding privilege because unconsciously it just seems normal.

Diversity work is hard and scary for people of all backgrounds. Most of us strive to be inclusive and feel ashamed when we have a prejudiced thought and act in a biased manner. It is fair to say that we all will make erroneous cultural assumptions. Given that cultural mistakes with clients are inevitable, the bigger issue is learning to recognize these mistakes and take steps to correct them. Counselors who acknowledge their mistakes are more likely to strengthen the therapeutic alliance by validating the client's feelings and the counselor's commitment to be more culturally sensitive. An example of a common pitfall is helpers being so afraid of messing up that they never explore the issue of race/ethnicity with their clients of different racial/ethnic backgrounds. At the other extreme, helpers may be so intent on being inclusive and politically correct that they continuously bring up culture and see everything through that lens. It is crucial for helpers to become aware of their feelings of guilt, fear, shame, repulsion, and anger, then to become aware of the origins of these feelings, and then to consciously choose what attitudes to strive for and behaviors to implement. Each time we slip up (and again, we will slip throughout life), we can use these opportunities to reexamine ourselves and deepen our therapeutic relationships.

My Own Experiences of Culture

To set an example of exploring cultural self-awareness, let me describe my own cultural background and the influence I think it might have on my being a helper. I was born in 1948 in the United States, a time right after World War II when the United States was quite insular from other cultures and values were very conservative. My parents were European American, and I had almost no exposure to people from different cultures until I was in my 20s. Although my parents were kind, caring, and giving people, they were a product of their time and held what we would now consider racist attitudes. They were very religious, with my father having been trained to be a Baptist minister, and so my siblings and I were raised to be good and moral, give back to society, view most everything pleasurable as sinful, and also to try to convert others to our beliefs. Another major cultural emphasis was in terms of eating only healthy food, which was very countercultural at that time and made us very different from others. We moved a lot and were poor, with my father taking a menial factory job to support four children. My mother went to work as a social worker (even though she had no degree) after I (the youngest of four) went to elementary school. I had to work to put myself through college, given that my parents could not provide any financial support.

In my family, communication was not open and immediate; rather, people talked about each other behind their backs. But everyone was very interested in dynamics and tried to understand ourselves and other people. We were all very interested in reading, especially about other people's lives. Yet another important factor is that as a teenager, I rebelled strongly against my family's religion and began to question everything involved with their style of life. Although dysfunctional in many ways, my family was loving, and I experienced no major traumas.

Given this background, it was not surprising that I chose psychology as a major when I went to college. When I earned my doctorate and became a psychologist, I shifted from a lower middle-class, religious background into being upper middle class, professional, and nonreligious, all of which was a culture shock. Furthermore, I have spent my entire adult life in the relatively protected, albeit competitive, academic world. I am married, have two adult children and one grandchild, and believe that family and work are both equally important. Meanwhile, the world has also shifted, and the United States has become incredibly diverse, such that I have neighbors from all over the world.

Given that I am White, American, heterosexual, well educated, not disabled, and now of a comfortable socioeconomic status, I have a lot of privileges. I have experienced discrimination because of my gender, but I have also experienced special treatment because of being a woman. I experienced poverty as a child and have had to work hard to achieve my academic and financial success, but I have been fortunate to work within a university and community that values diversity and equality.

Obviously, all of these components influence who I am as a helper. When someone is different from me (and most people are on some dimension), I have to work hard to make sure that I do not project my beliefs and worldview on them. I have to consciously try to understand their perspectives. I have to become aware of biases that may get activated and stereotypes that automatically get activated. I pay attention to my dreams about my clients, and I talk about my clients in a peer supervision group. The two hot buttons I am most aware of right now and willing to reveal are an uneasiness around brilliant people from wealthy backgrounds who have had elite educations because I immediately get tongue-tied and feel like a poor child, and a lack of understanding of people who are not interested in deep exploration and insight because it is hard for me to empathize with people who are not psychologically minded. It is a work in progress, obviously, to become aware of my biases and assumptions, and I know that I often fail.

I hope that you will engage in a similar process of thinking about your background and your biases. Although it is hard and can be painful to admit these weaknesses, it is crucial so that you understand what impact they might have on your clients.

What Do You Think?

- What is your definition of culture?
- Debate the role of culture in functioning.
- Many wars have been fought over culture and religion. Debate the notion that we define ourselves by feeling similar to our group (the *in* group) and better than the others (the *out* group). What can be done to reduce the number of religious wars?
- Would you emphasize similarity or diversity in your thinking about culture?

RESEARCH SUMMARY

Working With LGBT Clients

Citation: Israel, T., Gorcheva, R., Burnes, T. R., & Walther, W. A. (2008). Helpful and unhelpful therapy experiences of LGBT clients. *Psychotherapy Research, 18,* 294–305. doi:10.1080/10503300701506920

Rationale: Lesbian, gay, bisexual, and transgender (LGBT) clients often face stigma, prejudice, and discrimination, and as a result have higher rates of mental health problems and seek out mental health services at a higher rate than do their heterosexual peers. Unfortunately, mental health professionals do not always respond to LGBT clients in a therapeutic way, which could exacerbate their problems. The authors' goal in this study was to identify LGBT clients' descriptions of helpful and unhelpful events in therapy to enable future therapists to provide better treatments for sexual minority clients.

Method: LGBT clients currently in therapy were interviewed about what they found helpful and unhelpful in therapy (clients had been in therapy an average of 4.6 different times, and about two thirds of their experiences were positive). Data were analyzed using ethnographic content analysis (a qualitative method).

Interesting Findings:

- Helpful situations were characterized by therapist warmth, respect, nonjudgmental attitude, trustworthiness, confidentiality, caring, and listening. Therapists were described as knowledgeable, helpful, and affirming in dealing with sexual orientation or gender identity. It was also viewed as helpful when therapists helped clients gain insight, alleviated symptoms, provided structure, taught skills, were available outside sessions, instilled hope and optimism, were reassuring, helped gain access to medication, and focused appropriately on client concerns.
- Unhelpful situations were characterized by therapists being cold, disrespectful, disengaged, distant, or uncaring. Some unhelpful interventions were meditation, "why" questions, excessive self-disclosure, excessive silence, and withholding feedback. In addition, therapists sometimes imposed their values, judgments, and decisions on clients; did not focus on what clients wanted to focus on; mismanaged medication; breached the client's trust or confidentiality; pushed clients too much to explore or disclose; were not available; or sexually violated clients.

Conclusions:

- There are clearly some things that are helpful and unhelpful with LGBT clients.
- A caring relationship and basic helping skills are both important with LGBT clients.

Implications for Therapy:

- Therapists need to be warm and accepting of LGBT clients.
- Therapists need specific training in working with LGBT clients.
- Therapists need to evaluate their values about working with LGBT clients.
- Therapists need to remember that sexual orientation and gender identity are not the only problems that LGBT clients discuss in therapy.
- Therapists should not make assumptions about sexual orientation or gender identity, because clients are often in early stages of identity development.

BONUS MATERIALS   Practice exercises, labs, and other resources for students and teachers are available on the companion website: http://pubs.apa.org/books/supp/hill4.

EXPLORATION STAGE ‖

Overview of the Exploration Stage

6

When one pours out one's heart, one feels lighter.
—*Yiddish proverb*

Yusef was feeling miserable, lonely, and worthless after his recent move to the United States. He desperately wanted to have a close friend with whom he could talk about his deepest feelings. His parents were concerned about him and suggested that he talk with a helper. During his first session with the helper, Yusef indicated that he felt like he was going to "burst from loneliness." Since moving to this country, he had not talked to anyone other than his parents. He was hesitant to tell them how badly he felt because he worried that they would get too concerned, and he felt they could not really do anything to help him. The helper listened carefully and reflected Yusef's feelings of isolation, sadness, and rejection. Yusef began to cry and was able to talk about how he felt different from the other kids because he was from another culture. The helper let him talk and express all his feelings. She accepted him and listened nonjudgmentally, interested in understanding his experiences. At the end of the session, Yusef told the helper that he felt much better and had renewed energy to make friends. Talking to a caring, understanding person helped lift Yusef's burden and made him feel better.

http://dx.doi.org/10.1037/14345-006
Helping Skills: Facilitating Exploration, Insight, and Action, Fourth Edition, by C. E. Hill

T his overview chapter presents the theoretical background for and major goals of the exploration stage. Chapters 7 through 9 of this volume describe the major skills used to reach the goals of the exploration stage. Chapter 10 presents clinical issues new helpers face in implementing this stage.

Theoretical Background: Rogers's Client-Centered Theory

Much of what takes place in the exploration stage is influenced by Carl Rogers's theory of personality development and psychological change (see Rogers, 1942, 1951, 1957, 1959, 1967; Rogers & Dymond, 1954). Rogers had a profound influence on the field of psychology with his optimistic and hopeful assertion that all people have the potential for healthy and creative growth. His client-centered orientation was rooted in phenomenology, which places a strong emphasis on the experiences, feelings, values, and inner life of the client. Rogers believed that perceptions of reality vary from person to person, that subjective experience guides behavior, and that people are guided by their internal experience rather than by external reality. Similarly, he believed that the only way to understand individuals is to enter their private world and understand their internal frame of reference. In other words, to understand another person, one needs to suspend judgment and try to see things from that person's perspective.

According to Rogers (1942, 1951, 1967), the basic motivational force is the tendency toward self-actualization, which propels people to become what they are meant to become. He believed that each person has an innate *blueprint,* or set of potentialities, that can be developed. Just as plants and animals grow without any conscious effort provided that the conditions for growth are optimal, Rogers believed that people have an inherent ability to fulfill their potential. Furthermore, Rogers believed that people are resilient and can bounce back from adversity given this innate growth potential.

THEORY OF PERSONALITY DEVELOPMENT

According to Rogers (1942, 1951, 1967), infants evaluate each experience in terms of how it makes them feel; Rogers called this the *organismic valuing process* (OVP). Rogers believed that because behavior is governed by the OVP, infants can perceive experiences as they actually occur without distorting them. With the OVP, no experiences are more or less worthy; they just are. In other words, every event is interesting and open for investigation without prejudice. Infants thus evaluate experiences as to whether they enhance or maintain the organism. For example, if an experience (e.g., being hugged) enhances the organism, the infant feels good and is satisfied and might smile or laugh. However, if experiences do not enhance the organism (e.g., being cold or having a dirty diaper), the infant does not feel good, is not satisfied, and so might cry. Infants evaluate events by how they actually feel, not by how someone else tells them they should feel. The OVP, then, is an internal guide that everyone has at birth, and it leads the person toward self-actualization (see Figure 6.1). People freely seek those experiences that enhance them when they trust this internal guide. Rogers believed that because infants have positive strivings toward self-actualization and a natural curiosity about life, they can trust these inner feelings.

In addition to having the OVP, children also have a need for unconditional positive regard. In other words, they need acceptance, respect, warmth, and love without *conditions of worth* (COWs); that is, they need to be loved just because they are themselves and not because they meet certain standards or fulfill certain requirements. When children feel prized, accepted, and understood by significant others (usually parents), they begin to experience self-love and self-acceptance and develop a healthy sense of self with little or no conflict. A prized child is able to attend to his or her OVP and make good choices on the basis of inner experiencing.

Unfortunately, because parents themselves are not perfect, they place COWs on their children, demanding that children fulfill certain requirements to be loved. For example, parents may give messages such

FIGURE 6.1

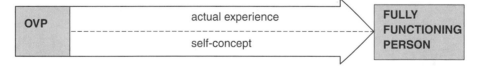

The self-actualizing tendency. Psychologist Carl Rogers's hypothesized path between the organismic valuing process (OVP) and the "fully functioning person." All people, Rogers believed, have a "self-actualizing tendency," a drive to encounter actual experience according to one's own self-concept. When there is such congruence, self-concepts are valued in terms of basic, genuine feelings and self-regard; experiences are evaluated according to the OVP—that is, according to the basic needs and desires of the organism.

as "I will not love you unless you are a 'good girl,' " "I will not love you unless you keep your room clean," or "You must be intelligent to receive my love." Because parents communicate (through words or actions) that children are lovable and acceptable only when they behave in accordance with imposed standards, children come to believe that they must be and act in certain ways to earn their parents' love.

Given the need for love, the COWs, rather than the OVP, come to guide a child's organization of her or his experiences (see Figure 6.2). In other words, children sacrifice their OVP to receive love from their parents (e.g., children give up being spontaneous and playful to sit "properly" and be "good" to please their parents). When a child introjects (i.e., internalizes) his or her parents' COWs, these conditions become a part of the child's self-concept.

The more COWs there are, the more distorted the person becomes from his or her own experiencing. For example, a mother may communicate to a young girl that it is not acceptable for her to hate her brother. The girl may feel that to be loved, she must be a good girl, and so she may disown the hate as not being part of herself. Hence, rather than learning that she may feel hate but cannot hurt her brother, she learns that her feelings are not acceptable. Another example is parents who punish or ridicule a boy for crying when he is hurt or needs help with a difficult task. The boy might repress his feelings of pain and dependency and become extremely independent to maintain his parents' approval.

FIGURE 6.2

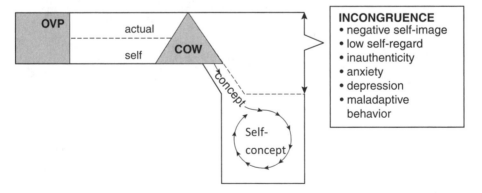

Conditions of worth and incongruence. The self-actualizing tendency can be derailed when the self-concept is altered by conditions of worth (COWs), which supplant a person's basic, positive self-regard with others' conditional evaluations of worth. The incongruence between actual experience and self-concept, according to Rogers, typically results in inauthentic expressions of feelings, low self-regard, defensiveness, anxiety, and depression.

These two examples illustrate how externally imposed values can substitute for the OVP. When feelings of hate or dependency get aroused, these children cannot identify or repress these feelings and thus are not in touch with their inner experiencing.

Children feel positive self-regard only when their experiences are consistent with feedback they receive from others (e.g., if a girl feels talented in playing the violin and others tell her that she is talented). Feelings of self-worth become dependent on the COWs that are learned in interaction with significant others. A child with too many COWs will not be open to experience, accepting of feelings, capable of living in the present, free to make choices, trusting, capable of feeling both aggression and affection, and capable of creativity. He or she will have a conflicted sense of self.

Obviously, children must become socialized to live in their families and society. Children cannot act on all their innate desires or get all of their needs met immediately because the world is not a perfect place and also because other people have needs that sometimes conflict with theirs. Parents, for example, cannot always immediately meet the infant's needs because they have other demands on their time. In addition, parents cannot allow a child to hurt a sibling or another child. The manner, however, in which parents socialize their children is crucial. For example, a parent can empathize with a young girl but still place limits on her (e.g., "I know you are angry at your brother, but you cannot hurt him"). The girl may feel frustrated but does not learn to deny her feelings. Instead, she learns to experience her feelings but channel them in a more socially acceptable direction. In contrast, when parents humiliate a child (e.g., "Real men don't cry," "Shut up, or I'll give you something to cry about") or deny that the child has feelings (e.g., "You don't hate your teacher," "You don't feel hurt"), the child becomes confused about her or his feelings. The child may feel sad or feel hatred, but the parents say he or she does not have these feelings. What should the child trust, the inner experience or what parents tell him or her to feel? If the child does not pay attention to his or her parents, she or he risks losing parental approval and love. If she or he does not pay attention to inner feelings and instead tries to please others, the child loses her or his sense of self. One can easily see how children come not to trust their inner experiences. Children must survive, so they often choose parents' attention and "love" over inner experiencing.

When COWs are pervasive and the OVP is disabled, the sense of self is weakened to the point at which a person is unable to experience or recognize feelings as belonging to the self. For example, a woman might not even be aware of feeling angry and hurt when being verbally and physically abused by her husband because she thinks she deserves the abuse. When people cannot allow themselves to have their feelings, they often feel a sense of emptiness, phoniness, or lack of genuineness. This lack of genuineness about one's feelings reflects a split or incongruence between the real and ideal self and is the source of anxiety, depression, and defensiveness in relationships.

DEFENSES

Rogers (1957) suggested that when there is an incongruence between who one is and who one thinks one ought to be, the person feels threatened. For example, a person who acts pleasant and happy but is actually feeling grumpy and depressed is in danger of losing touch with his or her inner self. If she or he were to perceive her or his depression accurately, his or her self would be threatened because he or she has built an image of self as always happy. When a person feels such a threat, she or he typically responds with anxiety, a signal that the self is in danger. Feeling this anxiety, the person invokes defenses to reduce the incongruity between experience and sense of self, thereby reducing anxiety.

One major defense is perceptual distortion, which involves altering or misinterpreting one's experience to make it compatible with one's self-concept. By distorting experiences, clients avoid having to deal with unpleasant feelings and issues and can maintain their perceptions of themselves. For example, a man may perceive himself as being of average weight even though he is quite overweight and no longer fits into chairs. He might tell himself he does not eat any more than other people. As another example, a person with a sense of worthlessness who is promoted at work might misinterpret the reason for the promotion to be congruent with her negative sense of self. She might say that the only reason she got the promotion was that "the boss had to do it" or "no one else wanted the job."

A second defense is denial, which involves ignoring or denouncing reality. In this situation, people refuse to acknowledge experiences that are inconsistent with the images they have of themselves. By denying their experiences, clients avoid anxiety. For example, a woman who is treated unfairly at work might ignore her anger at her boss because she has internalized her parents' belief that anger is bad and that she will not be loved if she expresses anger. Rather than allow herself to experience her anger, she may say she is not trying hard enough or is not smart enough for the job.

Defenses block incongruent experiences from full awareness and minimize threats to one's sense of self and thus allow the person to function and cope. A certain level of defenses is necessary for coping, but excessive use of defenses can take a toll on the self in at least three ways. First, the subjective reality (what one allows oneself to experience) can become incongruent with the external reality (the world as it is). At some point, the person may no longer be able to distort or deny the experience, which could lead to overwhelming feelings of threat and anxiety and disintegration of the self. For example, a child might struggle to maintain the illusion that things are fine between his parents despite hearing their nightly battles. However, when his mother leaves without warning, the boy may not be able to handle the loss and may stop attending school and talking to others. In another example, a person might partition off parts of self that are unacceptable and exclude them from awareness (e.g., deny to oneself that sexual abuse occurred). Second, a person might develop a rigidity of perception in areas in which she or he has had to defend against perceiving reality. For example, a woman might have such a strong need to believe in the curative effects of a quack medicine for cancer that she does not listen to any disconfirming evidence, resulting in her not seeking proven strategies for treating her cancer. Third, the real self can become incongruent with the ideal self, suggesting a discrepancy between who one is and who one wishes to be. A woman might be average in intelligence but feel a need to be super smart (particularly if she has internalized parental COWs that she should be extremely intelligent). If the discrepancy between the real and the ideal is large, the person may feel dissatisfied and become maladjusted (e.g., depressed, anxious).

REINTEGRATION

According to Rogers (1957), to overcome disintegration, rigidity, or discrepancies between real and ideal selves, a person must become aware of the distorted or denied experience. In other words, a person must allow the experience to occur and accurately perceive the event. The woman described above must acknowledge to herself that she has average intelligence and accept and value herself rather than distort or deny her feelings. Rogers theorized that for reintegration to occur, the person must (a) reduce the COWs and (b) increase positive self-regard by obtaining unconditional positive regard from others. COWs lose their significance and ability to direct behavior when others accept the person as he or she is. In effect, individuals return to the OVP and begin to trust the inner self, thus becoming more open to experience and feelings (see Figure 6.3).

A person can reintegrate without unconditional positive regard from another person if there is minimal threat to the self and the incongruity between self and experience is minor. Typically, however, individuals respond to years of having COWs imposed on them by becoming increasingly defensive. Once developed, defenses are difficult to let go because the person anticipates being vulnerable and hurt again. In effect, defenses

FIGURE 6.3

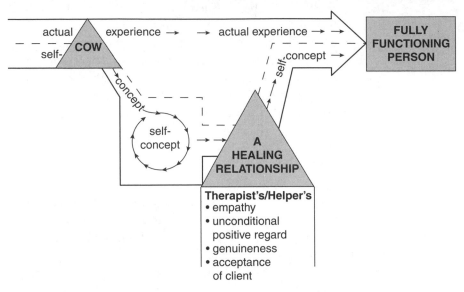

A healing relationship. Only through a healing relationship that offers empathy, unconditional positive regard, genuineness, and acceptance—typically from a therapist or helper—can the self-concept be restored to congruence with actual experience, according to Rogers (1957). The self-concept returns to evaluations of actual experience based on the organismic valuing process (OVP), thereby facilitating self-actualization and the drive to become a "fully functioning person"—one who can realize the self's maximum potentiality for independence, creativity, authentic expressions of feelings, and love. COW = conditions of worth.

are adaptive to help children cope, but fear and habit make them difficult to shed when they are no longer needed.

A helping relationship, then, is often crucial for overcoming defenses and allowing the person to return to trusting the OVP. A helping relationship allows the individual's self-actualizing tendency to overcome the restrictions that were internalized in the COWs. In a helping relationship, the helper attempts to enter the client's subjective world and understand the client's internal frame of reference. The helper also tries to provide an experience in which the client is accepted and cared for without COWs. Thus, genuine acceptance from helpers begins to enable clients to accept themselves. This helping relationship does not necessarily need to be from a professional helper, and in fact, people often seek healing relationships from supportive people in their environment (e.g., friends, relatives, rabbi, minister, priest).

Rogers (1951) believed that the helping relationship, in and of itself, produces growth in the client: "I launch myself into the therapeutic relationship having a hypothesis, or a faith, that my liking, my confidence, and my understanding of the other person's inner world, will lead to a significant process of becoming" (p. 267). Rogerian helpers believe that most clients benefit greatly from being listened to, understood, and accepted. The power of this kind of relationship can be highly therapeutic and constructive. In the Rogerian approach to helping, the helper enters the therapeutic relationship with the facilitative attitudes of congruence (genuineness), unconditional positive regard, and empathy.

Rogers (1957) postulated six conditions that he considered to be necessary and sufficient for change to occur.

1. *The client and helper must be in psychological contact.* A therapeutic relationship or emotional connection between the helper and client is essential.
2. *The client must be in a state of incongruence.* There must be a discrepancy between self and experience that leads the client to feel vulnerable or anxious. If a client feels no anxiety, she or he is unlikely to be motivated enough to engage in the helping process.
3. *The helper must be congruent (genuine) or integrated in the relationship.* The helper must be open to her or his own experiences and be genuinely available to the client. The helper cannot be phony in the helping relationship.
4. *The helper must feel unconditional positive regard for the client.* The helper values all feelings (although not necessarily all behaviors) and places no judgment on the feelings. Essentially, a helper is trying to understand a client's feelings and experience but is not trying to judge whether the person "should" or "should not" have the feelings or whether the feelings are "right" or "wrong."
5. *The helper must experience empathy for the client.* The helper tries to immerse herself or himself in the client's feeling world and understand the client's inner experiences. The understanding comes out of the helper's experiencing of the client's feelings, using the helper's inner processes as a referent. The helper not only experiences the client's feelings but also has his or her own reactions to the client's feelings; the helper is thus able to go beyond words to understanding the client's implicit feelings (Meador & Rogers, 1973). The helper tries to feel as if she or he were the client and temporarily living in the client's life, without ever losing the awareness that they are separate individuals. The helper tries to sense and uncover feelings of which the client is unaware because of the threatening nature of these

feelings. Rogers emphasized that empathy is not passive but requires thinking, sensitivity, and understanding. He described *empathy* as follows:

> It means entering the private perceptual world of the other and becoming thoroughly at home in it. It involves being sensitive, moment by moment, to the changing felt meanings which flow in this other person, to the fear or rage or tenderness or confusion or whatever that he or she is experiencing. It means temporarily living in the other's life, moving about in it delicately without asking judgments. (Rogers, 1980, p. 142)

Empathy can be distinguished from sympathy, in which the helper feels pity for the client and often acts from a position of power rather than as an equal. Empathy also differs from emotional contagion, in which a helper feels the same feelings as the client (e.g., becomes just as depressed as the client) and cannot maintain objectivity. Empathy involves a deep understanding of the client's feelings. Bohart, Elliott, Greenberg, and Watson (2002) indicated that empathy is effective because it creates a positive relationship, provides a corrective emotional experience, promotes exploration, and supports the client's active self-healing efforts.

Another construct that is similar to empathy is compassion, which means to resonate with the client's suffering (see Vivino, Thompson, Hill, & Ladany, 2009). I think of compassion as caring deeply for another person and accepting that person while being fully aware of his or her frailties and humanness. Thus, it is more than just feeling others' feelings; it is being able to feel deep understanding of what it must be like to be them. When I have trouble connecting with clients, I try to gain compassion for them, to accept and understand why they are as they are. Rogers probably considered compassion as a part of empathy, but it is helpful for therapists to cultivate compassion in addition to empathy because it allows them to feel deeply for what their clients are going through.

6. *The client must experience the helper's congruence, unconditional positive regard, and empathy.* If the client does not experience the facilitative conditions, they do not, for all practical purposes, exist for the client, and the sessions are not likely to be helpful.

Rogers (1951) stated that a facilitative attitude (being genuine, unconditionally positive in regard, and empathic) on the part of helpers is what is most beneficial for clients. He indicated that skills were important but that the facilitative attitude served as the basis for the skills. Skills without a facilitative attitude might not only be unhelpful but might be harmful.

In summary, Rogers speculated that if helpers can accept clients, clients can come to accept themselves. When clients accept themselves, they can allow themselves to experience their real feelings and accept that the feelings come from themselves. Hence, the OVP is unblocked, and the person becomes open to his or her experiences. The client can begin to experience love, lust, hatred, jealousy, joy, competitiveness, anger, pride, and other feelings; accept the feelings; and come to accept self. It is important to remember that acceptance of feelings is distinct from decisions about what to do about those feelings. Allowing oneself to have the feelings provides a basis for making decisions about what to do because the actions are then based on inner feelings rather than on "shoulds."

CURRENT STATUS OF CLIENT-CENTERED THEORY

Meta-analyses have shown that client-centered therapy and humanistic therapy are indeed effective and that they are just as effective as other approaches to psychotherapy (Elliott, Greenberg, Watson, Timulak, & Freire, 2013). In addition, reviews of the empirical literature have confirmed the importance of the facilitative conditions, particularly of empathy, in leading to positive outcome of therapy (Farber & Doolin, 2011; Kolden, Klein, Wang, & Austin, 2011). It appears that the facilitative conditions are important for allowing clients to feel safe and supported, to help clients have a positive relationship experience, to promote exploration, and to support clients' active self-healing efforts.

Recent research has focused more on the working alliance, or the relationship between the therapist and the client, rather than just the therapist-offered facilitative conditions (e.g., Horvath, Del Re, Flückiger, & Symonds, 2011). Thus, contemporary researchers consider the interaction between therapist and client to be more important than just looking at what the therapist offers. In fact, it is hard to imagine the therapist being empathic without the client being responsive and engaged, given that both therapist and client are involved in the interaction.

THE RELATIONSHIP OF ROGERS'S THEORY TO THE HELPING SKILLS MODEL

Rogers's theory forms the foundation for the exploration stage and informs the insight and action stages. I agree with Rogers that helpers should maintain an empathic client-centered stance of trying to understand the client's experience as completely as possible with as little judgment and as few prior assumptions as possible. Empathy, compassion, and a therapeutic relationship can be effective in helping clients begin to accept themselves and trust their experiences.

In contrast to Rogers's assertion that a facilitative attitude is more important than the specific skills, I believe that a facilitative attitude and skills are inseparable (Hill, 2005b, 2007). Skills are used to express a facilitative attitude, and a facilitative attitude is needed to express the skills. In addition, as articulated in Chapter 4, awareness (including self-knowledge, in-the-moment awareness, and cultural awareness) is also crucial because without awareness, the helper is likely to act out unconscious impulses in a way that could damage clients. Client involvement is also important but of less focus at this point because we are concentrating on the helper's contribution to the helping process. Thus, a facilitative attitude, awareness, and skills are all important components of the helper's contribution to the helping process.

Another point on which I diverge somewhat from Rogers's theory relates to his assertion about the helpful components of the therapeutic process. For some clients, being understood and encouraged to express their feelings is enough to get them back to a self-healing mode so they can function again and make needed changes. Others, however, need more assistance in learning how to deal with feelings and experiences, many of which may be new to them. Furthermore, some clients need to be assisted in moving toward insight and action. In addition to maintaining the facilitative conditions, then, I posit that helpers need to be able to facilitate insight and action. Additional theories (psychoanalytic, cognitive, behavioral) are needed to assist some clients in moving beyond exploration of thoughts and feelings; these are described in later chapters.

Furthermore, I do not completely agree with Rogers that people are inherently good and striving for self-actualization. There seems to be minimal evidence for these postulates. My assumption is that people are neither good nor bad at birth but rather develop depending on temperament, genetics, the environment, parenting, and early experiences (see Chapter 2, this volume). More is known now about genetic and biological contributions to human functioning than was known when Rogers proposed his theory. Despite these differences in beliefs about human nature and biological contributions, though, I agree with Rogers about the importance of the facilitative conditions for establishing the therapeutic relationship and helping clients explore concerns and achieve self-acceptance.

Finally, Rogers did not attend closely to cultural considerations in his theory, probably because the United States was not as diverse then as it is now. Culture certainly fits into Rogers's theory, however, in that being truly empathic and compassionate assumes a major interest in the person, awareness of who the person is, and an acceptance of the person. Thus, I would assert that multicultural awareness is important to genuinely being Rogerian.

Goals for the Exploration Stage

The goals for the exploration stage are establishing rapport and a trusting relationship; attending, listening, and observing; helping clients explore their thoughts and narratives; facilitating the expression of emotion; and learning about clients. The sections that follow define these goals in more detail.

ESTABLISHING RAPPORT AND DEVELOPING A THERAPEUTIC RELATIONSHIP

Helpers establish rapport (i.e., an atmosphere of understanding and respect) with their clients so that clients feel safe to explore. Rapport sets the stage for development of the therapeutic relationship, which is important in helping. Clients are most likely to reveal themselves when they believe they have a caring, therapeutic relationship with their helpers. Clients generally need to feel safe, supported, respected, cared for, valued, prized, accepted as individuals, listened to, and heard in their interactions with helpers. In everyday relationships, people often do not fully listen to others, so it is a gift to clients for helpers to listen attentively to them without rushing to say something next (e.g., telling a competing story, as friends often do).

During the exploration stage, helpers strive to understand their clients from the clients' frame of reference. They aspire to "walk a mile in the client's shoes" and view the world through their clients' eyes. Helpers try to understand clients' thoughts and feelings without imposing their thoughts or values on clients. They attempt not to judge clients and figure out whether they are "right" or "blameworthy" but instead have compassion and try to understand how clients came to be the way they are and how it feels to be who they are. Helpers try to align or attune themselves (i.e., feel what it is like to be the client) so they can understand the client's feelings.

If helpers can assist clients in becoming aware of their inner experiencing, clients can begin to trust and then to heal themselves. Rogers (1957) hypothesized that clients typically need to feel accepted and prized by others before they can begin to accept and value themselves. To do this, helpers need to accept clients as they are as much as possible and provide them with the facilitative conditions of empathy, uncon-ditional positive regard, and genuineness. As mentioned earlier, *empathy* refers to understanding another person and feeling as if you are the other person (i.e., trying to put yourself in her or his place even though you are not that person and can never understand the person completely). *Unconditional positive regard* refers to accepting and appre-ciating another person without judgment. *Genuineness* (or what has also been termed *congruence*) refers to helpers' being open to their own experiences and genuinely available to clients rather than being phony or inauthentic. A large part of establishing a relationship is having an attitude of acceptance, empathy, respect, and compassion. Helpers need to listen and understand clients without judging them. In addi-tion, having knowledge of helping skills, feeling competent in being able to use the skills, being aware of one's own feelings and motiva-tions, and being able to appropriately use the skills places helpers in the framework in which they are more likely to have a therapeutic attitude.

Helpers should not think they can simply establish a relationship at one point in time and ignore it thereafter. They need to be aware of maintaining the relationship throughout the helping process. At any time throughout the process, the relationship can, and often does, rup-ture and need repair (see Hill, Nutt-Williams, Heaton, Thompson, & Rhodes, 1996; Rhodes, Hill, Thompson, & Elliott, 1994; Safran, Muran, Samstag, & Stevens, 2002). In fact, relationships are often stronger after a rupture and repair.

Beginning helpers often worry about the possibility of not liking a client or not being able to establish rapport with a client. For example, many beginning helpers think they could never work with rapists or child abusers because they would be repulsed and horrified. However, the goal of being a helper is not to make friends with clients. Helpers do not need to "like" clients in the same way they like or choose to spend time with close friends. Rather, helpers have a responsibility to understand and assist clients and to feel compassion for the human beings underneath the exterior presentations. Often, if a helper can gain insight into how the client got to be how he or she is, the helper can begin to have compassion for the client.

For example, the greatest challenge for one helper was working with women in prison. The crimes committed by the women made it difficult for her to empathize and respect them. However, after getting to know the women and their life circumstances, she became aware that these women had feelings similar to hers. Even though she had not experienced the same life events as her clients, she had experienced many of the same emotions and thus could empathize with her clients' feelings, even if she did not condone their behaviors. We often like to think of people who make us anxious and defensive (e.g., prisoners, dictators) as evil and "other," as a different species than we are so that we do not have to encounter our own negative impulses, but in fact, it is always important to remember that we have many of the same feelings (e.g., a desire to manipulate, a desire for revenge).

ATTENDING, LISTENING, AND OBSERVING

The major way that we as helpers establish rapport and build a therapeutic relationship is through attending, listening, and observing. We orient ourselves nonverbally toward clients so that we are receptive to listening to whatever they say. We listen intently to what they say rather than assuming we know anything about them. We observe carefully to see how they are feeling and reacting to everything that happens in the session.

In addition, helpers monitor their reactions to clients, as described in Chapters 2 and 4. Helpers need to know what is going on internally as they work with clients and make a determination about whether the reactions are due to their own issues, due to what the client is eliciting from them, or more likely some combination of the two.

HELPING CLIENTS EXPLORE THOUGHTS AND NARRATIVES

Clients need a chance to talk about their problems. It often helps to talk out loud about what is going on inside. All too often, people just continue with their ordinary routines without exploring their problems in any depth. As Frank and Frank (1991) noted, "How can I know what I think until I have heard what I have to say?" (p. 200). Having a forum to express their thoughts allows clients to hear and think about the content of what they are saying. Clients need to realize what they are thinking and have a chance to express these thoughts out loud. This talking is similar to telling one's story or narrative.

Furthermore, by realizing what one is thinking, one has a better chance to hear the inconsistencies and logical fallacies. Talking about one's thoughts provides the client the opportunity to think about whether she or he really believes what is being said, especially when the client knows someone else is hearing it. In addition, the process of talking to a helper about a problem is useful because it allows the client to think about it, take it out and examine it, put thoughts into words, and get another person's reactions. Then clients can reevaluate what they are thinking, rewrite the script, and perhaps change the story or narrative.

ENCOURAGING EXPRESSION AND EXPERIENCING OF FEELINGS

Emotions are a key element in the helping process because they represent fundamental experiencing and are connected integrally to cognitions and behavior. In fact, mental health could be defined as allowing oneself to have a whole range of feelings and expressing these feelings in an appropriate manner (e.g., laughing when happy, crying when sad).

One major goal of the exploration stage is for helpers to assist clients in experiencing feelings about their presenting problems. Many clients learned as children to suppress their feelings. They had to distort or deny their actual feelings to survive and gain approval from parents or other significant persons, so many clients are not aware of their feelings. For example, if clients cannot allow themselves to feel hurt, they limit their range of emotions and might feel hollow or empty inside. Some clients feel that their "inner cores" are rotten or nonexistent. Clients might not know who they are and might rely on other people to tell them how they feel. In significant relationships, they might ignore their feelings and feel distant without knowing why. Hence, being able to feel their true feelings and put words onto the feelings can be liberating for clients and help them develop a sense of self.

Sometimes the content of what the client says is not as important as the feelings about the topic, particularly if there is a discrepancy between content and feelings. Helpers need to listen to the "music" (i.e., the underlying message) in addition to listening to the words. They need to try to hear both the content and what the client feels.

In addition, clients need to focus on what they are feeling immediately in the present moment. Experiencing immediate feelings is often not comfortable, so clients may want to run away and avoid their feelings. Through support and encouragement from helpers, clients often are able to tolerate the anxiety and discomfort of exploring their immediate feelings. For example, Joel spent much of the session telling the helper about events that occurred during the week. When the helper gently encouraged him to explore his feelings in the present regarding these past events (e.g., "How do you feel right now about the event?"), Joel talked about his feelings, and the session became more intense and productive than it previously was.

Helpers sometimes need to be assertive and ask about feelings that clients are not discussing. For example, clients might need to be invited to talk about difficult feelings such as shame or being depressed or suicidal. In friendships, people often do not probe beyond what their friends choose to reveal because they feel that would be overstepping implicit boundaries. In helping relationships, by contrast, helpers encourage clients to explore painful feelings that are hard to express. However, helpers need to respect the rights of clients not to go any deeper than they choose. Helpers thus walk a fine line between inviting clients to disclose feelings and not forcing them into unwanted disclosure.

Another reason for encouraging clients to talk about feelings is that emotional arousal seems to be necessary for change to occur (Frank & Frank, 1991). Without emotional arousal, clients typically are not involved in the helping process and are not motivated to change. Many times, people deny or defend against their feelings because they do not want to deal with the overwhelming or painful nature of their feelings. In contrast, when people have strong emotional arousal (e.g., fury, despair), they are most aware of feelings and more likely to change.

LEARNING ABOUT CLIENTS

The exploration stage provides an important opportunity for helpers to learn about their clients. When a client first comes to a session, the helper has no way of knowing how to help that particular person. Helpers cannot assume that they know anything about a particular client or his or her problems, even (or perhaps especially) if the helper has similar problems. Encouraging an individual client to explore often requires a substantial amount of time because most people and problems are quite complex, and it is often difficult to be aware and able to articulate the experience. In addition, because our goal is to help clients come to their own conclusions and decisions, helpers need to listen carefully to what clients say and how they feel before constructing an action plan to help them solve their problems.

In learning about clients, helpers must follow the lead of the individual client. Helpers can be prepared in general by knowing theories of therapy and practicing the helping skills, but they must learn more specifically about how to help each client from that client. A parallel example is having a baby. Expectant parents can read many books about babies and generally be prepared for having a child, but they really learn parenting skills from attending to the needs of their own unique infant (i.e., the baby teaches them how to be a parent because every baby has different needs). Similarly, each client is different because of culture, family, and experiences; helpers cannot make assumptions about who the client is or what she or he needs and has to learn from the client how to be responsive to that individual.

Furthermore, on the basis of observing and learning about the client, the helper starts to conceptualize the client and the client's problems during the exploration stage. This conceptualization enables the helper to implement the insight and action stages. Knowing something about the origin of and factors maintaining the problem can aid helpers in deciding whether clients can profit from insight and action.

Exploration Stage Skills

In the next few chapters, I focus on three sets of skills that helpers can use to attain the above goals. The goals of establishing rapport and building the therapeutic relationship and learning about the client are meta-goals—they happen as a result of applying the more specific goals in a facilitative manner. So in the next chapters, we focus on the goals of attending, listening, and observing; exploring thoughts and narratives; and exploring feelings.

Within each goal, helpers can use several skills somewhat interchangeably. To attend, listen, and observe, helpers use eye contact, facial expression, head nods, open body posture, body movements, space, grammatical style, silence, no or minimal interruptions, no or minimal touch, encouragers, and approval-reassurance. To facilitate exploration of thoughts and narratives, helpers use restatements or open questions/probes about thoughts. To facilitate exploration of feelings, helpers use reflections of feeling, disclosures of feeling, or open questions/probes about feeling. It is not so much which skill within the set is used as that the skills are used for the right goal and are implemented in a helpful manner (i.e., with good attending skills and empathy). See Exhibit 6.1 for a list of goals and skills used to facilitate these goals.

Concluding Comments

The exploration stage is important to facilitate the development of the helping relationship, give clients a chance to explore concerns and immerse themselves in their immediate experiencing, and provide helpers with an opportunity to learn about clients' presenting issues and assess clients' appropriateness for what helpers can offer. For Rogerians, the exploration stage is all that is needed for helping. Rogerians believe that the facilitative attitudes of empathy, unconditional positive regard, and genuineness allow clients to begin to accept themselves, which releases the inner experiencing and unblocks the potential for self-actualization. Indeed, some clients need only a listening ear to get them back to their own self-healing processes. Hence, helpers generally spend a considerable amount of time in the exploration stage because it can be so helpful. However, because many clients cannot make progress with exploration alone, insight and action are

EXHIBIT 6.1

Skills for Facilitating the Goals of the Exploration Stage

Goal	Skill
Attending, listening, observing	Eye contact
	Facial expression
	Head nods
	Body posture
	Body movements
	Space
	Grammatical style
	Silence
	No interruptions
	No touch (or minimal touch)
	Minimal encourager
	Approval-reassurance
To explore thoughts	Restatement
	Open question or probe about thoughts
To explore feelings	Reflection of feelings
	Disclosure of feelings
	Open question or probe about feelings

often necessary to help them change. In this case, exploration sets the stage for everything that follows. In addition, exploration skills are used throughout all three stages. Thus, even when helpers move to insight and action, the most frequently used skills are the exploration skills because these skills help clients continue to feel safe and encourage deeper exploration.

It is important for beginning helpers to remember how difficult it is for some clients to open up and explore. Simply telling them to feel comfortable and saying that helping is a safe environment is not enough to reduce the fear of some clients in forming a relationship. In Chapter 10, we explore some of the difficulties that helpers have creating a safe setting, encouraging clients, and implementing the exploration skills.

An important caveat throughout the exploration stage (and the rest of the helping process) is that there are no absolute "right" interventions to use. Although there are general guidelines, it is not possible to provide a cookbook to tell helpers exactly what to do in different circumstances with different clients. Individual clients require different things at different times from helpers. It is up to helpers to determine which interventions are productive and which are not useful by paying attention to the individual client's reactions and responses (refer back to Chapter 2 for a review of the moment-by-moment process).

What Do You Think?

- Rogers has been charged with being too optimistic about human nature and as reflecting American culture in the mid-20th century (compared with the pessimistic view of Europeans such as Freud). Debate whether Rogers's view is too simplistic and optimistic.
- Take each of Rogers's six conditions and debate its merits.
- Do you think that it is the therapist's facilitative conditions, the relationship between the helper and client, therapist awareness of needs and motives, or client involvement that is most crucial for the success of the exploration stage?
- How well do the tasks of the exploration stage fit your personal style?
- Discuss whether establishing a relationship is more a matter of facilitative attitudes or of implementing helping skills.
- Describe the challenges you would face in developing a relationship with someone you believe has done awful and despicable things (e.g., rape, murder).
- Do you believe that it is necessary for clients to "tell their stories"?

RESEARCH SUMMARY

Therapist Skills and Innovative Moments

Citation: Cunha, C., Goncalves, M. M., Hill, C. E., Mendes, I., Ribiero, A. P., Sousa, I., Angus, L., & Greenberg, L. S. (2012). Therapist interventions and client innovative moments in emotion-focused therapy for depression. *Psychotherapy, 49*, 536–548. doi:10.1037/a0028259

Rationale: Narrative theorists suggest that the major change clients make in therapy involves how they talk about or tell their stories. They measure this change by identifying innovative moments (IMs) in client speech. Five types of IMs have been identified: *action* (the client acting in ways that are discrepant with the problematic self-narrative), *reflection* (new understandings that undermine the dominance of the problematic self-narrative), *protest* (challenging the problematic self-narrative), *reconceptualization* (a shift between two positions and a transformation process), and *performing change* (new activities or experiences that become possible because of changes). Previous studies have found more IMs in successful than unsuccessful therapy, in particular, with more occurrences of reconceptualization and action IMs. Cunha et al. wondered whether specific therapist skills facilitated IMs. Therapist skills were conceptualized as exploration (includes approval-reassurance, closed questions, open questions and probes, restatements, reflections of feelings), insight (includes challenges, interpretations, self-disclosures, and immediacy), and action (includes information and direct guidance).

Method: Three good-outcome and three poor-outcome cases of emotion-focused therapy for depression were selected based on examination of a number of outcome measures. The first two sessions, two sequential middle sessions, and the two final sessions of these six cases were coded for therapist skills and client IMs.

Interesting Findings:
- Exploration skills were used more often, whereas insight skills were used less often, in good- compared with poor-outcome cases across all three phases of therapy. Action skills were used more often in initial phases of good- than poor-outcome cases but more often in the final sessions of poor- than good-outcome cases.
- IMs more often followed skills in the good- than poor-outcome cases. In good-outcome cases, the connection between skills and IMs increased from the initial to middle phase of therapy and was maintained in the final phases. In poor-outcome cases, the connection between skills and IMs increased from the beginning to middle but then decreased in the final phase.
- In terms of types of IMs, the authors divided these into easier IMs (action, reflection, protest) and more advanced IMs (reconceptualization, performing change). In the initial and middle phases of the good-outcome cases, all three types of skills were associated more with easier IMs but not with more advanced IMs; in the final phase, exploration and insight skills were more often associated with easy IMs than with the more advanced IMs. In the final phase of poor-outcome cases, all skills were more associated with the easy than advanced IMs.

Conclusions:
- Therapists used the skills more effectively in good- than poor-outcome cases (i.e., all three types of skills led to more IMs in good- than poor-outcome cases).
- Experiential therapists used mostly exploration skills, which fits with this theoretical perspective as being client centered. However, exploration skills did not lead to more IMs than did insight skills.
- Insight skills were used more often in poor- than good-outcome cases. The authors speculated that therapists were trying to engage clients when the more theoretically preferred exploration skills were not working.

(continued)

RESEARCH SUMMARY *(Continued)*

- Exploration and insight skills led mostly to the easier IMs in the initial and middle phases of therapy, whereas they led mostly to the more advanced skills later in therapy. It appears that the foundation must be set early in therapy with the easier IMs before the complex IMs can occur.
- Action skills were used more in the beginning and middle phases of good-outcome cases, which the authors speculate was because therapists were engaging in in-session experiential activities such as chair work. They speculated that action skills were used less in the final phase because therapists were helping clients consolidate gains. In contrast, in poor-outcome cases, action skills increased steadily across phases, perhaps because therapists continued to try to engage clients in therapeutic tasks even when they were not working. Action skills led more often to the easier than the more complex IMs.

Implications for Therapy:
- Therapists should pay attention to the immediate effects of their interventions.
- Therapists can use both exploration and insight skills to promote easy IMs in the early and middle phases of therapy and the more complex IMs in the final sessions of therapy.
- Therapists can use action skills (remember that these were usually the in-session directives) to promote the easy IMs throughout therapy.

BONUS MATERIALS

Practice exercises, labs, and other resources for students and teachers are available on the companion website: http://pubs.apa.org/books/supp/hill4.

Skills for Attending, Listening, and Observing 7

The one who listens is the one who understands.
—*African (Jabo) proverb*

The students in one class prearranged to manipulate their professor's behavior through nonverbal responding. Whenever the professor moved to the right, they looked up, paid rapt attention, and smiled encouragingly. Whenever the professor moved to the left, they looked down, rustled their papers, coughed, and whispered. The professor soon had moved so far to the right, he fell off the stage! This example illustrates the power of attending skills.

The skills covered in this chapter rarely show up on transcripts of helping sessions because they are mostly nonverbal rather than verbal. They are what has been called the "back channel" of communication, similar to the oil that greases the mechanism to make a machine run smoothly or the glue that holds the elements of a collage together. Helpers attend to clients, listen to them, and observe them carefully so that the process of helping moves forward. These skills help clients feel safe and comfortable, which allows them to explore their thoughts and feelings. Helpers do not usually think consciously about and are not aware of these skills, but they can have a big impact on clients.

http://dx.doi.org/10.1037/14345-007
Helping Skills: Facilitating Exploration, Insight, and Action, Fourth Edition, by C. E. Hill

Overview of Attending, Listening, and Observing

Attending refers to helpers orienting themselves physically toward clients. The goal of attending is for helpers to communicate to clients that they are paying attention to them so that clients feel safe to talk openly about their thoughts and feelings. In effect, attending lays the foundation for the implementation of the verbal helping interventions. Clients feel they are valued and worthy of being listened to when helpers attend to them. Attending can also encourage clients to verbalize ideas and feelings because they feel helpers want to hear what they have to say. Furthermore, attending behaviors can reinforce clients' active involvement in sessions.

Attending is communicated mostly through nonverbal and para-verbal (i.e., how we say the words) behaviors, which help convey both what helpers are trying to express and what they do not intend to express (or might be trying to hide). For example, although a helper might try hard to be empathic and look concerned, he or she might feel bored and irritated with the client, which might be expressed through foot tapping or stifled yawns.

Attending orients helpers toward clients, but listening goes beyond just physically attending to clients. *Listening* refers to capturing and understanding the messages that clients communicate (Egan, 1994). Listening involves trying to hear and understand what clients are saying. Reik (1948) talked about listening with a third ear, or trying to hear what the client really means, not just what she or he says overtly. In effect, the helper puts the verbal and nonverbal messages together and hears what the client is thinking and feeling at a deep level.

Attending behaviors set the stage for allowing helpers to listen, but attending does not necessarily ensure listening. Helpers could attend physically but not listen (e.g., they could be thinking about dinner that night and not hear what clients are saying).

Listening provides the raw material from which helpers develop their verbal and nonverbal interventions, but listening should not be confused with the ability to deliver helpful interventions. Helpers could listen without being helpful, but it would be difficult to be helpful without listening. Thus, from watching sessions, one could not actually tell if helpers were listening; however, one could infer they were listening if they were able to produce statements that reflected what they heard.

Observing involves paying attention to what is going on overtly with clients in terms of nonverbal behaviors and mannerisms. Whereas listening focuses more on the words and nuances of what the client is saying, observing focuses on trying to pick up on the behavioral cues of the client and how the client is coming across. Observing is particularly important for noting times when clients have negative reactions, feel ambivalence, have difficulty expressing emotions, or are distracted or uninvolved.

Clearly, there is a lot of overlap among the attending, listening, and observation skills, which is why they are presented together in this chapter. As a helper, you will want to do all of these to build a relationship with clients. Before I describe nonverbal behaviors, let's think about cultural issues in attending, given that such issues can have a profound impact on the helping process.

Cultural Issues in Attending, Listening, and Observing

Each culture develops rules for nonverbal communication (Harper, Wiens, & Matarazzo, 1978). An example of such a rule is the pattern of greeting that might take no more than one third of a second. This pattern involves looking at the other person, smiling, lifting the eyebrows, and nodding the head. These behaviors act as a releaser in that they elicit the same response from another person. Rules for nonverbal behaviors are typically outside of conscious awareness. Most people probably could not articulate the nonverbal rules in their own culture because they learn these rules as young children through social interactions and example rather than by explicit verbal instruction.

Nonverbal behaviors that are appropriate in one culture might not be appropriate in another. A whole industry has developed to teach diplomats and travelers about nonverbal rules of other cultures. For example, in Asia, it is important for people not to praise themselves and instead to appear humble (Maki & Kitano, 2002). Therefore, an American who boasts might not be well received in Asian countries.

If you are involved in interpersonal interactions in which your rules for nonverbal behaviors are not followed by the other person, you might feel intense discomfort. You might not be able to understand or articulate why you feel uncomfortable, but you probably know that something does not feel right. For example, if someone stares at you, you might feel uncomfortable because it is inappropriate in your culture to stare for a long time. If someone stands too close and grabs your arm when you are talking, you might feel an urge to move away because the person has violated your personal space.

Helpers need to adapt their style to fit clients' nonverbal styles rather than expect clients to adapt to them. Helpers can take their cues from clients as to what makes them feel comfortable. For example, if a client acts nervous when the helper initiates eye contact, the helper might look away and observe whether the client responds differently. We cannot stereotype that clients from certain cultures will behave in specific ways; rather, we have to observe to see how each individual client responds.

Relax and Be Natural but Professional

It is important not to just appear relaxed but to actually be relaxed. Many beginning trainees try so hard to maintain an attending stance that they come across as artificial or posed. They perform all the "right" behaviors but end up being too attentive, which makes clients feel they are being examined too closely. One of the most difficult tasks facing helpers is to relax and be themselves. However, when helpers integrate attending and listening behaviors into their way of being, clients often respond by exploring their concerns.

When you are not able to relax, it can be helpful to step back and try to learn more about what is going on inside you. For example, if you feel your muscles tensing or note you are withdrawing physically from clients, you might reflect about what is going on inside you at that moment. Awareness is the key to handling situations (refer back to Chapter 4). Once you know how you feel, you can make informed decisions about how to act rather than having the reactions "leak out." Paying attention to bodily reactions provides an incredible amount of information about clients. If you feel bored, anxious, attracted, or repulsed by a client, chances are other people feel this way toward the client. See Chapter 14 for ideas about how to use these reactions therapeutically during the insight stage.

Nonverbal Behaviors That Facilitate Attending

Helpers typically communicate much of their attending and listening through nonverbal behaviors, and helpers observe what clients may be experiencing through noting their nonverbal behaviors. Indeed, some researchers (e.g., Archer & Akert, 1977; Haase & Tepper, 1972) have discussed the importance of nonverbal behaviors in the communication of emotions. These researchers have suggested that people communicate true emotions more through nonverbal than verbal expressions, and that nonverbal behaviors are more reliable indicators of true emotion when there is a discrepancy between verbal and nonverbal behaviors. In my opinion, there is not enough empirical evidence to indicate the relative importance of verbal and nonverbal behaviors; however, enough evidence exists to suggest that helpers should pay attention to what they and their clients communicate nonverbally as well as verbally.

So let us examine the different kinds of nonverbal behaviors. *Kinesics* refers to the relationship of bodily movements (arm and leg movements, head nods) to communication. Bodily movements can be categorized into several types, each of which has a different function (Ekman & Friesen, 1969). *Emblems* are substitutes for words (e.g., a wave is a universal greeting). *Illustrators* accompany speech (e.g., measuring the size of a fish with the hands). *Regulators* (e.g., head nods, postural shifts) monitor the conversation flow. *Adaptors* are habitual acts that are often outside awareness and have no communicative purpose (e.g., head scratching, licking one's lips, playing with a pen).

Helpers can use emblems, illustrators, and regulators to accompany verbal messages, but they should avoid using adaptors that detract from the helper's effectiveness by turning the focus away from the client to the helper. Too many adaptors or an inappropriate use of emblems, illustrators, or regulators is often a sign of "nonverbal leakage" (i.e., the person does not want to communicate or is trying to hide, but the feeling leaks out through nonverbal channels).

In the next sections, I review several nonverbal behaviors that are important for enabling the helper to attend to the client. These behaviors are also important for the helper to be aware of when observing the client. Obviously, these nonverbal behaviors all operate together, and sometimes one nonverbal behavior can compensate for another, but here I break them apart to describe how each one operates. Note that all of these behaviors can be used too much or too little with any given client; there is typically an optimal level that the helper and client have to negotiate, often implicitly.

EYE CONTACT

Eye contact is a key nonverbal behavior. Looking and gaze aversion are typically used to initiate, maintain, or avoid communication. With a gaze, one can communicate intimacy, interest, submission, or dominance (Kleinke, 1986). Eyes are used to monitor speech, provide feedback, signal understanding, and regulate turn taking (Harper et al., 1978). One could say we meet people with our eyes or that "the eyes are the windows into the soul." In contrast, gaze avoidance or breaking eye contact often signals anxiety, discomfort, or a desire not to communicate with the other person. In general, a person who violates the rules of eye contact will have a hard time communicating with others.

In typical noncounseling interactions, people make eye contact with each other (i.e., mutual gaze) in 28% to 70% of their interactions (Kendon, 1967), although usually for no more than 1 second at a time. Dyads typically negotiate when and how much to look at each other, although this is not a conscious negotiation and takes places at a nonverbal level. Too little eye contact can make one feel the listener is uninterested in the conversation and is avoiding involvement. By contrast, too much eye contact can make the other person feel uncomfortable, intruded on, dominated, controlled, and even devoured. Likewise, staring can feel rude, insulting, and threatening.

Norms for eye contact differ among cultures. In White middle-class North America, people tend to maintain eye contact while listening but look away when speaking, checking back from time to time to get feedback. In some Native American groups, sustained eye contact is considered offensive and a sign of disrespect, especially if by a younger to an older person (Brammer & MacDonald, 1996). Several cultural groups (some Native American, Inuit, or Aboriginal Australian groups) avoid eye contact, especially when talking about serious topics (Ivey, 1994). And, as noted in Chapter 5, a lack of eye contact signifies respect for an authority figure in some cultures.

FACIAL EXPRESSION

Darwin (1872) speculated that before prehistoric people had language, they communicated threats, greetings, and submission through facial expressions. He believed that this shared heritage explains why all humans express basic emotions through similar facial expressions. He wrote,

> the movements of expression in the face and body, whatever their origin may have been, are in themselves of much importance for our welfare. They serve as the first means of communication between the mother and her infant; she smiles approval, and thus encourages her child on the right path, or frowns disapproval. The movements of expression give vividness and energy to our spoken words. They reveal the thoughts and intentions of others more truly than do words, which may be falsified. . . . These results follow partly from the intimate relation which exists between almost all the emotions and their outward manifestations. (p. 366)

The face is perhaps the body part most involved in nonverbal communication because people communicate so much emotion and information through facial expressions (Ekman, 1993). People pay a lot of attention to facial expressions because they give clues about the meaning of the verbal message. In Shakespeare's (1623/1980) *Macbeth*, Lady Macbeth says to her husband, "Your face, my thane, is a book whereon men may read strange matters" (Act 1, Scene 5, p. 17).

The following are some common facial expressions and possible meanings (remember that these are only possible meanings), according to Nirenberg and Calero (1971):

- A frown might indicate displeasure or confusion.
- A raised eyebrow may suggest envy or disbelief.
- An eye wink might indicate intimacy or a private matter.
- Tightened jaw muscles may reflect antagonism.
- Eyes squinted might reflect antagonism.
- Upward rolling of the eyes may imply disbelief or exasperation.
- Both eyebrows raised may denote doubt or questioning.

Ekman and Friesen (1984) showed photographs of facial expressions to people around the world and found that several facial expressions had the same meaning across cultures. People around the world cry when distressed, shake their heads when defiant, and smile when happy. Even blind children who have never seen a face use the same facial expressions to express emotions as sighted people (Eibl-Eibesfeldt, 1971). In addition, fear and anger are expressed mostly with the eyes and happiness mostly with the mouth (Kestenbaum, 1992).

Although people in different cultures share a universal facial language, they differ in the manner and depth of expression of their emotions. For example, emotional displays are often intense and prolonged in Western cultures, whereas Asians display emotions of sympathy, respect, and shame but rarely display self-aggrandizing or negative emotions that might disrupt communal feelings (Markus & Kitayama, 1991; Matsumoto, Kudoh, Sherer, & Wallbott, 1988).

An important facial feature used in helping is smiling. Although smiling makes a person look friendly and can encourage exploration, too much smiling can be perceived as ingratiating or inappropriate when clients are talking about serious concerns. Helpers who smile excessively could be seen as not genuine, mocking the depth of clients' problems, or uninvolved.

HEAD NODS

The appropriate use of head nods, especially at the end of sentences, can make clients feel helpers are listening and following what they are saying. Indeed, verbal messages are sometimes unnecessary because helpers communicate through head nods that they are "with" clients and that clients should continue talking. Too few head nods can make clients feel anxious because they might think that helpers are not paying attention; too many can be distracting.

BODY POSTURE

An often-recommended body posture is for helpers to lean toward clients and maintain an open body posture with the arms and legs uncrossed (e.g., Egan, 1994). This leaning, open body posture often effectively conveys that the helper is paying attention, although helpers can appear rigid if they stay in this position too long. Also, if the open, leaning position is uncomfortable, it can be hard for helpers to attend to clients.

BODILY MOVEMENTS

Bodily movements provide information one often cannot obtain from either verbal content or facial expression. As Freud (1905/1953a) eloquently stated, "He that has eyes to see and ears to hear may convince himself that no mortal can keep a secret. If his lips are silent, he chatters with his fingertips, betrayal oozes out of him at every pore" (p. 94). Van den Stock, Righart, and de Gelder (2007) found that body expressions were particularly important in addition to those of the face and voice in helping responders recognize emotions. Similarly, Beattie and Shovelton (2005) suggested that spontaneous hand gestures enabled people to get their messages across more clearly.

Ekman and Friesen (1969) noted that leg and foot movements are the most likely sources of nonverbal leakage because they are less subject to conscious awareness and voluntary inhibition. The hands and face are the next best sources of clues for nonverbal leakage. Hence, if a helper finds him- or herself repeatedly tapping his or her foot, the helper might think about what he or she is feeling.

Gestures often communicate meaning, especially when they are used in conjunction with verbal activity. According to McGough (1975), the following are some possible meanings (again, remember that these are just possible meanings):

- Steepling of fingers might suggest that a person feels confident, smug, or proud.
- Touching or rubbing the nose tends to be a negative reaction.
- Hand to mouth often occurs when a person has blurted out something that should not have been said.
- Finger wagging or pointing implies lecturing or laying blame.
- Tugging at the collar suggests that the person feels cornered.

- Pinching the bridge of the nose implies that the person is deep in thought.
- Locked arms or crossed legs can be a defensive or critical position.
- A clenched fist is sometimes a defensive or hostile gesture.
- Hand over the eyes can be a gesture of avoidance.
- Sitting back in chair with hands behind the head may communicate confidence or superiority.

SPACE

The term *proxemics* refers to how people use space in interactions. E. T. Hall (1968) described four distance zones for middle-class Americans: intimate (0–18 inches), personal (1.5–4 feet), social (4–12 feet), and public (12 feet or more). If rules for prescribed distances are not followed, people can feel uncomfortable, although they are not usually aware of what is making them uneasy. Hall noted that once these patterns for space are learned, they are maintained largely outside of conscious awareness. Typically, the personal to social distance is considered appropriate for seating arrangements in helping relationships, although individuals vary in the amount of distance that feels comfortable for them. Some helpers place chairs close together, whereas others, when they have control over the arrangements, place the chairs far apart. Some helpers place a number of chairs in their offices and allow clients to choose where they sit; where the client sits then provides information that the helper can later use in speculating about the client's needs (e.g., to be close or to be distant).

Space is used in different ways in different cultures (E. T. Hall, 1963). American and British people generally prefer to be relatively distant from other people and rarely touch. In contrast, Hispanic and Middle Eastern people generally prefer less distance. For example, Arabs and Israelis often stand close, touch, talk loudly, and stare intently. In their review of the literature in work environments, Ayoko and Hartel (2003) found consistent evidence that space violations triggered conflict for people from different cultural backgrounds. In addition, Norman (1982) noted that space is a specialized elaboration of culture. He claimed that space reflects status, power, and expressions of personality. For example, a client would probably very differently to a helper sitting behind a desk than to a helper sitting without a barrier in between, given that desks can communicate power.

Helpers also need to take cultural considerations into account rather than just reacting unconsciously to someone who uses different proxemic patterns. However, helpers need to be avoid stereotyping given the vast range of differences within cultures. For example, a helper should not assume all Latino/Latina clients want to be hugged at the beginning and end of each session just because Latino people often hug when greeting and leaving. Differences exist within cultures, and acculturation to the dominant culture may influence clients' comfort with physical closeness.

Paraverbal Behaviors That Facilitate Attending

In addition to nonverbal behaviors, there are also paraverbal behaviors that accompany interventions. In other words, the manner in which helpers speak makes a difference. We consider here tone of voice and grammatical style.

TONE OF VOICE

Consider how you feel when someone speaks with a soft, gentle, inviting voice as opposed to when a person speaks in a loud, brash, demanding voice. You might have strong reactions to the two helpers based on their different speech mannerisms. Similarly, clients are more likely to explore when helpers speak gently rather than loudly and demandingly.

In addition, it can be helpful for helpers to somewhat match the client's pace of speech. Helpers might use a slower pace of speech with clients who speak slowly. In contrast, helpers might use a somewhat faster pace with clients who talk rapidly. If a client is speaking too rapidly, however, the helper might use a slower pace to encourage the client to slow down.

GRAMMATICAL STYLE

Another way helpers communicate attending is by matching the client's language and grammatical style. Language must be appropriate to the cultural experience and educational level of the client, so the helper can form a bond with the client. If a client says, "I ain't never gonna make it with chicks," it would probably be better for the helper to say something like, "You're concerned about finding a girlfriend," rather than "Your inferiority complex prevents you from establishing relationships with appropriate love objects." The latter statement sounds too discrepant from the client's language. Helpers should not compromise their integrity by using a language style that feels uncomfortable to them, but they can modify their style to be more similar to that of their client. Each of us has a comfort range of behaviors, and helpers need to find the place within that range to meet each client.

Behaviors That Facilitate Active Listening and Observing

Listening and observing involve verbal, nonverbal, and paraverbal channels of communication. Furthermore, helpers observe each of these types of communication to try to determine what the client is thinking and feeling.

VERBAL MESSAGES

Helpers can listen carefully to the words clients use to communicate thoughts, feelings, and experiences. Helpers get into a listening stance by using attending skills (e.g., "um-hmm") and freeing their minds from distractions. Helpers can imagine themselves in the client's position. Thus, helpers listen by seeking to understand what a client is experiencing from the client's perspective rather than from the helper's viewpoint. For example, an adolescent client, Kathleen, complained she felt devastated and worthless because she had not been asked to the prom. From the perspective of the helper, a 35-year-old married woman, not being asked to the prom was not a catastrophic event. However, by listening to Kathleen with a third ear, the helper could imagine that Kathleen felt awful.

A key to listening is for helpers to pay attention to clients without formulating the next response. All too often, people are half listening to what someone is saying because they are thinking about what to say next. It is better to listen and say nothing (especially if the client is exploring productively) than to rush in and say something that interrupts the client's exploration.

In addition, clients who have different verbal styles than their helpers can cause confusion for their helpers. Helpers who are introverted might assume that talkative clients are comfortable, when they could be talking too much out of anxiety. It is important for helpers not to project their feelings and personal style onto their clients.

NONVERBAL AND PARAVERBAL MESSAGES

Not only is it important that helpers listen to clients' words, they also can learn a lot by "listening" to clients' nonverbal behaviors. Clients who are nervous often use a lot of adaptors, are quiet, stutter, or cannot speak coherently. Clients who are defensive or closed often cross their arms and legs, almost as a barricade to the helper. Clients who are ashamed might look down as they speak. Clients who are scared might speak softly, look away, or have a closed posture. In contrast, clients who are comfortable and feel safe with their helpers often lean forward and talk with animation and feeling in their voices.

As noted earlier, helpers should not interpret nonverbal behaviors as having fixed or standard "meanings." Fidgeting can reveal anxiety, but it can also reveal boredom; folded arms can convey either irritation or relaxation. For example, if a client sits with arms and legs crossed, he or she is not necessarily withholding or defending. It could mean he or she is cold or just habitually sits with arms and legs crossed. Helpers cannot "read" another's body language as having universal meaning but can use body language as providing hints or clues about what a client might be feeling. If a client is sitting with arms and legs crossed and has scooted the chair back, the helper might hypothesize that the client needs distance from the helper. The helper needs to investigate this hypothesis further, however, by talking about it with the client (using skills covered in this book). Thus, helpers can use nonverbal data to form hypotheses and then gather more data to determine the accuracy of these hypotheses.

It also appears that some emotions are hard to read. Results from two studies (A. P. Atkinson, Dittrick, Gemmell, & Young, 2004; Van den Stock et al., 2007) suggest that fear and anger are harder to recognize than happiness and sadness. In addition, fear and anger are difficult to distinguish. These results indicate the importance of helpers not making assumptions about what clients are feeling.

Helpers also need to be aware of possible misinterpretations when someone from another culture uses nonverbal behaviors differently than they do. For example, if a European American helper greets an African American client who does not make eye contact, the helper should not assume the client suffers from guilt or low self-esteem but should pay close attention to whether this nonverbal behavior has a different meaning in the client's culture.

Helpers are often confused when clients have different nonverbal styles from theirs. For example, a helper who does not like to make a lot of eye contact might assume that a client who makes eye contact feels comfortable and in control of the situation. However, too much eye contact can be as much a defense or indication of anxiety as too little eye contact; both styles make it difficult for people to get close to others.

A key to listening is to pay attention to context. Rather than becoming fixated on the meaning of specific nonverbal behaviors, helpers need to pay attention to everything about the client: the verbal and nonverbal behaviors, the setting, the culture, and the presenting problem. For example, Archie appeared angry and hostile to the helper, but his behavior made sense when he revealed that he had just been stopped and frisked by a police officer for no apparent reason other than that he was an African American man in a White neighborhood.

When Rosenthal, Hall, DiMatteo, Rogers, and Archer (1979) showed clips of emotionally expressive faces and bodies, they found that some people were better at detecting emotion than others and that women were generally better at detecting emotion than men. J. B. Miller (1976) used social learning theory to explain why women might be better at detecting emotion than men:

> Subordinates (women), then, know much more about the dominants than vice versa. They have to. They become highly attuned to the dominants, able to predict their reactions of pleasure and displeasure. Here, I think, is where the long story of "feminine intuition" and "feminine wiles" begins. It seems clear that these "mysterious" gifts are in fact skills, developed through long practice, in reading many small signals, both verbal and nonverbal. (p. 10)

It is interesting to note that although some people are better than others at picking up nonverbal cues, some evidence showed that counselors were no better than noncounselors at nonverbal acuity (Sweeney & Cottle, 1976).

Helpers who are aware that they are not as natively sensitive to nonverbal cues can try harder to pay attention to these behaviors. A few studies have suggested that trainees can be taught to increase their sensitivity to nonverbal communication (e.g., Delaney & Heimann, 1966; Grace, Kivlighan, & Kunce, 1995). It seems that self-awareness and practice can help people become more sensitive to nonverbal cues.

MINIMAL VERBAL BEHAVIORS

There are two minimal verbal behaviors that helpers can use to facilitate client exploration: minimal encouragement and approval–reassurance.

Minimal Encouragers

Helpers encourage clients to keep talking through nonlanguage sounds, nonwords, and simple words such as "um-hmm," "yeah," and "wow." Helpers use minimal encouragers to acknowledge what the client has said, communicate attentiveness, provide noninvasive support, monitor the flow of conversation, and encourage clients to keep talking. Minimal encouragers are often used in conjunction with and serve the same purpose as head nods.

Too few minimal encouragers can feel distancing, whereas too many can be distracting and annoying to the client. I suggest helpers use minimal encouragers and acknowledgments, mostly at the end of client sentences or speaking turns (i.e., everything a client says between two helper interventions), to encourage clients to keep talking (assuming they are actively involved in exploration). A minimal encourager here suggests that you are giving up your speaking turn and would like the client to continue speaking. Interrupting a client to provide minimal encouragers, however, can be distracting, so helpers should pay attention to the appropriate timing of this intervention.

Approval–Reassurance

Approval–reassurance is a helpful skill that can be used occasionally (and I stress occasionally) to provide emotional support and reassurance, indicate helpers empathize with or understand clients, or suggest that clients' feelings are normal and to be expected. The key is to use approval–reassurance to foster exploration and to make clients feel safe enough to keep talking at a deep level about their concerns. For many clients, approval-reassurance that their problems are normal and that they are not alone in their feelings can be empowering and help clients in deeply exploring their concerns. The following are some examples of approval–reassurance that could be helpful depending on the situation:

- "That's really hard to handle."
- "That's a devastating situation."
- "How awful!"
- "Wow! That's an awesome opportunity!"
- "Good try!"
- "It was really terrific that you were able to express your feelings to him!"
- "Yeah, I know what you're going through."
- "I've been there too."

Approval–reassurance can also be used to provide reinforcement, indicating that the helper values something the client has said or done and wants to encourage the client to continue the effort to change. Some clients need support or acknowledgment that they have done something well. In addition, approval, reassurance, and reinforcement can help some clients persist in exploring because they know someone is listening and sympathetic; this is especially important if clients are exploring difficult or painful topics.

When using approval–reassurance, it is important that the helper stay close to where the client is and know the client well enough to know what behavior is being approved. For example, Beth had been working on being assertive came into her session and said that she finally told her boss that she wanted more control over her schedule. The helper immediately said, "Wow, that is great that you were able to stand up for yourself." Beth burst into tears and said that she was fired from her job. It perhaps would have been more helpful for the helper, instead of assuming that the experience was positive and thus giving approval-reassurance, to say something like, "And how did that go for you?"

Approval-reassurance is especially inappropriate if used to minimize or deny feelings (e.g., "Don't worry about it," "Everyone feels that way"). When used in this manner, approval-reassurance stops rather than facilitates clients' exploring and accepting feelings. Such statements can make clients feel they have no right to their feelings. Helpers sometimes use these interventions as misguided attempts to reassure others that everything is okay. Unfortunately, problems typically do not go away because they are minimized or denied. Most of us have heard the old sayings, "Give it time" or "Time cures all." It is not "time" that makes feelings go away; in fact, feelings often fester when they are bottled up or denied. Rather, it is awareness, acceptance, and expression of feelings that aid in resolution of painful affect. To reiterate, our goal as helpers is generally to help clients identify, intensify, and express feelings rather than minimize or deny them.

Furthermore, approval–reassurance can sound false if used excessively, prematurely, or insincerely. If such interventions are used to promote helper biases (e.g., "I think you're right to feel guilty about getting an abortion"), they can also be problematic because they stop client exploration or make clients feel compelled to agree or comply.

In general, then, if done judiciously and sparingly, approval–reassurance can encourage clients and facilitate exploration of thoughts, feelings, and experiences. Approval–reassurance should not be used, however, to diminish feelings, deny experiences, stop exploration, or provide a moral judgment. When helpers find themselves using approval–reassurance in a counterproductive way, they may want to think about what is going on in their own lives.

Here is an example of a positive use of approval–reassurance (in italics):

Client:	I just learned that my sister needs to have a kidney transplant. She's been sick a lot lately and hasn't been getting better.
Helper:	*That's too bad.*
Client:	Yeah, I feel terrible for her. She's only 21 and has always been active, so this is a real shock for her. I feel guilty that she got this horrible disease while I'm healthy and able to function.
Helper:	*It's pretty natural to feel some guilt.*
Client:	Really? I'm glad to hear that. I have been trying to do more for her. I'm thinking of organizing a campaign to find a donor and raise money for her treatment. Because she has an unusual blood type, it will be difficult to find the right person, and it's going to cost a lot of money.
Helper:	*That's terrific that you would do that for her.*

Client: I feel like it's the least I can do. It does interestingly bring up a lot of issues for me about obligation versus doing things because I want to. (Client continues exploring her thoughts.)

AVOIDING INTERRUPTIONS

One particularly distracting behavior is interruptions. When the client is exploring productively (i.e., talking about innermost thoughts and feelings), the helper does not need to interrupt. Often in the exploration stage, the helper simply has to attend and listen and stay out of the client's way, so that the client has the opportunity to keep talking. Matarazzo, Phillips, Wiens, & Saslow (1965) stressed that helpers should not interrupt and should delay talking for several seconds after the end of client statements. This pause (noninterruption) allows clients to continue thinking and talking without undue pressure from helpers. Matarazzo et al. found that inexperienced helpers interrupted far more often than did experienced helpers.

Interruptions can occasionally be helpful, however. If the client is stuck, cannot think of what to say, or is rambling or talking nonstop but not exploring in much depth (e.g., is telling stories in a bland tone), the helper may need to interrupt to help the client get back on track through the use of exploration skills (see Chapters 8, 9, 10, and 19).

SILENCE

A silence is a pause during which neither helper nor client is speaking. The silence can occur after a client's statement, within a client's statement, or after a simple acceptance of the helper's statement. For example, after the client says something like "I just feel so confused and angry and don't know what to say," the helper might pause to allow the client time to reflect on the feelings and see if the client has anything new to add. If the client pauses in the middle of saying something and is obviously still processing the feelings, the helper might be silent to let the client think without interruption. If the client responds minimally to something the helper said, the helper might be silent to see if the client can think of something else to say. It is important to note that to say nothing is not necessarily to do nothing. Helpers can be attentive and supportive, and they can listen without saying anything. In fact, sometimes the most useful thing a helper can do is to say nothing.

I often recommend the use of brief silences for beginning helpers because it gives them a chance to listen to clients without having to formulate an immediate response. Thus, when clients pause, the helper ponders how to reflect all that has been said while of course still attending to the client. Often, beginning helpers are surprised to discover that clients keep talking, indicating that they just need permission to talk.

Silence can be used to convey empathy, warmth, and respect and to give clients time and space to talk (Hill, Thompson, & Ladany, 2003; Ladany, Hill, Thompson, & O'Brien, 2004). Silence can also allow clients time to reflect or think through what they want to say without interruption. Some clients pause for a long time because they process things slowly and thoroughly or because they are in the middle of thinking through something and need time to get in touch with their thoughts and feelings. At such times, silence is respectful because it provides space for clients to think without feeling pressured to say anything. Warm, empathic silences give clients time to express their feelings. By allowing clients the space, helpers can encourage clients to express feelings from which they might otherwise run away. Silence can indicate to clients that helpers are patient and unrushed and have plenty of time to listen to whatever comes out. During these empathic silences, helpers can sit attentively focused on being with the client while the client is deeply immersed in thoughts and feelings. Hence, I suggest that helpers avoid interruptions and give clients several seconds after speaking to see whether they have anything else to say. Likewise, some empirical evidence suggests that clients talk more when therapists delay speaking (Matarazzo et al., 1965).

Silence also is often inadvertently used for negative or inappropriate reasons (Hill et al., 2003; Ladany et al., 2004). Some helpers are silent because they are anxious, angry, bored, or distracted. Many beginning helpers are uncomfortable with silence. They do not know what to do and are often concerned about how clients might perceive them. To relax, helpers can breathe deeply, relax, and think about the client and what might be going on inside the client. In other words, helpers should try to establish an empathic connection with clients during silence rather than focusing on themselves. If silences go on for a long time (i.e., more than a minute) or if a client is obviously uncomfortable, the helper should consider breaking the silence and asking the client how she or he is feeling.

As with other skills, the acceptability of silence varies by culture. D. W. Sue and Sue (1999) noted that in Japanese and Chinese cultures, silence can indicate a desire by the person to continue talking after making a point. In contrast, European Americans are less comfortable with silence and often rush to fill the space.

Here is an example of how silence might be used therapeutically when the client is actively exploring and engaged in the process:

> *Client:* My dog Sam just died. I'm really upset because I've had that dog since I was very little. I grew up with the dog.
>
> *Helper:* (Silence of about 1 minute) *How are you feeling?*
>
> *Client:* I was just thinking about how I got the dog. I begged my parents forever to get me a dog. I said

> I would take care of it. Of course, I didn't much at
> first, but I did later. Sam was kind of like Red Rover
> in the comics—he waited for me at the bus stop,
> and we had great adventures together. I could tell
> Sam everything.
>
> *Helper:* (Silence of 30 seconds)
>
> *Client:* Sam helped me get through my parents' divorce. I
> felt like I could rely on him then like no one else.
> It's like losing my best friend—we went through so
> much stuff together. I felt so terrible when I left for
> college and couldn't take him with me. He looked so
> sad, and I didn't even say goodbye to him.

AVOIDING TOUCH

Touching is a natural inclination when helpers want to indicate support to their clients and in fact can make clients feel understood and involved in a human relationship (Hunter & Struve, 1998). Montagu (1971) noted that touch is a natural physical need and that some people hunger for touch because they do not receive enough physical contact. Unfortunately, touch can sometimes have negative effects. Clients can feel that their space has been invaded. If the touch is unwanted or if clients have a history of unwanted touch, touch can be frightening and make clients feel unsafe.

Highlen and Hill (1984) reported that the few studies conducted on touching in therapy were inconclusive. Some studies have shown positive effects of touching, whereas others have found no effects. A survey of practicing therapists indicated that about 90% never or rarely touched clients during sessions (Stenzel & Rupert, 2004). The only type of touch that was used much at all was a handshake, typically before or after a session. Some therapists, however, were reluctant to even shake hands due to concern that any touch could be misinterpreted as sexual or exploitative and result in harm or litigation. Furthermore, therapists indicated that they were more likely to accept a hug or handshake than to initiate such behaviors.

Given the potential benefits, misunderstandings, and harm related to touch, it clearly requires clinical judgment to know when to use touch. It is better for beginning helpers to refrain from touching to avoid ethical and clinical problems that may arise. General guidelines for touch for more advanced helpers, as suggested by Kertay and Reviere (1998) and E. W. L. Smith (1998), are to

1. seek consent from the client before touch,
2. explain the use of touch to the client, and
3. discuss the experience with the client afterward.

Examples of Inappropriate and Appropriate Attending, Listening, and Observing

It helps to have an example of what these attending and listening behaviors might look like in practice. The first example is of an inappropriate use of these behaviors, whereas the second example is an appropriate use (although remember that these will vary based on the client and helper).

EXAMPLE OF INAPPROPRIATE ATTENDING, LISTENING, AND OBSERVING

In the following example, the helper is distracted by other events and has a hard time paying attention to the client:

Helper:	(leaning back, arms folded, and looking at the ceiling) So, how come you came today anyway?
Client:	(very softly) Well, I'm not sure. I just haven't been feeling very good about myself lately. But I don't know if you can help me.
Helper:	(shifts forward in seat and looks intently at client) Well, so what is happening?
Client:	(long pause) I just don't know how to . . .
Helper:	(interrupts) Just tell me what the problem really is.
Client:	(long pause) I guess I really don't have anything to talk about. Sorry I wasted your time.

EXAMPLE OF APPROPRIATE ATTENDING, LISTENING, AND OBSERVING

In this example, the helper is fully present with the client and able to attend and listen to the client, as well as observe what is going on with the client:

Helper:	Hi. My name is Debbie. We have a few minutes to talk today so that I can practice my helping skills. What would you like to talk about?
Client:	(very softly) Well, I'm not sure. I just haven't been feeling very good lately about myself. But I don't know if you can help me.

Helper: (matches the client's soft voice) Yeah, you sound kind of scared. Tell me a little bit more about what's been going on lately.

Client: I've been kind of down. I haven't been able to sleep or eat much. I'm behind on everything, and I don't have the energy to do any schoolwork.

Helper: (pauses, softly) It sounds like you feel overwhelmed.

Client: (sighs) Yes, that's exactly how I feel. It just seems like there's a lot of pressure in my first year of college.

Helper: Um-hmm (head nod)

Client: (continues talking)

Difficulties Helpers Experience in Attending, Listening, and Observing

Many beginning students reading this chapter have said that it is difficult to observe another person and decide how to intervene. They feel intimidated in trying both to monitor themselves and to pay attention to the client, let alone figure out what to say. It makes sense that bringing these behaviors up to awareness initially feels strained and tense because these are things that we have done automatically all our lives. Once we focus on them, it feels almost surreal and like an out-of-body experience. After focusing on them for a while, however, and paying attention to what you observe and how you come across, you will hopefully again begin to feel comfortable in your new stance. The key is practicing with lots of feedback.

Another difficulty is that some helpers are not sensitive to cultural differences in nonverbal behaviors. When someone from another culture does something nonverbally that is different from their custom (e.g., using eye contact differently), some helpers judge these clients according to their own cultural standards. It is important to become aware of this tendency and try not to judge clients using your own cultural standards. I want to again emphasize that there are no right nonverbal behaviors. The key is figuring what helps the client relax and explore. Within the bounds of looking professional, each helper needs to determine which attending behaviors feel comfortable and natural to use. For example, sitting in an uncomfortable but technically correct counselor posture will probably communicate discomfort rather than professionalism to the client.

Concluding Comments

Attending behaviors set the stage for helpers to listen and to let clients know they are being heard. Helpers also need to listen carefully to clients' verbal and nonverbal behaviors to hear what clients are saying and observe to pick up clues about underlying thoughts and feelings. In addition, attending and listening provide the foundation for all the other skills taught in this book, so helpers should be particularly attentive to learning these skills.

What Do You Think?

- Do you think that attending is different from listening?
- What are some rules for nonverbal behavior in your culture?
- How do you think rules are established for nonverbal behaviors? Can these rules be changed?
- What do you think about the role of culture in attending and listening?
- What are your thoughts about manipulating your nonverbal behaviors to achieve desired goals with clients?
- How much of communication is nonverbal versus verbal?
- How do you feel about using silence? How was silence used in your home?
- How might touching help or hinder the helping process? How was touching used in your family?

RESEARCH SUMMARY

Nonverbal Communication

Citation: Hill, C. E., Siegelman, L., Gronsky, B. R., Sturniolo, F., & Fretz, B. R. (1981). Nonverbal communication and counseling outcome. *Journal of Counseling Psychology, 28,* 203–212.

Rationale: Nonverbal behavior is thought to be an important component of helpful therapy, but it is unclear exactly how it works. The authors indicated three areas that they wanted to study: nonverbal abilities (skills of interpreting and communicating nonverbal messages), nonverbal behavior (specific behaviors that are helpful in sessions), and congruence (the consistency between verbal and nonverbal messages).

Method: Twenty doctoral student therapists were each paired with one male and one female undergraduate student who volunteered to talk about a personal problem. Therapists conducted a 30-minute session with the volunteer client, and then they both evaluated the session. Next, they watched a tape of the session. For each 1-minute interval during the tape review, therapists and volunteer clients rated, using a list of 13 possible affects (e.g., calm-relaxed, angry-hostile), the following: (a) one overall feeling of their own; (b) one feeling expressed through words; (c) one feeling expressed through voice tone; (d) one feeling expressed through movements, facial expressions, gestures, or a combination of these; and (e) one feeling they thought the other person had. Two weeks later, therapists and clients completed measures assessing their encoding and decoding abilities (abilities to send and receive nonverbal messages). Trained judges coded the following nonverbal behaviors in each 5-second interval of sessions (with sound muted): affirmative head nods, smiles, direct facing of the body, forward trunk lean, leg position (ankle on knee), and horizontal and vertical arm movements.

Interesting Findings:
- Therapists were better at decoding (interpreting nonverbal messages) than clients were.
- Encoding and decoding abilities were not related to session outcome measures.
- Therapists did more head nods, forward trunk leans, leg movements, and vertical and horizontal arm movements but smiled less often than did clients.
- The more vertical arm movements the therapist made, the worse the clients rated the credibility of the therapist.
- The more the therapist smiled and leaned forward, the more the therapists judged themselves as being empathic and warm.
- If the therapist was consistent in affect between the verbal and nonverbal channels, the therapists viewed themselves as facilitative.
- If the client accurately perceived the therapist's affect, the client rated the therapist as facilitative.
- Clients rated sessions better when they rated themselves as consistent in their verbal and nonverbal affect.

Conclusions:
- Nonverbal abilities were not related to session outcome.
- The amount therapists used various nonverbal behaviors was only minimally related to session outcome (but timing, which is probably more important than amount, was not investigated).
- Both therapists and clients evaluated sessions as having been better if they each felt consistent in their verbal and nonverbal displays of affect. It may be that inconsistency or incongruence is a manifestation of anxiety.

Implications for Therapy:
- Therapists need to be aware of what they are communicating through their nonverbal behavior.
- Therapists need to pay attention to what clients are communicating through their nonverbal behavior.

BONUS MATERIALS   Practice exercises, labs, and other resources for students and teachers are available on the companion website: http://pubs.apa.org/books/supp/hill4.

Skills for Exploring Thoughts and Narratives | 8

> The world is made of stories, not atoms.
> —*Muriel Rukeyser*

After Jason's parents were killed in a random drive-by shooting, he needed a chance to talk with someone who would not judge him. His helper listened supportively, showed appropriate and encouraging attending behaviors, rephrased the content of what Jason was saying (e.g., "You're still trying to understand what happened," "You can't make sense of their deaths," "You want to hurt their murderer") and asked open questions to help Jason clarify his thoughts. Jason left feeling better about having someone listen and being able to express what he was thinking.

Rationale for Exploring Thoughts and Narratives

When clients come into a helping situation, we as helpers need to hear what they think about their problems, what stories they are telling themselves about how they got where they are, and what explanations they have for their problems. Once

http://dx.doi.org/10.1037/14345-008
Helping Skills: Facilitating Exploration, Insight, and Action, Fourth Edition, by C. E. Hill

we understand, we can help clients challenge and change the thoughts and narratives and thus lead to changing their behaviors and rewriting their stories. In this chapter, I focus on the content of the narratives (the thoughts), and I focus on the feelings in Chapter 9. Obviously, thoughts and feelings cannot really be separated, but I have separated them into two chapters to provide maximum attention to each.

A whole new form of therapy has recently been developed called *narrative therapy* (Madigan, 2011; White, 2007). Narrative therapy is based on the assumption that people are storytelling creatures. In every culture, people tell stories that shape who they are and how they think about themselves. Only by taking those narratives out and examining them can people begin to reshape who they are and how they think about themselves. Narratives are often ill defined or rigid and need to be reevaluated. A small change can be big in the long run because it changes the course of the narrative and all other narratives. The goal in working with narratives in the exploration stage is to bring them out in open and explore them, whereas we aim to change the narrative in the insight stage (although clients well may change narratives on their own).

I am not just referring here to the client telling stories to entertain us. The purpose of helping is not for the helper to be entertained but for the client to think deeply about his or her concerns. And I am not referring to just obsessing about problems and endlessly listing complaints. A study found that adolescent girls tend to coruminate (Rose, Carlson, & Waller, 2007) or endlessly obsess and worry about issues and bring each other down. Ruminating obviously does not help but rather seems to perpetuate the same old story. Rather, helpers want to hear about what troubles clients about these issues. Helpers want clients to slow the process down and think about their situation, to have a chance to talk about the different pieces of the problem in a supportive, nonjudgmental setting. By explaining things to someone else, clients often hear themselves in a new way.

When I talked about this issue in class recently, a student asked me how we can tell whether a client is truly exploring versus ruminating versus telling a story to entertain us. Good question! If a client is telling a story (at least if she or he is a good storyteller), there is often a polished quality to it—there is a clear beginning, a build up to a climax, and then a conclusion. The goal of the storyteller is to perform, and so the attention is focused on getting the other person's attention. If the client is ruminating, there is a steady tone, often boring, and often a monotone voice, with a lot of repetition. The goal of the ruminator is to worry or justify. In contrast, when a client is truly going inward and exploring thoughts and narratives, there are often pauses to check things out, and the voice tone varies as the person is discovering new things as he or she talks. The goal of the explorer is to think about, evaluate, consider, reflect, and see new aspects.

The primary skills for helping clients explore thoughts and narratives are restatements and summaries because they help clients feel heard, encourage them to continue talking, and help to focus on the most important aspects of their stories. Open questions and probes for thoughts are also helpful, especially if not used too often and if interspersed with restatements. Closed questions and disclosures of similarities are occasionally helpful and are used in rare circumstances.

Restatements and Summaries

Restatements are a repeating or paraphrasing of the content or meaning of what a client has said (see Exhibit 8.1). Restatements typically contain fewer but similar words as the client's, are more concrete and clear

---

EXHIBIT 8.1

Overview of Restatement

Definition	A *restatement* is a repeating or rephrasing of the content or meaning of the client's statement(s) that typically contains fewer but similar words and is more concrete and clear than the client's statement. Restatements can be phrased either tentatively or as a direct statement. Restatements can paraphrase either the immediately preceding material or material from earlier in session or treatment (i.e., summaries).
Examples	"You want to be an effective helper."
	"Your parents are breaking up."
	"To summarize, you seem clearer on what you would like to do about attending the wedding."
Typical helper intentions	To clarify, to focus, to support, to encourage catharsis (see Web Form D)
Possible client reactions	Supported, understood, clear, negative thoughts or behaviors, stuck, lacking direction (see Web Form G)
Desired client behavior	Cognitive–behavioral exploration (see Web Form H)
Helpful hints	Focus on the content of what the client is trying to communicate
	Pick the most important part of the client's statement to paraphrase—the "cutting edge," the part that is most salient, for which the client has the most energy
	Keep restatements short and simple
	Pause before restating to see if the client has finished talking
	Give restatements slowly and supportively
	Focus on the client rather than on other people
	Vary the manner in which you deliver restatements

than the client's statement, can be phrased either tentatively (e.g., "So you seem to be saying that maybe you were a little bit late?") or more directly (e.g., "You were late"), and refer to things the client just said or to things the client said earlier in the session or treatment.

Summaries, a kind of restatement, tie together several ideas or pick out the highlights and general themes of the content expressed by the client. Summaries do not go beyond what the client has said or delve into the reasons for feelings or behaviors (these would be interpretations; see Chapter 13) but rather consolidate what has been said. For example, after listening for several minutes, the helper might say to an adolescent:

> So here's what I think we've learned so far. You have a strong reaction when your parents are intrusive. They barge in your room without knocking and give you no privacy. You feel like they don't listen to you. And then you start acting annoyed and shut them out.

RATIONALE FOR USING RESTATEMENTS AND SUMMARIES

The use of restatement goes back to Rogers (1942), who believed that helpers need to be mirrors or sounding boards, enabling clients to hear what they are saying without judgment. Thinking about one's problems alone is often difficult because one can get blocked or stuck, may not have enough time or energy to examine problems thoroughly, may rationalize behaviors, or may give up and quit trying. Having another person who listens and serves as a mirror of the content offers clients a golden opportunity to hear themselves think.

Given that clients often feel confused, conflicted, or overwhelmed by their problems, hearing accurate restatements allows them to gain feedback about how their concerns sound to others. It is important that clients hear back what they have said, so they can evaluate what they are thinking, add things they have forgotten, think about whether they actually believe what they have said, and think about things at a deeper level. Because statements often sound different when repeated by someone else, restatements allow clients to ponder what they really think. Restatements can also enable clients to clarify matters, explore aspects of the problem more thoroughly, and think about aspects they had not considered before. Just taking the time to think through a problem carefully with the benefit of an interested listener can lead to new understanding. In fact, with relatively healthy clients who are trying to understand major problems or make decisions, helpers might never need to go beyond this type of intervention because these clients only need an opportunity to hear what they are thinking.

The helper typically uses restatements to reflect on new thoughts as they arise. Successive approximations enable the helper to help the client get closer to what he or she is trying to say. So the first things out of the client's mouth may sound confused, but after a few times trying with the help of gentle restatements, the client is often better able to express what she or he is thinking.

An additional reason that helpers use restatements is to put their listening into words and to play an active role in the helping process. Rather than assuming they have understood what clients have said, helpers use restatements to check out the accuracy of what they think they have heard. Having to listen to clients and summarize their words in fewer and more concise terms requires that helpers attend carefully and determine the key components of what clients have revealed. Saying "I understand how you feel" or asking questions can be easy but does not convey any actual understanding; restating what the client has said is much harder and requires that helpers not only listen but also struggle to understand enough of what clients have said so they can restate the essence of their messages. Although at first it may seem that restatements are a passive mode of responding, helpers are actively engaged in trying to capture the essence of clients' experiences and paraphrase it back for clients to hear. It is actually quite hard to figure out what people are saying given that they often are not completely sure what they are thinking and so cannot articulate it clearly.

Restatements and summaries are most appropriate to use when clients are talking cognitively about their problems (i.e., are trying to explain a situation or thought, trying to sort out what they are actually thinking) rather than when they are actively exploring emotions. Interestingly, although helpers are typically oriented more toward working with emotions, clients spend most of their time talking about thoughts and narratives, and some do not like to or cannot engage at an emotional level, so being able to engage with clients at this level is important. Such clients like to analyze their thoughts about problems and might be threatened if asked to focus too much on feelings, especially early in a helping relationship.

As with restatements, helpers also use summaries to reassure clients that they have been listening and to check the accuracy of what they have been hearing. Summaries can be particularly useful when clients have finished talking about a particular issue or at the end of sessions as a way of helping clients reach a sense of closure regarding what has been explored. Summaries also can be helpful at the beginning of subsequent sessions to recap past sessions and provide a focus for the upcoming session if the client is not quite ready to talk. Not all clients want or need such summaries, especially if issues seem clear-cut to them, but summaries can be helpful when clients are diffuse or confused.

HOW TO RESTATE

The goal of restatements is to enable clients to focus and to talk in more depth about an issue, as well as to assist clients in figuring out issues. Just restating what the client already knows would not help the client go deeper. Rather, helpers try to capture the "cutting edge" of what clients have revealed—what clients are most uncertain about, what is still unexplored, or what is not completely understood. A student used a metaphor of Wayne Gretzky, a star hockey player, saying that it is important in hockey to go to where the puck is going, not where it has been. Helpers, then, should pick out a salient message or an issue that clients are uncertain about to facilitate further exploration on this issue.

Clues for determining what is valuable to restate can be gathered by attending to what the client focuses on most, what the client seems to have the most involvement in talking about, what the client seems to have questions or conflicts about, and what is left unresolved. Attention to nonverbal messages (e.g., vocal quality might indicate that the client is deeply engaged in what he or she is talking about) can also assist helpers in determining the salient content of the client's message.

Helpers sometimes worry that selecting an important part of the client's statement requires a judgment call and removes them from a client-centered approach to helping. I would argue that restatements in fact allow helpers to stay within a client-centered approach because they are trying to use their empathic skills to figure out the most important aspect of the message for the client. Helpers have to listen to clients at a deep level to hear what clients are most concerned about. The attitude of being client-centered is thus important in formulating restatements.

Beginning trainees often think they need to capture everything the client has said, but capturing everything not only would be impossible but would probably be counterproductive. The focus would shift from the client to the helper because the repeating would take too much time. The momentum would be lost in the session. The client would be put in a position of trying to remember everything he or she said to determine whether the helper repeated everything accurately. In contrast, an effective restatement keeps the focus on the client and is almost unnoticeable in subtly guiding and encouraging the client to keep talking. Focusing on one piece of an issue at a time is important to allow clients the opportunity to delve deeply into a concern. Helpers can return later to other aspects of the problem after one part is explored thoroughly.

Restatements are generally shorter and more concise than clients' statements, focusing on important material rather than repeating everything verbatim. For example, if the client has been talking at some length about the many things that have been getting in the way of studying, the helper might give a restatement such as, "So you have not been able to study lately" or "Studying has been difficult for you lately," because these statements focus on what is important for the client to explore at a deeper level. A restatement essentially orients the client to what the helper wants him or her to talk about.

The emphasis of restatements typically is on the client's thoughts rather than on other people's thoughts. This focus enables the client to focus inwardly rather than blaming others or worrying about what others think. For example, Janet was discussing her decision to move to the West Coast. During the session, she continuously focused on her colleagues' and friends' reactions to her decision. The helper worked to focus the restatements on Janet ("You would like to move") rather than on her friends and colleagues ("Your friends don't want you to move").

The emphasis is on helping clients explore more deeply without having an agenda for what content should emerge. Helpers work to be nonjudgmental and do not assume they know or understand what clients are experiencing but rather take the stance of helping the client explore whatever emerges. Helpers are not invested in solving problems or disclosing their own problems but are focused on facilitating client exploration.

To reduce the tendency to become repetitive, helpers can vary the format of restatements. There are several ways to introduce restatements, for example:

"I hear you saying . . . "
"It sounds as though . . . "
"You're saying that . . . "
"So . . . "
"What you seem to be saying . . . "
"If I'm hearing you accurately, . . . "
"Let me see if I got what you're saying . . . "
"I'm not sure I got that completely, let me try to summarize and see if I got it . . . "

Alternatively, helpers can just repeat and slightly draw out a key word a client has said, such as *divorce, music,* or *headache.* If the key word is presented in a questioning or inviting tone, it encourages the client to tell the helper more about the topic. For example, if a client has been talking about her daughter having just been tested and found to have an incredibly high IQ score, and the helper wants the client to explore more about IQs, she might simply say, "IQ . . . ?," thereby inviting the client to tell her more about what IQ means to her.

Although it is typically helpful when restatements are relatively close to what the client has said, it is not necessary (or often even possible) for the restatements to be perfectly accurate. For example, if a client presents a confused and jumbled statement of her of his concerns and the helper provides restatements that do not encapsulate the content accurately, the client can clarify what she or he means so both the client and helper can understand the situation better. Restatements thus allow clients a chance to clarify helpers' mistaken impressions.

If your restatement or summary is totally wrong, that is not necessarily a disaster for the relationship (unless of course the helper has been dismissive, judgmental, or critical). One misstep does not undo the therapeutic relationship, as long as the helper demonstrates the willingness to keep listening to try to understand more.

EXAMPLE OF RESTATEMENTS

The following shows a helper using restatements (in italics) in a session:

Client: I have to go on a pilgrimage to Mecca. I don't really want to go because it's the middle of my last semester in college and I'm worried that my grades will suffer if I leave for 2 weeks, but I don't have much choice. According to my religion, I have to go.

Helper: *You have to go.*

Client: Yeah, for my religion, we all have to do a pilgrimage before we get married. It's just expected. My father has to go with me because a man has to be on the pilgrimage, but I don't have a very good relationship with him, and he's not well, so I don't know if he can withstand the rigors of the trip. The last time he went with my brother, it was pretty disastrous.

Helper: *You said you don't have a very good relationship with your father.*

Client: Right. He wasn't around much when I was growing up. He was always too busy. And now to spend 2 weeks with him is a lot. I don't even know what we could talk about. I feel like I don't know him. I get anxious just thinking about spending a lot of time with him. But on the other hand, I wish I knew him better, so maybe this is an opportunity to get to know him.

Helper: *You wish you knew him better.*

Client: Yeah, really know him. I've always wanted to have a good relationship with him. People say that we're a lot alike. And he could teach me a lot about my religion and culture, things I don't know much about, given that I came to the United States when I was very young.

Helper: *So you could learn something from your father.*

> *Client:* Oh, yeah, I think I could learn a lot from him. He is a wise person. I just hope I can be myself with him. I've always felt like such a little kid, and I would rather feel like an adult with him the way I can with my mother.
>
> *Helper:* *Feel like an adult.*
>
> *Client:* Yeah, I want to feel like myself when I am around him. I want to be able to behave like I do with other people. I want to get to know him as a person instead of feeling afraid of him. (Client continues to explore.)

DIFFICULTIES HELPERS EXPERIENCE IN RESTATING

Many helpers initially feel awkward and stilted using restatements because in everyday social communication people do not typically paraphrase what another person has said. Many beginning helpers worry that clients will feel annoyed and say something like "I just said that." In fact, the reaction of clients is usually quite different when they are given a good restatement—they feel heard and are eager to explore more. Once students learn how to use restatements, they can be useful not only in helping relationships but also with friends and family to demonstrate that one is really listening.

Another difficulty beginning helpers face is sounding like parrots if they continually use the same format to introduce restatements (e.g., "I hear you saying . . . ") or if they repeat clients' messages verbatim. Clients often get annoyed with parroting and become distracted from focusing on their concerns. In a related vein, some helpers are so afraid of making a mistake when choosing key aspects of clients' messages that they repeat everything, taking the focus off the client and halting the flow of the interchange. Not surprisingly, clients quickly become bored and annoyed with such restatements, saying things like, "That's what I just said." Moreover, clients might feel stuck and aimless when restatements are mere repetitions of what they have said. By choosing the key components, focusing on the "cutting edge" of clients' concerns, varying the format, and keeping the restatements short, helpers can deal with these problems. It is also important to focus on being empathic rather than restating robotically. Some helpers get so caught up in capturing the content accurately that they forget the most important thing is to show the client that they are struggling to hear and make sense of what the client is saying.

Some helpers feel frustrated when they use restatements because they feel they are not "doing" anything or giving the client specific answers. Restatements are used to help clients explore and tell their stories rather than come to insight or action, so helpers rarely feel brilliant when using them. In fact, clients often are not able to remember restatements because the focus is on them rather than on the helper.

Open Questions and Probes for Thoughts

Questions come to most of us naturally. We are curious and want to get to know other people, and questions are a most direct way to elicit information. Exhibit 8.2 provides an overview of the different types of questions that are used in the helping process. In this chapter, the focus is only on open and closed questions about thoughts, but other types (e.g., open questions and probes for insight) are presented and discussed later in the book.

RATIONALE FOR USING OPEN QUESTIONS AND PROBES ABOUT THOUGHTS

Open questions and probes about thoughts help clients clarify and explore their thoughts. When using these leads, helpers do not want a specific answer from clients but instead want clients to explore whatever comes to mind. In other words, helpers do not purposely limit the nature of clients' responses to a "yes," "no," or one- or two-word answer, even though clients may respond that way (see Exhibit 8.3). Whereas open questions are phrased in the form of a question (e.g., "What are your thoughts about that?"), probes are phrased in the form of a statement or directive (e.g., "Tell me more about your thoughts"). The phrasing is different, but the intent for both is to facilitate exploration.

WHY USE OPEN QUESTIONS AND PROBES TO GET AT THOUGHTS?

Many researchers have found that open questions are used frequently in therapy and are generally perceived as being moderately helpful for the therapy process (Barkham & Shapiro, 1986; Elliott, 1985; Elliott, Barker, Caskey, & Pistrang, 1982; Fitzpatrick, Stalikas, & Iwakabe, 2001; Hill, Helms, Tichenor, et al., 1988; Martin, Martin, & Slemon, 1989). These studies suggest that open questions and probes can be a useful intervention for encouraging clients to talk longer and more deeply about their concerns. I recently heard a person say that the three kindest

EXHIBIT 8.2

Types of Questions and Probes

Format of question	Open ("How do you feel about that?")
	Probe ("Tell me about that.")
	Closed ("Did you get an A?")
Related to specific skills	Thoughts (clarification, focus, explanation, meaning, example)
	Feelings
	Insight
	Immediacy
	Strategies
Time frame	Past (memories, childhood experiences)
	Present (current)
	Future (anticipations, expectations)
Focus	Self
	Other

EXHIBIT 8.3

Overview of Open Questions and Probes About Thoughts

Definition	*Open questions and probes about thoughts* ask clients to clarify or explore thoughts. Helpers do not request specific information and do not purposely limit the nature of the client response to a "yes," "no," or one- or two-word answer, even though clients may respond that way. Open questions and probes can be phrased as queries ("How do you think about that?") or as probes ("Tell me your thoughts about that"), as long as the intent is to help the client clarify or explore.
Examples	What were you thinking when you said that?" "Tell me more about your thoughts about that."
Typical helper intentions	To focus, to clarify, to encourage catharsis, to identify maladaptive cognitions (see Web Form D)
Possible client reactions	Clear (see Web Form G)
Desired client behaviors	Recounting, cognitive–behavioral exploration (see Web Form H)
Helpful hints	Make sure your questions are open instead of closed
	Vary the format of the open question and probe
	Avoid multiple questions
	Avoid "why" questions
	Focus on the client rather than on others
	Focus on one part of the issue rather than trying to cover everything
	Have an intention for every question
	Observe client reactions to your questions

words you could hear are "Tell me more." Indicating curiosity and interest through judicious use of open questions and probes for thoughts or
probes can truly be a gift.

Open questions and probes serve several purposes. They can be particularly useful when clients are rambling, repeating the same thoughts
but not really exploring deeply. They can also be used to help clients
clarify their thoughts when they are confused, lead clients to think
about new things, help clients unravel conflicting thoughts, or provide
structure for clients who are not very verbal or articulate. Clients often
get stuck describing their problems, and open questions and probes help
them think about different aspects of the problem. Open questions and
probes can also be used to clarify or focus and are particularly helpful
when clients are starting the session, rambling, being vague or unclear,
or stuck. As with restatements, open questions and probes demonstrate
that the helper is listening and interested in the client. They show that
the helper is tracking what the client says and is interested enough to
encourage the client to keep talking.

In addition, if a client cannot think of what to talk about, open
questions and probes are a good way for helpers to provide direction.
For example, if Justin has been talking about receiving a bad grade and
has explored his feelings and then the dialogue stops, the helper might
ask Justin what a bad grade means for the future. Other possible open
questions and probes might be to ask Justin to compare how this situation relates to past experiences with grades or how this grade affects his
relationship with his parents. These open questions and probes could
help Justin talk more completely about other important aspects of the
problem. I like comparing problems to a ball of yarn; with each open
question or probe, helpers encourage clients to take out a bit of the
yarn and talk about it. When one piece is explored thoroughly, helpers
gently guide clients to pull out another piece of the yarn (i.e., talk about
another aspect of the problem).

In addition, open questions and probes about examples are helpful
when clients are talking generally and vaguely about problems. Asking
for specific examples can give helpers a clearer picture of what the client is talking about (e.g., "Tell me about a specific time when you felt
distant from your father").

HOW TO USE OPEN QUESTIONS AND PROBES ABOUT THOUGHTS

There are several ways that open questions and probes can be used. For
example:

- "Tell me about the last time you thought x."
- "Tell me more about x."

- "What's that like for you to think x?"
- "What do you think about that?"
- "What do you mean by that?"
- "What does x mean?"
- "Can you give me an example of that?"
- "What comes to mind when you think about x?"

Appropriate attending behaviors are important when delivering open questions and probes. If the tone of voice is low and soft, the rate of speech is slow, and the open question and probe is phrased tentatively, the client is likely to perceive the helper as conveying concern and intimacy. Helpers should be supportive, nonjudgmental, and encouraging no matter what clients say because there are no right or wrong topics to explore and no right or wrong answers to questions.

Open questions and probes should be short and simple. Clients may have difficulty responding to lengthy or multiple questions because they might feel confused. Multiple questions ("What did you do next, and what were you thinking, and what did you mean by that?") can have a dampening effect on the interaction if clients do not know which question to respond to first or feel bombarded. Clients might ignore important questions if there are too many of them because they cannot respond to all of them. Helpers can come back later and ask other questions if they still seem relevant.

Thus, open questions and probes about thoughts are most effective when helpers focus on one part of the problem at a time. Clients cannot talk about everything at once and may have difficulty choosing a single topic, so it can be helpful for helpers to pick the most important or salient issue to focus on and return to others later. As with restatements, it is best to focus on the areas for which clients have the most energy or affect, or for what is at the "cutting edge" of a client's awareness. For example, if Juan is talking about several different topics, the helper might ask Juan a question about the topic that seems most unresolved or pressing.

In addition, it is useful to keep the focus of the open question or probe on the client ("How did you feel about your mother's behavior?") rather than turning the attention to other people ("What did your mother do in that situation?"). Keeping the focus on the client helps the client explore what is going on inside him or her rather than deflecting the attention to other people. For example, if Jean often argues with her mother, the helper can ask about Jean's thoughts ("What are your thoughts when your mother starts yelling at you?") rather than asking Jean about her mother's thoughts ("What do you think your mother would say about this?"). Although it could be helpful to understand more about the mother, she is not in the room, and the helper is likely to get a one-sided view of her. The person the helper is most likely to help is the client, so it is typically better to focus on the client.

It is also important to keep the client focused on current thoughts, although these current thoughts may be about past events. So rather than asking, "What did you think then?" the helper would ask, "What do you think now about what happened then?"

It is not necessary to ask open questions or probes if the client is exploring at a deep level. Rather than interrupting just to get a chance to say something, it is better to keep quiet and allow the client to keep talking and only ask questions when the client is stuck or needs guidance about what to explore further.

One particular kind of probe I like is "Tell me your memories about that." This probe is particularly helpful when a client is describing a troubling current situation that you suspect might be influenced by past experiences. Thus, when Selina was talking about the effects of her father and stepmother breaking up, I asked about her memories of her mother and father's divorce. Selina was able to talk about painful memories that obviously were still affecting her and influencing how she was dealing with the current situation.

Helpers generally also avoid "why" questions (e.g., "Why did you blow up at your boyfriend the other night?" "Why are you not able to study?") in the exploration stage because they are difficult to answer and can make the client defensive. As Nisbett and Wilson (1977) indicated, people rarely know why they do things. If they knew why they act as they do, they probably would not be talking to helpers. When someone asks why you did something, you might feel she or he is judging you and deriding you for not being able to handle the situation more effectively. Instead of "why" questions, helpers could use "what" or "how" questions (e.g., instead of "Why didn't you study for your exam?" the helper could ask, "What was going on that kept you from studying?" "What was going through your mind when you were trying to study?" or "What is going on that makes it difficult for you to study?"). Why questions are more appropriate in the insight stage and are discussed in Chapter 13.

Finally, helpers should be aware of cultural differences in receptiveness to questions. D. W. Sue and Sue (1999) noted that people from some cultures may be uncomfortable when they are questioned or asked to initiate the dialogue (e.g., "What would you like to talk about today?") because it may be disrespectful. In such cases, helpers may have to be more direct, either in educating the client about the helping process or in suggesting topics to discuss. Helpers cannot assume, however, that clients from other cultures will not like open questions or probes, but if they observe that clients seem uncomfortable with them, they can instead try restatements.

EXAMPLE OF OPEN QUESTIONS AND PROBES ABOUT THOUGHTS

The following shows a helper using open questions and probes about thoughts (in italics) and probes (in italics) in a session:

Client:	My younger sisters are fighting a lot with each other. They really get nasty and have been hurting each other. My youngest sister was caught stealing from a store recently. My parents aren't doing anything about it, and my sisters are just going wild. I wish there was more I could do to help them. If I were still at home, they would listen to me. I think they don't have anyone to turn to. My parents are divorcing, so they're just not available to my sisters.
Helper:	*Tell me more about what it's like for you not to be there.*
Client:	On one hand, I'm delighted to be away from the mess. On the other hand, I feel guilty, like I survived the *Titanic* crash and came out alive but they're sinking.
Helper:	*What is it like when you are with your family?*
Client:	My parents are still living together, but they fight all the time. Things are pretty scary around the house because my parents get pretty violent with each other. I have to look out for my sisters. I am really more their parent than either of my parents are. I got to be pretty strong by having to fend for myself so much.
Helper:	*Give me a specific example of a time when you had to look after your sisters.*
Client:	Oh, yeah, just last night when I called home. My younger sister said that mom has started to throw dishes around and dad left the house in a huff and they haven't talked. No one even asks them about their schoolwork any more and they are running around wild. I don't know what to do for them from here. (Client continues to explore.)

DIFFICULTIES HELPERS EXPERIENCE IN DELIVERING OPEN QUESTIONS AND PROBES ABOUT THOUGHTS

A common problem is that helpers tend to ask the same type of open questions and probes repeatedly, most often "What do you think about that?" Many clients become annoyed when they continually hear the same type of question or probe and have a hard time responding.

Similarly, some beginning helpers use only open questions and probes rather than interspersing these with restatements. Helpers tend to use open questions and probes excessively when anxious because this skill is relatively easy and already exists in most helpers' repertoires. Unfortunately, the interaction can become one-sided if helpers use too many open questions and probes. In this situation, helpers are not demonstrating that they are listening to what the clients are saying or struggling to understand the clients. The tone of the session can become stilted rather than being a mutual struggle to explore and understand the client's concerns.

Closed Questions About Thoughts

Closed questions typically request a one- or two-word answer ("yes," "no," or a confirmation) or ask for specific facts (e.g., "What was your test grade?" "How old were you when your parents were divorced?" or "Did you call the counseling center?"). Such questions are asked to gather specific information, presumably because the helper is going to use the information for some reason (e.g., to assess the client, to figure out an action plan).

Closed questions have an important but limited role in the helping process. Occasionally, the helper needs to obtain specific information, perhaps because the client has been vague and the helper needs more information to understand the situation. The most direct way to get this specific information is through closed questions. For example, when a client is vague about his or her family situation and the helper is struggling to understand the family dynamics, the helper might ask, "Are you the oldest child?" or "Where are you in the birth order?" In such situations, asking for needed information is better than making assumptions or being confused. The key is that the information is important for the therapeutic process.

Helpers can also use closed questions occasionally to ask for clarification, because they did not hear what the client said, or because they want to determine if clients understood or agreed with what they said. For example:

"What did you say?"
"Am I right?"
"Is that what happened?"

"Does that sound right to you?"

"Did I understand you correctly?"

Another situation in which closed questions are important is during a crisis situation. If there is a crisis (e.g., the potential for suicide, homicide, violence, or abuse of any kind or decompensation into serious mental illness), the process changes from helping to crisis management. In these situations, helpers need to ask clients directly about what is happening so they can make appropriate referrals (see also Chapter 19). If such a situation occurs while you are in training, it is best to immediately seek out supervision from someone who can help you figure out how to handle the situation.

Closed questions are appropriate for certain types of interview situations, such as a medical doctor gathering information to make a diagnosis, interrogations by lawyers during courtroom trials, or job interviews. In these situations, the roles between the interviewer and interviewee are often distinct. The interviewer asks the question to get the desired information; the respondent answers the questions. The control of the interview usually stays with the interviewer, who directs the interaction by asking questions.

An example of an interview situation in which closed questions are useful is in academic advising. When a student comes to me in my role as an academic advisor asking about her or his chances of being accepted into graduate school, my goal is to gather enough information about the student's credentials (e.g., grade point average, Graduate Record Examination [GRE] scores, research and clinical experience, career goals) to make an assessment. The best and most efficient way of gathering such information quickly is typically through closed questions (e.g., "What are your grade point average and GRE score?" "What research experiences have you had?" "Where do you hope to be employed after graduate school?"). I try to ask the closed questions in a supportive, empathic, nonjudgmental fashion, without attempting to determine what students should do with their lives or pass judgment on their effectiveness as human beings. Once I have the information, I can assess how likely it is that the student will be admitted to graduate school. If I think the student needs help exploring values, feelings, options, and talents, I typically refer him or her to the campus counseling center because these tasks are not part of my role as an academic adviser.

Although closed questions can be helpful in interview situations, they have limited applicability in helping settings because they typically do not help clients explore. Helpers slip into an interviewer role and quickly become responsible for directing the interaction. They become interviewers rather than helpers. Once trapped in the interviewer role and having to think about the next question, helpers often have difficulty changing the course of the session and encouraging exploration. In these situations, clients can become dependent on helpers for the next question. Rather than exploring problems deeply, clients often respond passively and wait for the next question.

Given the theoretical premise of the model presented in this book that helpers are trying to facilitate clients in their self-healing efforts rather than acting as experts who diagnose and "treat" clients, I would assert that helpers do not typically need much specific information. Specific information does not help facilitate exploration of values, feelings, options, and talents. Before asking questions, I thus recommend that helpers think about what they are going to do with the information once it is provided. Helpers can ask themselves, "Whose need am I fulfilling with the information I gain from closed questions?" If the information will be used to facilitate the process of client exploration, helpers should go ahead and ask the question. If the information is desired for voyeurism, curiosity, to fill the silence, or to make a diagnosis and fix the problem, helpers should probably not ask the closed question during the exploration stage.

When helpers use closed questions, they follow the same guidelines for implementation as were proposed for open questions and probes. In other words, helpers should use an empathic and inviting manner to encourage the client to explore rather than just answer the simple question. Furthermore, helpers should refrain from asking multiple closed questions. As with too many open questions and probes asked at once, clients can feel bombarded and have a hard time knowing which questions to answer first. Helpers should also avoid closed questions (questions that have a specific desired answer, e.g., "yes," "no," or specific information) that limit exploration. More important, helpers need to notice what happens when they use closed questions. Helpers should determine for themselves whether control of the interaction shifts back to them when they use too many closed questions. Do closed questions make you feel like a grand inquisitor? Helpers can also ask clients for their reactions to determine the effects of the closed questions.

Most beginners use too many closed questions because this skill is a familiar way of interacting outside of the helping situation. In social interactions, people often ask a lot of closed questions to get the details of exactly what happened. The goal in these social interactions is to get the facts of the story rather than to help the person express and explore thoughts, as it is in the helping process.

Helpers sometimes use closed questions inappropriately to satisfy their curiosity. They might ask for information out of voyeurism rather than to help the clients explore. For example, Martha was working on her feelings of jealousy of and competitiveness with her older sister.

Martha came into the session and announced that her sister had a date with a "hot" movie star. The helper exclaimed, "Wow, how did she meet him?" or "What was he like?" Although extreme, this example illustrates how helpers can get carried away with asking for specific information to satisfy their own curiosity rather than to help clients explore. It also illustrates how the focus can easily shift away from the client to others.

A particularly egregious type of closed question occurs when the helper is condescending or tries to coerce the client into responding a particular way (e.g., "You really don't want to keep drinking, do you?"). Such questions take the focus away from the client and make the helper seem like an expert who knows how the client should behave.

I would not go so far as to say that helpers should never use closed questions, given that they can occasionally be helpful. I do, however, encourage beginning helpers to reduce the number of closed questions they use and instead use more open questions and probes and restatements. When helpers do need to use closed questions to gather specific necessary information (sometimes history is important for gaining awareness of context), they can follow up with the other exploration skills to help clients get back to exploration.

Finally, I should note that I have known some helpers who use closed questions that lead to productive client exploration. How can that be? When I have thought about such interventions, the helper is usually phrasing another intervention in the format of a closed question or is just incredibly empathic and conveying via nonverbal behaviors that the client should explore. I do not necessarily recommend this but say it to note that closed questions are not uniformly bad.

DISTINGUISHING BETWEEN OPEN AND CLOSED QUESTIONS

A major distinction is between open and closed questions. Closed questions ask for specific information and thus have a specific answer, whereas open questions ask the recipient to explore or say whatever comes to mind. In helping, we generally use open questions as much as possible because we are trying to facilitate client exploration. Closed questions are used more frequently in interviews (e.g., job interviews, medical consultations) where specific information is required.

To distinguish between closed and open questions, I suggest that you see whether the question can be made to be more open. If it can be made more open, it is probably a closed question. For example, the closed question "Did you get an *A?*" can be changed to "How do you feel about how you did on the test?" The latter question is more open. One important thing about open questions is that they allow the client

EXHIBIT 8.4

Examples of Transforming Closed into Open Questions/Probes

"Have you thought about calling a friend tonight?" → "What could you do tonight?"
"How many siblings do you have?"→ "Tell me about your family."
"Did you talk to your mother about it?" → "How did you feel after the event?"
"Do you want to talk about your reactions?" → "What were your reactions?"
"What time did you get up this morning?" → "How are you feeling about the amount of sleep you get?"
"Did you have a happy childhood?" → "Tell me about your childhood."

to explore what is important to them. For example, Mary was wondering where her client, Sam, was in the family birth order. She almost asked him this as a closed question but decided to practice making it open. She said, "Tell me more about your siblings," which led to Sam's exploring in detail the many conflicts and tensions in the family and how he felt everyone babied him because he was the youngest. Mary got far more information than she probably would have with a closed question. Exhibit 8.4 shows how closed questions can be transformed into open questions or probes.

Disclosures of Similarities

In disclosures of similarities, helpers reveal personal information about ways in which they are like the clients to help clients feel less alone or different (see Exhibit 8.5). Yalom (1995) described how universality is an important mechanism of change because it enables clients to feel that they are not the only ones who have been in similar situations. In later sections of this volume, I cover other types of disclosures (of feelings, insight, and strategies) that are more appropriate for helping.

THEORETICAL PERSPECTIVES ON THERAPIST DISCLOSURE

There has been a great deal of theoretical and empirical interest in therapist disclosure. Because this is the first chapter in which I discuss disclosures, I present here some of the theoretical perspectives on it.

Humanistic theorists (e.g., Bugental, 1965; Jourard, 1971; Robitschek & McCarthy, 1991; Rogers, 1957; Truax & Carkhuff, 1967) have long valued therapist disclosure. Because they value transparency,

EXHIBIT 8.5

Overview of Disclosure of Similarities

Definition	A *disclosure of similarities* refers to the helper's presentation of personal information about ways in which they are like the client to help the client feel less isolated or alone.
Examples	"I too have had nightmares." "I used to have social anxiety when I was younger." "I am a spiritual person."
Typical helper intentions	To focus, to support, to encourage catharsis, to relieve therapist's needs (see Web Form D)
Possible client reactions	Supported, understood, clear, negative thoughts or behaviors, stuck, lacking direction (see Web Form G)
Desired client behaviors	Recounting, cognitive–behavioral exploration (see Web Form H)
Helpful hints	Use disclosure infrequently. Disclose only for client needs, not for own needs. Disclose only about things that have been resolved. Disclose only about things that do not make you feel too vulnerable. Keep it short and simple. Turn the focus back to the client immediately after the disclosure.

realness, and genuineness in the therapeutic relationship, they think that helper disclosure can have a positive effect on treatment. Humanists believe that a personal and transparent style of intervention benefits both the process and the outcome of therapy because it allows clients to see helpers as real people who also have problems, as fellow travelers in the journey of life. In addition, humanists believe that when helpers disclose, there is more of a balance of control in the relationship, in that clients are not the only ones who are vulnerable. Humanists also contend that disclosure enhances rapport because clients feel more friendly toward and trusting of helpers who disclose. Interestingly, humanists think that disclosure can help to correct transference misconceptions as they occur because helpers are direct and honest with disclosures and, hence, challenge distortions as they arise. Additional benefits claimed by humanists for disclosures are that helpers are able to be more spontaneous and authentic and can model appropriate disclosure. Moreover, helpers' disclosures can facilitate client disclosure and repair ruptures in the therapeutic relationship. In effect, humanists believe that helpers' disclosures encourage an atmosphere of honesty and understanding between helpers and clients that fosters stronger and more effective therapeutic relationships.

Similarly, cognitive–behavioral theorists advocate for the use of helper disclosure. They believe that helper disclosure within sessions, when used with appropriate boundaries, can strengthen the therapeutic bond and facilitate client change (see Goldfried, Burckell, & Eubanks-Carter, 2003).

In contrast, traditional psychoanalytic theorists (e.g., Basescu, 1990; Greenson, 1967; Simon, 1988) view psychotherapy as focused on working through patients' projections and transferences. They believe helpers should be neutral or blank screens so that clients can project onto them their feelings and reactions toward significant others. For example, a client's childhood experiences might prompt the client to transfer onto the helper a fear that the helper is going to be punitive. An analytic helper might sit behind the client to enable the client to focus inwardly rather than watching the helper's face for cues about his or her reactions. If a helper is in fact being neutral, she or he can assist the client in seeing that the belief that the helper will be punitive is a projection. If helpers deviate from neutrality, it is difficult to distinguish client projections from realistic reactions to what the helper is actually doing. For example, if a helper is consistently late, it would be difficult to determine whether the client's anger was a distortion based on previous experiences or legitimate anger at the helper's tardiness. Readers should not confuse neutrality with a lack of empathy, however, because competent analytic helpers are appropriately warm and empathic. It is not too surprising, given this emphasis on neutrality, that psychoanalytic helpers typically do not disclose.

In fact, psychoanalysts propose an inverse relationship between the client's knowledge of the helper's personal life, thoughts, and feelings and the client's capacity to develop transference to the helper (Freud, 1912/1959). They believe that helper revelations contaminate the transference process and deleteriously demystify the therapy, thereby reducing the helper's status (Andersen & Anderson, 1985). In addition, Cornett (1991) suggested that helper disclosure might represent unresolved countertransference difficulties on the part of the helper, which would seriously compromise the client's ability to profit from treatment. Furthermore, psychoanalysts argue that helper disclosure can expose helper weaknesses and vulnerabilities, thereby undermining client trust in the helper and adversely influencing outcome (Curtis, 1981, 1982).

I should note, however, that some current psychoanalytic theorists advocate the use of disclosure (see Geller, 2003), especially related to the therapeutic relationship (see Chapter 14). In fact, many current psychoanalytic theorists would argue that there is no way not to disclose, in that even nondisclosure reveals a great deal about the therapist.

I agree more with the humanistic thinkers than with the traditional psychoanalytic thinkers about the value of helper disclosures. I have seen the power of disclosures in helping settings. But we should also heed the concerns the psychoanalytic thinkers have about disclosures and make sure that disclosures are used for the benefit of clients rather than for the needs of helpers.

In sum, helpers can disclose beneficially for clients if they do it for the appropriate intentions (not for their own needs) at the right moment. If helpers disclose in a manner in which they maintain an objective stance (i.e., are not overinvested), focus on the client, and observe client reactions, disclosures can be helpful. In fact, sometimes disclosures can be more helpful than other skills because helpers are not "putting something on" clients but are respectfully offering different possibilities to help clients gain insight.

HOW TO DISCLOSE ABOUT SIMILARITIES

A major caveat is for the helper to determine whether the disclosure is for her or his own needs or for the client's needs. It is also critical to keep the disclosure short and turn the focus back to the client. The tone of the disclosure should be "We're all human and imperfect" rather than "You think you have it bad, let me tell about my experience." It is also important for the helper to disclose only problems that are relatively resolved rather than ones that they are currently troubled by (see also Hill & Knox, 2002). For example, when the client expresses feeling like she is the only one who has ever had a difficult time adjusting to college, the helper might say, "I had a difficult time too when I first came to the university. Tell me more about your experience."

A specific situation that requires a bit more attention is how to respond when a client asks the helper for a disclosure. For example, a client might ask where the helper went for vacation or whether the helper is married or has children. A general rule would be to briefly provide information (if it feels comfortable) but also to then be curious about what motivates the client's desire for this personal information. Helpers might ask clients about their thoughts, fantasies, or concerns about them to learn more about what motivated clients to ask for information. In addition to providing the personal information, helpers can thus use the situation as an opportunity to investigate why clients want the information. Processing these issues in a gentle and supportive manner can provide the client with insight and strengthen the relationship.

A Comparison of Skills for Exploring Thoughts

Restatements help clients hear what they have been saying and enable them to clarify and expand. With restatements, clients often feel that helpers are listening to them and trying to understand them. In contrast, open questions and probes about thoughts directly ask the client to explore more, so they give guidance about what the helper wants the client to talk about at that given moment and therefore can be helpful when the client is not sure what to do or needs direction. Closed questions ask for specific information and are helpful if the helper plans on using the specific information in some way (e.g., developing a diagnosis, assigning homework), although such interventions rarely help clients explore. Disclosures of similarities can help clients feel that they are not the only ones who have ever faced difficulties and can be effective if the focus is quickly returned to the client. I recommend using mostly restatements, with occasional sprinkles of open questions and probes, closed questions, and disclosures of similarities. One guideline is to use restatements when the client is exploring thoroughly and you want to help her or him keep going, whereas it is perhaps better to use open questions and probes about thoughts when the client seems to need more direction.

What Do You Think?

- Debate the efficacy of restatements compared with responses that are more typically used in friendships, such as advice and disclosure.
- Compare and contrast restatements and open questions and probes about thoughts.
- In his early theorizing, Rogers (1942) promoted restatement at the most important skill, whereas later he focused more on other skills. What do you think about restatements?
- How do you respond when people use restatements or open questions and probes with you?
- What cultural considerations can you think of in using restatements or open questions and probes?
- Do you agree that helpers should not ask "why" questions in the exploration stage?
- Debate the merits of focusing on thoughts versus feelings.

RESEARCH SUMMARY

Self-Disclosures

Citation: Knox, S., Hess, S. A., Petersen, D. A., & Hill, C. E. (1997). A qualitative investigation of client perceptions of the effects of helpful therapist self-disclosure in long-term therapy. *Journal of Counseling Psychology, 44,* 274–283. doi:10.1037/0022-0167.44.3.274

Rationale: In the theoretical literature, the use of therapist self-disclosure is controversial, with psychoanalytic theorists cautioning against it and humanistic therapists advocating for it. Given that a previous study (Hill, Helms, Spiegel, & Tichenor, 1988) found that clients rated self-disclosure as the most helpful therapist intervention even though it was used infrequently, Knox et al. wondered how clients experienced therapist self-disclosures.

Method: Clients currently in long-term therapy were interviewed about their experiences of therapist self-disclosure (which was defined for the participants as "an interaction in which the therapist reveals personal information about him/herself, and/or reveals reactions and responses to the client as they arise in the session," p. 275), both generally and in a specific example of a helpful disclosure. Transcribed interviews were analyzed using a qualitative methodology.

Interesting Findings:
- Clients typically believed that their therapists disclosed to normalize their experiences or to reassure them.
- Helpful therapist disclosures were primarily of facts (recall in the current book that there are also disclosures of feelings, insight, and action). The disclosures were mostly of events in the past, about family, leisure activities, or similar experiences. None of the disclosures were about the immediate therapy relationship (which is called immediacy in this book).
- Disclosures typically resulted in positive consequences. More specifically, clients said that they gained insight or a new perspective; viewed their therapists as more real and human, which improved their relationship; felt better because they felt normalized and reassured; and could use therapists as models.
- Although not typical, clients occasionally had negative or neutral reactions to therapist disclosures (they felt wary of the therapist or feared the resulting closeness).

Conclusions:
- Disclosures in which a helper reveals ways in which she or he is similar to a client to reassure the client of being normal can be helpful if used cautiously and in the right context. Importantly, these disclosures were of past events that had been resolved.
- There can be some negative effects, particularly of clients becoming nervous about therapists crossing boundaries and wanting to be too close.

Implications for Therapy:
- Used infrequently and at the right time (e.g., when clients are talking deeply about personally distressing thoughts), disclosures can help reassure clients that they are normal, help clients gain greater insight, make the therapeutic relationship stronger, and serve as a model for clients about the benefits of disclosure.
- Helpers need to be careful about not disclosing for their own needs.

BONUS MATERIALS

Practice exercises, labs, and other resources for students and teachers are available on the companion website: http://pubs.apa.org/books/supp/hill4.

Skills for Exploring Feelings 9

It seems to me that clients who have moved significantly
in therapy live more intimately with their feelings of pain,
but also more vividly with their feelings of ecstasy; that
anger is more clearly felt, but so also is love; that fear is an
experience they know more deeply, but so is courage.
—*Carl Rogers*

Tyler, an aspiring actor, had been in an automobile
accident that left him with a disability and made it
unlikely he would ever be able to act again. Throughout the session, his helper used a number of reflections (e.g., "You feel angry because you can no longer
do what you love to do," "I wonder if you feel afraid
that people will laugh at you," "It sounds like you feel
anxious about going out in public") to help Tyler talk
about his many feelings so he could identify and accept
what was going on inside him. The helper also asked
some open questions (e.g., "How do you really feel
about that?") that helped Tyler stop and think about
what he was really feeling and then try to express his
feelings. Once he was able to express his feelings, Tyler
felt relieved.

I n this chapter, I identify four skills that can be used to help
clients explore feelings. Helpers can use reflections of feelings, disclosure of feelings, open questions and probes about
feelings, or focusing.

http://dx.doi.org/10.1037/14345-009
Helping Skills: Facilitating Exploration, Insight, and Action, Fourth Edition,
by C. E. Hill

Rationale for Exploring Feelings

As Rogers noted (see Chapter 6), emotions are a key part of our experience. They tell us how we are reacting to stimuli and what we need to do. Often we ignore, deny, distort, or repress feelings because we have been told they are unacceptable (e.g., being told "big boys don't cry"). Hence, we grow apart from our inner experiencing and cannot accept ourselves. We need to return to and allow ourselves to feel our emotions because only then can we decide what to do about them.

From an evolutionary perspective, emotions are important because they inform us about what actions to take, whether to fight or take flight. Thus, the emotions serve as an immediate trigger that informs one how to behave. From a biological perspective, verbalizing feelings is also important. Functional magnetic resonance imaging research by Lieberman et al. (2007) showed that verbalizing feelings is helpful. Putting feelings into words (affect labeling) helps to diminish negative emotional experiences by decreasing the response of the amygdala and increasing the activity in the right ventrolateral prefrontal cortex as mediated by the medial prefrontal cortex.

Summers and Barber (2010) provided a good justification for encouraging clients to experience their feelings at a deep level. They suggested that

> by experiencing old feelings and understanding their context, patients begin to work through the meanings (sometimes unconscious) attached to these events. Slowly, the old feelings and perceptions reenter consciousness, and once they are conscious, patients' natural problem-solving capacities can be engaged. This process unites insight or self-understanding and emotional re-experiencing. Some have characterized this aspect of therapy as habituation or desensitization to the painful feelings. . . . Becoming distant from (or habituated to) these feelings or thoughts is therapeutic, increasing the patient's sense of mastery, control, and autonomy. The patient is no longer afraid of them and can be more emotionally open and flexible. (p. 34)

Feelings are at least as important as content or thoughts in client communication. Clients seem to be most able to solve their problems when they get in touch with their feelings (see also Elliott, Watson, Goldman, & Greenberg, 2004). Experiencing feelings allows clients to evaluate events in terms of their inner experiencing.

Furthermore, clients' expression of emotions enables helpers to know and understand them. People respond differently to events, so helpers need to know how experiences are interpreted by individual clients. For example, when Varda came to a helper's office because her father died, the helper initially assumed that Varda felt sad, depressed, and lonely because that is how the helper felt when her father died. But in fact, Varda felt angry because she had been having intrusive memories of childhood sexual abuse since her father died. It was safe for Varda to remember the abuse only when her father was no longer able to hurt her. In addition, Varda felt relief that her father was dead because she no longer had to deal with him. This example illustrates the importance of listening carefully and not imposing assumptions on clients.

If clients experience, accept, and own their emotions, they can become open to new feelings and experiences. Feelings are not static but change once they are experienced. When a person experiences a feeling fully and completely, new feelings often emerge. For example, once Varda experienced her anger, she became aware of other feelings such as sadness, which then led eventually to feelings of acceptance and peace. The goal of helping is not to make the client feel "better" but rather to help the client experience emotions more deeply: to laugh when happy, cry when sad.

Clients do not have to act on the feelings, but they can make more informed decisions about what to do when feelings are out in the open. In fact, being aware of one's feelings makes one less likely to act on them unintentionally. In contrast, unaccepted feelings are likely to "leak" out, sometimes in destructive ways. For example, Robert unintentionally was rude and hostile to a friend who was accepted into a prestigious law school because Robert's own application had been rejected. Consciously, he was happy for his friend, but he had not worked through his own wounded feelings. All of us know people who do not directly say they are angry but indirectly communicate subtle, nasty messages that make it difficult to respond to them. Other people get stuck because they cannot accept their feelings. Similar to the obstruction that occurs when a river gets dammed up, these people get blocked if they do not allow themselves to have and express their feelings.

Feelings are rarely simple or straightforward; therefore, it is important to note that clients might have several conflicting feelings about a topic. For example, Diana might feel excited about taking a new job and pleased that she was selected over other candidates. However, she might also feel anxious about what is required of her, afraid of working too closely with the boss (who reminds her of her father), insecure about how others may view her, and worried about whether she can make enough money to pay the rent. It is important for helpers to encourage clients to experience and express as many feelings as possible without worrying about whether the feelings are rational, ambiguous, or contradictory.

Anger, sadness, fear, shame, pain, and hurt seem to be the most important emotions involved in therapeutic change (Greenberg, 2002). These negative emotions are often bottled up and not expressed or experienced because of shame and fear of disapproval. Many people cannot allow themselves to even think about such feelings. Hence, clients require a supportive environment to feel safe enough to express these feelings openly.

In addition, it is important to note that sometimes emotions exist in layers (Greenberg, 2002; Teyber, 2006). For example, after anger is expressed and experienced, sadness and shame often emerge. Inversely, after sadness is expressed and experienced, anger and guilt often emerge. Similarly, gestalt therapists believe every feeling has two sides. If clients talk only about fear, helpers might wonder about wishes; if clients talk only about love, helpers might wonder about hate. By fostering exploration of the feelings, helpers enable clients to admit the multitude of feelings they might not otherwise have been able to acknowledge.

Helpers need to remember that feelings are multifaceted and change over time. New feelings emerge as old feelings are experienced and expressed. Understanding and reflecting feelings at one point in time is just the beginning of entering into an experiential process; helpers need to constantly look for new feelings that emerge during the exploration process.

Cultural Considerations in Working With Feelings

Helpers should also be aware of cultural considerations in working with feelings, given that cultures differ in beliefs about how much emotion should be expressed. In the United States, people are generally encouraged to be open about their feelings and experiences. One only needs to turn on radio and television talk shows to see how people share their innermost feelings freely. People from non-American cultures, however, are often more reserved about admitting and expressing feelings, especially with nonfamily members (Pedersen, Draguns, Lonner, & Trimble, 2002).

There are also gender differences in the expression of emotion, in that men often have a harder time expressing feelings than women do. Men are not typically socialized to be sensitive to feelings and often feel threatened if asked to say what they are feeling (Cournoyer & Mahalik, 1995; Good et al., 1995; O'Neil, 1981). Helpers may need to proceed more slowly with clients who are not comfortable with emotions, remembering that emotions occur cross-culturally but that some people have a hard time expressing emotions.

Before working with feelings, it may be important to educate some clients about why you are focusing on feelings. My friend EunSun Joo in Korea pointed out that Korean clients need such information about the importance of feelings because they worry about losing respect if they express feelings.

Reflection of Feelings

A *reflection of feelings* is a statement that explicitly labels the client's feelings (see Exhibit 9.1). The feelings may have been stated by the client (in either the same or similar words), or the helper may infer the feelings from the client's nonverbal behavior or from the content of the client's message. The reflection may be phrased either tentatively (e.g., "I wonder if you're feeling angry?") or more directly (e.g., "It sounds to me like you're feeling angry"). The emphasis can be just on the feeling (e.g., "You feel upset") or on both the feeling and the reason for the

---

EXHIBIT 9.1

Overview of Reflection of Feelings

Definition	A *reflection of feelings* is a repeating or rephrasing of the client's statements, including an explicit identification of feelings. The client may have stated the feelings (in exactly the same or similar words), or the helper may infer feelings from the client's nonverbal behavior, the context, or the content of the client's message. The reflection may be phrased either tentatively or as a statement.
Examples	"You feel angry at your husband for not being home." "You seem pleased that you told your boss you didn't want to work late."
Typical helper intentions	To identify and intensify feelings, to encourage catharsis, to clarify, to instill hope, to encourage self-control (see Web Form D)
Possible client reactions	Feelings, negative thoughts or behaviors, clear, responsibility, unstuck, scared, worse, misunderstood (see Web Form G)
Desired client behaviors	Affective exploration (see Web Form H)
Helpful hints	Listen for the underlying feelings. Capture the most salient feeling to reflect to the client. Reflect only one feeling at a time. State the feeling tentatively, with empathy, and without judgment. Match the intensity of the feeling. Reflect what the client is feeling at present. Keep the reflection short and simple. Focus on the client's feelings rather than on the feelings of other people. Vary the format of reflections. Vary the feeling words you use.

feeling (e.g., "You feel upset because your teacher did not notice all the work you have done recently").

Helpers use reflections to help clients identify, clarify, and experience feelings. In addition to labeling feelings, helpers try to facilitate clients in experiencing the feelings in the immediate moment (i.e., an experience is more important than an explanation). For example, a couple might recount an incident in which they became angry with one another. The helper would encourage them to express their current feelings and talk to each other about how they are feeling about the incident now. Cathartic relief occurs when feelings begin to flow rather than being stuck or bottled up and when clients accept their feelings.

BENEFITS OF REFLECTIONS OF FEELINGS

Reflections of feelings are ideal interventions for enabling clients to enter into their internal experiences, especially if delivered with concern and empathy for clients' reluctance to experience painful feelings. Clients often have difficulty identifying and accepting feelings on their own, perhaps because they do not know how they feel, are ambivalent or negative about the feelings, or have been punished for having had such feelings in the past.

It can be difficult to articulate feelings because emotions are often sensations rather than fully understood awareness. People often do not have words to symbolize feelings, so working together with helpers to struggle to label feelings helps clients identify the feelings. In effect, clients do an internal search (Gendlin, 1996); in other words, clients focus inward and identify sensations and then try put words or labels on the sensations (e.g., "I feel a something in the pit of my stomach. I'm not sure what it is . . . I guess it's kind of worry . . . no, maybe it's more fear, kind of like I'm not sure what will happen. Everything seems up in the air . . . yes, I definitely feel apprehensive about the meeting.").

Hearing reflections enables clients to rethink and reexamine what they really feel. If a helper uses the term *disgusted*, this forces the client to think about whether *disgusted* fits his or her experience. This searching can lead to deeper exploration of the feelings in an attempt to clarify the feeling. It is often difficult for clients to verbalize their deepest, most private thoughts and feelings. In a safe and supportive relationship, they can begin to explore the feelings, which are often complex and contradictory. They can feel a combination of love, hatred, and guilt toward the same person in the same situation. Being allowed to admit these ambivalent feelings to another person without rejection can enable clients to accept feelings as their own.

Reflections also validate feelings. Laing and Esterson (1970) suggested that people stop feeling "crazy" when their subjective experience is validated. It is easy to feel that one is the only person who has ever felt a certain way, so hearing helpers calmly label feelings can help clients believe that such feelings are acceptable and that helpers accept clients as they are.

Reflections can also be used to model the expression of feelings, which could be useful for clients who are out of touch with their emotions. Many people experience an emotion but do not have a label for the feeling. For example, the intervention "I wonder if you feel frustrated with your sister" suggests that frustration is a feeling that a person might have in this situation. By labeling feelings, helpers also imply that they are not afraid of feelings, that feelings are familiar, and that clients are acceptable regardless of their feelings. By suggesting a feeling, especially if delivered tentatively and respectfully, reflections might circumvent clients' defenses or possible embarrassment about having the feelings. Helpers thus indicate through reflections that the feelings are normal and that they accept the person who has the feelings.

Coming up with reflections requires that the helper work at least as hard as the client is working and demonstrate that he or she is actively engaged in trying to understand the client. In delivering a reflection, the helper is forced to communicate his or her understanding of the client's feelings and check out the accuracy of his or her perceptions. The helper could say, "I understand exactly how you feel," but this statement does not demonstrate that understanding to the client. Reflections, in contrast, provide an opportunity for helpers to show their understanding. Beginning helpers quickly discover that accurately perceiving and communicating how another person feels is difficult. Although we can never truly understand another person, as helpers, we can struggle to get past our own perceptions and try to immerse ourselves in the client's experiences and empathize with the client. Finally, reflections can help to build the relationship because helpers are working hard to understand their clients. If clients feel the helpers' empathy and understanding and are able to talk with them openly and explore their feelings, the therapeutic relationship is likely to build.

Reflections of feelings are thus ideal interventions for encouraging client expression of feelings because helpers give examples of what clients might be experiencing. Clients can then begin to recognize and accept feelings as natural and normal. In addition, if helpers clearly articulate what they think clients are feeling, clients can provide helpers feedback about what helpers did or did not understand.

HOW REFLECTION OF FEELINGS RELATES TO EMPATHY

Some authors have equated reflection of feeling with empathy (e.g., Carkhuff, 1969; Egan, 1994). I disagree with this stance because it is too narrow to define *empathy* as just reflection of feeling (see also Duan

& Hill, 1996). I agree with Rogers (1957) that empathy is an attitude or way of being in tune with the experience of another person. If delivered appropriately, however, a reflection of feelings could be a manifestation of empathy. For example, if a helper says, "You must feel so devastated" in a compassionate tone, the client is likely to feel that the helper understands. A technically correct reflection of feelings, in contrast, could be unempathetic if delivered at the wrong time or in an inappropriate manner. For example, if a helper says, "you feel humiliated" in an all-knowing, firm voice, the client may feel put down or misunderstood. The client might feel that the helper understands her better than she understands herself, which could make her mistrust her own feelings.

There are also times when it is more empathic to use a helping skill other than a reflection. For example, a helper responding to a client who feels stuck in an abusive relationship might challenge the client's decision to stay in the abusive situation. This response might be empathic given the dangerous situation in the home and the helper's valuing of the client as a person deserving of a healthy relationship.

HOW TO REFLECT FEELINGS

Clients need to feel safe enough in the therapeutic relationship to risk delving into their feelings. They must feel that they will not be disparaged, embarrassed, or shamed but rather accepted, valued, and respected when they reveal themselves. Hence, reflections must be done gently and with empathy.

When learning to do reflections, a helpful format is to say:

- "You feel ____" or
- "You feel ____ because ____"

In other words, helpers can say just the feeling word to highlight the feeling (e.g., "Angry" or "You feel angry"). Or they can say both the feeling and the reason for the feeling (e.g., "You feel frustrated because you didn't get your way") to provide supporting data for why the client has the feeling.

Once helpers grasp how to do reflections, it is useful to vary the format so that clients do not become annoyed with repetitiveness. If the helper says, "It sounds like you're feeling . . . " 20 times in a row, it is not surprising that the client would notice, which would take away from the client's exploration. The following are some alternative formats:

- "I wonder if you're feeling ____"
- "Perhaps you're feeling ____"
- "You sound (or seem) ____"
- "Could you be feeling ____?"
- "From your nonverbals, I would guess you're feeling ____"

- "It sounds like you feel ____"
- "Perhaps you feel ____"
- "So you're feeling ____"
- "And that made you feel ____"
- "I hear you saying you feel ____"
- "My hunch is that you feel ____"
- "You're ____"
- "Upset" (or whatever feeling word is most appropriate)

Using a metaphor instead of a feeling word can also be helpful because metaphors often capture the imagination and express feelings in pictures in a way that engages other senses. For example, the helper might say, "It's like you're in a fog" or "It sounds like you felt like you were run over by a truck."

I suggest that helpers focus on one salient feeling in each reflection rather than try to reflect all of the feelings in a single statement. This focus enables clients to search inwardly about this one feeling and try it on for size, whereas reflecting multiple feelings could be overwhelming and distracting. Helpers can come back later and pick up on additional feelings for further exploration.

Not only is the specific feeling important, but helpers also need to try to match the intensity of the feeling to show greater empathy (Skovholt & Rivers, 2003). For example, the intensity of anger could range from a mild "irritated" to a stronger "mad" to an even stronger "enraged." Similarly, the intensity of happiness could range from "okay" to "happy" to "ecstatic." Helpers can also vary the intensity of a feeling word by using modifiers, such as "somewhat" or "very" (e.g., "somewhat upset" vs. "very upset").

It is also sometimes useful for helpers to state the feelings tentatively (e.g., "Perhaps you're feeling upset?") to encourage clarification. Stating feelings too definitely (e.g., "You obviously are angry at your mother") can preclude exploration because clients might feel that there is no reason to struggle to identify the inner feeling. Hence, it can sometimes be helpful to adopt a quizzical tone, such as "I wonder if you might be feeling ____?"

In addition, given that the goal of helpers is to allow clients to immerse themselves in their feelings so they can come to accept these feelings, helpers should focus on what the client is feeling in the present moment about the situation because these are the feelings that are very alive. By focusing on present feelings, helpers guide clients in experiencing their immediate feelings rather than in relating details about past feelings (e.g., "You sound irritated right now as you talk about your mother" rather than "It sounds like you were upset with your mother when that happened"). Remember that a person can have feelings in the present about something that happened in the past (e.g., "You still feel angry as you think about what he said"). Thus, the key is to stay with the feeling and be in the "now" with the client, helping the client navigate the ebb and flow of the feelings.

I also suggest that helpers allow clients time to absorb and think about the reflections that are presented rather than rushing quickly to the next feeling. If the client starts crying or getting upset, the helper can encourage him or her to experience and express these feelings rather than trying to "take away" the feelings or make the client feel better. Pause, go slowly, and do not interrupt when the client is experiencing feelings; at the same time, be there with the client and reflect her or his feelings.

Because the goal is to reflect feelings and keep the focus on the client, helpers need to be aware of staying in the background and facilitating exploration. Helpers can reach this goal by maintaining a supportive and listening stance. Clients should almost not notice good reflections because these interventions help them explore and focus inward on themselves rather than attending to what the helper is saying.

A great metaphor a student used is that it is not so much that the helper is using a metal detector to uncover the feelings; it is more that the helper and client are working together to construct the feelings. When things are going well, it is not clear who is following whom, but that the helper and client are working together to get at the feelings.

IDENTIFYING FEELING WORDS

Many beginning helpers have difficulty coming up with a variety of words to describe the emotions expressed in a given situation. Exhibit 9.2 is a checklist of emotion words developed from several sources (Greenberg, 2002; Hill, Siegelman, Gronsky, Sturniolo, & Fretz, 1981; student feedback; lists collected from various unknown sources). This list includes both positive and negative emotions, but the negative emotions outnumber positive emotions by about two to one, as is generally true with emotions (Izard, 1977). Feel free to highlight favorite words and also to add words to the list to personalize it. (The Emotion Words Checklist is available as a downloadable PDF on the companion website, at http://pubs.apa.org/books/supp/hill4.)

SOURCES OF REFLECTIONS

Clues about what a client is feeling can be found in four overlapping sources: (a) the client's portrayal of his or her feelings, (b) the client's verbal content, (c) the client's nonverbal behavior, and (d) the helper's projection of his or her own feelings onto the client. Helpers need to be aware that the last three sources only provide clues and may not necessarily accurately reflect a client's feelings.

EXHIBIT 9.2

Emotion Words Checklist

Calm–relaxed

at ease	at peace	calm	comforted	comfortable
complacent	composed	contented	easygoing	mellow
peaceful	quiet	relaxed	relieved	safe
satisfied	serene	soothed	tranquil	warm

Joyful–excited

amused	animated	blissful	captivated	cheerful
delighted	eager	elated	ecstatic	enchanted
energized	enthusiastic	euphoric	exhilarated	excited
fantastic	glad	gleeful	happy	high
hopeful	joyful	jubilant	lighthearted	loved
lucky	marvelous	optimistic	overjoyed	pleased
positive	superb	thrilled		

Vigorous–active

active	adventurous	alert	alive	ambitious
animated	bubbly	busy	daring	energetic
free	invigorated	lively	motivated	reckless
refreshed	renewed	revitalized	spirited	vibrant
vigorous	vivacious	wild		

Proud–competent

accomplished	admired	attractive	beautiful	bold
brave	capable	competent	confident	courageous
deserving	effective	efficient	empowered	fearless
forceful	gifted	handsome	heroic	important
independent	influential	intelligent	invincible	looked up to
lovely	mighty	pleased	powerful	prosperous
proud	purposeful	respected	responsible	satisfied
self-reliant	steady	strong	successful	sure
talented	triumphant	victorious	wise	worthy

Loved–loving

accepted	affectionate	attached to	cared for	desire for
devoted to	encouraged	fond of	included	love/loved
needed	protected	safe	secure	supported
trust/trusted	understood	wanted		

Concerned–caring

accepting	caring	charitable	comforting	compassionate
concerned	considerate	cooperative	empathic	forgiving
generous	gentle	giving	helpful	interested
kind	loving	nice	pity	protective of
receptive	responsive	responsible for	sensitive	sorry for
sympathetic	tender	understanding	unselfish	warm
worried about				

Luck–deserving

appreciative	deserving	entitled	fortunate	grateful
justified	lucky	thankful	warranted	

(continued)

EXHIBIT 9.2 (Continued)

Inspired

enlightened	enriched	impressed	inspired	transported uplifted

Completed–finished

completed	done	finished	fulfilled

Surprised–shocked

amazed	astonished	astounded	awestruck	flabbergasted
immobilized	numb	paralyzed	shocked	shaken speechless
	startled	stunned	surprised	taken aback

Anxious–afraid

afraid	agitated	alarmed	anxious	apprehensive at a loss
	defenseless	desperate	dread	edgy
fearful	fidgety	frantic	frightened	horrified hysterical
	ill at ease	impatient	insecure	jumpy jittery out of
control	overwhelmed	panicky	petrified nervous	on edge
	restless	scared	stressed	
tense	tentative	terrified	threatened	uncomfortable
	vulnerable	worried		uneasy

Bothered–upset

annoyed	bothered	burdened	distressed	disturbed perturbed
	troubled	rattled	restless	shaken shook
	uptight	unbalanced	worried	upset

Angry–hostile

aggravated	agitated	angry	bitter	defiant displeased
	dissatisfied	enraged	exasperated	frustrated furious
	hateful	heartless	hostile	incensed indignant
	infuriated	irate	irked	irritated mad miffed
	nasty	outraged	pissed off provoked	rebellious
	resentful	resistant	ruthless spiteful	unforgiving
	vehement	vengeful	vindictive violent	vicious

Contempt–disgust

better than	contemptuous	disgusted	indignant	look down nauseated
	repelled	repulsed by	revulsion	righteous scornful
	sickened	superior	turned off	

Sad–depressed

blue	distraught	down	defeated	dejected
demoralized	depressed	despondent	discouraged	down gloomy glum
	grief	heartsick	low melancholy	miserable
	morose	mournful	numb pessimistic	resigned sad
	somber	sorrowful tearful	unhappy	

EXHIBIT 9.2 *(Continued)*

Shame–guilt

apologetic	ashamed at	fault	bad	belittled
				blameworthy
	culpable	degraded	disgraced	embarrassed
exposed	foolish	guilty	humbled	humiliated
mortified	naughty	put down	mocked	regretful
remorseful	ridiculous	rotten	scorned	shamed
sorry	stupid			

Inadequate–weak–helpless

cowardly	deficient	feeble	fragile	helpless
hopeless	impaired	inadequate	incapable	incompetent
ineffective	inefficient	inept	inferior	insecure
insignificant	overwhelmed	pathetic	powerless	rejected
small	stupid	unable	unacceptable	unfit
unimportant	unqualified	unworthy	useless	vulnerable
weak	worthless			

Intimidated–controlled

bossed	bullied	controlled	dominated	intimidated
intruded on	obligated	overpowered	picked on	pressured
pushed around	put upon			

Lonely–unloved–excluded

abandoned	alienated	alone	apart	cut off
discounted	distant	empty	homesick	ignored
isolated	left out	lonely	lonesome	neglected
overlooked	rejected	uncared for	unimportant	unloved
unpopular	unwanted	unwelcome		

Hurt–cheated–criticized–blame

abused	accused	belittled	betrayed	blamed
cheated	criticized	crushed	degraded	deprived hurt
devastated	disappointed	disliked	forsaken	misunderstood
judged	injured	let down	mistreated	victimized
overlooked	pained	put down	rejected	
wounded				

Burdensome–tolerated–obligated

| burdensome | endured | indebted | in the way | obligated |
| put up with | tolerated | | | |

Manipulated–exploited

| abused | exploited | imposed upon | manipulated | managed |
| maneuvered | overworked | placated | pressured | used |

Tired–apathetic

apathetic	bored	disinterest	drained	exhausted
fatigued	indifferent	lukewarm	resigned	run down
sleepy	sluggish	tired	unconcerned	unimpressed
uninterested	unmoved	weary		

(continued)

EXHIBIT 9.2 (Continued)

Confused–bewildered

baffled	bewildered	conflicted	confused	disorganized
doubtful	flustered	hesitant	lost	mixed up
mystified	perplexed	puzzled	stuck	torn
uncertain	undecided	unsure		

Reluctant

cautious	guarded	hesitant	inhibited	reluctant
shy	timid	wary		

Compelled–determined

compelled	determined	driven	haunted	obsessed
obstinate	stubborn	tormented		

Jealous–mistrustful

envious	jealous	mistrustful	paranoid	suspicious

Client's Expression of Feeling

Sometimes clients are aware of their feelings and express them openly. For example, Amanda might say, "I was really upset with my teacher. I was so mad that she wouldn't even listen when I told her my feelings." The helper might use another word (e.g., "furious") to describe the feelings so that Amanda can experience feelings at a deeper level or explore other aspects of the feelings. Amanda has signaled her or his readiness to talk about feelings, so the helper can help her expand on the feeling and identify other feelings.

Client's Verbal Content

Another source of clues about feelings is verbal content. Although the client may not be mentioning feelings directly, it is sometimes possible to infer the feelings from the client's words. For example, clients often respond to a major loss with feelings of sadness, respond to success with feelings of pleasure, and respond to anger directed at them with fear or hostility. Hence, helpers can make preliminary hypotheses about what clients might be feeling based on their knowledge of how people typically respond in similar situations. For example, an adolescent client might mention that she received her report card and had improved her grades in almost every subject. The helper might tentatively say, "I wonder if you feel proud of yourself for raising your grades." Helpers need to be cautious and ready to revise their reflections, however, on the basis of feedback and added information from the client. Helpers cannot know everything about clients and will need to amend their reflections as they gather more information and as the feelings emerge and change in sessions.

Nonverbal Behaviors

How the client appears nonverbally is a third and major source of clues for feelings. For example, if the helper observes that the client is smiling and looks pleased, the helper might say, "You seem happy about that." Or if the client has a composed facial expression but is kicking his or her foot vigorously (see Chapter 7, this volume, noting that people have less control over arm and leg movements than they do over facial expressions), the helper might wonder out loud if the client is nervous or angry. The meaning of nonverbal behaviors is not always the same (see Chapter 7), however, so it is good to use nonverbal behaviors as clues to possible feelings rather than assuming that nonverbal behaviors have fixed meanings.

Another valuable clue is when the client uses an atypical nonverbal behavior. For example, if the client is usually open and has good eye contact but all of a sudden will not look at the helper and frowns, something relevant to the helping process could be going on inside the client (e.g., the client might feel misunderstood).

Projection of Helper's Feelings

A final source for detecting client feelings is ourselves: How would I feel if I were in that situation? For example, if a client is talking about an argument with a roommate over cleaning their apartment, helpers can recall how they have felt in similar arguments with roommates, siblings, or friends. Helpers are not judging how the client "should" feel but are attempting to understand the client's feelings by remembering and imagining themselves in a similar situation. Helpers can use these projections as long as they remember that the projections are possibilities rather than accurate representations of the client's reality. Indeed, the helper's feelings might not apply to the client. However, the helper can hypothesize about the client's feelings using her or his own projections and then search for supporting and nonsupporting evidence in the client's verbal content and nonverbal behaviors.

ACCURACY OF REFLECTION OF FEELINGS

The feeling word provided by the helper does not have to be perfectly accurate to be helpful, but it does need to be "in the ballpark." As long as the feeling word is relatively close to what the client is feeling, the client can clarify the feeling. For example, if a client has been talking about feeling scared and the helper uses the word *tense*, the client can clarify and say the feeling is more like *terror*. Clarifying the feeling gives the helper a clearer understanding of the client and allows the client to articulate or clarify what he or she is experiencing internally. One could even argue that reflections that are too accurate could halt client exploration because there would be no reason for the client to try to clarify or explore the feelings. However, feeling words that are "not in the ballpark" can be damaging. If a helper uses the word *happy* after the client has said *tense*, the client might feel that the helper is not listening or does not understand, and the client might give up on the helper and quit exploring.

Helpers are rarely accurate with every reflection because it is so difficult to understand another person. More often, helpers struggle each time to understand the changing emotional territory that the client inhabits and presents. Clients often appreciate the helper's struggle to understand as much as valuing the specific reflection. Understanding another person's feelings is something helpers strive for but remain humbly aware of how difficult it is to achieve. Hence, helpers should not be as concerned with assessing the accuracy of a particular reflection as with trying to understand clients and communicating to clients that they are working to understand.

An additional concern is that clients might accept the helper's reflection as accurate not because it necessarily is but because the helper is in a position of authority. Clients might feel their helpers know more about them than they actually do. Helpers thus need to observe whether clients comply too readily with what helpers say rather than experiencing their own feelings. As tempting as it might be, acting as an omniscient authority with regard to clients' feelings often leads to dependency, misunderstandings, or a difficult realization of the helper's limitations. On the other hand, clients might disagree with a reflection just because the helper is in a position of authority. They may feel a need to resist if the reflections are presented to adamantly.

WHEN TO USE REFLECTIONS OF FEELINGS

Reflecting feelings can have positive benefits by helping clients explore the affective component of the problems, experience relief from tension, come to accept their feelings, and feel proud that they had the courage to express and face their feelings. According to Greenberg (2002), a good time to focus on emotions is when

- there is a therapeutic bond between a helper and a client,
- the helper and client agree on the task of working on emotions (remember that the client may need to be provided with a rationale for why emotions are focused on),
- a client is avoiding feelings (e.g., the client obviously has a feeling but is interrupting it or is avoiding emotion by intellectualizing, deflecting, or distracting),

- a client behaves maladaptively because of a lack of awareness of feelings (e.g., becomes passive when abused, depressed when angry, overly inhibited from feeling happy or sad and so lacking vigor), or
- a client needs to reprocess traumatic experiences (although not usually immediately after the event).

WHEN NOT TO USE REFLECTIONS OF FEELINGS

Reflection of feelings can be problematic if clients reveal more feelings than they can tolerate at the time. If their defenses are overwhelmed, clients can deteriorate under prolonged emotional catharsis. They may not be ready for the feelings and may not feel supported enough to risk deep exploration. It is probably better not to focus on emotions in the following situations (Brammer & MacDonald, 1996; Greenberg, 2002):

- The therapeutic relationship is not strong (e.g., the client does not feel safe or does not trust the helper, the helper does not have enough information about the client);
- the client feels overwhelmed by emotions due to severe emotional disorder, delusional thinking, or extreme anger;
- the client is going through severe emotional crises, and discussing feelings would add more pressure than he or she could handle;
- the client has a history of aggression, falling apart, substance abuse, self-harm, not being able to regulate emotions, or lack of coping skills;
- the client shows strong resistance to expressing feelings;
- there is not enough time to work through the feelings; or
- the helper is not experienced in dealing with emotionally distraught clients.

During crises or when the client is feeling emotionally overwhelmed or distraught, it is often more appropriate to help clients regulate their emotions rather than pressing them to go deeper into feelings (Greenberg, 2002). Emotion regulation techniques such as relaxation training (e.g., suggest that the client take a deep breath) are discussed in Chapter 17 of this volume.

My intent in presenting these cautions is not to discourage helpers or make them fearful about dealing with client feelings but to increase helpers' awareness about potential hazards of reflecting feelings. In general, reflection of feelings is appropriate and beneficial but can occasionally lead to clients feeling overwhelmed by uncontrollable feelings, so helpers need to be aware and responsive to client reactions.

EXAMPLE OF REFLECTION OF FEELING

The following shows a helper using reflection of feelings (in italics) in a session:

Client: I had to miss classes last week because I got a call right before class that my father had been in a serious car accident. He was on the highway and a truck driver fell asleep at the wheel and swerved right into him, causing a six-car pileup. It was really awful.

Helper: *You sound very upset.*

Client: I am. All the way to the hospital, I kept worrying about whether he was OK. The worst thing is that he already had several bad things happen to him recently—his third wife left him, he lost money in the stock market, and his dog died.

Helper: *You're concerned because of all the bad things that have happened lately.*

Client: Yeah, he doesn't have much will to live, and I don't know what to do for him. I try to be there, but he doesn't really seem to care if I'm there or not.

Helper: *It hurts that he doesn't notice you.*

Client: Yeah, I have always tried to please my father. I always felt like I couldn't do enough to make him happy. I think he preferred my brother. My brother was a better athlete and liked to work in the shop with him. My father just never valued what I did. I don't know if he liked me very much.

Helper: *Wow, that's really painful. I wonder if you're angry too?*

Client: Yeah, I am. What's wrong with me that my father wouldn't like me? I think I'm a pretty nice guy. (Client continues to explore the situation.)

DIFFICULTIES HELPERS EXPERIENCE IN DELIVERING REFLECTION OF FEELINGS

Beginning helpers are often nervous about dealing with clients' expressions of intense negative feelings, such as sadness or anger. They get anxious when clients cry because they are uncomfortable with crying, uncertain about how to handle deep negative emotions, and unsure about how to respond to show understanding. Feelings of guilt might also emerge when clients cry, because helpers might think their interventions upset the clients or caused the pain. Furthermore, helpers might be afraid that if they encourage clients to express their feelings, the clients will get stuck in the feelings and not be able to emerge from them. Helpers might also have difficulty accepting intense negative feelings in themselves and thus have difficulty allowing clients to have such feelings. It is important to stress, however, that feelings are natural and clients need to express their feelings so that they can begin to accept them. When helpers accept clients' feelings, it conveys to the clients that their feelings are okay. I encourage helpers to learn to accept and cope with their anxieties so they can enable clients to express and accept their feelings. Many helpers find that taking a deep breath and focusing on the client and the client's feelings rather than focusing on themselves helps them encourage clients to express and accept their feelings (Williams, Judge, Hill, & Hoffman, 1997).

At the other extreme, helpers sometimes have difficulty working with feelings when clients are reluctant to experience their feelings. We always want to respect the client's right to not do something in helping, but at the same time, we need to remember that clients are sometimes reluctant because they are scared and need encouragement to go further. If clients go around the edges of their feelings and then retreat and then come back again, we can sometimes take this as an indication that they want to go further but are scared (always checking our own intentions and motivations to ensure we have the client's best interests in mind).

At times, beginning helpers have difficulty capturing the most salient feeling to reflect back to the client. They might hear several feelings and be confused about which to reflect first. Helpers should pay attention to the feeling that seems to elicit the most intensity or depth of feelings and the ones that they think the client can tolerate experiencing and exploring. They can always come back later and reflect other feelings when they become more salient. There is time in the exploration stage to cover many feelings in depth, so it is better to focus on each feeling individually and thoroughly. Practice helps tremendously. Helpers can practice by guessing the most salient emotions displayed in movies, reflecting strong feelings of friends when they are talking about problems, and role-playing in practice exercises.

Some helpers also have difficulty separating their own feelings from the client's feelings. They assume clients must have the same feelings they do. Other helpers overidentify with a client and feel the client's emotion so strongly (i.e., feel sympathy or emotional contagion) that they cannot be objective and helpful. Helpers need to become aware of their own feelings so that they can differentiate what is coming from clients and what is coming from them. As mentioned before, self-reflection, personal therapy, and supervision can help with this task.

Finally, helpers sometimes state the client's feelings too definitely (e.g., "You obviously feel angry") rather than tentatively (e.g., "I wonder if you feel angry"). If clients are passive and have difficulty disagreeing with their helpers, direct statements of feelings by helpers can be problematic because clients are not thinking for themselves or examining their experiences. A tentative statement about feelings can be more respectful and encourages clients to verify, dismiss, or modify the feeling words.

Disclosure of Feelings

Disclosure of feelings can be defined as the helper revealing a feeling that he or she had or has (see Exhibit 9.3). This disclosure can be real ("When I have been in that situation, I felt stressed"), hypothetical ("If I were in your situation, I would probably feel stressed"), or how the helper feels in the moment hearing the client talk (e.g., "Just hearing you talk about your situation makes me feel stressed"). For the rationale regarding the use of disclosures, refer back to the section on disclosures in Chapter 8.

Disclosures of feelings can be used to model for clients what they might be feeling, especially if the focus is returned to the client after the disclosure (e.g., "When I was applying for my first job, I felt terrified about what I would say in the interview. I wonder if that's how you feel?"). After hearing a disclosure of feelings, clients might recognize

EXHIBIT 9.3

Overview of Disclosure of Feelings

Definition	A *disclosure of feelings* is a statement about a feeling that the helper had in a similar situation as the client.
Examples	"When I was breaking up with my boyfriend, I felt sad."
	"If I were in your situation, I might feel angry."
Typical helper intentions	To identify and intensify feelings, to encourage catharsis, to clarify, to instill hope, to encourage self-control (see Web Form D)
Possible client reactions	Feelings, negative thoughts or behaviors, clear, responsibility, unstuck, scared, worse, misunderstood (see Web Form G)
Desired client behaviors	Affective exploration (see Web Form H)
Helpful hints	Listen for the underlying feelings.
	Choose feelings that you think the client is experiencing.
	Disclose only one feeling at a time.
	Disclose feelings that are not too "hot" at the moment for you (this is about the client, not about you).
	State the feeling tentatively, with empathy, without judgment
	Keep the disclosure short and simple
	Turn the focus back to the client immediately (e.g., I wonder if you feel that way?")

that they had similar feelings. In other words, disclosures of feelings can stimulate clients to recognize and express their feelings. In effect, the disclosure of feelings is similar in intention and consequences to reflection of feelings. Disclosure of feelings can be helpful for clients who are afraid to experience their feelings, especially feelings of shame and embarrassment.

An additional goal of disclosure of feelings is to help clients feel more normal because they learn that other people have similar feelings. Many of us think we are the only ones who ever feel lousy, inadequate, phony, or depressed. Hearing that others have felt the same way can be a tremendous relief. In fact, Yalom (1995) posited that universality (i.e., a sense that others feel the same way) is a curative agent in therapy.

HOW TO DISCLOSE FEELINGS

Disclosures of feelings can be a good way for helpers not to impose feelings on clients. Rather than saying "You feel _____," the helper says "I felt _____ in the past, and I wonder if you might feel that way?" Helpers are being respectful by owning that they are the ones who have the feelings. They acknowledge their projections and then ask how the client feels. Importantly, after the disclosure, the helper returns the focus to the client.

I do not recommend that helpers make up feelings just to be able to use disclosures of feelings. Such disclosures are not authentic and thus defeat the purpose of disclosures. Hypothetical disclosures, however, can be used because then it is clear that the helper is projecting feelings (e.g., "If I were you, I might feel worried").

Many of the same suggestions as were discussed under reflections of feelings apply to disclosures of feelings. For example, it is best to disclose only one feeling at a time and to match the intensity of the feeling. I would add that it is wise for helpers not to disclose anything that makes them feel too vulnerable. Furthermore, many of the same suggestions as were discussed under disclosures of thoughts apply to disclosures of feelings. For example, it is important to disclose for the client's rather than for the helper's needs, keep the disclosure short and turn the focus back to the client.

EXAMPLE OF DISCLOSURE OF FEELINGS

The following shows a helper using self-disclosure of feelings (in italics) in a session:

> Client: How did you learn to be a therapist?
> Helper: *I am just in the process of learning to be a helper. It will be many years and lots of training before I am qualified*

to consider myself a therapist. You seem to be curious about my credentials. I wonder what is going on for you?

Client: I just wonder if you're going to be able to help me.

Helper: I can understand that fear. *I was very nervous about going to see a therapist the first time too.*

Client: I am a bit nervous. This is the first time I've talked to anyone about my problems. I feel like I'm weak if I talk to anyone. My father always used to say that only crazy people go to therapists.

Helper: *That would make me angry.*

Client: It did make me angry. My father is hardly one to talk given his problems. I really want to have an opportunity to talk more about my feelings about my family—they are pretty messed up, and I guess I am too.

The helper might shift at this point to using other helping skills (e.g., reflections and restatements) to help the client explore more about her feelings about her family.

Open Questions and Probes About Feelings

If the helper wants clients to express feelings, the most reliably efficient skill is probably probe for feelings (see also Goates-Jones, Hill, Stahl, & Doschek, 2009; Hill & Gormally, 1977) because this skill specifically instructs the client about how to respond. With a probe for feeling, the helper asks something like, "I wonder how you're feeling about that?" Thus, the helper directly asks clients to talk about feelings (see Exhibit 9.4). I use the term *efficient* advisedly, however, because it is more difficult to show empathy with open questions and probes than it is with reflections or disclosures of feelings, so helpers need to be careful to maintain their caring and facilitative attitude when using questions and probes.

One way to think about coming up with open questions and probes for feelings is to formulate a reflection to get to the salient topic and then replace the feeling word with the open question/probe. For example, if the reflection would be, "You seem worried about what your mother might say," the helper might instead say, "How do you feel about what your mother might say?"

EXHIBIT 9.4

Overview of Open Questions and Probes About Feelings

Definition	*Open questions and probes about feelings* ask clients to clarify or explore feelings. Helpers do not request specific information and do not purposely limit the nature of the client response to a "yes," "no," or one- or two-word answer, even though clients may respond that way. Open questions and probes can be phrased as queries ("How do you feel about that?") or as probes ("Tell me how you feel about that"), as long as the intent is to help the client clarify or explore.
Examples	"What are you feeling right now?" "Tell me more about your feelings."
Typical helper intentions	To focus, to clarify, to encourage catharsis, to identify maladaptive feelings (see Web Form D)
Possible client reactions	To focus, to clarify, to encourage catharsis, to identify maladaptive feelings (see Web Form D)
Desired client behaviors	Recounting, affective exploration (see Web Form H)
Helpful hints	Convey empathy with your question.
	Make sure your questions are open instead of closed.
	Vary the format of the open question and probe.
	Avoid multiple questions.
	Avoid "why" questions.
	Focus on the client rather than on others.
	Focus on one part of the issue rather than trying to cover everything.
	Have an intention for every question.
	Observe the client's reactions to your questions.

The material presented in Chapter 8 for open questions and probes about thoughts also applies to open questions and probes about feelings. I would highlight the need to vary open questions and probes about feelings, so that helpers are not continually saying, "How do you feel about that?" Instead, helpers might say, "What was that like for you?" or "Tell me about that experience."

EXAMPLE OF OPEN QUESTIONS AND PROBES ABOUT FEELINGS

In the following example, open questions and probes about feelings (in italics) are intermingled with reflections of feelings and disclosures of feelings:

> *Client:* I think I want to go to the local community college when I graduate from high school because my parents don't have enough money to send me anywhere else.

Helper: *What are you feeling right now?*

Client: I feel a little disappointed because I had always assumed that I would go to a big university. I've gotten good grades, and it doesn't seem fair that I cannot go wherever I want.

Helper: You sound angry.

Client: I probably am. My parents told me I could go wherever I wanted, but then they got divorced last year and nothing has been the same.

Helper: I know that when my parents got divorced, I felt totally abandoned. *I wonder if you feel like that?*

Client: I do. They are both into their own stuff now. They are both dating other people and acting like silly teenagers. I feel older than them. But because they got divorced, we no longer have enough money for me to go to the university.

Helper: *What might you feel about that?*

Client: I feel betrayed. They always promised me I could go to the university. I was always the smartest kid, and they praised me a lot for that. But now, they don't even know I exist. It just feels like the bottom has fallen out. (Continues)

Focusing

Focusing is a specific method for helping clients experience feelings at a deeper level (Elliott, Watson, Goldman, & Greenberg, 2004; Gendlin, 1981, 1996; Wolfe, 2005). It provides a structure whereby the client turns inward, experiences his or her feelings, and then attempts to put the feelings into words. Focusing is similar to mindfulness or meditation in that the client sets aside expectations and waits receptively for feelings to emerge. The helper directs the client to go inward and be curious and encourages him or her to be open and tolerant of whatever emerges.

Before embarking on focusing, however, the helper and client must have a good, solid therapeutic relationship. Because it can be scary for clients to go into uncharted territory and allow themselves to experience feelings that they had previously been blocking, the client needs to trust the therapist.

A good time to use focusing is when the client expresses unclear feelings. Clients may be blocked by their feelings or have trouble allowing themselves to get into their feelings in depth. The client may have the vague sense that something is not right but not quite be able to identify the affect. The client may feel in a fog or have a foreboding sense of anxiety or discomfort.

To facilitate focusing, the helper listens carefully and empathically to all aspects of the client's communication, tracking the feelings as they shift and evolve. The helper also tracks the client's feelings about the experience and the therapist, particularly in terms of whether the client feels ready and able to continue with the focusing process. The helper gently and slowly guides the client through the process. The helper also tries privately to be aware of his or her own experiencing and uses that to further the client's experiencing.

The following steps can be used to facilitate focusing:

1. When the client has identified a vague feeling that the helper thinks would benefit from deeper exploration, the helper asks the client if she or he would like to try an exercise that might help him or her get more in touch with the feelings.

2. If the client agrees, the helper asks that client to close her or his eyes or concentrate on a point on the wall, focus on her or his breathing, and notice the sensations of how it feels to inhale and exhale.

3. The helper then directs the client to try breathing slowly from the diaphragm (e.g., "You can feel your stomach move in an out when you are breathing from your diaphragm") and continue to focus on the sensations of your breathing. The helper then asks the client to be open to whatever thoughts and feelings arise during this experience.

4. After a pause, the helper asks the client to look inside (e.g., "Ask yourself what's going on right now"). After another pause, the helper might say, "Don't rush, just see whatever comes to mind, just let it come." [During this step, the helper is not expecting the client to say anything out loud.]

5. After another pause, the helper might say, "Tell me what comes to you."

6. When the client presents a feeling, the helper asks the client to talk about the feeling in greater depth. The helper might ask the client to give a word or image that describes the feeling. The helper might then restate or reflect back what the client is saying. When the client thinks of a word or image, the helper asks the client to check out how the word or image fits. If it doesn't quite fit, the helper asks the client to keep exploring and check in with his or her body. If the client is stuck and the helper has a strong image in mind, the helper might offer the image and ask the client how it fits, always respecting whether it fits for the client.

7. Sometimes describing the feeling helps the client feel a new feeling (recall from earlier in the chapter that feelings change as we experience them). Getting unstuck from the old blocked feelings can bring a sense of relief, often signified by a deep sigh. But if the client does not experience a shift to a new feeling at this point, the helper can further query the client about the feeling (e.g., "When you think about that, how does it feel?" "What else might you be feeling?" "What is the worst part of the feeling?" "What would it feel like if this feeling were resolved?"). If memories come up, the helper can ask the client to talk more about the memories and the feelings they evoke. In effect, the helper keeps working with the client until the client feels some sense of relief or indicates that she or he would like to stop.

8. During this whole process, the helper also needs to focus on his or her own breathing. Notice the sensations of how it feels when you inhale and exhale. Now try breathing slowly from your diaphragm. Continue to focus on the sensations of your breathing. Try to be open to whatever thoughts and feelings arise during this experience. Focus on the area of your body where you experience the feeling.

9. Stay with the imagery and help the client experience her or his feelings.

10. After the exercise, the helper can ask the client to reflect on the experience.

A common difficulty for helpers during the focusing exercise involves sticking too closely to the specific instructions provided here and not attending to the client's experience. Given that some clients have trouble focusing on their bodies and may have strong reactions to the exercise, it is important to modify the exercise to fit their needs. Other difficulties involve being impatient and rushing the client, being self-critical when the shift does not happen, or being overwhelmed or distracted. The instructions are provided a general guideline and are meant to offer a structure but are not meant to be followed precisely. Helpers can shift from the exercise to asking about the client's feelings about the experience and modify it to fit the client's needs at the moment.

A Comparison of Skills for Exploring Feelings

My favorite skill is for exploring feelings is reflection of feelings because, when used appropriately, it conveys empathy, that the helper is listening to the client, and that the helper is struggling to understand the client. Reflections of feelings help clients immerse themselves in their feelings, come to accept these feelings, and then move to new feelings. With reflections, clients often feel that helpers are listening to them and understand them. Sometimes, it can be helpful to soften the reflection by using a disclosure of feelings, especially if the helper turns it back to the client (e.g., "Does that fit for you?").

Of course, using only reflections or disclosures of feelings could be boring and tedious for both the client and helper. There are times, for example, when clients would benefit more from an open question or a probe to help them talk about feelings. In this situation, an open question or a probe about feelings is a good way to encourage clients to talk about specific feelings. If clients have difficulty identifying their feelings, though, they might feel anxious and unsure when helpers ask, "How are you feeling about that?" Such questions can confuse or concern clients because they are not sure what helpers want to hear or how they "should" feel. Sometimes asking how they feel stimulates defenses and makes clients shut down. Clients can also feel annoyed that helpers are not really listening to what they are saying or trying to empathize with their feelings.

It can also be helpful to follow up reflections with open questions or probes about feelings. For example, the helper might say, "You sound sad," give the client a chance to respond, and then say, "Can you tell me more about the feeling of being sad?"

In addition, focusing can be useful when the client seems open to exploring feelings at a greater depth and seems especially tuned in to inner sensations. For some clients, exercises can be off-putting, so helpers need to be careful about introducing the exercise.

What Do You Think?

- Compare and contrast the effects of using reflections of feeling, disclosures of feelings, open questions or probes about feelings, and probes in terms of their ability to help clients explore.
- Compare and contrast focusing on feelings versus thoughts for exploration.
- How does your culture influence how you feel about experiencing and expressing your feelings and talking about other people's feelings?
- What are your thoughts about the importance of accuracy in reflections of feelings?
- Some therapists do not like to ever disclose anything. What would be their reasoning? Do you agree?

RESEARCH SUMMARY

Eliciting Feelings

Citation: Hill, C. E., & Gormally, J. (1977). Effects of reflection, restatement, probe, and nonverbal behaviors on client affect. *Journal of Counseling Psychology, 24,* 92–97. doi:10.1037/0022-0167.24.2.92

Rationale: Given that client expression of affect is typically viewed as desirable in psychotherapy, the authors wondered what therapist skills can help clients express affect. Furthermore, the authors wondered if therapist nonverbal behavior influences client affect.

Method: Volunteer clients who were interested in talking with a counselor were paired with a trained counselor, who first assured the client of confidentiality and then asked the client to discuss feelings about a problem. The study then followed a classic a–b–a–b experimental design in which there was a no-intervention phase to allow a baseline assessment (a), followed by the intervention (b), with a return to baseline (a), and then a return to the intervention (b), so that we could determine the effects of the intervention. During the 6-minute baseline, the counselor responded to the client with only minimal nonverbal and verbal stimuli ("Mm-hmm," "I see"). During the 9-minute intervention phase, the counselor was cued via a light behind the client to deliver either the nonverbal (head nods and smiles at appropriate times) or no-nonverbal (no head nods or smiles) condition; via another set of lights, the counselor was cued to deliver approximately one reflection (e.g., "You feel angry because your father doesn't support you anymore"), restatement ("Your father doesn't support you anymore"), or probe ("How do you feel about your father not supporting you anymore?") per minute. Volunteer clients were debriefed after sessions. Interviews were transcribed and divided into response units (grammatical sentences). Trained judges coded whether the client gave an affective self-referent (expressed a feeling, e.g., "I feel angry that my father doesn't support me") in each client statement.

Interesting Findings:
- Clients produced more affective self-referents during the probe condition than they did during the reflection or restatement conditions.
- Clients talked more during the intervention phases than during the baseline phases.

Conclusions:
- Probes elicited more client affect than did reflections or restatements, perhaps because they directly asked the client to talk about feelings.
- It was uncomfortable for volunteer clients to talk without any feedback from the counselor during the baseline period.
- It is important to recognize that the findings may not generalize to actual psychotherapy given that this study involved an experimental manipulation.

Implications for Therapy:
- Probes are a good way to get clients to talk about feelings. Of course, reflections and restatements may have other impacts not measured in this study.

| BONUS MATERIALS | Practice exercises, labs, and other resources for students and teachers are available on the companion website: http://pubs.apa.org/books/supp/hill4. |

Integrating the Skills of the Exploration Stage

10

It is a luxury to be understood.

—*Ralph Waldo Emerson*

Dmitry, a new helper, was in his first session with a client, Joe. He asked several closed questions, and Joe answered them briefly, then sat waiting for more questions. Dmitry panicked because he did not know what to do next. He felt himself sweating and wanted to run out of the room. Instead, he paused, took a deep breath, and thought about what he had learned about helping. His teacher's words echoed in his head: "Try to feel what the client is feeling." So he said, "I wonder if you're scared right now?" and was amazed when the client started talking about feeling depressed because he was doing poorly in his courses. Joe went on to talk about how his father was critical and shamed him when he did not meet his unrealistic standards. Dmitry quickly became so engaged in listening to Joe that he forgot his own anxiety.

To summarize the last few chapters, the goals of the exploration stage are to establish rapport and help clients explore thoughts and feelings. It is important foremost for helpers to be empathic and to accept clients unconditionally so that clients can then begin to accept themselves and return to a

http://dx.doi.org/10.1037/14345-010
Helping Skills: Facilitating Exploration, Insight, and Action, Fourth Edition, by C. E. Hill

self-healing process. In addition, helpers lay the foundation during the exploration stage to move to insight and action. By keeping an awareness of these goals in this stage, helpers can be more grounded in trying to facilitate the process. Otherwise, it is easy for helpers to get lost and let clients talk aimlessly or in circles.

This chapter covers issues that arise for helpers during the exploration stage. First, I review more completely the goals and skills of the exploration stage. I then talk about the difficulties that helpers typically face in the exploration stage and present several possible strategies for coping with the difficulties. Finally, I present an example of the exploration stage.

Choosing Goals to Facilitate Exploration

In trying to decide what to do during the exploration stage, the helper has to first ponder what his or her goals are for helping the client. In general, the helper wants to put the client at ease, help the client feel safe, create an atmosphere in which the client can talk, listen attentively to the client, and observe the client for clues about what he or she might be thinking or feeling but not willing or able to articulate. This set of goals is accomplished primarily through the nonverbal and minimal verbal attending, listening, and observation skills discussed in Chapter 7.

The helper also wants to help the client explore the content of the problem by telling the narratives about what is troubling him or her. For clients to be able to talk openly and figure out what they are trying to say and what they mean, it helps to have someone listening attentively and collaborating with them. The use of restatements, open questions and probes about thoughts, and disclosures of similarities can be helpful in pursuing this goal.

The experiencing of emotions is also important. The client needs to focus not only on the stories but also on the feelings attached to the stories, to experience and express what is going on internally. Experiencing the emotions within the context of an accepting relationship allows the client to accept the emotions and thus come to trust his or her inner experiencing. To facilitate this emotional experiencing, the helper often uses reflections of feelings, disclosures of feelings, open questions or probes about feelings, and focusing.

Of course, the goals of establishing a relationship, facilitating exploration of content, and intensifying feelings often overlap. So how do helpers decide which skills to use at any given moment in the session? There are no fixed rules, but I can share with you some ideas based on my clinical experience.

Choosing Skills to Match the Goals and Intentions

To help clients explore deeply, helpers typically rely mostly on reflection of feelings (e.g., "You feel tense because you're not sure how your daughter-in-law is reacting to you") to demonstrate that they are listening and struggling to understand the client's experience. Reflections are particularly helpful when clients need encouragement to keep talking, when clients need to experience their feelings (whether or not they are actively expressing the feelings), or when helpers want to show support or understanding. Reflection of feelings is also a useful way to identify possible feelings for clients who are out of touch with their feelings. In addition, helpers can disclose about their own feelings as a softer, more tentative way of proposing feelings that clients might have. Or helpers can use focusing to deepen feelings.

Most clients respond to reflections or disclosure of feelings by talking about their feelings. However, some clients do not, perhaps because reflections do not direct clients to talk about their feelings. For these clients, helpers can alternate reflecting feelings with asking open questions or probing about the feelings ("Tell me more about how you feel when your daughter-in-law drops the baby off"). In this way, helpers not only suggest possible feelings but also actively encourage clients to identify and express their own feelings.

If helpers want to help the client articulate and explain their narratives or stories, they might use restatements (e.g., "So you flunked your exam" or a repetition of the key word *exam*) to facilitate the discussion. When clients are confusing, rambling, or just need to talk, restatements can serve as mirrors that reflect back to clients what they are saying. Restatements help clients clarify and think more deeply about what they are saying. Similarly, helpers can use open questions and probes about thoughts to guide or focus the discussion and help the client examine different parts of the narrative (e.g., past, present, future thoughts; thoughts about self or other).

Throughout the session, a helper can use open questions and probes to maintain the session's flow (e.g., "How are you feeling about that?" "Tell me more about that"). If clients seem stuck or are repeating the same material over and over, helpers can use open questions and probes to ask about other aspects of problems the client has not addressed. Using a variety of open questions and probes helps clients explore the complexity of situations and think about things they might not have considered.

Helpers can follow clients' responses to open questions and probes with a reflection of feelings or restatement to show they understand what clients have said and to encourage them to say more. Open questions and probes request that clients respond in a particular way, whereas reflections of feelings are a gentler way of suggesting feelings without seeming as demanding. Restatements and reflections shift the responsibility for initiating dialogue back to clients and show that helpers are listening to clients. Alternating among open questions and probes, restatements, and reflections can keep helpers from getting stuck in an interviewer mode and can make the session seem less contrived and more engaging.

On rare occasions, helpers ask closed questions to gather specific, important information from clients (e.g., "Is your mother alive?" "When did you graduate from high school?"). Helpers need to remember to use closed questions to benefit clients rather than to satisfy their own curiosity. Before using closed questions, then, helpers need to be clear about what they are going to do with the information and whose needs are being met (the helpers' or the clients'). Generally, however, I recommend that helpers try to rephrase closed questions into open questions and probes, restatements, or reflections of feelings.

Implementing the Skills of the Exploration Stage

Helpers typically face a number of problems in trying to integrate the skills of the exploration stage. One problem that many beginning helpers have is not being able to facilitate exploration. Their clients go around in circles, repeating themselves over and over rather than going deeper into their problems. Generally, circling occurs when helpers use too many closed questions or use restatements or reflections that are focused on someone other than the client, are too general or vague, or do not ask about other aspects of problems. Because they worry about being too intrusive, beginning helpers often skim the surface of issues rather than helping clients explore deeply with the skills suggested in this book.

Another difficulty is that beginning helpers often focus too much on the skills and forget to attend and listen, or they might forget to be empathic and caring. It is not enough just to use the right skills; helpers must use them in an empathic manner to fit what clients need at the time. Even more than using the skills, helpers need to genuinely care, feel compassion for the client, and be present and engaged in the moment.

One way to tell whether interventions are working is to pay attention to clients' reactions to them. If the client is exploring and going deeper into problems, that's great, and you are obviously on the right track. However, if the client becomes very quiet, passive, or does not explore, the helper should assess what is not working. Perhaps the helper is not attending or listening, is asking too many closed questions, is focusing on someone other than the client, or is giving inaccurate restatements and reflections. The client might be bored, confused, or overwhelmed with negative feelings and retreat from further exploration. By assessing the problem, a helper can change what she or he is doing and try different skills. It is crucial that helpers pay close attention to client reactions to select appropriate interventions.

When the client is productively exploring, the helper fades into the background as much as possible. The client is obviously able to work and needs the helper just to be there supporting the work. Jung (1984) phrased this well in talking about dream interpretation: "The greatest wisdom [a dream analyst] can have is to disappear and let the dreamer think [the dream analyst] is doing nothing" (p. 458). Our job as helpers is to have clients so immersed in exploration that they do not notice our skills—the interventions should facilitate, rather than intrude on, the process. This might involve the helper giving head nods, being silent, and working to be empathic and to communicate empathy.

Finally, it is important not only to observe the client to see how she or he is reacting to the process but also to ask the client about their reactions (remember that clients often hide negative reactions; see Chapter 2, this volume). By checking in with the client frequently, the helper can modify the process to make it more suitable for the client.

The Process of the Exploration Stage

In this section, I describe several steps that helpers can use in their first session. These steps include getting started, facilitating exploration, dealing with difficult client situations, and developing one's own style.

GETTING STARTED

Before the session, it is ideal for the helper to take some time to "center," to get in touch with current feelings and take some time to relax (use deep breathing), put aside (bracket) other issues and concerns, and focus on being present in the moment with the client. At the beginning of the session, the helper can also take a deep breath and assume a helping posture that is comfortable yet professional. The helper then introduces himself or herself to the client, explains what will happen in the session, and describes confidentiality. Then the helper turns the floor over to the client by asking the client what him or her to the session today or what she or he would like to talk about today. The helper listens attentively and allows the client to do most of the talking.

The helper can never know or be prepared for everything that will occur in any given helping session. This lack of control is often hard for beginning helpers who are used to doing well and mastering situations. My best advice is to prepare by practicing the skills a lot, and in different situations, so that they become automatic, and then go into the helping situation without a specific agenda. In other words, the helper goes in prepared to attend and listen and focus on the client using whatever skills come naturally given all the practice she or he has done. In Chapter 19, I focus on intakes, which is a different version of an initial session.

FACILITATING EXPLORATION

If the client seems focused mostly on talking about ideas, stories, or narratives without much emotional content, the helper might start by listening carefully. When the client pauses (try not to interrupt and make sure that the client is done talking), the helper might use a mix of restatements and open questions and probes about thoughts to demonstrate understanding and to encourage further clarification and exploration. If the client has difficulty continuing, the helper might ask open questions and probes to encourage exploration of other aspects of the problem. After establishing some rapport, the helper might tentatively introduce reflections of feelings and open questions and probes about feelings to gently help the client think about feelings.

If the client is clearly in touch with feelings and able to experience and express them, the helper might start with reflections of feelings and open questions and probes about feelings to help the client go deeper into the feelings (remember to go with the cutting edge of the feelings). The helper will probably occasionally intersperse these feeling-oriented interventions with restatements and open questions and probes about feelings to help the client explore other aspects of the problem.

At the end of the session, helpers might summarize what the client has said to see whether the client has anything else to add and provide closure. For example, a helper might say,

> You've been talking a lot today about your feelings about your roommate. You seem concerned that the two of you are not as close as you have been in the past. You are not sure what you can do to fix the relationship. How does this summary fit for you?

Alternatively, helpers might ask clients to summarize (e.g., "Could you sum up what you learned so far?") to get a sense of how much clients have absorbed. Ideally, summaries are a joint effort, with helpers and clients trying together to explicate what has been learned. Sometimes, of course, summarizing is not necessary because clients naturally move directly to insight.

CONCEPTUALIZING THE CLIENT

In addition, the helper observes the client throughout the session and begins to formulate hypotheses about what is going on for the client. In other words, the helper begins to conceptualize how the client got to where she or he is (e.g., what contributed to his or her current state) and what the helper can do to get the client unstuck and functioning better. These observations and conceptualizations form the basis for interventions during the insight stage. Some questions that the helper can ask him or herself after each session:

- What is the client's problem?
- What is motivating the client to seek help now?
- How does the client think and feel about the problem?

In the previous editions of this volume, I talked about determining when the client had explored enough so that the helper could know when to move onto the insight stage. I now think that the idea of having explored enough was somewhat misguided. Clients continue exploring throughout all three stages of the helping process, so it is not quite right to talk about an adequate amount of exploration. I now think a more appropriate construct is to determine whether the client is ready for deeper exploration and insight. In other words, there are sometimes windows of opportunity in which clients are open enough to go deeper. Thus, rather than helping involving a linear process in which clients go through exploration, then insight, and then action, it is more typical that clients spend the majority of their time in exploration and occasionally are able to venture deeper into insight or action and then go back to exploration.

DEALING WITH DIFFICULT CLIENT SITUATIONS

I can hear trainees asking, "But what do I do when the client won't talk, or when the client is too talkative, or when the client is suicidal, or when I'm attracted to the client?" and so on. For now, I'll ask you to hold off on the questions and focus on developing your skills. Once you begin to master the skills, it is time to turn to focus on difficult client situations—these are covered in Chapter 19.

DEVELOPING YOUR OWN STYLE

There is no "right" way to implement this (or any other) stage in this helping model. Each helper has to modify the skills to fit his or her personal style, and then modify that style to fit the needs to individual clients (all of whom have different needs and reactions). I suggest that you try out the skills and see how they work for you. Practice a lot. Get feedback from clients and observers. Become a personal scientist—see what works and what does not work.

Cultural Considerations

There are a number of cultural considerations to consider when implementing the exploration stage. First, the humanistic theory behind the exploration stage is in tune with a Western philosophy that encourages open examination of thoughts and feelings and emphasizes self-healing and self-actualization. Other cultures, particularly Eastern cultures, value collectivism more than a strong emphasis on self (Pedersen, Draguns, Lonner, & Trimble, 2002; D. W. Sue & Sue, 1999). Clients from non-Western cultures may thus be less amenable to exploration than to action, so the exploration stage may need to be shorter than it would be with a Western client (note that many Western clients are also uncomfortable exploring feelings). Helpers must be mindful of not imposing their own values about open communication on people from other cultures. I caution, however, that some exploration is necessary to get a firm foundation of understanding before rushing to action. Furthermore, helpers must be careful not to stereotype clients from other cultures or assume all people from a given culture have similar values. Remember that there is more variation within a given culture than between cultures (D. R. Atkinson, Morten, & Sue, 1998; Pedersen, 1997).

Another important cultural consideration in the exploration stage relates to gender. Although in general women are more comfortable expressing feelings than men, given that men are typically socialized to hide feelings of sadness and fear, helpers should not assume that all women will enjoy exploration and all men will not.

A general guideline is that it is important to explore cultural differences when these seem salient to the client. The helper can mention cultural differences in the first session and ask about these (e.g., "I am aware that we are from different cultural backgrounds. I wonder how that is for you?"). The helper can also be attentive to client discomfort throughout the helping process and ask the client whether this discomfort is due to cultural differences (e.g., "I notice you seem uncomfortable when I probe for feelings. I wonder if opening up to a stranger is frowned on in your family or culture?"). In addition, it can also be helpful to ask about cultural values related to the helping process (e.g., "What is the reaction in your family and culture to people seeking help from counselors or helpers?"). Finally, helpers can ask clients to talk about their culture, so that they can learn more about the experience for each client uniquely (e.g., "Tell me about what it is like for you to be a Korean student who has just arrived in the United States").

Difficulties Implementing the Exploration Stage

Here are some difficulties that beginning helpers have talked about when they are first learning to implement the exploration stage. If you are aware of these obstacles ahead of time, you will be more likely to cope when difficulties inevitably arise.

It is important to remember that none of us are perfect, and even experienced therapists have difficulties, given that helping is a human endeavor. Indeed, my purpose in talking about these difficulties is so that novice helpers can become aware that these difficulties are normal.

INADEQUATE ATTENDING AND LISTENING

Several factors might interfere with helpers' ability to attend and listen adequately to their clients. Many helpers get distracted from listening because they are thinking about what to say next ("I wonder if I should bring up that she seems sad?") or are distracted about something unrelated to the session (e.g., "What's for dinner tonight?"). Helpers sometimes judge the merits of what clients are saying rather than listening and understanding them. One type of judgment that is hard to avoid is evaluating clients using one's own cultural standards. For example, a European American, middle-class, female helper might have difficulty listening to and understanding an upper class African American man or a very poor Asian woman. Sympathy can be another impediment to listening because helpers sometimes become so involved with and feel so badly for clients that they cannot maintain objectivity; they try to "rescue" clients instead of attending to feelings.

ASKING TOO MANY CLOSED QUESTIONS

Beginning helpers often ask too many closed questions because they feel they need to gather all the details of a problem. Many helpers think the helping process is similar to a medical model in which they should collect a lot of information to diagnose the problem and provide a solution for the client. However, in this stage the helper's task is to aid clients in coming to their own solutions, so there is little need to know all the details. Instead, such skills as facilitating exploration of thoughts and feelings are important for helping clients explore.

Some helpers ask too many questions simply because they do not have anything better to say. These helpers do not necessarily want to hear the answers to their questions; they just want to fill time or satisfy their curiosity. When asking questions, it is important to clarify for whom the question is being asked (i.e., to assist the client or to fulfill the helper's need).

TALKING TOO MUCH

Some helpers talk too much in helping sessions. They might talk because they are anxious, want to impress clients, or like to talk in general. However, if helpers are talking, clients cannot talk and, hence, cannot explore their concerns. Research has found that clients generally talk about 60% to 70% of the time (Hill, 1978; Hill, Carter, & O'Farrell, 1983). In contrast, in nonhelping situations, each person in an interaction ideally talks about 50% of the time; therefore, it can be difficult for beginning helpers to adjust to listening more than talking.

NOT ALLOWING SILENCE

One of the most daunting tasks for beginning helpers is to cope with silence. Trainees often rush to fill voids in sessions out of fear that clients are bored, anxious, critical, or stuck. Rushing to fill voids can result in superficial and unhelpful comments. Helpers should try to understand their fears about silence in sessions, asking themselves what concerns they have (e.g., not appearing competent, not helping the client). Once they figure out these concerns, they can work on these fears outside of sessions, rather than rushing to fill silences in sessions.

FEELING AN URGE TO DISCLOSE TOO MUCH

One of the biggest problems beginning helpers have is the urge to disclose too much. Because client issues are often similar to their own, beginning helpers want to share their experiences with their clients. It seems natural to disclose and tell one's stories, as one would with friends. Helpers also may want help for themselves and may be distracted by their own problems while listening to clients. It can be difficult to listen to someone else's issues when one is going through the same thing. For example, beginning helpers in their early 20s often have difficulty listening to students their own age talk about identity issues, relationship difficulties, problems with parents, and plans for the future because helpers have these same problems. Beginning helpers who are older might have difficulty listening to problems about parenting and aging. Adopting the professional identity of a helper who listens but does not disclose much is a major and challenging shift in perspective for beginning helpers. However, because inappropriate self-disclosure can be detrimental and can hinder the therapeutic relationship, helpers need to learn to restrain themselves and only disclose for the client's benefit.

GIVING TOO MUCH (OR PREMATURE) ADVICE

Beginning helpers often rush into giving advice. They feel pressured to provide answers, fix problems, rescue clients, or have perfect solutions. Many clients and beginning helpers are under the misguided notion that helpers have a responsibility to provide solutions to problems. Giving clients answers or solutions is often detrimental because clients have not come to the solutions on their own and therefore cannot own them. Furthermore, when given answers, clients do not learn how to solve future problems without depending on other people. Clients most often need a sounding board or someone to listen to them think through their problem or help them figure out how to solve their problems, rather than someone telling them what to do. It is critical to realize that the need to provide answers often originates in the helper's insecurity and desire to help, which are normal feelings at the start of learning helping skills.

It is important, however, to recognize that some clients *do* want answers from helpers and do not want to explore. It is sometimes appropriate to move relatively quickly to the action stage with such clients. Sometimes such clients will be more eager to explore after they have made specific changes in their lives; other clients, however, just want changes without deep exploration and understanding. Helpers can educate clients about the benefits of coming to their own solutions after a thorough exploration of their problems, feelings, and situation, but helpers need to be responsive to client's preferences and needs in terms of exploration versus action.

BEING "BUDDIES"

Sometimes beginning helpers err by acting like "buddies" with clients instead of being helpers. The role of helper necessitates providing a connected yet clearly defined relationship to maintain objectivity and offer maximum assistance. Being a buddy can be limiting because helpers might choose interventions to make clients like them rather than to help clients change. For example, Sam, a beginning helper, began every session by talking with his client, Tom, about recent sporting events. Tom responded enthusiastically to talking about sports but was reluctant to discuss more personal issues. Sam avoided changing the topic because he wanted to maintain a friendly connection with Tom. Unfortunately, because of his desire to be buddies, Sam was not able to help Tom explore his personal issues.

DISCOURAGING INTENSE EXPRESSION OF AFFECT

Beginning helpers sometimes feel awkward when clients express intense affect, such as despair, intense sadness, or strong anger (especially if the anger is directed toward the helper). Sometimes helpers are uncomfortable with negative feelings because they do not allow themselves to feel their own negative feelings. They may deny or defend against their internal "demons." For these helpers, hearing clients' negative feelings can be stressful. Sometimes helpers feel a need to make clients feel better immediately because they do not want their clients to suffer. They mistakenly think that if clients do not talk about their feelings, the feelings go away. They might be afraid to have clients get into the negative feelings because they feel inadequate to help. Guilty feelings might emerge for helpers if their interventions result in clients crying. These helpers err on the side of keeping things "light" or minimizing feelings so they do not have to face "tough" situations in which they feel helpless. Recently, an attractive adolescent client told her helper she felt totally fat and ugly. She expressed disgust with her body and astonishment that anyone would want to be around her. A helper who is uncomfortable with intense negative feelings might give the socially sanctioned response of reassuring this client that she is attractive and suggesting that her feelings are not accurate. Ironically, this response would negate the client's feelings and could make the client feel worse because she would feel angry and misunderstood.

Now might be a good time to ask yourself how you feel about overt expressions of affect. What do you instinctively want to do when someone begins to sob? Most of us feel an urge to get the person to stop crying and to feel better. How do you react when someone is acting hostile and angry toward you? Many of us get defensive or react with hostility. Helpers need to be aware of their tendencies to respond in these types of situations so they can practice other, more therapeutic ways, to respond. The exploration skills can be particularly valuable tools for helping clients stay with their intense emotions.

DISSOCIATING AND PANICKING

Sometimes novice helpers become so anxious about their performance that they feel like they are outside their bodies observing themselves, instead of being fully present and interactive in the helping session. At the worst, these helpers become completely frozen and cannot say anything. These experiences can frighten helpers, who then panic and tell themselves they can never be good helpers. In fact, anxiety is often more of a problem than lack of skills, but fortunately I have seen many students overcome their anxiety and become gifted helpers.

FEELING DISCOURAGED ABOUT YOUR ABILITY TO BE A HELPER

At about this point in the course, some students say they feel like they are getting worse at being able to be a helper rather than getting better. They are so focused on each skill and on watching everything they do that it is hard to perform at all. An analogy can be drawn to learning to ski. When you first learn to ski, you are conscious of every little thing you do. Like beginning skiers, beginning helpers focus on each thing they do in the helping encounter. In learning helping skills, helpers practice the individual skills (and often unlearn habits that were not facilitative to helping) and then put all the skills together. Although difficult initially, it often begins to feel easier when you put them all together. Students often feel better after practicing for a few more weeks, although some students come to realize that they do not want to be helpers.

Coping Strategies for Managing Difficulties

For most students, it is possible to overcome these difficulties! I offer several coping strategies in this section, primarily based on findings of research with beginning helpers (Williams, Judge, Hill, & Hoffman, 1997). I hope all helpers find some strategies they can use.

PRACTICE THE SKILLS

First and foremost, helpers can practice the helping skills taught in this book. Over and over, students in the past have said the practice is what helped them learn (see also Chui et al., 2013; Jackson et al., 2013; Spangler et al., 2013).

The skills can be compared to tools in a toolbox; helpers learn about the various tools available for different tasks. Some tools work better than others for some helpers and some clients. It is important that helpers have many tools (e.g., helping skills and methods for managing anxiety) in their toolbox.

Before sessions with clients, helpers can role-play using specific helping skills. Helpers can also role-play the mechanics of sessions, such as starting and stopping the session, responding to silence, and dealing with anger directed toward the helper. By using role-plays with supportive partners (e.g., classmates), helpers are more likely to learn the skills at a comfortable pace. The more helpers practice and pay attention to what they do well and how they can improve, the better and more comfortable they are likely to become in helping sessions.

DEEP BREATHING

One way helpers can manage anxiety during sessions is to breathe deeply from the diaphragm instead of taking short breaths from high in the chest. To determine whether you breathe from the diaphragm, put your hand over your stomach. When you breathe, you should feel your hand move in and out. Deep breathing serves several functions. First, it allows one to relax. When the diaphragm is relaxed, it is harder to be anxious physiologically. Second, taking a deep breath gives helpers a moment to think about what they want to say. Helpers can take time to focus their energy instead of being distracted by thinking about what to say in the next intervention. Third, deep breathing gives clients a chance to think and consider whether they have anything else to say.

FOCUS ON THE CLIENT

All too often, beginning helpers are so concerned with their own behavior that they cannot listen attentively to clients. By shifting focus to be more concerned with the client than with themselves, helpers can listen more attentively (Williams et al., 1997). The goal is to facilitate clients in exploring feelings, not for helpers to show off how much they understand clients. By focusing on the client and attempting to immerse oneself in the client's world, many helpers forget about their anxiety.

POSITIVE SELF-TALK

We all talk to ourselves as we do things. We sometimes say positive things like "I can do this" or negative things like "I think I am going to panic." Some people have called this the "inner game" because it occurs beneath the surface. Positive self-talk has a positive influence on performance in helping sessions, whereas negative self-talk has a negative influence on performance (see Nutt-Williams & Hill, 1996), so helpers need to be attentive to what they are saying to themselves. Helpers can practice using positive self-talk before sessions so they have positive sentences ready to use to coach themselves. Alternatively, helpers can write down positive self-statements (e.g., "I know the skills," "I am competent") on index cards and glance at them before or during practice sessions.

OBSERVING MODELS

Watching skilled helpers in helping sessions is an excellent way to observe skills being used appropriately. The skills come alive when one sees them demonstrated by experts. Although reading about theories and skills is important, imagining how they come across is hard unless models are available. Bandura (1969) showed the effectiveness of watching a model as one step in the learning process. I recommend watching many different helpers to illustrate that there are many ways and styles of helping (especially see this book's accompanying DVD, *Helping Skills in Practice: A Three-Stage Model* and the new one on dreams, *Dream Work in Practice,* both published by the American Psychological Association).

IMAGERY

Through sports psychology, we know that when athletes have the requisite skills, practice through imagery can be a beneficial addition to actual practice (Suinn, 1985). Helpers can imagine themselves using appropriate attending behaviors and helping skills in different situations. For example, a beginning helper who feels uncomfortable with silence might close her eyes and visualize herself in a session with a quiet client. She might imagine herself sitting comfortably with the client and allowing the silence to occur. She might also visualize breaking the silence after a period of time by asking how the client is feeling.

Example of the Exploration Stage

The following is a sample of an interchange in which the helper facilitates client exploration through an integration of the exploration skills. This example is not meant to be perfect but rather a realistic example of what might occur with a beginning helper. After each helper response, I label the skills used and give an explanation of what the helper was trying to accomplish. As you go through the example, cover the helper's responses and formulate your response first. You can then see how similar the helper's response is to yours and determine which is most effective and which you would be most comfortable trying.

Helper: Hi! My name is Sandra. We have 30 minutes today to explore whatever you would like to talk about. (The helper intends to set limits by providing information about what the client can expect from the session.)

Client: Okay.

Helper: So, where would you like to begin? (The helper uses an open question to focus.)

Client: I'm feeling anxious about a paper I have to write. I always end up waiting until the last minute to begin, and then I panic because I don't have enough time to write it. I know I do this, but I can't seem to stop myself.

Helper: You're really upset with yourself. (The helper gives a reflection to help the client experience feelings.)

Client: Yeah, I'm worried that I'm going to ruin my chances of getting into graduate school because I'm not doing as well in my courses as I should be.

Helper: You feel scared because your current behaviors might limit your future goals. (The helper gives another reflection because she wants to stay with the feelings and help the client explore further.)

Client: Exactly, I really think I could succeed in graduate school, and I know I need a graduate degree to do what will make me happy. I'm so worried that I'll stay in this rut and ruin everything I've worked for.

Helper: Tell me about the last time you had a paper to write. Take me through what went on inside your head. (The helper wants information about what goes on and wants to get the client to talk more concretely about the problem, so uses open questions and probes about thoughts.)

Client: Well, actually, I have a paper due Friday, and I haven't started it yet. I've gathered all the material I need, and I've taken notes on the books, but I haven't written anything. And I've been up late several nights already this week, so I'm short on sleep.

Helper: I can hear the panic in your voice. (The helper reflects nonverbal behavior to help the client recognize feelings.)

Client: Yeah, I'm scared that I won't be able to pull it off this time. Usually I can just pull an all-nighter and get

	it done, but it seems too big this time. The paper's supposed to be 20 pages.
Helper:	What are your plans for this evening? (The helper wants the client to get more specific about the situation to provide a clearer picture and again focuses by using an open question about action.)
Client:	Well, I just want to go home and sleep. I just don't want to do it.
Helper:	Is anything else going on in your life that makes it difficult for you to work on the paper right now? (The helper notes that the client seems stuck and thinks that perhaps the situation is more complicated than the client has expressed. Hence, the helper uses an open question to ask about other issues.)
Client:	It's funny you should ask about that. I just had a big fight with my boyfriend, and I feel very upset. He wants to get married and have kids right away, but I really want to go to graduate school. But if I go to graduate school, I will have to move away, at least for a while.
Helper:	So you feel conflicted between being with your boyfriend and going on to school. (The helper feels pleased that the client has opened up about other parts of the situation. Because the helper wants to get the client to talk about her feelings about this conflict, the helper uses a reflection that focuses on both parts of the problem.)
Client:	That's really true. It just feels like everything has to go his way. Just because he's already finished his school and is working, he wants me to be done too.
Helper:	I wonder if you're somewhat confused. (The helper's intent is to identify feelings through reflection, but the helper has inappropriately projected her confusion onto the client because she is in a similar situation.)
Client:	No, not really. As I think about it, I feel angry. I shouldn't have to give up my career for his. My mother did that, and she is very unhappy. She never even learned how to drive. She did everything for her kids, and now that we have all left home, she's depressed and lonesome. I think I want to have a career, but I don't know. I don't know if it's fair, and I don't want to risk losing my relationship with my boyfriend.

Helper: (in a softer voice) It sounds like you are really torn up inside. (The helper realizes that the last intervention was inaccurate and shifts focus back to the client's feelings by using a reflection.)

Client: (cries softly) Maybe I can't write the paper because I'm so confused about this fight with my boyfriend and what's going on with my mother.

Helper: (The helper is silent for 30 seconds to give the client a chance to experience her feelings of sadness.)

Client: (cries and then blows her nose)

Helper: (softly) I'm sure this is very difficult for you to talk about. (The helper wants to support the client and gives approval-reassurance.)

Client: Yeah, it sure is. What do you think I should do?

Helper: Well, I think you should go talk to your instructor and see if you can get out of writing the paper tomorrow. Then I think you need to talk to your boyfriend and try to work things out. Perhaps you should encourage your mom to get counseling. (The helper inappropriately gets caught up in the client's request for help and gives direct guidance about what client should do.)

Client: Oh. (silence) Well, I don't know. (The client stops exploring and becomes quiet.)

Helper: Sorry, I got carried away with too much advice. How do you feel about a career? (The helper realizes the client has stopped exploring and so apologizes briefly. She then tries to go back to the exploration by using an open question to return to the last major issue they were discussing before the client got stuck.)

Client: (Client continues to explore.)

What Do You Think?

- How would you have handled the situation as the helper in the extended example?
- How do you explain the client's being able to gain insight (i.e., "Maybe I can't write the paper because of my fight with my boyfriend and what's going on with my mother") in the example when the helper did not provide interpretations?
- Discuss whether you think helpers need to go on to the insight stage or whether the exploration stage is necessary and sufficient for clients' change.

▪ Is it possible for clients to explore too much?
▪ Check the obstacles you are likely to face in your development as a helper:

_____ inadequate attending and listening
_____ asking too many closed questions
_____ talking too much
_____ giving too much or premature advice
_____ being "buddies"
_____ not allowing silence
_____ inappropriately self-disclosing
_____ discouraging intense expression of affect
_____ dissociating and panicking
_____ feeling inadequate

▪ Identify strategies you might use to cope with obstacles as a helper:

_____ developing compassion
_____ be supportive and listen attentively
_____ practice the skills
_____ observing models
_____ imagery
_____ role-playing
_____ deep breathing
_____ focusing on the client
_____ positive self-talk

RESEARCH SUMMARY

Silence in Therapy

Citation: Hill, C. E., Thompson, B. J., & Ladany, N. (2003). Therapist use of silence in therapy: A survey. *Journal of Clinical Psychology, 59,* 513–524. doi:10.1002/jclp.10155

Rationale: Silence is a difficult skill for many beginning therapists, who may feel uncomfortable with knowing when and how to use it. The theoretical literature provides little guidance for beginning therapists, given the contradictory advice ranging from suggestions that silence can be used to communicate tender concern to warning that silence can convey cruel inhumanity. Likewise, the empirical literature suggests that silence has been associated with both positive outcomes (e.g., client perceptions of rapport, increased client involvement in the session) and negative outcomes (e.g., perceptions of therapist as unempathic, dropout). The current study is a follow-up to a qualitative study conducted by the same authors (Ladany, Hill, Thompson, & O'Brien, 2004) in which they found that 12 experienced, mostly psychodynamic therapists used silence in various ways: to convey empathy, facilitate reflection, and gain time for themselves to think about what they wanted to say. These therapists thought that a solid therapeutic relationship was a prerequisite to using silence. Hill et al. wanted to replicate Ladany et al.'s (2004) qualitative findings with a larger, more theoretically diverse sample.

Method: Eighty-one therapists from a range of theoretical orientations, most of whom were in full-time practice, completed a survey. The survey, which was developed based on the results of the Ladany et al. (2004) study, asked about a silence event (which could have ranged from several seconds to a few minutes in which neither the client nor the therapist was speaking) in a recent session with an adult client in individual therapy. They were asked to describe the event, indicate their reasons for using silence, report their thoughts and feelings during the silence, and judge the consequences of the silence on the therapy process and outcome.

Interesting Findings:
▪ Ninety-three percent of therapists reported a recent silence event, most of which had occurred within the previous 4 weeks, were used intentionally, were less than 1 minute, occurred in the middle of sessions and in the middle phase of long-term treatment, and did not involve an explanation of the rationale for using silence.
▪ Therapists most often used silence to facilitate reflection, encourage responsibility, facilitate experiencing of feelings, not interrupt the flow, and convey empathy and support. They rarely used silence to create productive anxiety, to avoid a power struggle, to put up a shield, or because of anxiety or distraction.
▪ During silence events, therapists reported that they were most often focusing on what was going on with the client, observing the client, thinking about the therapy, and conveying interest. They were rarely trying to minimize client reactions or daydreaming.
▪ Therapists estimated that they generally intentionally used silence with approximately a third of their clients, with 12% never using silence and 4% using it with all clients. Of those therapists who used silence, it was used on average once every other session, with each silence lasting under 1 minute.
▪ Therapists indicated that they were most likely to use silence when clients were actively in a problem-solving mode. They avoided using silence when they thought clients might misunderstand the silence, the client was psychotic or paranoid, there was a poor therapeutic alliance, the client was exhibiting danger to self or other, or the client had a history of using silence as a punishment.
▪ Therapists typically indicated that the silence event was helpful given that it enhanced the therapeutic relationship and the therapeutic work during the session.

Conclusions:
- Therapists are thoughtful and judicious about using silence.
- Therapists seemed to have a great awareness that silence can be misunderstood and thus needs to be used with caution.
- Therapists were internally active during silence. They were thinking about their clients and the therapy process.
- Therapists would not use silence if they thought clients could not handle it.

Implications for Therapy:
- Silence can be helpful in circumscribed situations but can also create misunderstanding if not used at the right time.
- Therapists may need to educate clients about why they use silence (e.g., to facilitate clients going deeper into their feelings).
- Therapists may need to check with clients about how they experienced the silence.
- Therapists need to think carefully about their intentions for using silence.

BONUS
MATERIALS

Practice exercises, labs, and other resources for students and teachers are available on the companion website: http://pubs.apa.org/books/supp/hill4.

INSIGHT STAGE

Overview of the Insight Stage

11

Daring as it is to investigate the unknown, even more so is it to question the known.

—*Kaspar*

Juan had been to a helper who taught him relaxation, assertiveness skills, and time management skills. He was more organized, relaxed, and better able to carry on a conversation, but he still felt empty inside. He could not understand why he felt life had no meaning. He went to a different helper, who helped him explore his feelings about himself and his childhood. Through the new helper's gentle challenges and interpretations, he came to understand that his anxiety and loneliness had origins in his mother's death and his father sending him to live with his grandparents when he was 2 years old. Although his grandparents were very loving, he had always felt that he was imposing on them. He realized that in social situations, he distanced himself so that others would not have the chance to reject him and he could not be hurt. He lived his life as a defense against being abandoned again. In sessions, he worried that he was boring and that his helper would rather be elsewhere. Through talking about their relationship, Juan came to understand that his feelings were a transference onto the helper of his feelings about his parents abandoning him. Once he understood more about himself and could accept that the helper

http://dx.doi.org/10.1037/14345-011
Helping Skills: Facilitating Exploration, Insight, and Action, Fourth Edition, by C. E. Hill

indeed cared about him, Juan began to feel more secure and. He also was able to see that his grandparents loved him and had chosen to raise him. Juan felt better because he now had some explanations for his feelings and behaviors.

During the exploration stage, helpers work to establish a therapeutic relationship with clients, help clients talk about their problems and tell their narratives, and help them experience feelings related to their problems. For some clients, this supportive, nonjudgmental listening is all that is needed to help them get unblocked and able to think about how they want to be and what they want to do about their problems. Their actualization potential is released, and they become creative and active self-healers and problem solvers. They no longer "need" outside intervention, although they might enjoy sharing their thoughts and feelings with a good helper and benefit from a deeper examination of their concerns to help them grow and develop.

Unfortunately, not all clients can progress on their own after exploring their thoughts and feelings. Some clients get stuck and need someone to help them get past obstacles and defenses that protect them against internal pain and external harm. When painful events occur, these clients often compartmentalize experiences in their minds so that they do not have to think about them, making it difficult to integrate these experiences into their lives. Other clients have a hard time understanding the origins and consequences of their feelings and behaviors. Some clients have done things a certain way for so long that they never question their actions or think about the reasons for what they do. Some clients have been so damaged by their parents that they cannot see the world as a safe place. Other clients are eager to learn more about themselves and their motivations but need an outside perspective to help them move beyond their blind spots. For these situations, it is important for helpers to use insight skills.

Of course, not all clients want or need insight. Some will just need exploration, others will just need action. Likewise, some helpers will not feel comfortable using insight skills because they do not fit their personal style. However, it is good for helpers to be aware of the insight skills and practice them so that they can use them if needed.

The insight stage builds on the foundation of the exploration stage. Going beyond exploration to insight and understanding requires a deep sense of empathy and belief in clients. In this stage, helpers see beyond defenses and inappropriate behaviors and help clients come to accept and understand themselves more deeply.

The helper's role in the insight stage involves coaching the client to gain insight rather than the helper being the one who provides the insight. Often, clients are capable of coming up with their own insights when helpers provide the appropriate atmosphere and ask thoughtful questions. In fact, clients often feel better about insights they have attained on their own rather than interpretations that are foisted on them. Some clients, however, want more input from helpers, and such input can be helpful if offered in a collaborative, tentative, empathic manner.

What Is Insight?

When clients gain insight, they see things from a new perspective, are able to make connections between things, or have an understanding of why things happen as they do (Castonguay & Hill, 2007; Elliott et al., 1994). For a few clients, gaining insight is like a light bulb going on, a sudden feeling of "aha!" For example, after talking about it, Yinyin might suddenly realize her strong reactions to her boyfriend not wanting to go to a party stem from her rarely having gotten her way as a child. Her anger may be due to perceived past injustices and a belief that her boyfriend is doing the same thing to her that her parents did. For most clients, however, insight does not occur suddenly. Rogers (1942) noted that "insight comes gradually, bit by bit, as the individual develops sufficient psychological strength to endure new perspectives" (p. 177). For example, Robert might slowly, and only after several challenges and interpretations, come to realize that his indecision over his career choice might be due to conflicts with his wife. Hill, Knox, et al. (2007) talked about this range of insights as gold nuggets versus gold dust—sometimes clients are lucky and hit a gold nugget of insight, but more often there is a smattering of gold dust as they work hard to gain insight over time.

INTELLECTUAL VERSUS EMOTIONAL INSIGHT

Insight typically must be emotional as well as intellectual to lead to action (Reid & Finesinger, 1952; Singer, 1970). In other words, the insight must be deeply felt as well as cognitively understood. Intellectual insight provides an objective explanation for a problem (e.g., "I am anxious because of my Oedipal conflict"), but it has a barren, sterile quality that keeps clients stuck in understandings that lead nowhere (Gelso & Fretz, 2001). Many of us know people who can give a comprehensive history of their psychological problems and the sources of their difficulties but who cannot express their feelings fully. Emotional insight, in contrast, connects affect to intellect and creates a sense of personal involvement and responsibility (Gelso & Fretz, 2001). For example, when Nioud realizes that his conflict with his wife over having her own interests is really due to the hurt he felt because his father did not spend much time with him, he must also feel that hurt deep inside himself. This emotional and intellectual insight might help Nioud decide that it is okay for his wife to have some interests apart from him. Nioud might start thinking that he needs to develop his own interests and might begin to question why he allows his whole identity to be based on his wife. The deep insight Nioud achieves would not have been possible if he had been given an interpretation that sounded right "on paper" but was not something he could acknowledge as his own or feel at a deep level.

A client who understands only intellectually that she screams at her boyfriend because she is angry with her father is not likely to achieve the same kind of growth and change that emotional insight engenders. If this client were to experience the feelings associated with this intellectual understanding (e.g., how badly she feels about transferring negative feelings toward her mostly innocent boyfriend, and how deeply frustrated she is that her father continues to have a negative influence on her life), she might develop the motivation to change her behavior toward her boyfriend (which then might help her gain more insight about the problem). Emotional insight is typically easier for clients to attain when they are fully and actively involved in the helping process. They need to be personally involved and eager to experience their emotions and to try to understand themselves.

WHY IS INSIGHT NECESSARY?'

According to Frank and Frank (1991), the need to make sense of events is as fundamental to human beings as the need for food or water. Similarly, Wampold (2001) suggested that people need an explanation, sometimes any explanation, to make sense out of their lives. We need to understand why things happen around us to make sense of our world and to predict what will happen next.

Frank and Frank suggested that people evaluate internal and external stimuli in view of their assumptions about what is dangerous, safe, important, good, bad, and so on. These assumptions become organized into sets of highly structured, complex, and interacting values, expectations, and images of self that are closely related to emotional states and feelings. These psychological structures shape, and in turn are shaped by, a person's perceptions and behaviors. Frank and Frank thus viewed insight as a reworking of the past that leads to the discovery of new facts, as well as a recognition of new relationships between previously known facts and a reevaluation of their significance.

Similarly, Freud (1923/1963) believed that psychological problems are developmental and that resolution can only be reached by obtaining insight into the problems. He noted that symptoms generally make sense in the context of past and present life experiences. For example, Jenna's fear of public speaking made sense in the light of her reluctance to achieve and possibly outdo her passive and depressed mother. Her insight that she had been limiting herself to placate her mother led her to understand why she had made the choices she did throughout her life. This understanding gave her a sense that she could make different choices in the future.

Frankl (1959) emphasized the importance of having a life philosophy to transcend suffering and find meaning in existence. He argued that our greatest human need is to find a core of meaning and a purpose in life. Frankl's experience in a German concentration camp bears out his theory: Although he could not change his life situation, he was able to change the meaning he attached to this experience. By drawing on the strengths of his Jewish tradition, he was able to survive and help others survive.

Clients' interpretations of events determine subsequent behaviors and feelings, as well as their willingness to work on certain topics in a helping setting. For example, John, an 18-year-old client, is reluctant to learn to drive. If he believes his reluctance to drive is due to fears about having a major accident given that a friend was recently killed in an accident, John might say that fear is the main problem. If, however, John believes the fear is due to a reluctance to grow up and become independent and leave his depressed mother, he might feel more of a need to work on separation issues. Helpers need to learn how clients currently construe events (both consciously and unconsciously) so they can help them develop more adaptive constructs.

For many clients, it is ideal to attain insight before moving on to action. If clients did whatever helpers told them to do, with no understanding of or explanation for why these actions were important or fit into their worldview and values, they would not have a framework to guide their behavior when new problems develop. Clients would be dependent on others to tell them what to do as each new problem arose. In contrast, if clients learn how to think about their problems, they are more likely in the future to explore their problems, achieve understanding, and decide what they would like to do differently on their own. In effect, helpers are teaching clients a problem-solving approach. In the example of the reluctant driver, if John comes to understand that his reluctance is due to anxiety and guilt about leaving his sick mother, he can make an informed decision that fits his values about what he wants to do about his mother. Hence, insight is especially important in the helping process.

Theoretical Background: Psychoanalytic Theory

Psychoanalytic theory began with Sigmund Freud and has evolved through many subsequent theorists (notably Adler, Jung, and Sullivan). Over the time that psychoanalytic theory has existed, many changes have been made in the theory (Mitchell, 1993), with current emphasis given to the importance of the relationship between the therapist and client (e.g., Safran & Muran, 2000; Strupp & Binder, 1984; Wachtel, 2008).

I have often found that students are quite disdainful of Freud when they first take helping skills classes. Many have heard in introductory psychology classes that Freud is outdated and irrelevant. Yet as students progress through training, and particularly as they become master therapists, they often have increasing awareness of the richness and relevance of psychodynamic theory as a way of thinking about the complexity of human nature—people really are incredibly complicated and full of contradictions. So I encourage you to have an open mind about psychoanalytic theory and learn to think deeply about human dynamics.

Psychoanalysis presents a complex, rich description of the development of personality and treatment. In this section, the focus is on a few important aspects of psychoanalytic theory that are currently salient and applicable to the helping skills model. I encourage interested readers to explore other sources to learn more about other psychoanalytic theories (e.g., Basch, 1980; Gelso & Hayes, 1998; Greenson, 1967; Mahler, 1968; Maroda, 2010; McWilliams, 2004; Mitchell, 1993; Summers & Barber, 2010).

PSYCHODYNAMIC THEORY OF PERSONALITY

Freud (1940/1949) suggested that all children progress through stages of development. In the first stage, energy is focused on oral (eating) satisfaction, first with sucking and then with biting. As the child has to learn to control urination and defecation, energy shifts to the anal region, both with retaining and expelling. Then Freud suggested that a latent period occurs, in which the child is more free for other pursuits. As the child develops further, energy shifts to the genital region and children become attracted to parents of the opposite sex. The resolution of this conflict (the Oedipal conflict for boys, the Electra complex for girls) leads children to give up their fixation on the opposite-sex parent and instead identify and ally with the parent of the same sex and take on the morals and values of society. As children go through each stage, they can become stuck if they are either deprived (e.g., given too little to eat) or overindulged (e.g., given too much to eat). When people have difficulty, they tend to regress back to a stage in which they felt gratified (e.g., regress to overeating).

Looking back over 100 years from a different culture, it is clear that Freud's developmental sequence was heavily culturally bound and is not completely relevant for the present day. But rather than dismissing it out of hand, it is useful to recognize that psychological developmental sequences are important. Indeed, many theorists since Freud have built on these theories and offered different stage models (e.g., Erikson, Kohlberg, Mahler). So rather than focus on specifically whether there is an oral and anal stage, the message to take away is that we develop through different stages in our lives and that interactions with others during those stages has a huge impact. Another important notion here is that we can be either overindulged or underindulged at each of several developmental stages and that these early experiences influence us in later life.

Furthermore, Freud postulated that at birth, infants are totally governed by the *id*, or primitive urges that seek immediate gratification. As the child develops, the *ego* forms to help the child delay gratification and negotiate with the outside world. As the child develops further and internalizes society's morals and values through resolution of the Oedipal or Electra conflict, she or he develops a *superego* (which involves both morals and ideals). Throughout life, people struggle with conflicts among primitive impulses, the moderating ego, and societal restrictions and ideals. For example, Maria continually struggled with her weight. On the one hand, she wanted to eat whatever and whenever she wanted (influence of the id), but on the other hand, she relentlessly scolded herself for her lack of control (harsh superego) and compromised by allowing herself a small dessert every night if she had exercised during the day (the ego at work). It is important to remember that the id, ego, and superego are metaphors rather than actual physiological structures that can be found in the brain or body. Using these metaphors helps us tell a story of how and why people struggle to cope with life.

A related Freudian concept is consciousness. Freud divided awareness into the unconscious, preconscious, and conscious. He postulated that the largest percentage of mental activity is unconscious, or not available to immediate awareness. Some energy is in the preconscious, where a person can access some thoughts and experiences by attending to them. And a small amount of energy is readily available to conscious awareness. Freud proposed that most people act out of unconscious motivations and are unaware why they act the way they do. To illustrate the power of the unconscious, think about a recent time you did something that seemed out of character for you (e.g., became suddenly angry, acted differently from your values)—these feelings and behaviors may have been motivated by unconscious feelings.

Yet another important Freudian construct relates to *defenses*. Not everything goes smoothly in the development of personality. Because children do not receive everything they need to develop psychologically, they cope by developing defense mechanisms (see Exhibit 11.1 for a list of defenses). Freud (1933) and more recent psychoanalysts have theorized that defense mechanisms are unconscious methods for dealing with anxiety through denial or distortion of reality. Everyone has defense mechanisms because we all have to cope with the anxiety inherent in living. Defense mechanisms can be healthy if used appropriately and in moderation, but repeated and frequent use of defense mechanisms is problematic.

EXHIBIT 11.1

Defenses

Defense	Definition
Repression	Not allowing painful material into one's conscious thought
Intellectualization	Avoiding painful feelings by focusing on ideas
Denial	Actively rejecting painful affect
Regression	Engaging in behaviors from an earlier stage of development at times when one is anxious
Displacement	Shifting uncomfortable feelings toward someone who is less powerful and less threatening than the individual from whom the feelings originated
Identification	Emulating characteristics in others
Projection	Perceiving that others have the characteristics that are unconsciously disliked in one's self
Undoing	Behaving in a ritualistic manner to take away or make amends for unacceptable behaviors
Reaction formation	Acting in a manner that is opposite to what one is feeling
Sublimation	Changing unacceptable impulses into socially appropriate actions
Rationalization	Making excuses for an anxiety-producing thought or behavior

For example, Antonio has marital problems because he *projects* onto his wife that she is dominating like his mother. He is unable to see that her questions are motivated by concern rather than by a desire to control (of course she has issues of her own that play out in the relationship). He is afraid of telling his wife about his anger at her for being dominating, and so he *displaces* his feelings by kicking the dog. If asked about his anger, he *denies* it and *regresses* to acting like a whiny 7-year-old who expects to be punished. These defense mechanisms protect Antonio from the anxiety that comes from being aware of how he felt toward his mother when he was a child and from learning how to deal with his feelings more appropriately to the current situation with his wife.

A more current way of understanding the unconscious dynamics or the interplay between the id, ego, and superego is to consider the centrality of conflict in human functioning (Summers & Barber, 2010). From this perspective, all mental life can be conceptualized as inner turmoil arising from competing wishes, fears, and prohibitions, along with the attempts to resolve these contradictions is an acceptable way. Thus, we all have intense drives and impulses. Freud identified sex and aggression as the major drives, but Summers and Barber added attachment, bonding, mastery, and affiliation. These wishes can be in conflict (e.g., between love and aggression, between the wish to be close and the wish for independence), or the conflict can be between wishes and the outside world (e.g., the wish to be close vs. the lack of a suitable partner). The classic formulation is that the wish (impulse, drive), prohibition (fear or conscience), and defense (means of coping) all work together to lead to a compromise, which can be either negative, as in a symptom, or positive, as in creative expression. Thus, psychodynamic therapists look at the urges, their imagined consequences, and the associated fantasies, thoughts, and feelings, with the idea that examining this conflict openly can lead to compromise.

ATTACHMENT THEORY

Another important analytic construct is attachment, which has been the focus of much recent theorizing and research (e.g., Bowlby, 1969, 1988; Cassidy, & Shaver, 2008; Meyer & Pilkonis, 2002). Bowlby developed attachment theory to explain the behavioral and emotional responses that keep young children in close proximity to caregivers. According to Bowlby, infants are born with the ability to form attachment bonds with others. When facing threat, the attachment system becomes activated, and the infant seeks proximity and protection from the attachment figure.

In optimal attachment, caregivers provide a comfortable presence that reduces anxiety and promotes a feeling of security. From this secure base, infants feel a sense of security that allows them to "explore the environment curiously and confidently and to engage rewardingly with other people" (Mikulincer & Shaver, 2007, p. 21).

Unfortunately, the attachment system is disrupted when the attachment figure is unavailable, unresponsive, or ineffective in soothing the needy infant (Mikulincer & Shaver, 2007). When this happens, the child feels insecure and worries about whether she or he can rely on others, deal with emotions, or is worthy of care. If the caretaker repeatedly withdraws when the child seeks proximity, the child learns not to rely on others for help when threatened. In contrast, if the attachment figure is unpredictable, the child typically tries even harder to get a response from the caregiver.

Repeated experiences with attachment figures become organized into internal working models, which are mental representations of self, others, and relationships (Bowlby, 1969, 1988). These internal working models help people predict what they can expect from others, whether others will respond when needed, and whether the world is safe.

Through an observational study of young children, Ainsworth, Blehar, Waters, and Wall (1978) found three patterns of attachment: secure, anxious–ambivalent, and anxious–avoidant. Infants who were securely attached explored freely in their mother's presence, showed some anxiety upon separation, and were easily comforted when reunited. Infants with an anxious–ambivalent pattern were excessively anxious and angry, and they tended to cling to their mothers to an extent that interfered with their exploration. They were also distressed during separation and were difficult to comfort on reunion with mothers. Anxious–avoidant infants showed minimal interest in their mothers and displayed minimal affect throughout the observation. These observations have been replicated with other children, and the results have been extended to adulthood, suggesting that attachment patterns in childhood carry over to relationships in adulthood (Ainsworth, 1989). Indeed, extensive research has shown that the major determinant of attachment security is parenting (Fonagy, Gergely, & Target, 2008).

Thankfully, as Bowlby (1988) noted, "change continues through the life cycle so that changes for the better or worse are always possible" (p. 136). Bowlby specifically noted the possibility of change as a result of therapy in that the therapist becomes a safe haven for the client, giving comfort when the client feels threatened.

TREATMENT FROM A PSYCHOANALYTIC PERSPECTIVE

McWilliams (2004) had a nice way of conceptualizing psychodynamic treatment. She noted the importance of curiosity and awe, respect for complexity, a disposition of identification and empathy, a valuing of subjectivity and affect, an appreciation of attachment, and a capacity for faith. Thus, like Rogers (1957), she was more concerned with the helping attitudes than the specific techniques. I particularly like the emphasis on curiosity and awe, because this exemplifies what we try to do in the insight stage by engaging clients in deep thinking about their underlying dynamics.

A great deal has been written about specific interventions to use in psychodynamic work. Freud (1923/1963) believed that deep examination and insight into troubling issues could assist in the resolution of problems. As a foundation for treatment, the helper listens patiently, empathically, uncritically, and receptively to the client (Arlow, 1995). The helper focuses on incidents in the present reality, the past, and the relationship with the helper (Summers & Barber, 2010). Freud (1912/1958) spoke of helpers having an "evenly suspended attention," or of being aware both of what the client says and does as well as paying attention to his or her own internal feelings, thoughts, and fantasies.

To facilitate insight, the helper encourages the client to free associate—to say whatever thoughts come to mind without censure—to help the client get to underlying conflicts. When appropriate, the helper offers interpretations that are just beyond the client's current understanding to encourage the client to think more deeply about the issues (Speisman, 1959). The focus of interpretations is typically about the origins of behaviors and the influence of early childhood experiences on current behaviors.

Psychoanalysts talk about the importance of doing an "archeological dig" to determine the early reasons for current behaviors.

A goal of psychoanalytic treatment is to work with the unconscious conflicts (to replace the id with the ego) or to help the person become more rational and intentional rather than acting on primitive impulses. Thus, rather than just eating constantly to gratify oral urges, the helper works with the client to understand these urges and make a conscious decision to change. The goal is also to free the person up to feel and experience life as it happens (to laugh when happy, to cry when sad).

Another related goal is to make the unconscious conscious. Although the majority of the mind is unconscious, according to Freud, one can strive to make oneself as aware as possible of these primitive influences. Because of the difficulty of dealing with unconscious material, Freud proposed analyzing dreams, fantasies, or slips of the tongue, where the ego and superego do not have as strong a control. Psychoanalytic helpers also assist clients in developing an awareness of frequently used defense mechanisms and in gaining more control over the use of these unconscious strategies to reduce anxiety.

Freud believed that manifestations of unresolved problems from early in childhood are repeated (reenacted) throughout the client's life. Often, the reenactment is uncovered by analyzing how the client relates to the therapist. For example, a client whose mother was cold and unable to fulfill the client's attachment needs as an infant may demonstrate neediness in her relationship with the therapist. The client might call the therapist at home, ask for extra sessions, and try to get the therapist to extend the time limits of each session. The client might also project that the therapist is cold and unable to meet her needs. Placing on the therapist characteristics that belong to other people with whom one has unresolved issues is called *transference* (Freud, 1920/1943). Freud indicated that the analysis and interpretation of transference can be a powerful therapeutic tool to facilitate understanding of the client's relationships with others (see also Gelso & Carter, 1985, 1994).

The helper's unresolved issues (*countertransference*) can also influence the process and outcome of helping. Countertransference (see also Gelso & Hayes, 1998, 2007) can be defined as the helper's reactions to the client that originate in the unresolved issues of the helper. In the previous example, the therapist may have had unresolved needs to take care of others (perhaps related to having an alcoholic mother who relied on the helper to care for younger siblings) and so might respond to the client's neediness by allowing the client to call her at home, stop by the office at any time, and delay payment until the client earns more money. If unrecognized, countertransference behaviors can have a negative influence on therapy. However, awareness of countertransference feelings can actually facilitate the process. For example, if Jeff becomes aware that he has a hard time empathizing with a passive older female client because the client reminds him of his mother, Jeff can talk with his own therapist about his issues with his mother and talk with his supervisor about how to understand the client. Thus, Jeff can come to separate his reactions to the client from his own difficulties with his mother.

An important consideration is that both transference and countertransference can be influenced by cultural factors. We all clearly have prejudices and stereotypes about people who come from other cultural groups (refer back to Chapter 5), so we need to carefully examine our thoughts about our clients.

One change since Freud's time in psychoanalytic treatment is the recognition that the therapist is not a blank screen (what is called a *one-person psychology*) but rather plays a key role in the therapeutic relationship (referred to as *two-person psychology*). In Freud's time, it was thought that the therapist should be a blank screen so that the client could project (transfer) conflicts onto the therapist. There has been a growing recognition, however, that it is impossible for the therapist to truly be a blank screen. In addition, for many clients, having the therapist be a blank screen is not helpful because they need a genuine connection with another person.

Thus, the more recent theorizing emphasizes that both therapist and client contribute to the relationship based on their own issues (see the review in Hill & Knox, 2009). From this perspective, it is not possible to talk about client transference and therapist countertransference as separate issues. Building on this idea, relational psychoanalytic and interpersonal helpers view working on the therapeutic relationship as a central change mechanism within therapy. By talking openly about what is going on between the helper and client, it is possible to work through problems in the relationship, clarify distortions in the transference and countertransference, model healthy interpersonal functioning, and encourage clients to interact differently with others outside of therapy.

HOW PSYCHOANALYTIC THEORIES RELATE TO THE THREE-STAGE MODEL

The emphasis in psychoanalytic theories on the importance of early relationships, defenses, insight, and dealing with the therapeutic relationship is consistent with my thinking about the insight stage. More specifically, the emphasis on the importance of early childhood experiences is in concert with my thinking about the importance of early experiences, particularly with significant others. Similarly, the emphasis on defenses is important in helping clients cope with establishing moderate levels of defenses that protect them yet allow them to interact with others. I also believe strongly that insight is helpful in enabling clients to make lasting changes and to solve new problems as they arise. Furthermore, to me, psychotherapy would indeed be dull and lack depth if we just focused on exploration or behavior change instead of asking deeper questions about meaning. Finally, dealing with problems as they occur in the therapeutic relationship is crucial because it provides clients with corrective relational experiences and teaches skills to handle relationships outside of therapy more effectively.

One criticism I have with the classic Freudian model is that too much emphasis is placed on childhood. Although obviously childhood experiences are formative, experiences later in life can also have a huge impact on people. An example of a positive impact is a person who finds a loving relationship and becomes more trusting. An example of a negative impact is a person who is raped or caught in a terrorist attack and becomes fearful. In addition, the classic Freudian model does not focus on people's aspirations for the future as a driving force. As Yalom (1980) noted, we are also driven by our need to construct meaning in life and make sense of what we want to accomplish during life.

Another departure I make with psychoanalytic theory is with regard to helping clients move to the action stage. Helpers using psychoanalytic theories do not usually focus on helping clients make specific behavior changes (Crits-Christoph, Barber, & Kurcias, 1991). In contrast, I contend that the action stage can be very useful, especially when it follows the insight stage (although some clients want or need action before insight). Despite some differences in theoretical assertions, however, I stress that psychoanalytic techniques are helpful for guiding clients toward increased insight and self-understanding (which set the foundation for action).

Developing Conceptualizations About Client Dynamics

To make decisions about how to intervene in the insight stage, helpers need to have some idea about what is going on at a deeper level for the client (Eells, 2007). Helpers need to start thinking and hypothesizing about client dynamics. To do so, they rely in part on their perceptions and intuitions of the client dynamics. They use themselves as barometers of what is going on in the relationship. Helpers have to allow themselves to have inner reactions and then think about how the client contributes to these reactions. Helpers can ask themselves the following questions to begin to assess client dynamics:

- Is the client expressing discrepancies or contradictions in feelings, actions, or thoughts?
- What might be causing the client to behave this way at this time?

- What contributes to keeping this client from changing at this time?
- What defenses, resistances, and transferences are operating?
- How am I feeling in the therapeutic relationship?

Teaching students about conceptualization skills can be built into training programs. After role-plays, the instructor can ask students to begin to think about client dynamics. For example, in one training session, Kunal (a student in class who was the volunteer client) talked about not having been accepted into graduate school and feeling unsure about what he wanted to do—did he really want to go to graduate school, or did he want to do something else with his life? After we went through the exploration stage, I stopped the interaction, asked Kunal to sit quietly and observe but not respond, and initiated a discussion with the other students about their ideas about what might be going on with Kunal. We wondered, respectfully of course, whether Kunal had problems with indecision more generally, and we speculated about family pressures with regard to attending graduate school. These speculations were helpful in identifying issues for further probing in the insight stage. Our speculations were not all on target, but they did provide ideas about where to go, always recalling the need to be flexible and revise ideas based on emerging information. Similarly, it could be helpful for helpers to talk with supervisors about conceptualizations as a way to stimulate one's thinking.

On the basis of their conceptualizations, helpers can develop clearer intentions for how to intervene. Thus, by hypothesizing about the client's problem, the reason the client is talking about the problem at this particular time, and what the helper can do to help, the helper is able to better determine what to do next in the session. Conceptualization thus enables helpers to have a focus and intentions for interventions instead of just wandering aimlessly without a clear focus in sessions. Of course, one must always be tentative with conceptualizations because they can be wrong, especially when based on limited information, but just as clients need insight about their lives, helpers need conceptualizations about clients.

Goals and Skills of the Insight Stage

In the insight stage, I focus on three main goals to help clients move to new depths of self-understanding: challenging clients to foster awareness, facilitating insight, and working with the therapeutic relationship through immediacy. A number of skills are used to implement these goals. See Exhibit 11.2 for a list of the goals and the skills to facilitate those goals.

EXHIBIT 11.2

List of Skills to Facilitate Goals of the Insight Stage

Goal	Skill
Challenge client to foster awareness	Challenges of discrepancies
	Challenges of thoughts
	Challenge through chair work
	Humor as a type of challenge
	Silence as a type of challenge
	Challenge to take responsibility
	Using nonverbal behaviors to challenge
	Challenging through questions
Facilitate insight	Open questions and probes for insight
	Interpretation
	Disclose insight
Work on therapeutic relationship through immediacy	Open questions and probes for immediacy
	Immediacy

Not all of these skills will be used with any given client. Rather, help-ers look for markers to indicate that clients could profit from working in each of these areas. After describing the skills thoroughly in Chapters 12 through 14, I talk more in detail in Chapter 15 about how to recognize when each skill can potentially be useful and how to integrate the skills.

In addition, because clients (especially those from other cultures) are often not as familiar with these insight skills as they are with exploration and action skills, it can sometimes be helpful to educate clients about why and how insight skills are to be used. Thus, hearing that gaining insight can be helpful for providing a new way of looking at things, which can ultimately help the client make better decisions, can give clients a ratio-nale that makes it more likely that they will cooperate with the helper.

CHALLENGING TO FOSTER AWARENESS

It is important that clients become aware of their thoughts and behaviors. People have lived with themselves for so long and developed defenses to protect themselves from interpersonal injuries, so they are often unaware of thoughts and behaviors that are not adaptive. They need to hear how others honestly react to them so they can begin the self-examination pro-cess. For example, a client may be unaware that he comes across in a hos-tile manner, which makes others avoid him. Awareness involves becoming more conscious about one's thoughts, feelings, behaviors, and impact on others. Thus, awareness is often a precondition for insight. To facilitate awareness, helpers primarily challenge discrepancies and thoughts.

FACILITATING INSIGHT

In addition to gaining awareness of feelings, thoughts, or behaviors, it is important to help clients understand themselves at a deeper level. One of the hallmarks of our existence as human beings is the desire for an explanation for our thoughts, feelings, and behaviors. Explanations help most people feel more in control of their world and are a potent ingredient in therapeutic change (Hanna & Ritchie, 1995). In the insight stage, helpers search for clues regarding what motivates clients, what causes them pain and happiness, and what hinders them from achieving their potential, remembering to be empathic, compassionate, and tentative. Here, helpers use open questions and probes for insight, interpretations, and disclosures of insight.

WORKING WITH THE THERAPEUTIC RELATIONSHIP THROUGH IMMEDIACY

Another specific goal of the insight stage is for clients to gain awareness and insight into their interpersonal interactions by examining the therapeutic relationship. Because clients are often unaware how they come across to others, one goal of helping is to provide clients with feedback about how they come across in the helping relationship. The assumption is that they act toward others in similar ways as they do toward the helper, so looking closely at the therapy relationships provides a microcosm of clients' interpersonal relationships. Of course, clients do not behave exactly the same with everybody as they do with helpers (especially given that helpers do not necessarily have the same personal styles and countertransference issues as significant others), but observations of the therapy relationship provide an opportunity to work on one immediate relationship. Helpers can then work with clients in the action stage to generalize that learning to other relationships. To work on the therapeutic relationship, helpers use immediacy (again with empathy, compassion, and tentativeness).

Concluding Comments

In comparison with the exploration stage, in the insight stage helpers rely somewhat more on their own perspectives and reactions to help clients understand where they are getting stuck and what might be motivating them. Thus, helpers maintain their receptive, empathic stance of the exploration stage but occasionally present their own thoughts and conceptualizations when it seems likely to help the client go to deeper levels of awareness and understanding. I emphasize that helpers do not have "the" insight or right perspective and should not force clients to accept their perspectives. Rather, they primarily encourage clients to discover new things about themselves and occasionally and tentatively offer their own perspectives to help clients come to new awarenesses and insights.

There remains a sense of working together, with helpers aiding clients in discovering things about themselves. The goal is for clients to have a sense of discovery of the new understandings. Even when helpers suggest insights, clients need to try them out and explore how well they fit rather than accepting them unreservedly.

Helpers have to be careful when using their own perspective to make sure they are motivated by the best interests of the clients rather than by their own needs. When helpers are motivated by their own needs (i.e., countertransference), their interventions tend to be less helpful and are sometimes even harmful. Helpers need to be aware of their countertransference reactions so they do not inappropriately act on them in sessions.

Helpers also have to be prepared for clients not agreeing with their challenges or interpretations. Sometimes these skills are used prematurely or are inaccurate or inappropriate, some are done insensitively, and sometimes clients become defensive and anxious. Helpers need to pay attention to these reactions to see how they can intervene differently with the client. It is important not to blame the client (e.g., saying the client is resistant) but to figure out how to intervene in a way that the client can accept and use.

The skills unique to the insight stage (challenges, interpretations, disclosures of insight, open questions and probes for insight, and immediacy) are much harder to learn and use than the skills in the exploration stage (restatements, reflections of feelings, open questions and probes). Students tend not to master the insight skills in their initial exposure to the model. In fact, it takes most students many years and much practice to learn the insight skills and apply them in the appropriate situations in a helping setting. But it is important for beginning helpers to be aware of the insight skills, even though they should initially be appropriately cautious in using these skills. Similarly, helpers will not use every insight skill with every client, especially early in the helping process, but it is valuable to have an awareness of the various skills and learn how they can be used.

It is also important to remind beginning helpers that the exploration skills (attending and listening, restatement, reflection of feelings, open questions and probes about thoughts and feelings) are frequently used to help clients gain insight. Once the helper has presented a challenge, interpretation, disclosure of insight, or immediacy, the client needs help to work to think and explore the new ideas and so helpers return to using the exploration skills to help them explore this new level of awareness. It is also important to maintain empathy for the client and remember how difficult it is to change.

What Do You Think?

- What is the role of insight in your life? Describe several situations in which you naturally sought out (or avoided) insight.
- Describe your thoughts about whether insight is necessary before action.
- Describe your thoughts about how much interpretive input the helper should provide and how it should be done.
- Compare and contrast psychoanalytic theory with Rogers's client-centered theory. Which theory makes most sense to you in terms of personality development and therapy?
- Debate the role of defense mechanisms. What do you think about the idea that a certain amount of defense mechanisms can be healthy but that too many can be debilitating?
- Debate whether psychoanalytic theory has any relevance in today's world.
- How would you modify psychoanalytic theory to make it most relevant to you?

RESEARCH SUMMARY

Insight in Dreams

Citation: Baumann, E., & Hill, C. E. (2008). The attainment of insight in the insight stage of the Hill dream model: The influence of client reactance and therapist interventions. *Dreaming, 18,* 127–137. doi:10.1037/1053-0797.18.2.127

Rationale: Insight is an important outcome of therapy and particularly of dream work in therapy, so the authors wanted to examine factors related to insight gains during dream work. The authors were particularly interested in identifying the therapist skills and the client factors that might be associated with gains in dream work.

Method: Therapists were paired with undergraduates who volunteered to participate because they had a dream they wanted to understand. Before the session, clients completed a measure of reactance (i.e., amount they feel compelled to resist external demands). Therapists then guided the volunteer clients through one 90-minute dream session, using Hill's (2004) three-stage (exploration, insight, and action) model of dream work, which is similar to the helping skills approach. Before and after the insight stage, the therapist asked the client to say what the dream meant. Trained judges coded the amount of insight in the interpretations from before and after the insight stage. From the total data set of 157 cases, the authors selected for further analysis the 10 cases with high insight gains and high reactance, 10 cases with high insight gains and low reactance, 10 cases with low insight gains and high reactance, and 10 cases with low insight gains and low reactance. Trained judges listened to the insight stage and coded the therapist skills and client insight in each speaking turn.

Interesting Findings:
- Therapists used mostly probes for insight (45%), paraphrases (i.e., restatements or reflections of feelings, 21%), and interpretatives (i.e., interpretations or self-disclosures of insight, 7%) in the insight stage. ("Other" skills such as approval-reassurance, closed questions, open questions and probes other than for insight, challenges, self-disclosures other than for insight, immediacy, information, direct guidance, and other accounted for 28% of the skills.)
- Therapists did not differ in the skills used with clients high and low in reactance.
- Therapists used fewer probes for insight, more interpretatives, and more "other" with clients who gained more insight across the insight stage than with clients who gained less insight.
- The highest levels of client insight followed therapist interpretatives and probes for insight, somewhat less followed after paraphrases, and even less followed "other" skills.

Conclusions:
- Interpretations, self-disclosures for insight, and probes for insight all seemed to be effective means of helping clients gain insight. Restatements and reflections of feelings were somewhat less helpful but were still more helpful than other therapist skills (e.g., approval, reassurance, information).

Implications for Therapy:
- Therapists might consider using interpretations, self-disclosures of insight, and probes for insight to help clients gain insight.
- Although client reactance did not turn out to predict which therapist skills were used or how much insight was gained, other client variables may be relevant. It is always good to remember that clients do not all react the same way to various therapist interventions.

BONUS MATERIALS

Practice exercises, labs, and other resources for students and teachers are available on the companion website: http://pubs.apa.org/books/supp/hill4.

Skills for Challenging Clients and Fostering Awareness | 12

And the trouble is, if you don't risk anything, you risk even more.

—*Erica Jong*

Ethan says he wants to go to graduate school, but then he doesn't study and so ends up with bad grades. The helper gently challenges Ethan by saying, "Hmmm, on the one hand you say that you want to go to graduate school, but on the other hand, you don't seem to want to study." This challenge, which was presented in a gentle, nonthreatening manner, raised Ethan's awareness about his behaviors and encouraged him to think more about his commitment to attending graduate school. Ethan realized he was not ready for graduate school and began pondering why he might be sabotaging himself.

Rationale for Using Challenges

Challenges are used to help clients recognize maladaptive feelings, motives, and desires of which they are not aware or unwilling to change (see Exhibit 12.1). If a client is sad but

http://dx.doi.org/10.1037/14345-012
Helping Skills: Facilitating Exploration, Insight, and Action, Fourth Edition, by C. E. Hill

---

EXHIBIT 12.1

Overview of Challenge

Definition	A *challenge* points out maladaptive thoughts, discrepancies, or contradictions of which the client is unaware, unwilling, or unable to change.
Examples	"You're feeling sad that your husband died, but I wonder if you're also angry at him for leaving you."
Typical helper intentions	To challenge, to identify maladaptive behaviors, to identify maladaptive cognitions, to identify and intensify feelings, to deal with resistance, to promote insight (see Web Form D)
Possible client reactions	Challenged, unstuck, negative thoughts and feelings, clear, feelings, responsibility, new perspective, scared, worse, stuck, confused, misunderstood (see Web Form G)
Desired client behaviors	Observe the client to develop challenges (look for inconsistencies, maladaptive thoughts)
Helpful hints	Challenges should be done carefully, gently, respectfully, tentatively, thoughtfully, and with empathy.
	The helper's tone should be one of puzzlement and curiosity, trying to help the client figure out a puzzle.
	Work collaboratively with clients to raise awareness.
	Do not make judgments when you challenge.
	Be humble—remember how difficult it is to be aware.
	Present the challenge as soon as possible after the behavior occurs.
	Ask for client reactions.
	Vary the feeling words you use.

---

cannot bring himself to feel the sadness, he may end up feeling stuck and blocked emotionally. Similarly, if a client is angry at others but unable to admit it, she might make a lot of sarcastic comments and inadvertently wound others because her anger "leaks" out. Furthermore, clients might be invested in not being aware of their inappropriate behaviors. They may blame other people rather than take responsibility for their actions. For example, a middle-aged person might continue to blame his parents for all of his problems rather than take responsibility for them, because taking responsibility would mean he would have to give up his rage at his parents and change his unhealthy behaviors. Challenges are often needed to nudge such clients out of denial, help them see their problems in a different light, and encourage them to take appropriate responsibility for their problems.

Challenges can also help clients become aware of ambivalent feelings. Most of us have ambivalent feelings but cannot allow ourselves to feel both sides of issues because of beliefs about how we "ought" to be (e.g., "Nice girls don't get angry"). We also tend to compartmentalize unowned feelings and thoughts so that we do not have to think about them because we do not like what they reveal about us. Challenges can be used to unearth thoughts and feelings so that clients begin to experience and take responsibility for thoughts and feelings.

Challenges also enable clients to admit to having different or deeper feelings than they were previously able to acknowledge. Recall that we mentioned in Chapter 9 that feelings are often quite complex. For example, Angela said over and over that everything was going well until the helper challenged her about her poor grades. This challenge encouraged Angela to think about what might be going on at a deeper level and helped her realize that she was trying too hard to ignore problems.

These interventions can also be used to help clients become aware of their defenses (see Chapters 6 and 11 for more discussion of defenses). Defenses exist for a reason—they help us cope. All of us need some defenses to survive in the world. However, most of us have defenses that are not adaptive. We developed these defenses to protect ourselves from unreliable, punitive, or abusive parents or others, and we rigidly continue to use these defenses even when they are no longer needed. Although everyone needs defenses sometimes, the helper's goal is to help clients become aware of their defenses and make choices about when and how much to use them. For example, a helper might challenge a client by saying, "You say that you keep up a wall to protect yourself against everyone, but I wonder if you really need to keep it so high with everyone. Maybe there are some people you can trust." By providing a safe place to examine defenses, helpers can work with clients to distinguish situations in which defenses are needed to protect the client and when it is safe to let go of unnecessary defenses.

Our goal as helpers is not to break down or remove all of the defenses but to give clients the option of choosing when and how often to use defenses. We need to help clients look carefully at their reasons for maintaining defenses and determine whether the defenses are still needed. For example, in the face of a hostile attacker, a defense of withdrawal might be appropriate, whereas withdrawal might be counterproductive in an intimate relationship with a loving partner.

In the exploration stage, the emphasis is more toward support, whereas in the insight stage, once there is a relationship established and the helper thinks the client can tolerate being gently challenged, there can be more of a balance between support and challenge. A parallel can be drawn to how students want school to be challenging to help them learn but do not want it to be so challenging that they become anxious.

Even though the goal of challenges is to raise awareness (i.e., to become alerted to thoughts, feelings, and behaviors), sometimes challenges help clients gain insight. Although helpers are not interpreting or providing reasons when they challenge, sometimes simply hearing a challenge can lead clients to want to understand themselves at a deeper level. For example, a helper might challenge Jerald by telling him that he says he wants help, but he does not disclose anything about his situation. Jerald might be prompted to think about why he does not disclose; he might come to realize after exploration that he is reluctant to reveal anything because he is afraid of being rejected given that when he disclosed as a child, his father made fun of him. Being in a therapeutic relationship in which he feels safe can help Jerald question his assumptions and test whether his helper is actually like his father.

Furthermore, the need for challenges varies on the basis of where the client is in the change process. Clients who are at precontemplation and contemplation stages of change (see Chapter 2 for details) are more likely to need challenges to jolt them out of their complacency and encourage them to change but may be less likely to appreciate them (Prochaska, DiClemente, & Norcross, 1992). Clients in the later stages of the helping process (e.g., action, termination, and maintenance) may be less likely to require challenges to get them past defenses and barriers to changing and may be more open to examining themselves.

Theoretical Perspectives on Challenges

Several theorists have talked about the benefits of challenges. They have used the more traditional term *confrontation,* however, so I use both terms in this section.

Carkhuff and Berenson (1967), humanistic theorists, stated that the purpose of pointing out discrepancies is to help reduce ambiguities and incongruities in the client's experiencing and communication. They suggested that confrontations encourage clients to accept themselves and become fully functioning. Confronting clients with the discrepant facets of their behaviors challenges them to understand themselves more fully. As Carkhuff (1969) noted, "At the point of confrontation the client is pressed to consider the possibility of changing and, in order to do so, utilizing resources that he [or she] has not yet employed" (p. 93). Furthermore,

The challenge in a sense creates a crisis in the client's life. The crisis poses the client with the choice between continuing in his [or her] present mode of functioning or making a commitment to attempt to achieve a higher-level, more fulfilling way of life. (p. 92)

Another perspective about confrontation comes from Greenson (1967), a psychoanalyst. Greenson defined confrontation as a demonstration to the client of his or her resistance: "all the forces within the patient that oppose the procedures and processes of psychoanalytic work" (p. 35). He suggested that confrontations should be delivered before interpretations because defenses first need to be confronted and brought into awareness before they can be understood. For example, he noted that before he could interpret why a client was avoiding a certain subject, he would first have to get the client to face that she or he was avoiding something. Thus, the confrontation points out that the client is resisting; the questions of how and what the client is resisting are then addressed through clarification and interpretation.

Yet another relevant perspective is Stiles's (Honos-Webb & Stiles, 1998) notion about each of us being composed of a community of voices. He theorized that we incorporate significant others into ourselves such that each other person becomes a voice (e.g., Ashley might suddenly sound like her mother when she condemns herself for smoking, and then sound like her younger self when she whines about how she cannot be any different, and then sound like her father when she blames others). If voices are in discord, some may get silenced or rejected. The goal of therapy is to initiate a dialogue between the different voices and foster integration such that all voices can be heard and operate more harmoniously. This perspective reminds us that we all are complicated people with lots of opposing feelings and thoughts.

Types of Challenges

The most gentle and typical challenge is of discrepancies. I also briefly describe challenges of thoughts based on a cognitive therapy framework. Finally, I present chair work, humor, silence, taking responsibility, nonverbal behaviors, and questions as additional types of challenges.

CHALLENGES OF DISCREPANCIES

Discrepancies and contradictions are important because they are often signs of unresolved issues, ambivalence (mixed feelings), or suppressed (or repressed) feelings. Often these discrepancies come up because clients have not been able to deal effectively with feelings as they arise.

With challenges of discrepancies, helpers juxtapose two things to make the client aware of the contradiction between them, thus paving the way to understanding the cause of the discrepancy and making changes. Helpers can focus on several types of discrepancies:

- between two verbal statements (e.g., "You say there's no problem, but then you say you're annoyed with him"),
- between words and actions (e.g., "You say you want to get good grades, but you spend most of your time partying and sleeping"),
- between two behaviors (e.g., "You're smiling, but your teeth are clenched"),
- between two feelings (e.g., "You feel angry at your sister, but you also feel pleased that now everyone will see what kind of person she really is"),
- between values and behaviors (e.g., "You say you believe in respecting others' choices, but then you try to convince them that they are wrong about abortion"),
- between one's perception of self and experience (e.g., "You say no one likes you, but earlier you described an instance in which someone invited you to have lunch"),
- between one's ideal and real self (e.g., "You want to meet your mother's high standards, but you feel like you're just average"),
- between the helper's and the client's opinions (e.g., "You say you are not working hard, but I think you are doing a great job"), and
- between values and feelings (e.g., "You would like to be a good charitable person who volunteers for everything, but you feel angry about having to help out").

It is important to note that not all challenges of discrepancies relate to pointing out negative aspects that the client is not ready to face. Some relate to positive things that clients are not ready to admit to themselves. For example, Marita constantly put herself down in front of other people, making disparaging remarks about what a klutz she was or how anyone else could do things better. Her helper challenged her gently that in fact she was quite competent at expressing her feelings and interacting with him. She was surprised and then started crying, later saying that no one had ever said anything positive to her before.

A major task for helpers challenging discrepancies is to do so in such a way that clients can hear them and feel supported rather than attacked. Quite unlike the exploration skills that convey acceptance, challenges can imply criticism. With challenges, helpers indicate that some aspect of a client's life is incongruent or problematic and imply that a client should change to feel, think, or act differently, and so the helper needs to be careful about how the challenge is phrased and presented. Challenges should be done carefully, gently, respectfully, tentatively, thoughtfully, and with empathy.

One might think of the client as building a wall around himself or herself. Rather than attacking the wall directly with major weapons or armaments, the helper might do better to point out the wall. When the client is aware of the wall, the helper and client together can try to understand the purpose for the wall and decide whether the wall is needed. Rather than battering down the wall, the helper might encourage the client to build a door in the wall and learn when to open and close that door.

The helper's manner might reflect puzzlement, of trying to help the client figure out a puzzle and make sense of discrepant pieces. One can simply point out the discrepancy in a nonthreatening manner and ask the client to clarify. Similarly, Lauver and Harvey (1997) suggested using "collegial confrontations," which point out the helper's confusion about what he or she perceives as discrepant; they recommended against trying to persuade the client to come around to the helper's viewpoint. In essence, helpers empathically point out discrepancies and then follow these challenges with reflections of feelings and open questions and probes about how it felt to be challenged.

Furthermore, it is important that helpers not make judgments when they challenge. A challenge should not be a criticism but an encouragement to examine oneself more deeply. The goal is to work collaboratively with clients in raising awareness. If helpers are judgmental, clients may feel shamed and embarrassed and hence be more resistant to recognizing problems. Helpers need to remember that all of us have discrepancies and irrationalities and that we are not "better than" our clients. We need to be humble and empathize with how difficult it is to understand ourselves and make changes. It is usually easier to see someone else's inconsistencies than it is to see one's own.

Although sometimes painfully difficult to hear, if can be a gift for helpers to tackle obvious issues that others would shy away from. If you had spinach in your teeth, you would want someone to tell you. Similarly, if clients are doing things that turn others off, it is a gift to gently and lovingly point the behaviors out in a way that clients can hear. Clients often need someone outside to help them become aware of self-defeating behaviors, but they can only absorb the challenges if this is done in a way that they can hear.

When learning to challenge discrepancies, I recommend that helpers use the following formats to make sure they include both parts of the intervention:

On the one hand _____, but on the other hand _____.
You say _____, but you also say _____.
You say _____, but nonverbally you seem _____.
I'm hearing _____, but I'm also hearing _____.

Sometimes the first part of the discrepancy is implied, and the helper states only the "but" clause. For example, the client might say that there are no problems, and the helper might respond, "But you said he was angry at you" (implying "You just said there were no problems, but . . . ").

CHALLENGES OF THOUGHTS

Cognitive theorists suggest that irrational thinking keeps people from coping effectively and makes them unhappy. For example, Ellis (1962, 1995) suggested that people say irrational things to themselves, such as "I must be loved by everyone," "I must be completely competent and perfect to be worthwhile," "It is awful if things are not the way I want them to be," "There should be someone stronger than me who will take care of me," and "There is a perfect solution to human problems, and it is terrible if I don't find it."

Ellis noted that most clients make the assumption that events cause emotions, but he strongly argued that it is the irrational beliefs that lead to negative emotions. For example, if Sam gets a *C* on an exam, he might think that the failure makes him feel bad. But Ellis would have contended that it is what he tells himself about getting a *C* on the exam (e.g., "I'm a failure as a person; I should be perfect") that makes him feel bad rather than the *C* itself. Hence, Ellis suggested that if they replace the irrational beliefs with more rational cognitions, clients would have more positive emotions. In this example, Sam might be taught a more rational thought such as, "It's too bad that I got a *C* on the exam but that doesn't make me a bad person. It just means that I have to study harder next time, instead of going out drinking the night before."

Beck and his colleagues (A. T. Beck, 1976; A. T. Beck & Emery, 1985; A. T. Beck & Freeman, 1990; A. T. Beck, Rush, Shaw, & Emery, 1979; J. S. Beck, 1995) developed a cognitive theory that is slightly different from Ellis's theory. They postulated that automatic thoughts and dysfunctional interpretations are the major source of problems for clients and that clients misconstrue events on the basis of faulty logic and beliefs in the cognitive triad of the self, world, and future. Hence, clients often view themselves as defective, inadequate, or unlovable; the world as unmanageable, uncontrollable, or overwhelming; and the future as bleak and hopeless.

Beck's gentle therapeutic approach is quite different from Ellis's direct confrontational style. He recommended that helpers work collaboratively with clients as scientists to uncover faulty logic and examine its impact. Helpers ask a series of questions to help clients arrive at logical conclusions ("What happens when you say X to yourself?"). Helpers also actively point out cognitive themes and underlying assumptions that work against clients. Beck suggested that people often draw conclusions without having adequate evidence (e.g., a person might conclude that he is unlovable just because he has no one with whom to eat lunch one day). People also take details out of context (e.g., focus on one negative comment about a presentation in class and ignore several positive ones), develop general rules out of a few instances (e.g., because she made a mistake one time, a person generalizes that she cannot handle any responsibility), and make something more or less important than it needs to be (e.g., perceive a person's not saying "hello" as meaning that he is angry, minimizing the importance of failing a course). In addition, people attribute blame to themselves without adequate evidence (e.g., a secretary believing that a company's going out of business is due to her not coming into work one day) and engage in rigid, either–or thinking (e.g., a man may think that women are either goddesses or whores). For those who want to learn more about cognitive therapy, I recommend the widely used self-help book by Burns (1999).

Thus, we as helpers can challenge these irrational thoughts to help clients recognize their faulty thinking and change it. Helpers can ask, "What are you telling yourself now?" Or they might ask (remembering to only ask one question at a time), "What would be the worst thing that would happen if you did not succeed at being a physicist?" "What would be so horrible about that?" "You say you can't stand it, but is that true, would you fall apart?" "It might not be pleasant, but would it actually be catastrophic?" When asking such questions, it is important to remember that helpers attack the beliefs, not the person.

CHALLENGING THROUGH CHAIR WORK

Chair work can be particularly useful for challenging clients to become aware of conflicting feelings (e.g., love–hate) or unfinished business (e.g., feeling unresolved about a relationship ending). This technique originally comes from gestalt therapy (Perls, 1969; Perls, Hefferline, & Goodman, 1951) and more recently has been used in process-experiential therapy and emotion-focused therapy (Elliott et al., 2004; Greenberg, 2011; Greenberg, Rice, & Elliott, 1993) to help clients become aware of and integrate feelings. Sometimes doing and acting out feeling is easier and has more impact than talking about feeling.

Two-Chair Work

A two-chair technique can be used when the client expresses a major conflict between two opposing sides (e.g., "I wish I could, but I'm scared"; "I'd like to, but I stop myself"). These conflicts often arise due to internalized "shoulds," which come from early experiences of being told what to do. People begin to live according to these standards but typically have not thought through and determined for themselves how to live their lives based on their own feelings.

The helper asks the client to sit in one chair and try to experience and express the feelings from one side of the conflict. Once the client has expressed feelings, she or he is asked to move to other chair and talk from that side with full expression of feelings. Usually what happens is that one side, called the *topdog* in gestalt therapy because it is the controlling and dominant voice, engages in a lot of criticism (the "shoulds"), whereas the other side, called the *underdog* in gestalt therapy because it is usually the passive voice, whines, and acts helpless. Because of the conflict, the person feels stuck, immobilized, and angry, all of which are often outside of awareness. In typical conversations in the real world, when these two sides try to talk, they tune each other out and therefore cannot complete a dialogue. By having both sides speak fully and express their feelings as well as listen to the other side talk, the client comes to allow both sides to emerge and exist equally and thus can integrate them both into a more complete whole. The marker, or indicator, that a two-chair technique might prove beneficial to help the client explore more deeply, is when the client expresses having opposing feelings or seems to have feelings that she or he cannot seem to express because they seem unacceptable to him or her.

The following steps can be used to facilitate two-chair work. They need not be followed exactly but are provided here to give a clear sense of how this exercise can be done.

1. The helper identifies a conflict split in what the client says, for example, "I should love him, but I don't know how I feel" or "I should go to see my parents, but I just can't seem to make myself do it." Importantly, the helper first determines that the client has enough ego strength (resiliency) to be able to participate in the chair work given the potential intensity of this kind of work.

2. The helper asks the client if she or he would like to try an exercise to deepen the conflicting feelings so that they can try to understand them more. More education may be needed given that chair work can seem awkward to some people, but it is important for the helper not to be apologetic or unsure about whether chair work is a useful exercise.

3. If the client agrees, the helper pulls up another chair and invites the client to move to the new chair and talk directly to the other side of the self. It is important for the helper to be positioned equidistant from both chairs and be aligned equally with both sides, given that the ultimate hope is for both sides to express themselves openly and negotiate. The helper might start by asking the client to take the critic or topdog ("should") side. Alternatively, the helper could ask the client which side she or he

feels most in touch with or which side feels more alive and ask the client to start with that side. The helper directs the client to say what the chosen side would say to the other side (e.g., "You shouldn't do that" or "Don't say that"). The helper attends to making sure that this side expresses itself clearly and forcefully.

4. The helper then asks the client to move to the other chair and express what it feels like to hear what the other side said. Again, the helper encourages the client to be direct and clear about his or her reactions, perhaps asking the client to repeat if the client did not state the feelings strongly. If the client starts to talk to the helper instead of the other chair, the helper gently encourages the client to talk directly to the chair.

5. The helper again asks the client to switch chairs and respond. The switching continues with the helper encouraging each side to fully express the underling feelings and needs (this step often requires quite a bit of coaching from the helper). With both sides fully expressing themselves, the client can come to accept and negotiate the conflicting views. Typically, the critic softens, the passive side becomes stronger, and the struggle is resolved.

6. It is important to process the experience with the client. The helper can ask how it felt to engage in the exercise.

The following is an example of two-chair work. Jason has been talking about his depression and both his desire to change and resistance to change. He has been talking about being stuck for a couple of sessions.

Helper:	I wonder if you would like to try an exercise where we try to explore these two sides of yourself to try to get a better understanding of what's going on for you?
Client:	Well, I don't know if it will do any good, but I guess I'm willing to try if you think it will be helpful.
Helper:	Let's try it and see how it goes. You can stop at any time you wish. (Pause while helper moves another chair over) Okay, let's start with the side of you that wants to change. Would you be that side and talk to the other side of you that doesn't want to change; we'll put that other side of you in this other chair and you can talk directly to him.
Client:	What I would say is . . .
Helper:	Look directly at the other chair and talk as if that side of you were sitting there.
Client:	Okay. (Pauses and takes a deep breath) You are miserable right now. You really should do something about it (said rather meekly).

Helper:	Can you be a bit more indignant and express how you really feel?
Client:	(in a louder voice) You really are disgusting because you know you should change but you don't do anything about it. You say you're going to therapy, but then you get there and you clam up. How can you expect to change if you don't get into it?
Helper:	Okay, good. Now go to the other chair and respond from the side of you that doesn't want to change.
Client:	(to therapist) This feels a little silly.
Helper:	Yes, it does, but maybe try it and let's see how it goes.
Client:	(in a flat voice) Well, I don't know why you go on and on about this. Things aren't that bad. Just leave me alone.
Helper:	Can you try to get into it a little bit more? You sound a little whiny. Can you play that up some more?
Client:	I don't want to change. I wish you'd leave me alone. I like being depressed.
Helper:	Can you say that last part louder?
Client:	I like being depressed. It feels good. No one ever paid any attention to me, so at least I can pay attention to myself. I'm not so sure that I want to change.
Helper:	Okay, go back over to the other chair. Did you hear what the other side said?
Client:	Yeah, I'm feeling bad that you think no one ever paid attention to you. Can you say more about that?
Helper:	Switch chairs and respond.
Client:	I just felt left out a lot as a kid. My dad was pretty tough and beat me whenever he thought I got out of line. I felt sad a lot as a kid.
Helper:	Switch chairs.
Client:	I know that's been hard for you to even talk about your father. I'm sorry that I was so rough on you, always trying to make you change.
Helper:	Switch again.
Client:	Well, I do want to change, but I just feel so scared. And I'm not sure that I'm going to be able to really change. I feel so alone.
Helper:	Let's stop there for right now. What are you feeling right now?
Client:	Wow! I was surprised that so much came out so quickly. I guess I can begin to see why I feel so stuck. I would really like to explore more about my feelings about my father.

> *Helper:* Yeah, it's interesting that earlier you had told me that everything was so idyllic in your childhood, and now it seems like more was going on inside than you were comfortable admitting out loud.
>
> *Client:* Yeah, there's so much more there underneath.
>
> *Helper:* Tell me about how you felt in each chair.
>
> *Client:* In the chair demanding that I change, I could kind of hear my father's voice . . . that scares me because he was so mean. In the chair saying I couldn't change, I just felt so defeated. (session continues)

Notice how the first "You better shape up" side softened and listened to the other "whiny I can't change" side. Also notice how the "I can't change" side started to open up and explore a little more openly. Interestingly, talking between the two sides helped the client get away from "talking about" and into the experience of the conflict. Had the helper tried to interpret for the client what was going on, the client might have ignored it, but being in the situation allowed the client to experience the conflict more directly. Of course, this example is much shorter than would typically be true of an actual session, but I hope it gives an idea of how a helper could conduct this exercise.

Empty-Chair Work

Another version of this technique involves empty-chair work for clients with unfinished business, often feelings of anger, sadness, resentment, and hurt toward a significant other that the client has carried around since childhood. In this case, the helper works with the client to imagine what she or he wants to say to the person, talk to the person as if the person were sitting in an empty chair and then imagine how the other person might respond. The helper guides the client in expressing difficult feelings when talking to the significant other and coaches the client to express other possible feelings when talking from the side of the significant other. The same steps apply as above for two-chair work, such that the client goes back and forth between self and other.

Thus, two-chair work involves working with different parts of self, whereas empty chair work focuses on work with another person, although it is always important to remember that much of what we expect from another person involves projections. Note that although chair work is used in the insight stage to challenge clients to experience deeper feelings and conflicts, it is also appropriate in the action stage when the client is torn between different alternative actions (see Chapter 16).

Difficulties Helpers Experience When Doing Chair Work

One difficulty helpers have using chair work is a hesitance to try it because it is different from other skills and feels risky. It is also difficult to do without seeing a model of someone else demonstrating it. Another difficulty is figuring out how and when to do each step, so that for example, helpers might move too fast through the steps without giving the clients enough time to work through feelings. A concern that beginning helpers often voice is not knowing how much to push clients to do chair work if they seem reluctant or in knowing whether clients have enough ego strength to tolerate chair work. A final difficulty is in remembering to coach clients so that they learn how to do the steps and do them with adequate emotional expression. These difficulties can usually be overcome with adequate practice, and I highly recommend that beginning trainees practice chair work with peers before trying it on clients.

HUMOR AS A TYPE OF CHALLENGE

Sometimes challenges can be softened by using humor, as long as the client feels that the helper is laughing *with* rather than *at* him or her. Helping clients laugh at themselves can help them think about their problems in a different way. An example from Falk and Hill's (1992) study of the effects of therapist humor involved a case in which the therapist and client were dealing with issues related to control and perfectionism in the client's life, particularly with regard to eating and schoolwork. The client excitedly described her weekend in which she contacted several friends, coordinated their activities, and eagerly took on the role of the designated driver. She exclaimed, "I had so much fun." The helper commented, "And so much control." They both laughed, and the client began to talk about how her need for control pervaded many aspects of her life. If clients can start laughing, they can sometimes begin to see things in a different light. Of course, as with other types of challenges, helpers need to have established a relationship with clients and use the humor to raise awareness rather than to make fun of the client.

SILENCE AS A TYPE OF CHALLENGE

In contrast to the use of silence to provide empathy and warmth as described in Chapter 7, silence can also be used to challenge (Hill, Thompson, & Ladany, 2003; Ladany et al., 2004). In this use of silence, helpers challenge clients to take responsibility for what they want to say. Rather than rushing in and taking care of the client, helpers wait and encourage the client to say something. Silence sometimes increases discomfort and forces clients to rely on their inner resources and examine their thoughts or, as one therapist said, "to stew in their juices."

Although challenging silences may be helpful in long-term therapy when there is a good working alliance, it can be potentially damaging to use silence for these reasons if the client does not trust the helper or understand the purpose of the silence. Silence can be frightening for clients who feel isolated and out of touch with the helper or who do not know how to express themselves. Helpers have to assess what is going on for clients during the silence and determine whether it is better to continue the silence or break it.

CHALLENGING CLIENTS TO TAKE RESPONSIBILITY

Another way to challenge clients is to urge them to take appropriate responsibility for their behavior. One way of identifying whether clients are owning responsibility is to listen to the language they use. Some people in conversation use "you" and "everyone" instead of saying "I" (e.g., "Everyone gets upset at their parents" rather than "I am upset at my parents"). In other words, these clients make it seem that everyone feels or acts a certain way rather than taking responsibility for their own thoughts and feelings. Simply asking the client to say "I" and make the statement for himself or herself can raise the client's awareness and encourage him or her to take responsibility and differentiate from other people. Other phrases that indicate a lack of taking responsibility can also be challenged. For instance, the client can be asked to change "can't" to "won't" (e.g., "I can't ask for a raise" to "I won't ask for a raise") and "shouldn't" to "I choose to" (e.g., "I shouldn't play computer games" to "I choose to play computer games"). Once they change their language, clients can be asked to talk about how it feels to use different phrases. Once again, helpers should use such interventions gently and infrequently so that clients do not feel blamed and shamed.

USING NONVERBAL BEHAVIORS TO CHALLENGE

Helpers can also point out a nonverbal behavior that may reflect a discrepancy or underlying feelings that the client is denying. If we assume that sometimes feelings leak out through nonverbal behaviors, we might be able to encourage clients to examine what might be going on. Clients might thus be encouraged to become aware of what their bodies might be saying to them. The helper might direct the client who is tapping his foot to "be your foot. What are you saying right now?" And the helper might even ask the client to exaggerate the feeling to help him or her begin to identify the feeling. By asking the client to be the body part, helpers enable clients to get out of rationalization and into their experiencing—the client has to look inward to see whether there is something going on (e.g., "What am I feeling?"). Of course this intervention needs to be done cautiously and for the benefit of the client.

It is often easy for helpers to use this type of intervention to show-off (e.g., "Aha, I caught you").

CHALLENGING THROUGH QUESTIONS

The helper might also challenge by simply saying, "Really?" "Oh yeah?" or "Hmmm?" These interventions question the client in a gentle challenging manner and encourage the client to think about what he or she is thinking.

Guidelines for Presenting Challenges

Challenges are typically most effective if used in close proximity to the client's behavior. If a helper waits too long, the client might not remember what the helper is talking about. For instance, if the helper says, "Last session when you spoke about being angry at your mother, you smiled," the client is not likely to remember the incident. Thus, helpers should act fairly quickly (if they have enough data), while the behaviors and feelings are still recent (e.g., "Just then you smiled. I wonder what's going on?").

Helpers need to adapt their approach to using challenges to fit the client. For example, helpers can think about whether challenges are appropriate for the particular client. Direct, blunt challenges are not likely to be as effective with Asian, Latino/Latina, and Native American clients (Ivey, 1994) because they are not culturally appropriate. Ivey presented the example of a Chinese counselor's first efforts to counsel in China after training in the United States. He confronted an older Chinese man using the standard format for challenges: "On the one hand you do X, but on the other hand you do Y; how do you put these two together?" The older man politely said his farewell and never came back. The counselor had forgotten that when Chinese people see the need to express disagreement, they generally take great care not to hurt the other person's feelings or cause the other person to "lose face." His direct confrontive technique was considered ill-mannered and insensitive, especially because it came from a younger person. Ivey suggested that it is possible to confront a Chinese person but that helpers need to be sensitive and gentle when doing so, perhaps by presenting the challenge in a tentative manner and preceding it with something positive. On the other hand, direct (but still empathic and respectful) confrontation may be especially appropriate with some male European American or African American clients who find the soft and gentle approach meaningless and who may even denigrate the helper for using it. Ivey (1994) stressed the need for flexibility and responsiveness to each person.

Because challenges can have such a strong impact on clients, helpers need to observe clients' reactions carefully by listening attentively and observing the client's nonverbal behavior (recall the research cited in Chapter 2 that clients often hide negative reactions). Thus, helpers should not expect that they necessarily know when clients feel badly after a challenge. Clients could withdraw, and helpers would not know that they were upset. Hence, helpers often have to ask clients how they reacted to challenges and probe beneath the surface to understand the complete reaction (e.g., "You just got quiet. What are you thinking?"). In addition, helpers need to remember to reflect feelings to encourage clients to talk about their reactions to challenges (e.g., "You seem upset").

From observing the client's reactions, a helper can make more informed decisions about how to proceed:

- If the client responds to challenges with denial, the helper needs to rethink how he or she is presenting the challenges, whether the client is ready to hear the challenge, or whether a challenge was a good intervention.
- If the client says that she or he has no reaction to the challenge, the helper might evaluate whether she or he presented the challenges effectively, whether the challenge was accurate, or whether the client was defensive.
- If the client responds with partial examination or acceptance and recognition but no change, the helper can continue to confront gently to help the client move further. The helper also can reflect how scary it is to change and help the client to explore fears.
- If the client responds with new awareness and acceptance, the helper can summarize and then help the client explore more or move on to interpretation.

Helpers should not be surprised when clients react strongly to challenges. Instead, they should help clients express and work through their emotions. These reactions are the exciting and potentially potent, albeit scary for both clients and helpers, stuff of helping.

A final issue is the timing of challenges. If you think your challenge was accurate but your client denies or dismisses it, you may need to back off until the client can handle the challenge or until you have more evidence for your observations. For example, you may experience a client as being extremely hostile and pushy with you, although he perceives himself as being friendly and accommodating. Your first challenge, "You say you're easygoing, but you sound like you act somewhat aggressively with your friends," might be negated by the client ("Nah, they all love me").

You might want to obtain more examples from the client about how he behaves with friends, or you may want to ask the client to observe his own behavior or ask the client to ask his friends for feedback. Despite his reaction, you can trust your impression that this client was aggressive with you (although of course you need to search yourself for counter-transference issues related to aggression). In time, you might present another challenge with more specific behavioral evidence. For example:

> You say you are never hostile, but you sounded like you were hostile in your interaction with your friend yesterday. From what you said, you completely disagreed with everything your friend said and refused to talk about it. I wonder what your experience was?

The following shows a helper using challenges (in italics) in a session:

Client: My husband wants his parents to come and live with us. His father has Alzheimer's, and his mother takes care of his father, but she can't drive and is not feeling too well herself. They are both old and need more help around the house.

Helper: How do you feel about them moving in with you?

Client: Well, I think they need to do something. The situation is not improving, and they are getting old. My husband really wants to take care of them. He feels some obligation since he's the oldest child.

Helper: (gently) *I hear that your husband wants to take care of them, but I am not hearing what you want to do.*

Client: I have been brought up to believe that family takes care of family when they need help. I didn't take care of my parents, so I feel like we should do what we can to help them if they want it. They may not even want to move in. They might rather do something else.

Helper: *I'm struck by how hard it is for you to talk about your feelings.*

Client: That's interesting. You're really right. I feel like I don't have a right to my feelings. I feel like it's something I "should" do. I don't have any choice, so I'm trying not to have any feelings. If I'm really honest with myself, I'm terrified of what it will be like if they move in. His mother can be very critical.

Helper: You sound upset.

Client: Yeah, but it makes me feel guilty. I just don't know what to do. I guess I've always had a hard time standing up to his parents. Actually, I have a hard time standing up to most people, so this is just another example. I think it stems from my childhood. (Client continues to talk.)

Difficulties Helpers Experience Using Challenges

Challenges are difficult interventions for many beginning helpers. One set of difficulties relates to helpers not doing enough challenges. Many beginning helpers use too few challenges because they are afraid of being intrusive, forcing clients to examine their "dirty laundry," offending clients, sounding accusatory or blaming, destroying the therapeutic relationship, causing clients to feel unsupported, or afraid that clients will not like them. Furthermore, confronting people is not considered polite in some cultures, so helpers from such cultures may feel reluctant to use challenges. However, if clients are being contradictory or confusing or are stuck, it is difficult for them to clarify their thinking without outside feedback. In fact, if done appropriately, challenges can be a gift that lets the client know the helper is willing to say unpleasant things that others may not say (e.g., "You say you want to have friends, but you criticize everything anyone does"). Remember, however, that challenges need to be presented gently and with compassion, and that you may need to educate your client about why you are challenging because it can be such a change in style from the exploration stage.

Another set of difficulties involves using challenges inappropriately. Some helpers who feel afraid of negative feelings might use challenges to deny or minimize negative feelings. For example, if a client talks about suicidal feelings, a helper might use a challenge that indicates that the client has a lot to live for and should not be thinking about suicide. A statement that a client has a lot to live for might sound like the helper is pointing out strengths, but in this situation the helper is minimizing the negative feelings and falsely reassuring the client so he or she does not have to deal with the suicidal feelings. Such challenges can actually make clients feel misunderstood and worse about themselves.

A third set of difficulties involves using too many challenges or using challenges too harshly. Some helpers become too invested in having clients recognize their discrepancies. They might argue with clients to convince them of their observations. Or they become like detectives who present the evidence and want to force clients to admit their problems and confess that they are not being consistent. Or they might act like lawyers cross-examining witnesses in the courtroom; they seem eager to "catch" clients in their discrepancies. Other helpers use challenges, often unconsciously, as an opportunity to get back at clients they do not like or who upset them in some way. Because such challenges can make clients feel unsupported, helpers will probably want to become aware of their motives, intentions, and countertransferences so that they do not harm clients.

Finally, helpers often have trouble knowing how to respond when clients disagree and challenge the helper in return. For example, the helper might say it seems like the client is coming across hostilely or seductively, and the client might deny it and say it is the helper's problem (one client even told the helper to go see a therapist to work on her problems). Some helpers do not know whether to keep trying to get clients to see the evidence or whether to give up and try again later after they have more data to support the challenge. Helpers may even begin to distrust their perceptions when clients challenge them. At times, helpers might misperceive the situation because of their own issues or insufficient data. At other times, however, clients might be defensive, unwilling to examine themselves, or have a hard time acknowledging their behaviors. Having supervisors listen to tapes of sessions and provide feedback can be useful to allow helpers to determine whether they were distorting because of their own needs, whether the challenge was accurate but presented in a nontherapeutic manner, or whether the client was not ready to hear a challenge.

What Do You Think?

- Do you think that there is a benefit to awareness, or should helpers just focus on behavior change?
- Are challenges of discrepancies necessary and helpful?
- Compare and contrast challenges of discrepancies and challenges of thoughts.
- How can helpers maintain an attitude of curiosity and compassion for clients with their challenges rather than attacking them and getting invested in confronting clients?
- What types of helpers might be likely to use challenges inappropriately?
- Discuss the idea of a balance between support and challenge.
- How do you think culture plays a role in the use of these challenge skills?

RESEARCH SUMMARY

Effects of Confrontation Versus Support

Citation: Miller, W. R., Benefield, R. G., & Tonigan, J. S. (1993). Enhancing motivation for change in problem drinking: A controlled comparison of two therapist styles. *Journal of Consulting and Clinical Psychology, 61,* 455–461. doi:10.1037/0022-006X.61.3.455

Rationale: Client lack of motivation is a big problem in addiction work, leading clients to not comply with treatment recommendations, to not seek or to drop out of treatment, and leading to unsuccessful treatment outcomes. Although in the past this lack of motivation was blamed on client traits or defense mechanisms, Miller et al. wondered about the influence of therapist behaviors. In particular, addictions treatment used to emphasize a hard-hitting, directive, confrontational style meant to break through defense mechanisms, but Miller et al. suggested that a more empathic, supportive approach might be more effective. Therefore, they sought to compare a directive, confrontational approach with a client-centered approach.

Method: Participants, who were recruited for an assessment of their drinking behavior, first completed preintervention measures of their drinking behavior. They were then assigned to either an evaluation session to assess their alcohol risk and impairment within a week or to a delayed evaluation after a 6-week waiting period. Approximately one week after the evaluation, participants were randomly assigned to get feedback about their alcohol risk from interviewers who used either a directive (confronted about alcoholism, gave advice, and disagreed with clients about minimization of alcoholism) or client-centered approach (used empathy, reflective listening, deemphasized labeling of alcoholism in favor of considering the negative effects of alcohol and what the client might need to do about it). Tapes of sessions were coded for interviewer and client behavior.

Interesting findings:
■ Therapists in the directive condition confronted more, listened less, questioned less, and restructured (similar to interpretations) less than did therapists in the client-centered condition.
■ Clients who received the directive style were more likely than clients in the client-centered approach to argue with the therapist, interrupt or ignore the therapist, and deny or not acknowledge problems.
■ The more the therapist (in either condition) confronted the client (e.g., challenged, disagreed, engaged in head-on disputes, expressed incredulity, emphasized negative attributes, used sarcasm), the more alcohol the client drank 1 year later.
■ Clients gave positive, self-motivational statements more often when therapists listened and restructured.

Conclusions:
■ A confrontational style is associated with client resistance. Therapists may be more confrontational with resistant clients, and clients may become more resistant with confrontational therapists.
■ The authors noted that confrontation and empathy are not inherently incompatible, but from the description, it sounds like the therapists in the confrontation condition in this study were more argumentative than is advocated in the current text.

Implications for Therapy:
■ Challenges need to be presented carefully, with a lot of listening and empathy.
■ Helpers need to avoid being argumentative with clients.

BONUS MATERIALS   Practice exercises, labs, and other resources for students and teachers are available on the companion website: http://pubs.apa.org/books/supp/hill4.

Skills for Facilitating Insight

13

Men go abroad to wonder at the heights of mountains, at the huge waves of the sea, at the long courses of the rivers, at the vast compass of the ocean, at the circular motions of the stars; and they pass by themselves without wondering.

—*St. Augustine*

Jim told his helper that he was feeling depressed and aimless. He felt that nothing made sense and that he had no purpose in life. He also talked extensively about how his parents were anxious about him taking risks since his older brother had died in a motorcycle accident. On the basis of this and other information the helper had learned about Jim through several sessions, the helper said, "I wonder whether your lack of purpose in life is because you are still grieving the loss of your brother and you haven't been able to make your own decisions and figure out who you are as a person." This interpretation helped Jim make sense of his depression and aimlessness. After talking further with the helper and trying to understand what was going on inside, Jim was able to see his life in a new perspective and to think about how he wanted to be.

Helpers ideally begin the interpretive process with an attitude of empathic curiosity. They wonder what it is that makes clients act a certain way. And they invite clients to think more deeply about what causes and maintains their

http://dx.doi.org/10.1037/14345-013
Helping Skills: Facilitating Exploration, Insight, and Action, Fourth Edition, by C. E. Hill

problems. Furthermore, they help clients develop their own insights because discovered insights are typically better than those that are imposed. The skills that helpers use to facilitate insight are open questions and probes for insight, interpretations, and disclosures of insight.

Open Questions and Probes for Insight

Some clients come up with insights on their own if granted the space and support to do so. They just need helpers to give them permission to be curious and to join them in the process of trying to figure out what is going on. Open questions and probes for insight, which are questions or probes that invite clients to think about deeper meanings for their thoughts, feelings, or behaviors, can be used for this purpose (see Exhibit 13.1). These questions and probes gently guide the client to explore and become curious about possible explanations. These open questions and probes might be phrased in the following ways:

- "What are your thoughts about what is going on there?"
- "What do you make of your feelings about the ending of the relationship?"

EXHIBIT 13.1

Overview of Open Questions and Probes for Insight

Definition	*Open questions and probes* for insight invite clients to think about deeper meanings for their thoughts, feelings, or behaviors.
Examples	"What is your understanding about your lack of interest in sex?"
	"What do you think might be going on when you compulsively want to eat?"
Typical helper intentions	To promote insight (see Web Form D)
Possible client reactions	Clear, feelings (see Web Form G)
Desired client behaviors	Recounting, affective exploration (see Web Form H)
Helpful hints	Convey empathy and curiosity with your questions.
	Make sure your questions are open instead of closed.
	Avoid multiple questions.
	Focus on the client rather than on others.
	Observe client reactions to your questions.

■ "What connection do you make between your feelings and the event?"

Open questions and probes for insight are similar to those used for thoughts and feelings (see Chapters 8 and 9). The only difference is that the focus is on asking the client to think about insight rather than about thoughts or feelings. As discussed with open questions and probes for thoughts and feelings, open questions and probes for insight should be done gently and with an air of curiosity. The helper is collaboratively inquiring and helping the client to think about insight. Helpers do not ask too many questions at one time, do give clients time to respond, and vary questions with other skills so that they do not sound repetitive.

Whereas open questions are phrased in the form of a question (e.g., "What are your thoughts about that?"), probes are phrased in the form of a statement or directive (e.g., "Tell me more about your thoughts"). The phrasing is different, but the intent for both is to facilitate exploration.

One way to develop open questions and probes is to think about aspects of the narrative that do not quite fit. For example, in one session when a client was talking about her inexplicable and sudden bursts of anger at her boyfriend, the helper asked, "What is it about your boyfriend that allows you to blow up at him?" and then later "What might be some reasons that he doesn't deserve your respect?" These questions came directly from what the client was talking about and helped the client think about her anger in a different way.

Although I advised against asking "why" questions in the exploration stage, they are more appropriate in the insight stage if done tentatively and infrequently. Because the aim of the insight stage is to achieve insight, it can be useful to ask clients about their understanding, as long as helpers are careful not to sound blaming, accusatory, or demanding. Again, the goal is for the helper and the client to work together to construct meanings, so helpers need to be respectful, gentle, and genuinely eager to help the client attain insight when asking "why" questions. So rather than demandingly saying, "Why do you do that?" in an accusatory tone, the helper might empathically say, "I wonder if you could think about why you do that?" The helper's goal, of course, is to stimulate curiosity rather than defensiveness.

Open questions and probes for insight are ideal as a first step into the interpretive process because they allow helpers to find out what clients think and give clients a chance to integrate what they have learned in the exploration stage. Interspersed with open questions and probes, helpers can use a few interpretations and disclosures of insight.

Interpretations

Interpretations are interventions that go beyond what a client has overtly stated or recognized and present a new meaning, reason, or explanation for behaviors, thoughts, or feelings so clients can see problems in a new way (see Exhibit 13.2). Interpretations can work in the following ways:

- make connections between seemingly isolated statements or events (e.g., "Could your anger at your husband right now be connected to your grief over your mother's death?");
- point out themes or patterns in a client's behaviors, thoughts, or feelings (e.g., "It seems that you get fired from every job after about 6 months. I wonder if somehow your fear of success makes it difficult for you to keep a job longer");
- explicate defenses, resistance, or transference (e.g., "I wonder if you're expecting me to respond like your father does"); and
- offer a new framework or explanation to understand behaviors, thoughts, feelings, or problems (e.g., "You say you were spoiled as a child, but it seems to me that you often felt abandoned and anxious as a child and that leads you to cling to other people").

RATIONALE FOR GIVING INTERPRETATIONS

Interpretations can provide clients with a conceptual framework that explains their problems and offers a rationale for overcoming their concerns. Frank and Frank (1991) noted that interpretations increase clients' sense of security, mastery, and self-efficacy by providing labels for experiences that seem confusing, haphazard, or inexplicable. Frank and Frank asserted that interpretations relieve distress in part by relabeling client emotions to make them more understandable. They noted that the inexplicable loses much of its power to terrify when it is put in words. For example, if a helper interprets that Pablo's vague uneasiness at work is anger at the boss, who is a stand-in for the client's father, Pablo's uneasiness loses its power. Pablo is no longer unrealistically angry at his boss and instead can work on his feelings toward his father.

From a psychoanalytic perspective (e.g., Bibring, 1954; Blanck, 1966; Freud, 1914/1953b; Fromm-Reichmann, 1950), interpretations are used infrequently but are the "pure gold" of therapy—the central technique for producing self-knowledge and change in clients. Psychoanalytic therapists create interpretations from client material that has been repressed and is unconscious. They postulate that interpretations are effective because they stimulate insight, which can lead

EXHIBIT 13.2

Overview of Interpretation

Definition	An *interpretation* is a statement that goes beyond what the client has overtly stated or recognized and gives a new meaning, reason, or explanation for behaviors, thoughts, or feelings so the client can see problems in a new way.
Examples	"Maybe you don't want to clean your room or do your work because you're angry with your mother."
	"Ever since your friend committed suicide, you have been on edge and having a hard time coping. I wonder if you feel responsible for her death?"
	"I wonder if I remind you of your father. You said he acts like he knows everything."
	"Perhaps you're trying to get her to distrust you so you can get angry and leave. Otherwise it might be too hard to leave since she's alone."
Typical helper intentions	To promote insight, to identify and intensify feelings, to encourage self-control (see Web Form D)
Possible client reactions	Better self-understanding, new perspective, clear, relief, negative thoughts or feelings, responsibility, unstuck, scared, worse, stuck, lack of direction, confused, misunderstood (see Web Form G)
Desired client behaviors	Insight, cognitive–behavioral exploration, affective exploration (see Web Form H)
Helpful hints	Interpretations should be done carefully, gently, respectfully, thoughtfully, empathically, and infrequently.
	Make sure that client is ready for an interpretation. Carefully observe client reactions.
	Work collaboratively with clients to construct the interpretations.
	Keep the interpretation short.
	Follow up interpretations with open questions asking the client about his or her reactions.

to more reality-oriented feelings and behavior. Interpretations are thought to work by replacing unconscious processes with conscious ones, thus enabling clients to resolve unconscious conflicts. Although the exact mechanism through which insight works is vague and needs further explication, it is clear that insight plays a central role in the therapeutic change process.

In psychoanalytic theory, the role of early childhood is important because it serves as the template for everything that comes afterward. Hence, early childhood experiences are often the focus of interpretive behavior, although the childhood events that are focused on vary for different theorists. For Freudians (Freud, 1940/1949), the crucial early childhood event is the Electra–Oedipal conflict, in which the child seeks to have a romantic alliance with the parent of the opposite gender and to eliminate the parent of the same gender; the child must resolve this conflict to progress to maturity. Erikson (1963) postulated that the important early childhood events are interpersonal relationships, although he also believed that identity continues to develop across the life span. For Mahler (1968), the important early childhood event involves the symbiosis with the primary caregivers in very early years and the subsequent movement toward separation and individuation. Bowlby (1969, 1988) believed that attachment to the caregiver is the crucial event in childhood.

Because psychoanalytic helpers believe that early childhood relationships form the foundation for all ensuing relationships, interpreting the transference (i.e., a distortion by the client of the helper based on early childhood relationships) is an important type of interpretation. The assumption is that the client recreates the problematic early relationship patterns with the helper either as a way to confirm or reject that the helper will act in the same way as the early caregiver (Weiss, Sampson, & the Mount Zion Psychotherapy Research Group, 1986). The client might sometimes act as he or she did as a child (the passive victim) and expect the helper to play the complementary role (the dominant or oppressive dictator). Conversely, the client might sometimes take on the role that the parent played in the relationship (the dominant one) and expect the helper to act like the client did as a child (the passive victim). The helper's reaction to the client's behavior is crucial for confirming or disconfirming the client's expectations. For example, the helper might say to Amanda, "I wonder if you get so furious at me for seeing other clients because you always felt that your mother preferred your brother to you, and you don't like to have to share me with other clients."

Although psychoanalytic theory is the basis for our thinking about using interpretations, other theoretical orientations also use interpretations but postulate different mechanisms by which they work. From an information-processing perspective, Levy (1963) suggested that interpretations reveal discrepancies between the views of the therapist and client. In other words, an interpretation makes it clear that the helper has a different perspective than the client. The helper does not "buy" the client's view about the issue and postulates a different explanation. If there is a discrepancy in perspectives, the client has three choices: to change in the direction of the helper's viewpoint, to try to change the helper's mind, or to discredit the helper. If the client resolves the discrepancy in the direction of the helper's interpretation, the client is able to reconstrue how she or he views the issue. Research has shown that clients are more likely to change in the direction of the helper's interpretation if they view the helper as expert, attractive, and trustworthy (Strong & Claiborn, 1982).

An example may help to illustrate the information-processing perspective. Joe explained his depression as a chemical imbalance and thus sought help as a way to get medication. His helper suggested instead that Joe's depression was due to unresolved feelings about his mother's suicide and subsequent abandonment by his father. Because Joe valued the helper's opinion, he struggled to understand what the helper was saying about his depression. Initially, he argued with the helper, but then came to agree that in fact he did have anger at both of his parents. By shifting his perspective, he was then able to engage in the helping process to work through his feelings about his parents.

Cognitive psychologists (e.g., Glass & Holyoak, 1986; Medin & Ross, 1992) also construe the effectiveness of interpretations in different terms than do psychoanalytic theorists. Cognitive theorists believe that all thoughts, feelings, sensations, memories, and actions are stored in *schemas* (i.e., clusters of related thoughts, feelings, actions, and images). With interpretations, helpers attempt to change the way that schemas are structured. They bring back the memories and try to come to new understandings about them on the basis of more current and complete information. In effect, the schemas are changed and restructured. The client has a new way of thinking, which must be reinforced or else it erodes. Hence, repeated interpretations with expansions to different areas of the client's life may be necessary for the connections to be made and retained. In addition, action and behavior change may be necessary to consolidate the changes in thinking. In fact, new research on the brain suggests that there may actually be neurological changes in the brain resulting from psychotherapy (Etkin, Pittenger, Polam, & Kandel, 2005). These exciting findings suggest that memories that are raised and reexperienced in a new way get laid down differently back into brain, supporting the cognitive psychologists' theories about schema change.

An example for schemas relates to Katerina, who came to realize that she was lacking in self-esteem because she felt neglected as a child. However, she needed further interpretive work to understand the influences of the childhood experiences on her current life and change her schemas. In addition, making changes in her behaviors (e.g., getting a new job and leaving an abusive relationship) helped her begin to think more highly of herself and led her to understand why she had stayed in such a bad situation for so long. So interpretive work helped Katerina change her schemas (ways of thinking), and then action helped to reinforce or consolidate the schematic changes (connections).

Yet another perspective comes from narrative therapy, which suggests that we rewrite our stories in more productive ways in the helping process. In the exploration stage, helpers work with clients to tell their narratives, and then they use challenges to disrupt problematic narratives; finally, they use interpretations to help clients rewrite their narratives and to think about their concerns in new ways. For example, because in her family Joanna was cast in the role of the one who had to take care of the younger siblings after her father died, she might have come to tell herself that she could not expect much out of life. Because the helper helped her understand the role of her father's death, she was able to rewrite the narrative into a new way of thinking about her family and how she wanted to be in current relationships.

To conclude this section, I should note that there is not enough evidence to support any one of these theories over the others. In fact, interpretations could work for all the reasons: because the unconscious is made conscious and more under ego control, because discrepancies between perspectives propel clients to change in the direction of resolving the discrepancy, because interpretations cause changes in schematic connections, because reprocessing memories helps change brain structures, and because we rewrite the narratives in more adaptive ways.

SOURCES OF DATA FOR DEVELOPING INTERPRETATIONS

There are several sources of data that helpers can use for developing interpretations: verbal content of clients' speech, past experiences, interpersonal patterns, defenses, developmental stages, existential concerns and spiritual issues, and unconscious activities.

Verbal Content of Clients' Speech

A rich source of data for developing interpretations is in making connections in the content of what clients talk about. Given that people often compartmentalize things, listening carefully to what they say can reveal connections between relevant things that they have not put together. For example, if a client says she is having a hard time performing at her job and then goes on to talk about the seemingly unrelated topic of anxiety over her parents' health, the helper might connect the two if it seems probable that they are related (e.g., "Perhaps you're having a hard time concentrating at work because of anxiety about your parents' health").

Past Experiences

Helpers can speculate about how a client's behaviors is influenced by interactions in the past with significant others. When the client's responses to the helper seem distorted because of experiences with others in the past or present, helpers have material for making a transference interpretation. For example, Keisha responded with silence and tears every time her helper provided positive feedback. Silence and tears are not typical responses to positive feedback, so the helper made some guesses about what might be going on with Keisha. The helper knew about Keisha's history with her father and suggested that perhaps Keisha was afraid of what might follow positive feedback, given that her father often told her something good and then yelled at her for her mistakes. (More discussion of transference interpretations is available in several texts: Basch, 1980; Freud, 1923/1961; Gelso & Carter, 1985, 1994; Greenson, 1967; Malan, 1976a, 1976b; Stadter, 1996; Strupp & Binder, 1984.)

Transferences occur to other people in clients' lives. For example, Alan was having extreme angry reactions to his female boss. As we talked about these reactions, Alan described his boss in terms that were very similar to those he used when talking about his mother. When I gently wondered if his boss reminded him of his mother, he was able to see the connection and could then understand why he was having trouble interacting with her. The research suggests that transference interpretations work best with clients who are functioning pretty well, especially in terms of interpersonal relationships (Crits-Christoph & Gibbons, 2002). These findings suggest that helpers need to be careful about using such interpretations with distressed clients.

Interpersonal Patterns

Another way of developing interpretations is to look at the client's typical style of interacting and conceptualize what the client is trying to accomplish in these interactions. The core conflictual relationship theme method (Book, 1998; Luborsky & Crits-Christoph, 1990) describes how people engage in typical interpersonal patterns. Conflictual patterns have three components: (1) People have wishes or needs (e.g., the client may wish to control others or to have the approval of others), (2) they expect consistent responses from others (e.g., submission, approval), and (3) they consequently have a response from the self (e.g., depressed, pleased). For example, Keisha might wish for affection and love but also to be in control. She might expect others to hurt and control her as her father did, and hence she might feel anxious and lack confidence. Interpretations can thus be formulated about the client's characteristic way of interacting with others to help the client understand these patterns. Once the client understands the pattern, it is easier to challenge beliefs and make changes in the pattern.

Defenses

Helpers can also provide interpretations based on observations of a client's defenses, for example, "I wonder if your difficulty at work stems from your avoiding interactions with others, something you learned to do as a child to protect yourself from fears of abandonment." In the previous chapter on challenges, helpers were encouraged to point out defenses to raise the client's awareness of them. Now the helper can work with the client to understand the role that defenses play. People develop defenses early in life to help them cope with situations but then may fail to give up the defenses that are no longer needed. It is perhaps hardest to give up things that we believe protect us from harm, given that we perceive that these defenses protected us in the past. Through interpretive activity, helpers can help clients realize why they started using defenses and then make choices about the need to continue using them. For example, while Jon was talking about his inability to find a romantic relationship, the helper found himself feeling sleepy. After fighting off the sleepiness, the helper became curious and wondered to himself whether Jon was using a defense by speaking in a monotone to keep away his anxiety. Thus, the helper gently challenged Jon to bring this defense into awareness (e.g., "You know, I can't help but notice that when you start to talk about romantic relationships, you start talking in a monotone, and it's difficult to listen to you. Have you noticed a change in your behavior when you feel anxious?"). Jon was intrigued but could not think of what might be going on. After a pause to give Jon a chance to reflect, the helper gently speculated, "I wonder if talking about romantic relationships is hard for you because of your anger over your parents and how they handled their divorce and made you feel like you had to take sides?"

Developmental Stages

An additional source of material for interpretations is the client's life stage, within the context of his or her culture. Are clients on or off course for mastering the developmental tasks that are important for them in their cultural context (e.g., developing friendships, separating from parents, completing schooling, making decisions about life partners and children, developing a satisfying career, developing satisfying adult relationships, letting go of children and careers, adjusting to illnesses and dying)? Interpretations can be developed linking clients' current emotions and functioning to what they might be expected to be feeling or not feeling at this stage of life within their culture. For example, Ken, a 50-year-old White man, might feel depressed because he compares himself with other people his age who have accomplished more in their lives. He dropped out of high school to rebel against his parents, who were both physicians, and worked in construction his whole life; now he wonders if he made the right choices. As another example, as Melania turns 35 and is not involved in a serious romantic relationship, she is feeling anxious about whether she will ever be able to have children.

In thinking about developmental stages, it is important to recognize that these are somewhat culture-bound. For example, in Asian cultures, it is common for children to live at home through college. And it is becoming more common for young adults in the United States to return home to live with parents after college because they cannot afford the rent on apartments. To impose one's own demand for independence might not be appropriate in such cases.

Existential and Spiritual Issues

Helpers can also help clients understand themselves in terms of existential concerns. Yalom (1980), a well-known existential therapist, provided an excellent description of what he considered to be four universal existential concerns:

Death anxiety. The fact that everyone dies at some point means we all have to come to terms with our mortality. Feelings of vulnerability about death are particularly high at times of transition, when one is ill or has been in an accident or attacked, when a significant other is ill or has recently been hurt or died, or when there has been a recent major disaster. At such times, many people feel especially attuned to loss and death and need to talk about it.

Freedom. Freedom refers to the lack of external structure and the need to take responsibility for one's destiny. When people either have many talents or when they have no specific talents, it can be especially difficult to figure out one's calling and make choices.

Isolation. This includes isolation from both others and the world. Each of us enters and exits the world alone; therefore, we must come to terms with our isolation in contrast to our wish to be part of a larger whole, to be taken care of and protected.

Meaning in life. We must all construct our own life meanings, given that there is no predetermined path. We must all figure out what gives us a sense of purpose, why we want to wake up in the morning, and what legacy we want to leave.

Yalom (1980) noted the benefits of introducing a client with terminal cancer into a therapy group. Having a group member dealing with issues of death brings up the existential issues more saliently for the rest of the group members. But Yalom also noted that clients in individual work frequently give clues about existential concerns if helpers just pay attention. For example, clients complain about physical aches and pains, of aging, of not being able to do what they used to do, of not knowing what to do with their time, of wanting to leave a legacy, about the death of a pet, or of wondering about spirituality. All of these topics can be explored further to help people deal with existential crises. Interestingly, Yalom suggested that clients often feel more rather than less anxious after talking about existential issues because they realize they cannot control many things in life. But we hope that through talking about existential issues rather than defending against them, they gain in terms of living more meaningful lives.

Note that culture clearly plays a role in existential concerns, particularly in terms of religious beliefs. A person who believes in life after death will probably experience less death anxiety than will someone who does not believe in life after death. By listening carefully and nonjudgmentally to what clients say and asking them about relevant cultural beliefs, helpers can often hear underlying existential concerns and then assist clients, via interpretation, to understand these critical issues.

Unconscious Sources

Interpretations can be developed through indications of unconscious activities, most typically observable through dreams, fantasies, and slips of the tongue. Psychoanalytic theorists have long postulated that important unconscious material can be detected by looking at these manifestations. For example, if a client accidentally uses a former boyfriend's name when talking about her current boyfriend, one could wonder aloud with her whether there was some significance to the slip. Or if a client has a dream about the helper, this presents the helper with an ideal opportunity to look at what the client might be thinking about the helper. Similarly, if the helper has a dream about a client, this presents a valuable learning opportunity for the helper to speculate about the client, although helpers rarely reveal such dreams to clients, especially if they involve the helper's own unresolved personal issues (see Hill et al., 2013; Spangler, Hill, Mettus, Guo, & Heymsfield, 2009). For more detail on how helpers can work with dreams, I refer readers to a companion text that also uses the three-stage model (Hill, 2004) and a DVD demonstration of the dream model (American Psychological Association, with Hill, C. E., 2013).

ACCURACY OF INTERPRETATIONS

For psychoanalytic theorists, the accuracy of the helper's interpretation is important. The client and helper are on an "archeological dig" to uncover what actually happened in the client's past and understand how these events affect the client's current behavior. Of course, psychoanalytic therapists emphasize that what they hear in therapy is the client's perceptions about the events rather than actual events.

The problem is that accuracy can never be determined. We cannot go back and see what actually happened in the client's life, and even if we could, we would not know how the client absorbed the experiences. We know that people perceive events idiosyncratically and then distort memories of events over time (Glass & Holyoak, 1986; Loftus, 1988). Research shows that people can "remember" events that never happened (Brainerd & Reyna, 1998), so helpers need to be careful not to try to persuade clients that they have certain memories (e.g., repressed memories about childhood sexual abuse).

Many psychoanalysts have struggled with this dilemma about accuracy. Reid and Finesinger (1952) suggested that insight must merely be believed or make sense to have a therapeutic effect. They thought that the psychological relevance of the interpretation to the client's problems is more important than the truth per se (i.e., does the interpretation help the client understand more about his or her problems?). Similarly, Frank and Frank (1991) noted that interpretations do not have to be correct, only plausible. As an example, they cited a study by Mendel (1964) in which four clients responded with a drop in anxiety when they were offered the same series of six "all-purpose" interpretations (e.g., "You seem to live your life as though you are apologizing all the time").

I do not suggest that helpers ignore the "truth" and just have a set of standard interpretations to give clients. Quite the opposite: I believe that helpers should try as much as possible to develop interpretations that fit all of the information that clients present. Helpers should remain humble, however, about how difficult it is to know all the data and to determine whether an interpretation is accurate.

Basch (1980), a psychoanalytic therapist, indicated that whether clients agree or disagree with an interpretation is not a good indication of accuracy. Rather, he suggested, the criterion for accuracy should be whether clients subsequently bring up material that indicates they have gained insight into the problem. For example, if a helper interprets fear of intimacy as being based on feeling rejected by his father, the helper could conclude that the interpretation was facilitative (a better criterion than accuracy) if Lao brings in additional memories of his father being distant and rejecting. I would caution, however, that clients sometimes bring in (and even make up) memories to please their helpers.

Frank and Frank (1991) further noted that the client is the ultimate judge of the truth of the interpretation. They suggested that the helper's power to present an interpretation that is accepted by the client as valid depends on several factors:

- whether the interpretation makes sense out of all the material the client has offered;
- the manner in which the interpretation is offered—interpretations must be presented in ways that catch and hold the client's attention, such as with vivid imagery and metaphor, because clients need to be in a state of emotional arousal to be able to make use of interpretations;
- the client's confidence in the helper; and
- the beneficial consequences for the client's ability to function and for the client's sense of well-being.

In sum, as helpers we can never really determine the accuracy of interpretations. Thus, I suggest that perceived helpfulness is the important criterion for evaluating interpretations. The following criteria may be used for determining whether interpretations are helpful for clients:

- When an interpretation is helpful, the client typically feels a sense of "aha," of learning something that "clicks," and has a feeling that things make sense in a new way.
- Clients typically have a feeling of energy and excitement about their new discoveries, particularly when they feel they have discovered the insight themselves.
- Clients present additional important information that confirms the insight.
- Clients start thinking about what to do differently based on the insight.

In short, when interpretations are helpful, clients arrive at personally relevant insights and can use these insights to talk more deeply about problems (emotional insight) and move to action. In contrast, when interpretations are not helpful, the client might become silent, change the topic, feel misunderstood, feel angry or upset, or dismiss the therapist.

HOW TO INTERPRET

The major task is to engage in an interpretive process in such a way that the client and helper are working together to construct interpretations. As with challenges, interpretations should be done carefully, gently, respectfully, thoughtfully, empathically, and infrequently.

If you decide that a client is ready for interpretive work, you might begin by asking the client for her or his interpretation (e.g., "What do you make of your flunking out of school even though you are obviously very bright?"; "How do you make sense of your reluctance to retire even though your wife keeps pressuring you to do so?"). Asking clients for their interpretations before providing them with your thinking encourages clients to think about themselves, gets helpers out of the position of being the ones who provide all the interpretations, gives helpers more information from which to formulate interpretations, and allows helpers to assess clients' current level of insight.

If the client seems interested and engaged in the insight process, the helper might give a gentle, tentative interpretation to augment or extend the client's initial understanding. Helpers can develop these gentle, tentative interpretations by paying attention to what the client is half saying, saying in a confused way, or saying implicitly. The client may have almost put it all together and may only need a little help to begin to integrate the pieces.

Helpers should view this initial interpretation as a working hypothesis, which will be revised as the interpretive process ensues and more information is gathered. The purpose of the initial tentative interpretation is to help the client take the next step in the interpretive process and think about the reasons for his or her behavior.

The helper and client work together to construct insights that the client can hear and assimilate. The process is a creative attempt to understand a puzzling phenomenon. Natterson (1993) stressed that when a helper who wants to exert power over a client offers a shocking interpretation of a dream, it usually has an antitherapeutic effect because it discourages the client from sharing dreams. Similarly, Reik (1935) emphasized the deep, collaborative nature of the therapeutic encounter. He suggested that insights that clients construct as a result of interpretations should come as a surprise to both the helper and client, rather than because the helper has forced a predetermined interpretation on the client. Basch (1980) likewise noted that interpretations that are too obvious, easy, simplistic, or superficial are usually trivial or wrong, whereas the important insights are those that come as a surprise to both client and helper.

After effective interpretations, a client typically adds new information or suggests alternative interpretations. This new exploration is wonderful and gives a clear indication that the client is responding well to the interpretative process. Helpers can respond by reflecting feelings or asking open questions and probes to draw out the client's thoughts.

On the other hand, if a client does not respond or rejects an interpretation (says "Yes, but . . . "), the helper needs to reevaluate the situation. If the helper thinks the interpretation was right but the client was not yet ready to hear it, the helper can return to the interpretation at a later stage when she or he thinks the client is more able to tolerate insight (interpretations sometimes are painful to hear). If the helper is wrong (which is possible because helpers never have all the relevant information), the helper can use exploration skills to obtain more understanding of the client before attempting again to interpret. Alternatively, helpers can ask clients to provide an interpretation that fits for them. The key here is to be nondefensive and eager to work with the client collaboratively.

If the client accepts the interpretation and adds new information, the helper can extend the interpretation to a variety of situations to help the client reach greater understanding. For example, if the interpretation involves the client being unorganized and sloppy as a reaction to an overly neat and compulsive mother, the helper can extend this insight to how the client is messy in her apartment, unorganized in terms of her studying behavior, and late for appointments. By talking about all these areas, the client is more likely to begin to understand herself. Extending the interpretation to a number of situations also generalizes the learning, making it more likely that the client will begin to incorporate changes in thinking.

After hearing more from the client in reaction to the initial interpretation, the helper can summarize or offer a reformulated interpretation. The new interpretation might lead the client to new material that confirms or denies the validity of the reformulated interpretation. Thus, rather than helpers having and delivering the "correct" interpretations to clients, the helper and client work together to create or construct interpretations. This collaborative process requires that helpers be invested in the interpretive process rather than in specific interpretations, so they can revise interpretations when clients offer new information, explanations, or ideas.

Interpretations can be phrased as a direct statement (e.g., "You are worried about whether you should get married, so you are diverting your anxiety about getting married into trying to make the wedding perfect"); phrased more tentatively (e.g., "I wonder if your fear of failure could possibly be related to feeling that you are not sure you can please your mother"); or phrased as a question (e.g., "Could it be that you distrust men because of your bad relationship with your father?"). Although the last intervention is phrased as a question, it is clearly an interpretation because the content of the question assumes a relationship that the client had not articulated and provides an explanation for the behavior.

The phrasing of interpretations is crucial to their acceptance by clients. Phrasing the interpretation tentatively and without jargon makes it easier for clients to understand. For example, "I wonder if you might be afraid of what I say because I remind you of your mother, who was sometimes mean to you" is easier for a client to hear than "Your transference of your Oedipal rage onto me has caused you to distort my meaning." The latter interpretation is difficult for most clients to hear because it is stated too definitely and with too much jargon.

Psychoanalytic theorists suggest that it is important to provide interpretations that are not too far beyond what clients already have recognized (e.g., Speisman, 1959). If interpretations are too deep, clients cannot understand what the helper is talking about; interpretations that are slightly beyond the client's awareness make more sense to the client and give the client a manageable stimulus for thinking. In the first session with a client who procrastinates, for example, the helper might not want to interpret the cause of the procrastination back to early childhood events because the client may not be ready to hear such an interpretation. Instead, the helper might interpret just beyond the client awareness to gently encourage the client to go to slightly new levels of understanding (e.g., "Perhaps it's hard for you to study because you're afraid of succeeding"). Later, when the client is comfortable with this thought, the helper might push for deeper interpretations, such as the client's reluctance to supersede his or her parents.

EXAMPLES OF INTERPRETATION

A wonderful example of the whole working-through process comes from Hill, Thompson, and Mahalik (1989) in their examination of a single case of successful brief psychotherapy. The middle-aged client was the middle of 16 children. Her mother had married at a very young age; when her husband (the client's father) died, the mother abandoned the children. The client was divorced with three children and was depressed, blaming herself for being "spoiled." At the end of the therapy, the therapist and client both indicated that the most important interpretation was that the client's current difficulties resulted from a difficult childhood and inadequate parenting. Interpretations occurred only in the last half of the 12-session therapy, were of moderate depth, seemed to be accurate, and were interspersed with approval-reassurance, questions, restatements, and reflections aimed at catharsis. The therapist repeated the interpretation many times and applied it to many situations, which she referred to in postsession interviews as "chipping away" at the client's defenses. The client not only accepted the interpretation but also slowly began to incorporate it into her thinking (i.e., she changed from seeing herself as spoiled to seeing herself as neglected). The interpretation enabled her to disclose painful secrets (e.g., her father's attempted suicide and subsequent hospitalization in a mental institution). Finally, the therapist began to pair the interpretation with a suggestion that the client was a good parent to her children and thus could parent herself. The interpretation helped the client come to a greater self-understanding and, together with the direct guidance about parenting herself, enabled her to change in some fundamental ways (e.g., become a better parent, obtain a job, and begin an intimate relationship).

Here is another example with dialogue (interpretations are in italics). Note that the helper explores the problem before interpreting.

> *Client:* Lately, when I'm in church, I have been getting very anxious. I have been starting to panic when we have to hold hands to say a prayer. My palms get very sweaty, and I feel very embarrassed. I start worrying about it so much ahead of time that I cannot concentrate on the church service. I just don't understand why I should get so nervous. I wish I could understand it, though, because it is making my experience of going to church very unpleasant.
>
> *Helper:* It sounds like you feel upset about it.
>
> *Client:* I do. I feel foolish. I mean, who cares about my sweaty palms? I'm sure the other people are just interested in going to church and don't really care about me. I don't know the people very well though, because I just started going to this church when I moved here this fall.
>
> *Helper:* Tell me a little bit about the role of the church in your life.
>
> *Client:* I was hoping to have a community like we had in my hometown. I need something apart from the people I know at work. But it hasn't worked out. I haven't really met anyone there yet.
>
> *Helper:* So you just moved here and have been hoping to make friends in church.
>
> *Client:* Church was always important in my family. I don't know how much I believe in the religion, but I do feel a need for the connection that you get in church.
>
> *Helper:* So you want to make friends and find a community, but you also feel some ambivalence and you're not sure what you believe.
>
> *Client:* Wow, that is really true. I do feel like I'm supposed to go to church, but I'm not sure I really want to. I feel like my parents expect me to go. But I don't quite know what I believe. I haven't taken the time to figure out what I believe separate from what my parents told me to believe.
>
> *Helper:* *I wonder if worrying about your sweaty palms takes your mind off thinking about what you believe.*
>
> *Client:* Yeah, that's a good point. I sure cannot listen to much of the sermon if I'm worried about the person next to me and what they will think of me.

> *Helper:*   *Perhaps going to this new church is difficult because it reminds you so much of your family and what you were supposed to do as a child.*
>
> *Client:*   You're right. I feel like I've been trying to establish myself as an independent person. I moved across country to be on my own and make my own decisions, but I miss my family and my community. I don't know how much I want to be here. I feel like I'm struggling with trying to figure out who I am and what I want out of life. (Client continues to explore.)

DIFFICULTIES IN USING INTERPRETATION

Some helpers are hesitant to interpret because it feels intrusive to "poke around in clients' heads." They fear that their interpretations will be wrong or premature, will upset or anger clients, or will harm the therapeutic relationship. They err on the side of passivity and do not offer any of their own thoughts to the interpretive exchange. In addition, some helpers feel unable to put all the pieces together to formulate interpretations. If you feel this way, you might practice trying to understand your own behavior, focus more on asking the clients to come up with their own interpretations, and have patience that more interpretive ability will come with practice. I also suggest further readings in psychoanalytic theory (e.g., Basch, 1980; McWilliams, 2004; Summers & Barber, 2010).

Other helpers are too eager to give interpretations and err on the side of aggressiveness. The interpretation process brings out the worst in some helpers. They become invested in the intellectual challenge of figuring out clients and are eager to use their powers of insight. They lose sight of the need for empathy and a strong therapeutic relationship and charge into putting all the pieces of the puzzle together. I agree that people are infinitely intriguing, interesting, and fun to figure out, but helpers must temper such sentiments with a strong compassion for clients and a desire to help clients understand themselves.

I caution helpers in the use and potential abuse of interpretations because they can be powerful interventions. Helpers have the responsibility to use such power appropriately. I also caution helpers that clients may agree with interpretations because they want to please, but they may actually disagree with the interpretations and can feel wounded by them. Helpers thus need to observe client reactions and ask clients about their reactions.

Helpers also need to be careful to encourage clients to become actively involved in collaborating on constructing interpretations. In addition, timing is important, because clients need to be able to hear the interpretations and can build on them in constructing their own understandings.

Another problem helpers have is giving too many interpretations in one session. Clients often need time to absorb and think about each interpretation, so helpers should gauge their pace on the basis of clients' reactions.

Disclosures of Insight

Olga was emotional and upset when she revealed that her husband had left her for a younger woman. She felt abandoned and humiliated and did not want any of her friends to know that her husband had left. She talked in her helping session about feeling depressed, isolated, alone, and hopeless, and she said that she was too old to start over. The helper said, "You know, I got divorced several years ago, and I never thought I would recover. I came to realize that I had believed my worth was dependent on whether I had a man, rather than who I was. I wonder if that's true for you?" Olga was momentarily taken aback, and then said, "I never thought of it that way. I think you may be right. I was always taught that I needed to be married, and so I never prepared for anything else." The helper's disclosure thus enabled Olga to have an "aha" experience and think about why she was so upset about her husband's leaving her. She did not really miss him; they had not been getting along well for many years. Instead, she missed the sense of security that being married gave her. Once she understood that about herself, she could begin to adjust to the divorce.

In another example, Angela was a new mother who was having trouble getting back to a sexual relationship with her husband after the baby's birth. The helper disclosed that when she had been a new mother, it was gratifying to have the baby's affection and wondered if perhaps Angela was shifting all her attention from the husband to the baby. Because they had a good relationship and the helper was a mother, Angela was able to think about the possibility without feeling pathologized.

A disclosure of insight reveals an understanding the helper has learned about himself or herself and is used to facilitate the client's understanding of his or her thoughts, feelings, behaviors, and issues (see Exhibit 13.3). Instead of using challenges or interpretations, helpers share insights that they have learned about themselves in the hope of encouraging clients to think about themselves at a deeper level. Remember, though, that the intention is to facilitate client insight rather than to further the helper's understanding of himself or herself (refer back to discussion of disclosures in Chapters 8 and 9).

Some students confuse disclosures of insight with other types of disclosures. The key feature here is that the helper has a hint about an

EXHIBIT 13.3

Overview of Disclosure of Insight

Definition	*Disclosure of insight* refers to the helper's presentation of a personal experience (not in the immediate relationship) in which he or she gained some insight.
Examples	"In the past, I often did not want others to feel upset by my successes, so I would underplay anything I did well. I wonder if that happens for you?"
	"I indulge in some bad habits just like you. I know they're bad habits, but just like you, I don't want to change them. I discovered that I just don't like the feeling of anyone controlling me because my mother was very controlling. Does that fit for you?"
Typical helper intentions	To promote insight, to deal with resistance, to challenge, to relieve the therapist's needs (see Web Form D)
Possible client reactions	Understood, supported, hopeful, relief, negative thoughts or behaviors, better self-understanding, clear, feelings, unstuck, new perspective, educated, new ways to behave, scared, worse, confused, misunderstood (see Web Form G)
Desired client behaviors	Insight, affective exploration, cognitive–behavioral exploration (see Web Form H)
Helpful hints	Make sure that your intentions are to help the client gain insight rather than to get attention for your own problems.
	Choose things to reveal that seem similar to what the client is going through.
	Keep it short.
	Do not reveal things about yourself that have not been mostly resolved (i.e., about which you still feel troubled).
	Make sure to turn the focus back to the client after disclosing.

insight that might help the client and uses his or her experience to present this in a more tentative way than an interpretation.

WHY USE DISCLOSURE OF INSIGHT?

Helpers disclose their experiences to help clients attain realizations of which they had not been aware. This type of disclosure is useful when clients are stuck or are having a hard time achieving deep levels of self-understanding on their own. For example, if a client is talking about everything being just fine after leaving her abusive husband, but the helper suspects that the client has a lot of underlying turmoil, the helper might say, "I remember feeling like I wasn't sure if I made the right decision after I left my partner. It was real scary for me because my parents never allowed me to make my own decisions so I didn't trust myself. I wonder if something like that is true for you?" The helper hopes the client will understand more about herself by hearing about the helper's experience.

A reason for using disclosures of insight is to enable clients to hear things in a less threatening way than might happen with therapist challenges or interpretations. Hearing a disclosure such as "I also feel like a child when I go to visit my parents because I lose my identity and don't know who I am" or "I also have a hard time going to movies by myself because I feel like nobody loves me" provides an opportunity for clients to think about whether they have similar reasons for their behaviors. Rather than asserting an interpretation that may offend the client, helpers disclose personal insights and ask whether these insights might fit for the client, thus possibly facilitating new and deeper insight. By using disclosure, the helper admits that the insight may be a projection and allows the client to see if it fits. As with tentative interpretations, helpers are hoping that clients will feel freer to look for underlying reasons after they have heard helpers disclosing their insights. Thus, disclosures can have a modeling effect.

In addition, disclosures can alter the power balance of the helping relationship and lead to greater client participation. Rather than helpers being the experts with the answers and clients relying on helpers to solve their problems, disclosures make clear that helpers are also human and grapple with difficult concerns. In addition, in dyads in which cultures differ, disclosures can bridge the gap and make clients feel that their helpers understand them.

HOW TO DISCLOSE ABOUT INSIGHT

Helpers need to think honestly about their intentions before disclosing. If they had an experience that could help clients understand more about themselves, it might be useful to disclose it for all the reasons noted above. Disclosures should not be used, however, to discuss or solve the helper's problems (e.g., "You think you've got it bad, let me tell you how bad it was for me"). Harm can result if helpers disclose because they have unresolved problems or have a desire to get attention for themselves. In this case, the focus shifts from the client to the helper, perhaps resulting in the client taking care of the helper.

To develop appropriate disclosures, helpers can think about what contributed to their behaviors when they were in situations similar to those of their clients. By focusing on insights they gained about themselves, helpers use their experiences to help clients attain insight. If helpers decide that disclosures are appropriate for the client at a particular moment, they should keep the focus of the disclosure on the insight rather than on recounting details of the experience. For example, rather than talking about the details of how his father died, the helper might say, "When my father died, I didn't know what I was feeling so I relied on everyone to tell me what I should be feeling. In the process, I lost myself. I wonder if that's happening to you?"

When helpers disclose, it is best to choose something that occurred in the past and that has been resolved, resulted in a new perspective, can be helpful to the client, and does not make the helper feel vulnerable. Helpers should be honest about their experiences and should not make up things just to have a disclosure. If they have not had a similar experience that led to a new understanding, they should use a different skill rather than making up something or using a hypothetical example. A fabricated disclosure of insight would be inauthentic and cause great distance with the client. In addition, disclosures that are short and immediately turn the focus back to the client tend to be most effective. Helpers can follow disclosures with open questions and probes about whether the insight fits for the client (e.g., "I wonder how that fits for you?" or "I wonder if anything like that happens for you?").

If a disclosure does not work (e.g., the client denies or disavows having similar experiences or feels uncomfortable knowing information about the helper), it is probably best to refrain from making further disclosures. Several things could have happened. The helper could be right, but the client might not be ready to gain insight. Or the helper could be projecting insight onto the client. In addition, the client could become upset about learning anything personal about the helper because it alters the distance between them. In such instances, the helper can collect more evidence to determine whether the helper's projection, the client's lack of readiness, or the client's need for distance is at issue. If lack of readiness is the problem, the helper can try other skills (e.g., reflection of feelings or challenge). If projection is the problem, the helper can seek supervision or therapy. If the client prefers not to know anything about the helper, the helper can change strategies and limit disclosures. Of course, any extreme reaction should be investigated to assist in understanding and gaining insight into the client's underlying issues.

EXAMPLE OF DISCLOSURE OF INSIGHT

The following example shows a helper using disclosure of insight (in italics) in a session.

Client: I've been thinking a lot about death lately. I'm not thinking of suicide but more about the inevitability of death. There are so many senseless murders lately—the news is full of them. But I cannot quite grasp the idea of death—it doesn't make sense to me. It doesn't seem fair to be killed in the prime of life.

Helper: You sound scared about the idea of dying.

Client: Oh yeah, I really am. I really don't know what happens after death. Of course, my parents' religion talks about heaven and hell, but I can't quite buy all that. But if I don't believe what their religion says, I don't quite know what happens at death. And what is the meaning of life? I mean why are we here, and why does everyone rush around? What difference does it all make? I'm sure this all sounds very confusing, but I've been thinking about it a lot lately.

Helper: No, it makes a lot of sense. I think all of us need to grapple with the meaning of life and the fact that we are going to die. You know, though, let me make a guess about something. *When I have been most concerned about death and meaning in life is when I have been in moments of transition and trying to figure out what I want out of life.* I wonder if that's true for you now?

Client: Hmmm. That's interesting. I am about to turn 30, and it feels like a big turning point for me. I'm in a job I don't really like, and I haven't found the relationship that I always hoped I would find at this point. (Client continues talking about his personal concerns.)

DIFFICULTIES IN USING DISCLOSURES OF INSIGHT

One potential danger in using disclosure is that helpers might inappropriately project their feelings and reactions onto clients. For example, if a client has been talking about getting bad grades and a helper states, "I feel panicked when I get bad grades because I am still afraid of my parents' anger," the helper might have inappropriately projected his or her own insight onto the client. The client might confirm that this projection is not accurate by responding, "No, I feel more like I deserved the bad grade because I didn't study." Helpers need to remember that they are separate from their clients, have different experiences, and their personal insights might not apply to their clients.

Another problem is that some helpers use disclosure to satisfy their urge to reveal themselves, rather than using it intentionally to help clients gain insight. Similarly, some helpers mistake the notion of being open as an opportunity to say whatever is on their minds. Greenberg, Rice, and Elliott (1993) called such impulsive helper openness "promiscuous" disclosure. With these types of disclosures, clients may feel uncomfortable and lose respect for the helper. For example, Mary sought help to address her concerns about divorce. Unfortunately, her helper talked more about her own experiences with divorce than Mary did. Mary terminated and found a different helper who used disclosures more judiciously. Similarly, Greenberg et al. (1993) suggested that disclosures need to be done with disciplined spontaneity on the basis of the helpers' accurate self-awareness of inner experience shared in a facilitative manner at a therapeutically appropriate moment. In other words, helpers need to be aware of themselves and of their intentions and deliver disclosures that are likely to help clients.

Beginning helpers tend to use too many disclosures. As with medical students seeing themselves in all the syndromes described in their medical texts, beginning helpers connect with many of their clients' struggles. They have a hard time setting aside personal issues to focus on their clients' problems. It is indeed difficult to shift from the mutual sharing that ideally occurs in friendships to the reduced amount of sharing that occurs in helping relationships. Paying attention to how a client's problems differ from the helper's can facilitate the helper to differentiate himself or herself from the client and use disclosures judiciously.

Finally, some beginning helpers worry about making their disclosures perfect. They believe that disclosures could have negative effects if not done exactly right. They also worry about sounding patronizing, as if they have figured out everything for themselves whereas clients are still learning. They worry that they would feel too vulnerable and would lose any credibility they have as helpers if they disclose issues they are currently involved in and do not understand completely. Other helpers are concerned that they might not have an appropriate disclosure because they have not faced a similar situation or have not gained any insight into the situation—perhaps they really are in the same boat as the client. I recommend that helpers use other interventions if they feel uncomfortable or vulnerable using disclosures. I would also note that practice under close supervision helps greatly in terms of teaching beginning helpers the bounds of appropriate disclosures.

What Do You Think?

- What role do you think culture plays in the interpretative process?
- When do you think it would be appropriate or inappropriate to offer interpretations, disclosures of insight, and open questions and probes for insight?

- Do you agree about the necessity for developing a collaborative process of constructing interpretations with clients? Why or why not?
- Debate both sides of the idea that interpretations are a necessary prerequisite for change to occur.
- Argue for and against the idea that interpretations are the "pure gold" of helping.
- Discuss whether clients can be taught to be more introspective.
- Debate whether interpretations should only be given after challenges.
- Debate how to determine the accuracy of interpretations.
- What theoretical approach do you prefer as a basis for developing interpretations?
- Discuss the notion that disclosure reduces the power imbalance between helpers and clients. What are the advantages and disadvantages of having a power imbalance in a helping relationship?
- What types of helpers might feel most comfortable disclosing?
- Debate the importance of helper neutrality in the insight stage.

RESEARCH SUMMARY

Accuracy of Interpretations

Citation: Crits-Christoph, P., Cooper, A., & Luborsky, L. (1988). The accuracy of therapists' interpretations and the outcome of dynamic psychotherapy. *Journal of Consulting and Clinical Psychology, 56,* 490–495. doi:10.1037/0022-006X.56.4.490

Rationale: Given that psychodynamic therapists think of interpretations as the supreme agent of therapeutic change, we need to know more about the effects of interpretations. Crits-Christoph et al. argued that it is not just that any interpretations are helpful but rather that interpretations must be accurate. Interpretations were defined as providing reasons for thoughts, feelings, or behaviors and making connections between present circumstances and other life experiences. Accuracy was defined as the congruence between the interpretation and the client's core conflictual relationship themes (CCRT) as identified in narratives about events with others. The CCRT involves the client's wishes or needs toward the other, the response of the other, and the corresponding response of self (e.g., a wish to be close to others, being rejected by others, and consequently feeling lonely, depressed, and anxious).

Method: Clients completed outcome measures before and after therapy (averaging 53 weeks). The core conflictual relationship theme was identified by one set of judges in about 10 relationship narrative episodes in therapy sessions. Interpretations were identified by a separate set of judges in two early sessions of moderate-length psychodynamic therapy. Accuracy of interpretations (congruence between the content of the clients' CCRT and the content of the interpretation) was judged by a third set of judges.

Interesting findings:
- Treatment outcome was better when interpretations were accurate than when interpretations were not accurate.
- Of the three components of accuracy, wishes and responses of other were more related to outcome than were responses of self.

Conclusions:
- Interpretations about the client's persistent interpersonal problems can be helpful.
- It is important to know what the client wishes from another person and how he or she thinks the other person tends to respond.

Implications for Therapy:
- One way to formulate interpretations is by listening carefully when clients talk about what goes on in their relationships, particularly in terms of what they want or need from others and what they typically get back from others. The goal would be to make clients more aware of their typical patterns in relationships.

| BONUS MATERIALS | Practice exercises, labs, and other resources for students and teachers are available on the companion website: http://pubs.apa.org/books/supp/hill4. |

Skills for Immediacy

14

There are, in fact, no more important communications
between one human being and another than those
expressed emotionally, and no information more vital
for constructing and reconstructing working models of
the self and other than information about how each
feels towards the other . . . it is the emotional communications between a patient and his therapist that play the
crucial part.

—*John Bowlby* (1988, pp. 156–157)

Evita constantly got angry at her helper, Angela, and
criticized her for everything she said. Angela began to feel
inadequate and angry at Evita and did not look forward
to sessions. Angela consulted with her supervisor, who
helped her gain compassion for Evita by coming to understand that Evita's personal issues caused her to denigrate
Angela. The supervisor suggested that Angela use immediacy in the next session to let Evita know how she was
feeling. So in the next session, when Evita criticized her
for not saying the right feeling word, Angela said, "You
know, right now I'm feeling badly because it feels like
I cannot do anything right. I feel frustrated because I don't
know how to help you. I wonder how you feel about our
relationship?" Evita broke into tears and said that she
seemed to push everyone away. Angela was able to listen
and reflect that Evita felt criticized. Eventually they came
to realize that Evita pushed people away because she
feared rejection. Using immediacy allowed Angela to help
Evita understand more about how she acted with others,
and its use strengthened the therapeutic relationship.

http://dx.doi.org/10.1037/14345-014
Helping Skills: Facilitating Exploration, Insight, and Action, Fourth Edition,
by C. E. Hill

mmediacy occurs when the helper inquires about the client's feelings about the therapeutic relationship or discloses how she or he is feeling about the client, about self in relation to the client, or about the therapeutic relationship. Kiesler's (1988, 1996) term for immediacy was *metacommunication,* which he said occurs when helpers disclose to clients their perceptions of and reactions to a client's actions. He distinguished metacommunication from other helper disclosures of personal factual or historical information about life experiences because metacommunication relates specifically to the helper's immediate experience of the relationship with the client. Kiesler indicated that metacommunication is one of the most powerful interventions in the helper's repertoire because the helper responds to the client in a different manner from that to which the client is accustomed. Rather than ignoring inappropriate behavior, as is often the case in social interactions, for example, the helper tells the client directly but gently about the impact of the client's behavior on him or her. Similarly, Ivey (1994) called immediacy being "in the moment" with the client. He pointed out that most clients talk in the past tense about events but might profit from talking in the present tense about what is going on in the helping relationship.

Egan (1994) suggested that immediacy can focus on the overall relationship (e.g., "It feels to me that we are getting along well now that we have worked through our initial discomfort"), a specific event in the session (e.g., "I was surprised when you said that you appreciated the sessions because I wasn't sure how you felt about our work"), or present-tense personal reactions to the client (e.g., "I am feeling hurt right now because you reject everything I say"). See the overview of immediacy in Exhibit 14.1. For the insight stage, immediacy statements help clients gain greater understanding of how they come across in the therapeutic relationship, in the hopes that clients can use this information to change how they act in relationships outside of helping.

Immediacy overlaps somewhat with other skills. It can be thought of as a type of disclosure because helpers disclose personal feelings, reactions, or experiences about the client or relationship to help the client gain insight. Immediacy can also sometimes be a type of challenge because it can be used to confront clients about issues in the relationship (e.g., "I feel annoyed that you avoid my questions"). In addition, immediacy can sometimes be a type of information if it is used to point out patterns in a client's behavior in relation to the therapist (e.g., "Whenever I go on vacation, you cancel the first two sessions after I return. I wonder if we could talk about this pattern?"). However, immediacy differs from feedback about the client (a type of information covered in the action stage, see Chapter 16) because both people in the relationship are involved

---

EXHIBIT 14.1

Overview of Immediacy

Definition	*Immediacy* refers to the helper inquiring about or disclosing immediate feelings about the client, herself or himself in relation to the client, or the therapeutic relationship.
Examples	"Right now I'm feeling very tense because you seem to be angry at me."
	"I feel nervous too, but I'm pleased that you're sharing some very deep and personal feelings with me."
Typical helper intentions	To promote insight, to deal with the relationship, to challenge, to identify maladaptive behaviors, to identify and intensify feelings, to relieve therapist's needs (see Web Form D)
Possible client reactions	Relief, negative thoughts or feelings, better self-understanding, clear, feelings, responsibility, unstuck, new perspective, challenged, scared, worse, stuck, confused, misunderstood (see Web Form G)
Desired client behaviors	Affective exploration, cognitive exploration, insight (see Web Form H)
Helpful hints	Be aware of your own feelings about the relationship.
	Observe the client for possible feelings about the relationship.
	Cultivate a sense of curiosity and try to understand your and the client's reactions.
	Be gentle, tentative, and empathic.
	State your own feelings as well as noting what might be going on for the client.
	Be nondefensive and encourage an open discussion of the relationship.
	Return the focus to the client (e.g., "What do you think?" "What is your reaction?").

---

in immediacy interventions, whereas in feedback about the client, the focus is only on the client (e.g., "You did a really good job when you spoke up to your mother").

Types of Immediacy

In this chapter, I focus on four specific subtypes of immediacy. In the first subtype, *open questions and probes about the relationship,* the helper invites the client to share feelings about the therapeutic relationship. These inquiries are thus probes into the client's reactions to the relationship and have also been called *process statements* because they address what is going on in the immediate moment. These inquiries often involve the helper checking in with the client about feelings. For example, the helper might ask,

- "I wonder what reactions you had to the session today?"
- "How did you feel just now when I praised you?"
- "What would you like from me right now?"

The second subtype of immediacy is the helper's *statement of his or her reactions to the client.* Thus, the helper shares his or her own feelings and reactions in the moment and generally follows these up with an inquiry about how the client feels. For example, the helper might say,

- "I've been feeling a little disconnected from you today. I wonder how you're feeling?"
- "I feel so much closer to you today when you share your feelings so deeply. I feel so moved by what you have said. How has it been for you?"
- "I feel uncomfortable when you follow me around outside of sessions. I wonder if we could talk about that?"

Making the covert overt is the third subtype of immediacy. Often the client is saying something to the helper indirectly, and through this intervention the helper attempts to make the client's intention more open. In this subtype, anything that happens in the helping relationship is open for processing to see whether something is going on in the relationship. For example, the helper might say,

- "You are late again today. I wonder if anything is going on in terms of your feelings about being here?"
- "You keep looking at your watch. I wonder if you're eager to leave?"
- "You seemed angry when I said that. I wonder what's going on inside?"

A fourth subtype, which also might involve covert communications, is *drawing parallels with outside relationships.* Clients may talk about things that bother them about other people; they may or may not be covertly referring to things the helper, but it can be useful to check out. Again, the helper wonders aloud whether the client has reactions to him or her that are similar to those the client has to others. For example,

"You mentioned that no one seems to understand you. I wonder if you might be saying that I don't understand you?"

"You are talking about withdrawing from your friends lately. I wonder if that's happening in here with me?"

"You've said that you get upset if anyone criticizes you, and just now you pulled back when I talked about your procrastination. I wonder if you're worried that I will criticize you?"

Rationale for Using Immediacy

The helping relationship provides a microcosm of how clients relate in the real world. If a client is compliant with the helper, for example, he or she is probably compliant with others in the outside world. If a client is arrogant and shows off to impress the helper, chances are that she or he does similar things with other people. Often clients talk about how they get along with others but helpers cannot see both sides of the interaction; in the helping session, helpers can actually see how the client interacts. Therefore, the client's general interpersonal style can be examined, at least in part, by an investigation of his or her relationship with the helper. Of course, clients do not act toward all other people as they act toward the helper—it may be that they act a certain way to people in a position of authority and a different way to peers. But observing the behavior provides firsthand evidence of how the client comes across in interpersonal interactions, at least occasionally.

Helpers experience personally the impact of a client's behavior, which Kiesler (1988) and Cashdan (1988) called becoming "hooked" given that helpers are pushed into a constricted, narrow range of responses by the client's maladaptive behaviors. For example, dominant clients tend to "pull for" submissive behavior from helpers, whereas hostile clients "pull for" hostile behavior from helpers. If helpers become aware of feeling hooked (i.e., feeling a need to behave in a certain way) without critical judgment of the client, they can begin to understand how other people react to clients in interpersonal relationships and can feel freer to behave in a different and more therapeutic manner.

In addition to addressing problems in relationships in general, immediacy can also be used to discuss issues that arise in the helping relationship. For example, a helper could discuss with a client what has and has not been working in the helping process so that adjustments can be made, a helper might want to ask about a client's chronic lateness, or a helper might want to process feelings with a client about running into each other at a party. Many issues present themselves in a helping relationship, so immediacy is a critical tool for working through the inevitable interpersonal problems.

Immediacy can also be used to make covert communication more direct. In some cases, clients talk covertly about the helping relationship because they are not sure how helpers will react if they say something directly. For example, a client might say that no one can help him. Because the helper is trying to help him, it is not a huge leap to guess that at least part of the communication is directed toward the helper. In any communication, helpers can ask themselves what clients are trying to communicate to them about the therapy relationship, although they will decide whether to use immediacy based on the client's needs at the time.

Another reason for using immediacy is to challenge clients to change maladaptive behaviors. When helpers are honest about their reactions, clients learn how they come across to another person and thus might change their problematic behaviors. Some examples of interpersonal behaviors that can cause problems for clients in helping relationships (and other relationships) include being so talkative that the helper cannot speak, acting overbearing and arrogant and assuming that they are better than the helper, being passive and not saying anything without being asked, droning on and on in a monotone voice without maintaining eye contact, disagreeing with everything the helper says, constantly bringing gifts to the helper, or trying too hard to be helpful.

Resolving problems between the helper and client can also provide clients with a model of how to resolve interpersonal problems in relationships. If done well, clients learn that it is possible to talk about feelings, resolve problems, and develop closer relationships as a result of the discussion. Greenberg, Rice, and Elliott (1993) suggested that encountering another real human being who both cares and is authentic helps clients grow. Being able to resolve interpersonal problems can be a powerful experience, teaching clients that it is possible, although not always easy, to deal openly with issues.

In the world outside of helping, friends and acquaintances might not be honest with each other about how they feel about what is going on in their relationship because it is difficult, may hurt feelings, and takes time and effort. Because they do not receive feedback, however, clients often are not aware of how they come across to others. If oblivious to their own behaviors (which they often are because they are so used to them), clients cannot change, and there may be negative consequences (e.g., if a client is not aware that she speaks with a hostile tone, it could negatively affect her evaluations in the workplace). The helping relationship thus provides an opportunity for clients to become aware of how their behaviors affect another person and to make changes in a safe setting. Of course the ultimate goal is to help clients use immediacy in their relationships outside of therapy so that they can have more open communication.

Helpers who gently provide immediacy may be giving their clients a special gift. In effect, immediacy communicates that helpers are willing to take the time to let clients know about the effect of their behaviors so they can have an opportunity to increase awareness and change inappropriate behaviors. But it is important to emphasize that helpers must use immediacy in a caring way with deep compassion and empathy.

Immediacy can be a powerful, risky intervention that raises the temperature in the room; helpers need to know that immediacy has great power to heal but can also be damaging if done poorly.

Guidelines for Using Immediacy

Immediacy is a difficult and demanding skill. Helpers need to be aware of what is happening in themselves and in the therapeutic relationship and have enough self-confidence and self-understanding not to react defensively to a client's open expression of feelings. Because they do not always openly deal with immediate feelings in nonhelping situations, helpers often feel frightened about doing so in helping situations. It takes courage, as well as skill, to be immediate with clients. But most important, it takes compassion; rather than taking the client's behavior personally, helpers try to understand what is going on with clients that keeps them from relating effectively and then gently try to help client become aware of these behaviors so that they can change and have more satisfying relationships.

When using immediacy, helpers talk directly to clients about their interactions. In other words, helpers and clients metacommunicate about their communication. Kiesler (1988) stressed that the success of the metacommunication depends on the extent to which the helper balances the challenge of the metacommunication with being supportive and protective of the client's self-esteem. Helpers need to present the immediacy as a gentle examination of the process. Helpers communicate that they are committed to working with clients to understand their actions and the effects of their behaviors on relationships with other people.

Helpers might want to first educate clients about why they are using immediacy. Given that talking directly about the relationship is very different from what many people are used to, and it is often not sanctioned in families to have direct communication, clients may need a rationale for why it is important to use immediacy and what the effects might be. Often, when clients understand why an intervention is being used, they are more receptive to it.

It can also be important to comment about cultural differences in terms of dealing immediately with relationship difficulties. In cultures in which typical communication is indirect, it can be considered rude to directly communicate about the relationship. In shame-based and private cultures, it is often difficult to talk immediately about feelings. Helpers may still be able to use immediacy, but they may need to be gentle and tentative in their manner of delivery and carefully observe and ask about client reactions.

It is also often helpful for helpers take appropriate responsibility for their feelings when using immediacy by using "I" statements (e.g., "I feel uncomfortable with praise"; "I feel bad that I interrupted you") rather than "you" statements (e.g., "You shouldn't praise me"; "You talk too much"). Clients often have an easier time owning their responsibility (e.g., "I was probably talking too much") when helpers candidly admit their contribution to the interaction. Furthermore, it is only fair for helpers to admit responsibility (if justified) if they want clients to acknowledge their part. When helpers acknowledge their role in relationship problems, an open exchange can occur about how both people feel. Problems can be resolved, the therapeutic relationship can be enhanced, and clients can be encouraged to become actively involved in problem solving. For example, one client came into the session and, before he was even seated, asked if he could pray with the helper and then immediately proceeded to invoke God's help in guiding the helper in the session. The helper was taken aback, felt very uncomfortable, and needed to gently but honestly talk to the client about her reactions to his behavior before they could continue ("I feel a little uncomfortable praying in the session because it's not part of the way I operate. I wonder if we could talk about this").

It is crucial that helpers not prescribe how clients should change, because "should" statements imply that the helper knows more about the client than the client does. Instead, helpers simply point out how they react when clients act in a particular way. It is also important that helpers are aware that their feedback about clients is based on their perceptions and reactions and that others might react differently to the clients. Helpers might even suggest that clients gather feedback about how others react to the behaviors. An awareness of how they are perceived by others can enable clients to decide whether they want to make changes.

When the helper has a strong reaction to the client (e.g., hostility, attraction, envy, boredom), compassion can mediate the strong feeling. Thus, the helper first becomes aware of the strong feeling, allows it into awareness, ponders the feeling, and accepts it. Then, the helper steps back and tries to get some compassion for the client, trying to understand what might be going on that causes the client to behave toward the helper to elicit such strong reactions. The helper also tried to understand his or her own part in the interaction and takes appropriate responsibility and initiative to work on his or her part in his or her own therapy. Finally, the helper uses immediacy to approach the situation with the client when the helper thinks the client can tolerate it. The helper works hard to stay present in the moment in the interaction with the client and continue the discussion.

After being immediate with clients, helpers can ask clients about their reactions to the immediacy, so that the communication is two-sided.

Hence, after the helper says something like, "I felt uncomfortable when I saw you on the bus yesterday. I wasn't quite sure what to say, and I'm worried that you might have felt offended that I didn't speak to you," the helper can ask the client, "How did you feel about seeing me?" or "How do you feel talking about this right now?" Thus, the helper tries to engage the client in a discussion of the interaction. Research shows that it is important for helpers to be open about exploring the interaction (Rhodes, Hill, Thompson, & Elliott, 1994; Safran, Muran, Samstag, & Stevens, 2002).

Of course some clients will be happy to lay all the blame on the helper and turn the tables to talk about the helper's problems. If this happens, the helper can use that as an immediacy intervention (e.g., "You know, I'm feeling a little attacked. I wonder if we both can look at our parts in this interaction?").

Because helpers have indicated that it is permissible to process the relationship, they need to be aware that clients may give them feedback about what they do not like about the helper's behaviors. After all, helping is a two-way interaction, and helpers may be doing things that are not optimal for clients. Some of this information may be accurate and valuable—clients are wonderful sources of feedback because they are the recipients of what helpers do and know how the interventions feel. However, helpers also must be aware that feedback is sometimes distorted (i.e., transference). For example, Yutta may say that the helper is mean, not because of what the helper has done but because of unresolved feelings she has about her critical mother that she projects onto the helper. Helpers have to determine what feedback is genuinely related to their behavior and what is related to transference issues. There is usually at least a grain of truth in most client feedback, however, so helpers can investigate both their own behaviors and the client's contribution.

Example of Immediacy

The following shows a helper using immediacy (in italics) in a session:

Helper: *I have something to bring up with you that is a bit uncomfortable to talk about. At the beginning and end of each session, you want a hug, and I don't feel comfortable doing that on a routine basis.*

Client: (pause) I don't understand. I thought we were close, and it just feels natural to hug. What's the matter with hugging?

Helper: I do feel close to you, and I don't want to hurt our relationship, but I thought that talking about this could help
us clarify expectations. It makes me uncomfortable feeling
like I have to hug you. It doesn't feel professional.

Client: Hmmm, that's part of my culture. I always hug people when I meet them and when we leave. I feel
a little anxious when you don't want to, like you
don't care about me.

Helper: I do care about you as a client, but we're in a professional relationship, and it feels awkward to blur the
boundaries.

Client: I didn't realize that you felt that way. Is there anything I'm doing that is wrong?

Helper: You sound a little hurt.

Client: I guess I am. I didn't know that what I was doing is
wrong.

Helper: It's not wrong to hug, it just feels awkward in a professional relationship. I value our relationship, and I don't
want to be in a position where I feel uncomfortable. It feels
very important for us both to feel comfortable here.

Client: Okay, I think I understand. Are you angry at me?

Helper: No, not at all. I'm very grateful that you've been so understanding and that we could work through this difficult and
touchy situation. How are you feeling?

Client: I'm relieved that you're not angry. I think I can
change. I'm glad you told me.

Helper: Thanks. And please let me know if you have any more
feelings about this.

Difficulties Helpers Have in Using Immediacy

Beginning helpers often have fears about intruding and making clients
angry if they use immediacy, even if they do it empathically. Indeed,
clients do sometimes become angry. For example, a helper gently suggested that Olivia was acting helpless when she expected the helper to
take responsibility for her behavior and failures. Olivia became angry
and adamantly denied that her behaviors were similar to those of victims. Several sessions later, however, Olivia acknowledged that the
immediacy intervention was accurate and helped her become aware
that she was acting like her mother who typically played the martyr
role. If the helper had withheld the immediacy intervention for fear

of hurting Olivia's feelings, Olivia would not have learned a valuable lesson about herself. Although it is sometimes painful to hear, such feedback can be motivational and subsequently life-changing.

Another problem is that helpers often do not trust their feelings (e.g., "Maybe it is all my fault that I'm bored—if I were a better helper, I wouldn't feel bored"). They might feel unsure about their reactions and hesitant about communicating their feelings to clients appropriately and empathically.

Some helpers simply avoid immediacy because it is frightening to talk directly and honestly about the immediate relationship. They are not used to such open communication in their relationships, and they feel vulnerable when sharing immediate feelings. They might feel anxious about dealing openly with interpersonal conflicts because their families had strong rules against addressing conflicts openly. In fact, most helpers have an easier time being empathic with clients who are sad or depressed but are less skilled when it comes to talking directly with clients about negative reactions and working through interpersonal problems. Once again, personal therapy can provide an opportunity for helpers to come to understand their own issues. Supervision can also provide a reality check for helpers because they can learn how someone else reacts to the client.

Some trainees have trouble being immediate with clients who are very similar to them (e.g., from the same cultural or economic background or gender) because some situations trigger complex emotions such as anger, jealousy, disappointment, pride, and competitiveness. On the other hand, some trainees have difficulty when clients are dissimilar from them. One both sides, issues of diversity come up, and it is often hard to deal openly with diversity issues. Trainees often want to be completely accepting and inclusive and feel ashamed when they have politically incorrect feelings.

In addition, helpers sometimes inappropriately use immediacy to deal with their own needs. For example, a helper who had recently been divorced was feeling particularly vulnerable and needed affirmation that he was attractive, so he encouraged Ingrid to talk about her attraction to him. Usually, helpers are not aware that they are using immediacy to deal with their own needs. They might become aware that they are doing so, however, if their behaviors have negative consequences for their clients (e.g., a client quits after the helper gets angry at her for being too quiet). Hence, it is crucial that helpers try to be mindful of their needs so that they can get their needs met elsewhere instead of their needs intruding on the helping process.

It is often hard for beginning helpers to imagine using immediacy if they have only brief (e.g., 20-minute) interactions with clients as is typical in helping skills classes. Indeed, immediacy is often not appropriate in brief interactions. However, it is still valuable for beginning helpers to practice this skill in role-plays and be aware of how it could be used in actual sessions with clients with whom they work for longer periods of time.

What Do You Think?

- Discuss whether you think helpers can balance being direct with feedback and accepting clients as they are.
- How might helpers respond when clients are angry at them?
- Discuss the idea that immediacy can be an enactment of a deep level of empathy.
- Discuss the advantages and disadvantages of using immediacy compared with interpretations or challenges.

RESEARCH SUMMARY

Immediacy

Citation: Hill, C. E., Gelso, C. J., Chui, H., Spangler, P., Hummel, A., Huang, T., . . . Miles, J. R. (2013, July 12). To be or not to be immediate with clients: The use and effects of immediacy in psychodynamic/interpersonal psychotherapy. *Psychotherapy Research.* Advance online publication.

Rationale: People often seek psychotherapy because of problems in relationships. They may not be able to make or sustain relationships, or they may act in ways that make others angry at them or dismiss them. Because of these problems in relationships, people often feel isolated and alone but do not know how to change. Psychotherapy can help by analyzing patterns in relationships, exploring reasons for relationship problems, and suggesting alternative ways of behaving. But therapy is a relationship, so many of the problems that emerge in a client's relationships outside of therapy will also emerge in the relationship with the therapist. If the client is chronically hostile, deferent, seductive, or saintly, for example, she or he will probably also act that way with the therapist. Therapists can then use their reactions to help clients understand how others react and then figure out how to change. Given the theoretical importance of immediacy, we need to examine more closely when and how it occurs within psychotherapy.

Method: Sixteen cases of therapy lasting between eight and 59 sessions with community clients and doctoral student therapists were examined for immediacy events. Clients and therapists completed evaluations after each session. Each immediacy event was coded by a team of judges for type of immediacy, who initiated the event, duration, depth, appropriateness, resolution, quality, and consequences. Clients and therapists were interviewed after therapy about their experiences of immediacy.

Interesting Findings:
- Most immediacy events were initiated by therapists.
- Most involved exploration of unexpressed or covert feelings (e.g., "I wonder how you're feeling right now about our relationship?" "You seem a little angry at me right now."). Thus, most immediacy events focused on trying to help clients talk about what they might be feeling but not saying about the relationship so that they could learn to express themselves more freely in the relationship.
- Immediacy occurred during about 5% of time in therapy.
- Typical consequences
  - Clients expressed feelings about the therapist or therapy.
  - Clients opened up and talked in greater depth about themselves.
  - Clients gained insight.
- Therapists focused more on feelings and less on ruptures and initiated immediacy more often with fearfully attached (i.e., generally anxious and avoidant and insecure in their interactions with others) than with securely attached clients (i.e., generally nonanxious and nonavoidant and trusting in interactions with others).

Conclusions:
- Immediacy is often beneficial in psychotherapy. Although it is not used often and needs to be used well, it can facilitate the therapy process, and it can help the client gain insight.

Implications for Therapy:
- It is okay for clients to bring up feelings about their therapists. Even though it is often scary, it can help repair problems in the relationship and serve as a model for how clients can be more open in relationships outside of therapy.
- Therapists will need to tailor the immediacy interventions based on the client attachment style. Therapists may need to be a little more cautious with clients who have fearful attachment styles.

BONUS MATERIALS

Practice exercises, labs, and other resources for students and teachers are available on the companion website: http://pubs.apa.org/books/supp/hill4.

Integrating the Skills of the Insight Stage

15

He who has a *why* to live can bear with almost any *how*.
—*Nietzsche*

Monroe is able to experience and accept the depths of the anger and loss he feels because his sister will not speak to him. Benjamin, who has been unable to choose a career, comes to realize that he is afraid to compete with his father, a businessman who is extremely successful but distant from his family. Yvonne comes to understand that her feelings of inadequacy are based on other children making fun of her for having a slight speech impediment. Nigel gains the insight that he avoids all risks because of his fear of dying at a young age as his father did. Miji became aware that her hostility pushed people away from her. Neo becomes aware that his hostile humor pushes away other people. These are examples of new understandings that clients come to with the aid of helpers in the insight stage.

In the insight stage, helpers assist clients in developing new perspectives about themselves, their feelings, and their behaviors. Helpers choose which skills to use depending on their intentions, what the client is presenting at the moment, what the client can tolerate, and their overall goals for the session. They maintain an empathic connection with clients and primarily use exploration skills, but they also work to deepen

http://dx.doi.org/10.1037/14345-015
Helping Skills: Facilitating Exploration, Insight, and Action, Fourth Edition, by C. E. Hill

client experiencing, challenge clients to raise awareness, use open questions and probes to encourage clients to think about the reasons for their behaviors, use interpretations and disclosures of insight to facilitate new understandings of the underlying reasons or motivations for thoughts and behaviors, and use immediacy to help clients become aware of how they come across to others and to deal with tensions or misunderstandings in the therapeutic relationship. These interventions help clients achieve greater depths of self-understanding and insight about who they are, how they got to be the way they are, and how they are perceived by others.

We hope that clients gain some new understandings of themselves at a deep, emotional level by the end of the insight stage. We hope they see things in new ways or from different perspectives, are able to identify patterns or make connections, have ideas about why they do what they do, and have a deeper understanding of themselves. These insights sometimes have an "aha" quality to them, and clients feel relieved that they have explanations for their behaviors and thoughts. Clients "own" their new understandings because they have been instrumental in helping to construct them. Clients work to integrate these new understandings into their self-perceptions and may even start to think spontaneously about action.

Steps for Integrating Insight Skills

In trying to integrate the insight skills, helpers can follow several steps to help guide clients. Helpers need not follow these steps exactly but, rather, can use them as a general guideline for what can be accomplished in this stage.

STEP 1: SET THE STAGE

Helpers pave the way for the insight stage through empathy, reflections of feelings, and helping the client explore. There needs to be a good bond between the helper and the client, and the client needs to feel safe to explore the reasons behind feelings and thoughts, without fear of judgment. In addition, the need for empathy remains a key element of the insight stage. When dealing with difficult clinical situations, if helpers can put themselves in the client's shoes and try to understand what is going on with the client, they will often be able to avoid being judgmental and will be able to forge an alliance with their client. Relatedly, Vivino, Thompson, Hill, and Ladany (2009) found that experienced therapists who were able to step back and understand what was going on for clients were able to rekindle their compassion for difficult clients.

Another reason for taking adequate time is so the helper can observe the client. Helpers formulate challenges and interpretations from their observations of clients, so they must be alert and trust their observations. Before going into insight interventions, helpers need to collect an adequate amount of evidence to clarify what is going on rather than jumping to conclusions.

STEP 2: LOOK FOR MARKERS OF CLIENT READINESS FOR INSIGHT

The markers for readiness for challenges, insight work, and immediacy differ somewhat. Note that clients often do not present markers as clearly as indicated here, so helpers need to use their clinical intuition when necessary.

Markers for Challenging

Some markers for challenges are:

- ambivalence,
- contradictions,
- discrepancies,
- confusion,
- feeling stuck, and
- being unable to make a decision.

Helpers can also observe and listen to clients carefully for "sour notes"—things that do not sound right, make sense, fit, or go together or things that are done out of "shoulds," cause ambivalences, or result in struggles. These sour notes can point the way to issues about which clients feel contradictions and uncertainties. These markers suggest that clients are ready to allow the problem to "come into awareness."

Helpers try to think about why the client might feel confused or stuck. Rather than blaming or condemning the client, the helper tries to understand the client's dynamics. The empathy generated through this process can help the helper become curious about checking out the hypotheses rather than becoming invested in pointing out a discrepancy or trying to make the client change.

Markers for Insight Work

Possible markers of client readiness or eagerness are:

- a clear statement of awareness of a problem,
- a statement of a lack of understanding,

- a stated eagerness or willingness to understand, and
- a high level of affective distress experienced as a pressure to resolve the problem.

The client might say something like, "I just don't understand why I get so angry at my boyfriend. He usually does nothing wrong. I just suddenly get furious and I can't control my rage. I really wish I understood it because it is making me miserable and is about to destroy the best relationship I have ever had."

Possible markers indicating a lack of readiness are clients

- telling a story in a nonreflective manner,
- asking for advice, and
- blaming others for problems.

Skills for facilitating exploration or awareness are probably more suitable than insight skills when clients are not ready.

Some clients are psychologically minded and value probing into their dynamics and motives. Other clients, however, are not so interested in probing into the underlying dynamics and are more concerned with exploration or fixing problems. It is important, however, to stress that helpers should not assume from stereotypes that certain groups of clients (e.g., clients from a low socioeconomic class) are not suited for interpretations. Furthermore, some clients can be taught to be more introspective, particularly through open questions and probes for insight.

It is also important to be aware that some cultures may not value interpretive activity as much as the European American culture does. Some cultures (e.g., Asian, Hispanic) value action more than understanding, although sometimes education about why insight is valuable can be persuasive. Because it is important to respect others' values, helpers should not force clients to work on insight if they are not amenable after being educated about it.

Markers for Immediacy

Client Markers

One set of markers comes from observing the client:

- Does the client seem distraught, particularly quiet, unusually talkative, more vague than usual, acting hostile or too friendly toward you?
- Does the client mention references to other people that might be a reference to you (e.g., "No one understands me," "Everyone makes me feel bad")?

The client might directly confront the helper (e.g., "I'm angry that you're late," "I don't think I'm getting anything out of this relationship"). If so, these behaviors may be signs that something is going on inside the client about the helping relationship.

Helper Markers

Another set of markers is feelings that helpers have about clients. Typical markers are the following:

- feeling bored, angry, stuck, incompetent, prideful, or brilliant, especially if these feelings are extreme;
- feeling sexual attraction;
- feeling afraid and wanting to avoid certain topics with the client; and
- not using specific helping skills that would be appropriate (e.g., not exploring; not using insight skills).

Becoming aware of these feelings is often difficult for helpers, who like to think of themselves as being accepting and nurturing rather than as having negative feelings. To get into these potential feelings, helpers ask themselves the following questions:

- "What am I feeling when I am with this client?"
- "What do I want to do or not do when I am with this client?"
- "What keeps me from using skills that I know would be helpful with this client?"
- "How does this client affect me compared with the effect of other clients?"
- "Do I find myself blaming the client (e.g., saying that the client is not trying, is resistant, is bipolar)?"

Helpers need to allow themselves to have their feelings without judging themselves as "bad" or incompetent. Rather, helpers can view themselves as instruments and use their feelings to determine how they resonate with or react to clients. Supervision can be useful in facilitating helpers in their struggle with experiencing negative feelings toward clients because supervisors can normalize such feelings. For example, the supervisor might say, "If I were in this situation, I would feel sexually attracted to this client. She is so seductive that I would feel distracted in sessions." When supervisors are able to admit to having "politically incorrect" feelings, helpers often are then able to acknowledge their own feelings. Thus, supervision is invaluable for enabling helpers to become aware of their feelings and also for ensuring that helpers do not act out impulsively on their feelings.

Once the helper becomes aware of the automatic reactions, he or she can stop the reactions and try to understand them. Rather than taking it personally and feeling badly that they had these strong emotions or blaming the client for the reactions, helpers can try to cultivate a sense of curiosity about what contributes to clients acting as they do. Often, clients have developed these behaviors as defenses. For example, if a client is very talkative and does not let anyone else contribute to the discussion, he or she could be defending against letting anyone get close for fear of becoming engulfed. Thus, the constant talking may serve a defensive function of keeping others at a safe distance.

By coming to an understanding of what they are feeling with clients, helpers can regain some objectivity, which permits them to distance themselves from their reactions and begin to help their clients. For example, by becoming aware that a client's whining pulls for the helper to want to silence the client, the helper can begin to get curious about what causes the client to whine. The helper can then think about how to compassionately provide the client with feedback about the effects of her or his whining. By acting differently than expected or typical, the helper may be able to break the typical pattern so that a new type of interaction can occur.

Of course, helpers need to evaluate whether any of their own issues could be implicated in the feelings they have when they are with clients. For example, a helper might be sensitive to a client's talkativeness and aggressiveness because the helper's mother is dominant and talks incessantly. Furthermore, if helpers find they have similar feelings with several clients (e.g., being sexually attracted to several clients), this could be a clue that it is the helper's rather than (or in addition to) the client's problem.

STEP 3: DETERMINE INTENTIONS

Helpers need to think about their intentions at a particular moment in the helping process. The most appropriate intention here is to promote insight. Inappropriate intentions would be to make oneself look good at the expense of the client, to show off, or to punish clients for being frustrating. If helpers realize that they want to give a challenge or an interpretation to meet their own needs, they can pause, think about themselves and the client, and try to figure out what is going on in the relationship. Seeking supervision or consultation is often a good idea here.

STEP 4: ENGAGE IN AN INTERACTIVE, COLLABORATIVE INSIGHT PROCESS

Of overall importance is for the helper to be gentle, tentative, and empathic when using insight skills. The posture should be one of curiosity rather than one of showing off or being judgmental. Furthermore, it is important for the helper to collaborate with the client to discover meaning. Thus, there is a lot of back and forth with both people generating ideas about what might be going on: The helper might ask the client an open question and listen intently to the response, and then perhaps the helper offers a tentative interpretation, which the client adds to or modifies, and then the helper might challenge. Perhaps at this point the client has a glimmer of insight, which the helper restates and asks for more elaboration, and so on. The idea here is to help the client get unblocked so that he or she can go out and continue thinking on his or her own.

It is also important for the helper to carefully observe client reactions to insight interventions and make modifications if needed. And, because clients often conceal negative reactions, helpers might need to go beyond observing to asking explicitly about clients' reactions. Helpers should also remember to use exploration skills frequently during this stage because clients need the opportunity to process new information in a safe and supportive setting.

STEP 5: FOLLOW UP

Single challenges, interpretations, or immediacy statements rarely trigger new and lasting insight immediately. Clients typically require many reiterations before they begin to understand, incorporate and change cognitive schemas, and use insight to makes changes in their lives. At first, an insight intervention may seem strange and foreign, but as clients hears it numerous times in different ways, they begin to understand and integrate the ideas into their schemas (ways of thinking). Helpers thus need to plan enough time in sessions to work through the new insights. They also need to follow up on insight interventions in subsequent sessions. Clients typically continue the interpretative process outside of sessions (which of course is the goal of helping), so following up on what the client has been thinking in between sessions can be fruitful.

STEP 6: ASK THE CLIENT FOR HIS OR HER CURRENT UNDERSTANDING

Often what the helper thinks at the end of this stage can be quite different from what the client thinks. It is thus useful for the helper to check out what the client absorbed from the process. I recall one session in which I was sure that the client had gained a lot of insight but was surprised when she said that nothing much had changed. Knowing where the client is at can help you plan future interventions.

Caveats About Using Insight Skills

Several caveats apply to the use of insight interventions. First, the therapeutic relationship must be solid before insight skills are used. Clients must trust their helpers, and helpers must have a base of knowledge about clients from which to formulate insight interventions. A relationship can sometimes be established quickly, but it takes a long time with other cases before the relationship can withstand insight interventions. One way of determining whether the client is ready for insight is by trying a mild insight intervention to see how the client reacts. If the client rejects it adamantly, it is likely that she or he is not ready. If the client, however, responds positively, then the helper can proceed cautiously, always attending to how the client is responding. Helpers should always be attentive to client reactions to insight interventions. The most superb insight interventions are worthless if clients are not ready for them, and relationships can be damaged by premature insight interventions.

It is usually best to encourage clients to come to their own insights, if possible, through open questions and probes and interpretations that add just a bit beyond the client's current understanding. If clients are productively working on insight, helpers can stay in the background and encourage and coach clients. The process in the insight stage is thus just as collaborative as it was in the exploration stage. Helpers and clients work together to construct understanding rather than helpers being the experts who deliver insights to the clients.

When used, interpretive interventions need to be delivered gently and tentatively, with caring and empathy rather than with judgment or blame. They should be preceded by and interspersed with exploration skills (reflection of feelings, restatement, and open questions and probes). As clients contemplate what they learn from insight interventions, they are at a new level and need time and support to explore what they have discovered about themselves. Furthermore, helpers continually revise their insight interventions based on emerging information, treating them as working hypotheses rather than as fundamental truths.

In addition, insight interventions may need to be repeated many times, in diverse ways, over long periods of time, so that clients can begin to incorporate them, use them to change their thinking, and apply them to different parts of their lives. Altering ingrained ways of thinking is difficult, and repetition often assists clients in being able to hear and use the new insights. The first time often plants the seed, which starts the client thinking, and then the helper follows up on the idea and elaborates more at a different time.

Cultural Considerations

Given that helpers are relying more on their own reactions and thoughts in the insight stage than they did in the exploration stage, they have to be extraordinarily careful about imposing their values on clients from other cultures. For example, a Western helper might challenge a 22-year-old Asian student to be more independent and separate from her parents, but this suggestion might contradict the client's cultural value to be dependent on her parents until marriage. As another example, a helper might interpret a client's caring for an aging parent as self-defeating in terms of career advancement, whereas the client may feel a cultural obligation to sacrifice self for others, especially family. Western values promote individualism and self-actualization, whereas Eastern and Latino cultures value collectivism and familial obligations (Kim, Atkinson, & Umemoto, 2001; Kim, Atkinson, & Yang, 1999); these differences in values can lead to cultural clashes in terms of understanding dynamics and psychological problems.

Another cultural consideration related to the insight stage is that some cultures teach people to think that authority figures have the ultimate answers. Hence, interpretations may take on greater meaning to such clients as the "right" answer. In such instances, helpers have to be especially careful about what they say. In addition, clients from non-Western cultures might benefit from judicious disclosures of insight as a way of building trust (D. W. Sue & Sue, 1999). Disclosures of insight might provide a model for clients to ponder new ideas without dictating what the client should think.

An additional cultural consideration is that immediacy may seem quite rude and intrusive to people from cultures in which open, here-and-now communication is not valued. Again, helpers should be attentive to clients' reactions and ask about any discomfort and adjust their therapeutic interventions accordingly.

Although it is important to be sensitive to cultural considerations, this does not mean that helpers should not approach culturally laden topics. For example, even though culturally it may be appropriate for a woman to be meek and submissive, such behavior may get in the way of her moving ahead in her chosen career, and she may thus need help to think through this behavior and think about changing. Even though it may result in messy ruptures and temporary loss of trust, it may be necessary for the helper to challenge the client and then use immediacy to work on the relationship.

A final cultural issue is that it may be particularly difficult for a majority group client (e.g., a middle-aged White male) to receive a challenge or an interpretation from a minority individual (e.g., a younger biracial female). There may be resistance because such interpretation upsets the normative power differential in society. This same client may have no problem receiving a challenge or interpretation from an older female helper because he is used to getting maternal care and emotional support from older women but is not used to being in a one-down position with younger women.

Difficulties Helpers Might Experience in the Insight Stage

Becoming competent in the skills used during the insight stage is difficult, and these skills take many years to master. In addition, the skills cannot be applied in a rote, technical fashion to every client, which makes it challenging for instructors to teach and for students to learn these skills. Helpers have to use their intuition and rely on their reactions to clients, so there is danger of countertransference interfering with the insight process. Helpers need to proceed slowly and observe clients' reactions to their insight interventions, but I would encourage helpers not to avoid insight interventions because they would then miss opportunities to help clients understand themselves at deeper levels. Several difficulties can be identified.

MOVING PREMATURELY INTO INSIGHT

Helpers sometimes move into the insight stage before the therapeutic relationship has been firmly established, before the client has adequately explored the problems, or before the helper has a deep enough understanding of the problems. It is crucial that insight interventions be used within the context of a strong therapeutic relationship and be based on a strong foundation of understanding. Otherwise, these techniques have the potential for damaging clients. For example, if a helper challenges before the client trusts him or her, the client might doubt the helper's motives and terminate the helping relationship.

TAKING TOO MUCH RESPONSIBILITY FOR DEVELOPING INSIGHT

Beginning helpers often feel that they have to be the experts who "put it all together" and connect all the client's past experiences with the client's present behaviors in a new way. Or the helper may be impatient because the client cannot see what is blatantly obvious to the helper. To this helper, figuring out clients is more important than helping clients figure out themselves. From my perspective, the more important task is for helpers to empathize with clients, determine what contributes to clients having difficulty putting it all together, ask clients about their thoughts about insight, and work collaboratively with them to construct insights.

GETTING STUCK IN ONE THEORETICAL PERSPECTIVE

One of the dangers in the insight stage is that helpers may get stuck using only one theoretical perspective too rigidly. For example, a helper may try to apply psychoanalytic theory, even though the theory might not fit for an individual client. Thus, a helper could be convinced that every client is suffering from an Oedipal/Electra complex because Freud said so, rather than attending to the data that the client presents. Or as another example, a helper could conceptualize and treat the client from a cognitive viewpoint, assuming that maladaptive thoughts need to be challenged, even though the client is not receptive to cognitive work. It is helpful for helpers to be aware that theories are guidelines rather than cookbooks and that helpers need to be judicious in applying them.

FORGETTING TO BE EMPATHIC

Some helpers get so excited about figuring out the puzzle of the client's problems that they forget to be empathic. They do not remember the importance of keeping clients involved in the therapeutic experience. It is crucial to be constantly aware of how clients are feeling and reacting and to work at maintaining the collaborative relationship.

TAKING CLIENTS AT FACE VALUE AND NOT DIGGING DEEPER

Beginning helpers often have difficulty going beyond what clients present because they are not used to the idea of thinking of people as complex and as being motivated by conflicting unconscious forces. In addition, sometimes helpers are afraid of upsetting clients and being intrusive, so they fail to search deeper to help their clients. However, clients often value hearing another perspective about their problems because they feel stuck, so helpers need to be willing to help clients construct new understandings, always of course building on the basis of a good relationship and solid exploration.

FORGETTING THAT NOT ALL CLIENTS NEED OR WANT INSIGHT

No matter how much we as helpers personally value insight, not all of our clients are equally enamored. Some clients (and even some helpers) do not want or need insight. They prefer support without challenge and insight, or they want immediate behavior change without insight. They may want to feel better without understanding why they felt badly. Because the three-stage approach presented in this book is essentially client-centered and values empathy above all, it is important not to impose insight on such clients but to respect their choice not to understand themselves. For such clients, I recommend making an assessment about whether they primarily need support, behavior change, or something helpers cannot offer. If clients need support to make behavior changes, helpers can provide that and reduce the emphasis on the insight stage. If clients need other things (e.g., medication, support groups, welfare) that the helper is not competent to provide, helpers can refer them to other sources.

It is easy to blame the client for being resistant or reluctant if they are not "open" to what we want them to do. Rather than labeling clients, however, it is perhaps more helpful to think about how we as helpers have just not yet figured out how to reach this particular client.

COUNTERTRANSFERENCE

Finally, countertransference (defined and discussed in Chapters 2 and 11) can interfere with the helper's ability to deliver insight interventions effectively. For example, a client talking about abortion or divorce might stimulate unresolved feelings about these issues on the part of a helper. Similarly, a helper who has problems dealing with anger might withdraw when a client becomes angry at her. Once again, therapy and supervision can help to ensure that personal issues on the part of the helper do not unduly and negatively influence the helping relationship.

Strategies for Overcoming Difficulties in Implementing the Insight Stage

Helpers can overcome difficulties in the insight stage by focusing on empathy and using exploration skills, dealing with their personal feelings, and dealing with the helping relationship.

FOCUS ON EMPATHY AND USE EXPLORATION SKILLS

Often, when beginning helpers first learn insight skills, they get so anxious and focused on the insight skills that they forget to be empathic and focus on the client. Similarly, when helpers are in doubt or having problems coming up with insight skills, they can try to get back in touch with basic empathy for the client—how does the client feel? What would it be like to be the client? And, to facilitate empathy, the helper can refocus on the client using the exploration skills of attending and listening, open questions and probes about thoughts and feelings, restatements, and reflections of feelings. In effect, helpers need to backtrack, rebuild trust, and make sure they hear the client's real problems. Helpers can keep exploring until an idea for a challenge or interpretation emerges naturally and the client is ready to hear it.

DEAL WITH PERSONAL FEELINGS

It is important for helpers to be as aware as possible of what they are feeling (see Chapter 4). They need to sort out how much is a reaction to the client and how much is related to their own personal issues. Helpers can get personal therapy to deal with strong emotional reactions that arise when they are helpers. In addition, it is helpful to talk to supervisors about feelings that come up when working with clients.

DEAL WITH THE RELATIONSHIP

In one study (Rhodes, Hill, Thompson, & Elliott, 1994), satisfied clients were asked what their helpers had done to resolve major misunderstandings that arose in relationships. The clients reported that their helpers asked them how they were feeling about what was going on in the therapeutic relationship. In addition, helpers listened nondefensively to the clients and were willing to hear what they were doing wrong with clients. They apologized if they made a mistake or hurt the client's feelings.

If helpers acknowledge their part in problems in the helping relationship, they serve as models for how to deal with mistakes and how to respond in a compassionate way to another person. In addition, helpers can talk about their feelings about the relationship to let clients know how their behaviors influence others. Helpers can also ask clients to tell them if they feel offended or hurt. Providing a place where clients can discuss both positive and negative feelings toward the helper and the sessions is both challenging and critically important. Finally, helpers can thank clients for revealing their feelings. It is often painful and difficult to process the therapeutic relationship, so clients need to be assured that they can bring up both positive and negative feelings.

Example of an Extended Interaction in the Insight Stage

In this example, the helper has already established rapport, and the client has explored her feelings about her relationship with her daughter. The example starts at the beginning of the insight stage.

> *Helper:* So you said your daughter is not doing well in middle school and you're worried that she's going to flunk out of school. (The helper wants to tie together what the client has been talking about and so offers a summary statement.)

Client: Yeah, she just never does her homework. She watches television all the time, talks on the phone to her friends constantly, and eats. She's not even doing any extracurricular activities at school. I just can't get her to do anything. She just got her grades, which she wouldn't even let me see at first. I finally got them from her, and she's flunking two classes.

Helper: Have you considered getting her a tutor? (The helper jumps prematurely to the action stage here to offer suggestions for what to do about the problem.)

Client: We keep trying to get her to a tutor, but she doesn't want one. Last year we made her see a tutor, but it didn't help. She still flunked the course, and we wasted a lot of money.

Helper: You sound really frustrated. (The helper comes back to a focus on the client instead of on the client's daughter.)

Client: Yeah, I really am frustrated. I just don't know what to do. I feel so helpless. School was so important to me, and I feel that if she doesn't get a good education, she won't get anywhere in life. (The client really takes in the reflection and talks in more depth about her feelings about the problem with her daughter.)

Helper: You know, in my experience with my kids, it was really hard to separate myself from them. I wanted so much for them to be perfect to show that I was a perfect parent. (Helper uses disclosure to stimulate client insight.)

Client: Yeah, I get into that. I feel like I'm not a very good parent. Everyone else's kids are doing so well. They're all talking about their kids going to these expensive colleges. I want my kids to have all the things I didn't have and not feel as bad about themselves as adults as I do.

Helper: You really want the best for your children. (Helper restates to show support.)

Client: Yeah. Education wasn't a big thing in my family. My parents pushed me on religion and health food. In fact, they were really pushy; well, at least my mother was pushy about wanting me to be a missionary. We had such incredible fights when I was a teenager. They didn't even notice that I did well in school, so it was something I could do on my own.

Helper: Interesting—you wanted to be independent from your parents and make your own decisions in life, but you want your daughter to do what you tell her to do. (Helper challenges client with a contradiction of which the client seems to be unaware.)

Client: Wow, you're right! I can't believe that I would be doing the same thing to her that my parents did to me. I guess it seemed like such a different thing. I want her to do well in school, and my parents wanted to control me about religion. But I don't know how to be any different. I really try hard to be a good parent. It's so important to me.

Helper: I wonder if you think I'm judging you and maybe thinking you're bad for your parenting? (Helper picks up on the client's self-blaming and wants to see if she feels negatively toward her, so helper uses an immediacy statement.)

Client: Well, I don't know if you blame me. I blame myself. I just don't know how to quit doing what I'm doing with my daughter. I feel stuck. I don't know any other way to be a parent. I've tried as hard as I can.

Helper: You're feeling very discouraged. (Helper reflects feelings to support the client.)

Client: When I was younger, I didn't want to be a parent because I thought I would be rotten at it. I thought people should have to pass tests before they could become parents. There are so many rotten parents out there. But I was in therapy for a lot of years, and I thought I had solved a lot of my problems. But I guess I didn't solve them all. You know it was so much easier when the kids were younger.

Helper: Perhaps you're having problems now that your kids are teenagers because that's when you had your problems with your parents. You didn't get much of a model on how to be a parent of teenagers. (Helper interprets the client's current difficulties as related to past experiences.)

Client: That's really true. I sure didn't. You know, I still haven't forgiven my parents for some of the things they did. You wouldn't believe how controlling my mother was.

Helper: You still have a lot of anger at her. I wonder if you can identify with your daughter's anger? (Helper reflects feelings and interprets a parallel of the client's feelings with her daughter's to help the client get some empathy with daughter. Helper considers putting the client into an empty chair exercise to help work on the unfinished business with the parents but doesn't have enough time left in this session to be about to do it thoroughly.)

Client: Yeah, I know she feels angry at me. And you know, I feel good that she can express it. I used to just withdraw and get depressed when I was a kid. She at least can express herself pretty well sometimes. You know she does have a lot of spirit. She's different from me in some ways, yet in some ways she's a lot like me. School really is difficult for her. It's not fun for her to sit down and read a book like it is for me. She's just not academically oriented. But I guess she has to find her own way. She's not 5 years old anymore. Maybe I just have to trust that she will find herself. I have to accept her as she is just as I have to accept myself as I am. Maybe what I need to do is go back and do some more work on myself to see why I'm so controlling.

Helper: You've done a really good job of focusing on yourself. You've gone from blaming your daughter to looking at your part in this whole situation. (Helper wants to reinforce client for all the work she's done.)

Client: Yeah, it's not easy though. It's so much easier to blame her.

Helper: How do you feel about the work we've done today in trying to understand your conflicts with your daughter? (Helper asks how the client is feeling about their interaction.)

Client: I think I have a new understanding of my issues with my daughter. I'm not sure yet that I'll be able to stop having the fights, because they happen so quickly, but I do have a better idea what my part in the struggles is all about. I'll need to do a lot more thinking about what kind of relationship I want to have with my daughter.

What Do You Think?

- Several students have noted how difficult it is to learn and use the insight interventions. They have said that the exploration skills seemed easy, whereas now all of a sudden the insight skills seem hard. What is your experience?

- Many students forget to use the exploration skills when trying to use challenge, interpretation, disclosure, and immediacy. They revert to using lots of closed questions. What is your experience? What can you do to remember to integrate the exploration skills into the insight stage?
- How do you think clients from different cultures react to the insight skills as compared with the exploration skills?
- Debate the advantages and disadvantages of the insight stage. Identify the benefits and possible problems with moving clients to deeper awareness.
- Check which of the following obstacles you are most likely to face in your development of insight skills:
  _____ moving prematurely into the insight stage,
  _____ taking too much responsibility for developing insight,
  _____ applying psychoanalytic theory too rigidly,
  _____ taking clients at face value and not digging deeper,
  _____ forgetting to be empathic, and
  _____ forgetting that not all clients need or want insight from the helper.
- Which of the following strategies might help you cope with the potential obstacles you could face in the insight stage?
  _____ focus on empathy and use the exploration skills,
  _____ deal with personal feelings,
  _____ deal with the relationship.

RESEARCH SUMMARY

Training for Insight Skills

Citations: Chui, H., Hill, C. E., Hummel, A., Ericson, S., Ganginis, H., Ain, S., & Merson, E. (2013). *Training undergraduate helping skills students to use challenges.* Manuscript in preparation.
Jackson, J., Hill, C. E., Merson, E., Wydra, M., Liu, J., & Ericson, S. (2013). *Teaching undergraduates the skill of interpretation.* Manuscript in preparation.
Spangler, P., Hill, C. E., Dunn, M. G., Hummel, A., Walden, T., Liu, J., Jackson, J., Ganginis, H., & Salahuddin, N. (2013). *Helping in the here-and-now: Teaching undergraduates the skill of immediacy.* Manuscript in preparation.

Rationale: Given that students generally have much more difficulty learning insight skills than exploration and action skills, we wondered whether there might be particular methods that would help them learn these skills. The foundation for the studies was Bandura's (1979) theory that people learn by instruction, modeling, practice, and feedback. A secondary purpose was to determine whether some students benefit more from training than others do because this might have implications for selection of students for training programs.

Method: All three studies were conducted within semester-long undergraduate helping skills classes taught at one large public university in the United States. Each study involved three or four classes of about 30 students each taught by different instructors, all of whom had learned helping skills from me. The same basic design was used for each study, with some minor variations. At the beginning of the semester, students completed several measures. After the students had spent 6 to 8 weeks learning exploration skills, they were asked to read the chapter in the Hill (2004) text on the relevant skill (immediacy, challenge, or interpretation). They then participated in a 2-hour lecture and discussion class in which they heard a lecture about the target skill, saw video clips of expert therapists using the skill, and practiced the skill in the large class. A couple of days later, students participated in a 2-hour lab class, where they practice the target skill.

Interesting Findings:
- Some evidence was found across all three studies for the effectiveness of lecture, modeling, and practice. By far, the most effective component of training was practice.
- Students indicated some effects of culture on learning insight skills. Many felt that insight skills were not valued in their cultures (e.g., East Asians), making it difficult to learn these skills.
- Initial self-efficacy and previous helping experience predicted final immediacy self-efficacy. In addition, perceived cohesion among lab group members increased after learning and practicing immediacy.
- Students who initially reported low dominance had more gains in self-efficacy for using challenge than did students who were initially high in dominance.

Conclusions:
- Students really value practice in learning insight skills. We speculate that reading, lecture, and watching video clips of expert therapists using the skills set the foundation for learning but that practice is essential.
- Some components (e.g., reading, lecture, video clips, practice in large groups, practice in dyads) work well for some but not for others. Students vary in which components they like (e.g., some love reading, others do not).

RESEARCH SUMMARY (*Continued*)

Implications for Training:

- After reading, hearing a lecture, and watching video clips, students must have ample practice to learn how to implement the insight skills.
- Different types of practice seem to be beneficial (e.g., responding to written stimuli, responding to videotaped stimuli, practicing in large groups and hearing skills used by others, practicing in dyads).
- We suggest that a variety of components (instruction, modeling, practice, feedback) be used in training given that students differ in their learning styles.
- The quality of the video clips makes a big difference. Students need to feel that they can relate to the therapists in the clips. We also suspect that they need to discuss their reactions in class to benefit from the experience.
- We cannot select students for training based on these results. We suspect that performance-based measures (e.g., ability to respond facilitatively to a standard client) may predict better than self-report measures.

| **BONUS MATERIALS** | Practice exercises, labs, and other resources for students and teachers are available on the companion website: http://pubs.apa.org/books/supp/hill4. |

ACTION STAGE IV

Overview of the Action Stage   16

It is movement, not just insight, that produces change.
—*Waters and Lawrence* (1993, p. 40)

Not everything that is faced can be changed, but nothing can be changed unless it is faced.
—*James Baldwin*

Consuela sought help because she was feeling vaguely uninterested in life. During exploration with her helper, she described her situation as being devoid of close friendships. She also indicated that she had not been doing well in her job since she was promoted to a managerial position. She described her childhood as idyllic, with no major problems. After further exploration, Consuela revealed that her parents had been killed in a car accident a year ago. In the insight stage, the helper and Consuela began to piece together that Consuela had not had a chance to grieve the loss of her parents because she felt pressured to perform in her new job. She had moved to a new city to take the job right before her parents' deaths, and so she did not have friends to support her in the aftermath. In addition, Consuela's childhood was not as idyllic as she had initially indicated, in that she had gone through a rough adolescence with many fights with her parents. Through the helping process, she was able to understand that she felt angry at her parents because they had been so strict and had not allowed her to develop friendships outside the home. She was able to grieve her parents and the support they provided. At

http://dx.doi.org/10.1037/14345-016
Helping Skills: Facilitating Exploration, Insight, and Action, Fourth Edition, by C. E. Hill

this point, the helper decided to move into the action stage. Because Consuela indicated that she wanted to make new friends and deal with the stress of her job, they did assertiveness training to help her state more clearly what she wanted and needed from friends, relaxation training for helping her deal with stress, and some behavioral work to help to think about different ways of behaving in the work situation. After several sessions, Consuela started to make some friends and was feeling calmer about her work situation.

After clients have explored and gained insight, they are ready for the action stage, during which helpers collaborate with clients to explore the idea of change, explore options for change, and help them figure out how to make changes. These changes can be in thoughts (e.g., fewer self-defeating statements), feelings (e.g., less hostility), or behaviors (e.g., less overeating). The action stage also involves exploring feelings and examining values, priorities, barriers, and support in relation to change. The emphasis in this stage is on helping clients think about and make decisions about action rather than on dictating action to clients. Helpers are coaches rather than experts dispensing advice.

Rationale for the Action Stage

There are two important reasons for moving beyond insight to action. First, because most clients seek help to feel better or to change specific behaviors, thoughts, or feelings, it is important to help them attain these goals. Clients usually feel better if they not only gain insight but also develop some ideas about how to make needed changes in their lives. For example, Betty sought help because of problems with her roommate. She came to understand that it was hard for her to tell her roommate about her feelings because Betty's family was covert and indirect and never talked about feelings. This insight was important, but Betty also needed to translate the insight into action and change her behavior with her roommate.

Second, taking action is crucial for consolidating the new thinking patterns learned in the insight stage. Action makes insight more understandable and practical. New understandings can be fleeting unless something is done to help the client consolidate the insights. Old thinking patterns and behaviors easily resurface unless new ones are practiced and incorporated into existing schemas. For example, Miguel's old thinking pattern was that he was worthless unless he was perfect. When the helper challenged his thoughts, Miguel came to realize that he did not have to be perfect to accept himself. Miguel also came to understand that he acted needy and dependent because his parents never accepted him for who he was. His parents idealized his older, brilliant, and successful brother because they had never achieved much in their own lives. They had constantly put Miguel down for being only average in intelligence. Through the insight stage, Miguel came to realize that even though his parents did not accept him fully for who he was because of the comparison with his brother, he was still a worthy and lovable person. This insight was fragile and could have eroded, however, unless Miguel incorporated the learning into a new pattern of behavior and thinking. Thus, the helper worked with Miguel to think about possible changes. The two of them devised a list of things that Miguel wanted to do (e.g., sky-diving, rollerblading, going back to school) and developed a plan for how he could pursue these activities. Beginning to do things he wanted to do and at which he succeeded enabled Miguel to feel better about himself. The helper also worked with Miguel to help him meet friends with shared interests, so that he could receive social support. When he felt better about himself, Miguel began to question the things he had told himself about needing to be perfect. Hence, Miguel cycled back to insight after making changes.

Deterrents to Action

Sometimes newly gained insights lead spontaneously to action. Clients begin to say things such as,

> I can see that I've been so angry at the world because it felt unfair that I am not as smart and good-looking as my brother. I don't need to feel so angry now, because I can accept who I am and see that I have things to offer people. I am going to do the things that I want to do with my life"

or

> It makes sense that I had a hard time in my job if I kept treating my boss like my father. I don't need to do that anymore. I'm going to stand up to him and ask him for a raise.

Hence, moving to action comes naturally to some clients as they begin to talk about how they might apply what they have learned about themselves in the insight stage.

At other times, however, insight does not spontaneously lead to action, perhaps because clients feel stuck, understand the situation incompletely or only at an intellectual level, or do not take personal responsibility for their role in the maintenance of the problem. For example, Stefan might realize intellectually that he is upset about being fired, but he might not have allowed himself to feel the humiliation of the loss or experience his anger at his boss. He also might not have understood how he set himself up in self-defeating ways. Expressing, understanding, and accepting his feelings and his role in creating the situation are important tasks before moving to action, so Stefan and his helper might need to spend more time in the insight stage.

Another reason that insight might not lead directly to action is that clients might not have the necessary skills to take the next step. For example, even though Margarita understood why she was not assertive and wanted to change her behavior, she did not know how to stand up for herself. She could not behave more assertively because she did not have the skills needed for being assertive (e.g., maintaining eye contact, stating needs directly without blaming). Hence, clients may need to be taught these skills and may need to practice and get feedback about their performance to develop the skills adequately.

Even if they understand themselves thoroughly and have the skills to change, clients may lack the motivation to change. They may feel blocked from changing because old habits are hard to alter and they are afraid of trying anything new (e.g., a client learning to be more assertive might be reluctant to confront a friend for fear of losing the friendship). They may feel demoralized and not believe they can change. They may need encouragement to even begin thinking about change.

In addition, it is important to be aware that clients sometimes cannot make all the changes they may want or need to make because of limited talents and resources. For example, if Andrew has earned poor grades in college, getting into a high-ranking graduate program is an unlikely proposition. Hence, the goal of this stage is to enable clients to learn to make changes within the limits of the possibilities and to expand these possibilities as much as possible. For example, Andrew's helper might encourage him to explore advanced training in a related field so that he can pursue a career related to his goals. Although this view does not fit with the idealistic notion that every person can do whatever he or she wants, it fits with the more realistic idea of realizing one's limits and maximizing one's potentials within those limits.

Philosophical Underpinnings

The major philosophical underpinning of the action stage is that clients are the active agents of their own lives. They know when things are not going well and seek input to help them fix problems, but ultimately they make the decisions about how they want to be, and they are the ones who actually make whatever changes get made. The role of the helper in this stage is to serve as a coach, cheerleader, supporter, information giver, and consultant, but not to take over and "fix" the client.

This stage, then, is still client-centered, with helpers facilitating clients in thinking about change rather than imposing change on them.

Helpers do not have to know the best action plans for clients. In fact, helpers rarely need to form an opinion about what clients "must" or "should" do. The goal for helpers in this stage is to provide a support- ive environment and facilitate clients in resolving their problems and making their decisions. Hence, helpers need to be just as empathic and supportive as they were in earlier stages. Mickelson and Stevic (1971) found that behaviorally oriented counselors who were warm, empathic, and genuine were more effective with their clients than were those who were low in these facilitative conditions.

When clients decide for themselves what to do differently, they are more likely to take responsibility and ownership for their actions than if helpers dictate what they should do. Telling clients what to do, even if clients ask for advice, is often not helpful because clients become depen- dent on the helpers, especially if the client has a similar pattern in other relationships (see Teyber, 2006). Helpers cannot always be there for cli- ents, so they need to teach clients how to motivate themselves to change and how to implement changes in their lives. Thus, rather than solving clients' problems, helpers seek to enhance clients' problem-solving capaci- ties. With better coping skills, clients can address the problems that led them to seek help and are better equipped to solve problems in the future.

As you can see, helpers need to be supportive of clients and not be invested in whether and how they change. Whether the client chooses to change is her or his choice and responsibility rather than a reflection on the helper's skills and personal qualities. The helper's skills are involved in helping the client explore and make decisions about changes, not in which decision is made. Thus, the helper's goal is to encourage clients to explore whether they want to change, and if so, to assist them in making the changes they have identified as desirable. Otherwise, it is too easy for clients to replicate childhood patterns (e.g., acting or not acting) to please or defy helpers as they did their parents. Instead, helpers collaborate with clients in making choices, serving as facilitators of the process and helping clients explore the positives and negatives of the various choices rather than as experts who provide the answers and tell clients what to do.

Here is an example that illustrates the need for the action stage and shows how it is implemented. Casey acted silly (e.g., giggled uncontrol- lably) when she went out dancing because she was extremely nervous. Because Casey felt so embarrassed and panicked when she acted silly, she would leave dances early and then feel badly that she had missed all the fun. Through exploration and insight, she came to realize that her anxiety at dances arose from her fear of being with men. She was afraid no one would like her because her brothers had made fun of her when she was a child. Her brothers had told her that she was ugly and had taunted her about her face and hair. Insight was not enough, how- ever. Casey needed something to help her deal with the anxiety in the situation. The helper taught her relaxation and then strategized with her about how to handle specific situations at dances. When she felt a "silly" attack coming on, she and the helper planned that she would take a time-out in the bathroom, practice deep breathing, and watch what she was saying to herself. After practicing several times in sessions, Casey was able to attend a dance and enjoy it. She was even able to let a man touch her and allow herself to think that she was attractive. Being able to master the situation made Casey feel better about herself. She then began to reevaluate whether she was indeed ugly and wonder what had motivated her brothers to be so mean to her. Hence, insight led to action, which in turn led to more insight.

Markers for Knowing When to Move to Action

It is generally best to wait to move to the action stage until the client is ready for action. There are several indicators (markers) that a client might be ready to move on to action. The first is when the client has gained insight and starts spontaneously talking about action. This situation is the ideal because the helper is following the client's lead and providing what the client seems to need at the time.

Another situation in which action would be called for (sometimes at the beginning of the first session) is when the client presents with a specific problem and simply wants relief from that problem (e.g., a simple phobia such as fear of flying not complicated by other problems). In such cases, it makes sense for helpers to approach the problem straightforwardly and offer what help they know how to give (e.g., relaxation, exposure), after doing just enough exploration to make sure that they are working on the right problem. By giving clients what they ask for, helpers respect them and acknowledge their right to the type of services they want. Instead of trying to clients' their style and preferences, helpers respect these wishes and move to action. It may be that after making specific behavior changes, these clients will be curious about reasons for their behavior, but it is equally likely that they will just want to feel better.

Relatedly, some clients are in crisis and need to make some changes immediately. With these clients, helpers need to move quickly to action, shortening the exploration and insight stages. Such clients need more direct interventions because they are in crisis, are not psychologically minded, or cannot articulate their concerns. Some clients just want something or someone to make them feel better, and it is important for the helper to meet clients where they are rather than imposing her or his values on them. For example, a person who has been kicked out of his house, has no job or food, and has delusions may need immediate relief in terms of housing, food, and medication before he can focus on understanding. To rephrase Maslow's (1970) statement, "people cannot live on bread alone unless they have no bread." These clients, after they have received direct guidance about how to solve a pressing problem, might be willing to go back and understand what contributed to the problem or work on other problems.

Finally, another marker for moving to action is when the client is stuck in insight and not making changes. The classic example is the client who wallows in insight for years in therapy and knows exactly why she or he is dysfunctional (and often blames someone else) but then does nothing to accept the situation, take responsibility for the future, and change. Such clients can be gently encouraged to move to action.

Theoretical Background: Behavioral and Cognitive Theories

Behavioral theories lay the foundation for the action stage. In this section, I discuss the underlying assumptions of these theories, the principles of learning, and treatment strategies.

ASSUMPTIONS OF BEHAVIORAL THEORIES

Behavioral theories share several basic assumptions (Gelso & Fretz, 2001; Rimm & Masters, 1979):

- a focus on overt behaviors rather than unconscious motivations;
- a focus on what maintains symptoms rather than on what caused them;
- an assumption that behaviors are learned;
- an emphasis on the present as opposed to the past;
- an emphasis on the importance of specific, clearly defined goals;
- a valuing of an active, directive, and prescriptive role for helpers;
- a belief that the helper–client relationship is important to establish rapport and gain client collaboration but is not enough to help clients change;
- a focus on determining adaptive behaviors for specific situations rather than on seeking personality change; and
- a reliance on empirical data and scientific methods.

One of the defining characteristics of behavioral approaches is that behaviors, emotions, and cognitions (both adaptive and maladaptive) are learned (Gelso & Fretz, 2001); therefore, it is important to talk about how learning takes place. Rather than covering all behavioral theory, I cover those aspects that are most relevant to helping skills training: operant conditioning, modeling (also called observational learning), and cognitively mediated learning. Although the three types of learning are not as distinct as once thought, it is still useful to be aware of the different types.

OPERANT CONDITIONING

In operant conditioning, behaviors are thought to be controlled by their consequences (Kazdin, 2013; Rimm & Masters, 1979; Skinner, 1953). *Reinforcement* is anything that follows a behavior and increases the probability that the behavior will occur again. An event, behavior, privilege, or material object that increases the likelihood of a behavior occurring again is called a *positive reinforcer*. *Primary reinforcers* (e.g., food, water, sex) are biological necessities, whereas *secondary reinforcers* (e.g., praise, money) gain their reinforcing properties through association with primary reinforcers. An example of a positive reinforcer related to helping is an approval–reassurance given after a client talks about feelings if it leads to the client talking more about feelings.

Note that things are not always reinforcing (e.g., food is typically reinforcing only if a person is hungry) and that reinforcers are not the same for all individuals (e.g., a long bath may be reinforcing for one person but not another). Whether something is a reinforcer can only be determined by looking at whether the target behavior increases when the reinforcer is administered. Thus, a helper can determine whether something is reinforcing by observing the client's response.

To be effective, reinforcement must be contingent on, or linked directly to, the behavior (Rimm & Masters, 1979). An office worker who receives a raise every 3 months regardless of the quality of work is less likely to change his or her behavior than is the office worker whose raise is contingent on good performance.

For a behavior to be reinforced, it must first be performed. Hence, helpers often have to engage in *shaping,* which refers to the gradual training of a complex response by reinforcing closer and closer approximations to the desired behavior. Goldfried and Davison (1994) gave the example of training a developmentally disabled child to make his bed by first reinforcing him for fluffing up his pillow, then for pulling the top sheet forward, and so on. Each of these acts is a successive approximation of the final desired behavior. An example of shaping is how we teach exploration skills. We might first ask the trainee to practice listening empathically without saying anything, then ask him or her to repeat exactly what the client said, next ask the trainee to say the main word the client is communicating, and finally ask him or her to give restatements and reflections of feelings. Thus, we try to shape the helper's skills by starting with easier skills and moving on to more difficult ones only after the trainee has mastered the easier ones.

Punishment occurs after a behavior and reduces the probability that the behavior will occur again. Goldfried and Davison (1994) identified three punishment procedures: (a) presenting an aversive event (e.g., a frown when the client reports something undesirable), (b) removing a person from a situation in which she or he would otherwise be able to earn reinforcers (e.g., a time-out in a room away from anyone who could provide positive reinforcement), and (c) reducing a person's collection of reinforcers (e.g., taking away candy). The purpose of punishment in clinical situations is to decrease the frequency of maladaptive behaviors (e.g., inappropriate interrupting, nonstop talking).

It is difficult to deliver punishment immediately after the behavior. As a result, often a person is punished for being discovered rather than for the behavior itself. Hence, when punishment is used as the primary mode of behavior management, people often figure out how to avoid getting caught rather than decreasing the problematic behavior. For example, a child who steals cookies feels great (is reinforced) when he steals the cookies because they taste good, but he feels bad several hours later when he gets caught. Because the punishment is contingent on getting caught rather than on eating the cookies, the clever child figures out a way to get the cookies without getting caught.

Another important behavioral concept is *generalization,* which involves the transfer of learning from one situation to other, similar situations. For example, if kicking and hitting are punished with time-outs and cooperative behavior is positively reinforced at school, one would expect a decrease in kicking and hitting and an increase in cooperative behavior in the home setting. However, these behaviors are most likely to generalize if they are punished and reinforced in the same manner in the home setting as in the school setting. Another example of generalization is when a person acts frightened of a teacher or helper because she or he was punished by authority figures in the past (a concept similar to transference).

Extinction reduces the probability of a behavior occurring by withholding reinforcers after the behavior is established (Goldfried & Davison, 1994). For example, if a parent's attention reinforces fighting among siblings (when no other problems are apparent), a helper might instruct the parents to ignore the fighting and let the kids work out their problems on their own (unless one child is in danger of getting hurt) in the hopes that it will extinguish. Goldfried and Davison (1994) noted that extinction is best facilitated by concurrently reinforcing an incompatible and more adaptive behavior. Thus, in the previous example, the parents might suggest that the siblings play separately and then praise them if they play quietly.

Operant conditioning is often used when working with children because they are not usually amenable to insight-oriented approaches. For example, I used operant methods for several specific behavioral problems with my children (e.g., to reduce fighting, to help them get off to school on time in the morning, to help them sleep through the night in their own beds). It can also be useful for adults changing bad habits (e.g., nail biting, procrastination, overeating, underexercising, excessive drinking of alcohol or coffee). For more detail on self-help methods for dealing with behavioral problems, see Watson and Tharp (2006).

Although the concepts of operant conditioning sound relatively straightforward, helpers often have difficulty applying them because of the complexity of human nature and because helpers often have minimal control over the reinforcers and punishments in the environment. In fact, Goldfried and Davison (1994) aptly noted that helpers typically do not reinforce the actual changes but rather reinforce the client's talking about making specific changes. Clients have to transfer the reinforcement from talking about changing to implementing the changes outside the session. Thus, helpers act more as consultants, whereas clients are the actual change agents.

MODELING

People often learn things even though they have never been reinforced for performing them. One explanation for this learning is that they have learned through modeling or observational learning, which occurs when a person observes another person (a model) perform a behavior and receive consequences (Bandura, 1977; Kazdin, 2013). For example, children learn how to be parents by watching their parents and experiencing the effects of their child-rearing practices. Students learn how to be teachers by observing effective and ineffective educators. Helpers learn how to help by observing the behaviors of effective and ineffective helpers.

To understand how modeling works, learning and performance must be distinguished. A person can observe a model and thus learn a behavior. Whether the person actually performs the learned behavior, however, depends on the consequences at the time of performance. Bandura (1965) demonstrated this distinction between learning and performance with his classic Bobo doll study. Children observed a film in which an adult hit or kicked a Bobo doll (a life-size, inflatable, plastic doll that is weighted so it pops upright after it is punched down). The adult's behavior was rewarded, punished, or met with no consequences. When the children were put in the room with the Bobo doll, those who had observed the aggression being punished were less aggressive than were those who had observed the aggression being rewarded or ignored. When all children were given an incentive for performing the aggressive behavior, there were no differences among conditions, indicating that children in all conditions learned aggressive behaviors equally well. Bandura concluded that learning occurred through observation but performance depended on whether the child perceived that the adult was rewarded or punished.

Kazdin (2013) noted that imitation of models by observers is greater when models are similar to observers, more prestigious, higher in status and expertise than observers, and when several models perform the same behavior. Thus, helpers can learn about helping by watching videotapes of many experts. In addition, clients are probably more willing to listen to and accept suggestions from helpers whom they perceive to be credible and expert.

Modeling is an especially important component of helper training. Watching experts conduct therapy is incredibly useful (see the review by Hill & Lent, 2006). Students who have worked in my lab transcribing and coding therapy sessions often say that this experience was incredibly valuable in terms of learning what they liked and disliked about therapy.

COGNITIVE THEORY

Whereas early behaviorists such as Skinner believed in a stimulus–response model (meaning that people respond directly to environmental cues [e.g., noise leads to a startle response]), cognitive theorists (e.g., A. T. Beck, 1976; Ellis, 1962; Meichenbaum & Turk, 1987) introduced a stimulus–organism–response (S-O-R) model. In the S-O-R model, the organism (i.e., person) processes the stimulus before determining how to respond. Thus, people respond not to stimuli but to their interpretation of stimuli. For example, how Esteban reacts to a noise heard in the middle of the night is dependent on whether he thinks it is a benign noise (the house "settling") or whether he thinks the noise was made by a burglar. Thus, it is important to look for and dispute irrational thoughts (e.g., "I must be perfect," "Everyone must love me"). Theorists such as Beck, Ellis, and Meichenbaum have suggested that it is not so much events that cause a person to become upset but what the person thinks about the events.

Cognitive processes are of utmost importance to the helping situation. As discussed in Chapter 2, much of the helping process takes place at covert levels. Helpers' intentions for their interventions as well as their perceptions of clients' reactions influence their subsequent interventions. In addition, clients have reactions to helpers' interventions as well as intentions for how to influence helpers. Hence, a cognitively mediated model for understanding the helping process makes a lot of sense.

HOW BEHAVIORAL AND COGNITIVE THEORIES RELATE TO THE ACTION STAGE

Behavioral and cognitive theories fit well into the action stage of the helping model because they provide specific strategies for helping clients change. When clients have explored thoughts and feelings thoroughly and obtained insight about themselves, action allows them to determine how they would like to change their lives. When used in an empathic and collaborative manner at the appropriate time, behavioral and cognitive treatments can facilitate change. Core components of behavioral (e.g., reinforcement, modeling) and cognitive theories (e.g., intentions) are incorporated into the steps for working with the four types of action (see Chapter 17).

The major difference between behavioral and cognitive theorists on the one hand and the three-stage model on the other hand is that the former do not emphasize the importance of engaging in the exploration and insight stages. Helpers working from these models may engage in exploration and insight, but they do not view these as curative elements of the treatment.

Goals of the Action Stage

The goals of the action stage are for helpers to encourage clients to explore possible new behaviors, assist clients in deciding on actions, facilitate the development of skills for action, provide feedback about attempted changes, assist clients in evaluating and modifying action plans, and encourage clients in processing feelings about action (see Exhibit 16.1). While in the action stage, helpers need to remember to be empathic and pace themselves according to clients' needs. A stance of exploring, rather than prescribing, action is typically most helpful.

Skills of the Action Stage

The skills used uniquely in the action stage are open questions and probes for action, information, feedback about the client, process advisement, direct guidance, and disclosure of strategies. The purpose of the most frequently used skill, open questions and probes for action, is to stimulate clients in their thinking about action. Information is important to educate clients about options for action. Feedback about the client allows

---

EXHIBIT 16.1

List of Goals, Types, and Skills to Facilitate the Action Stage

---

Goals
    Explore possible new behaviors.
    Assist clients in deciding on actions.
    Facilitate the development of skills for action.
    Provide feedback about attempted changes.
    Assist clients in evaluating and modifying action plans.
    Encourage clients in processing feelings about action.
Types of action
    Relaxation
    Behavior change
    Behavioral rehearsal and assertiveness
    Decision making
Skills
    Open questions and probes for action
    Information
    Feedback about client
    Process advisement
    Direct guidance
    Disclosures of strategies

---

helpers to let clients know how they come across to the helpers. Process advisement is used to direct the process of sessions, particularly in doing therapeutic exercises (e.g., behavioral rehearsal) within sessions. Direct guidance is occasionally useful to give some advice to clients about the best strategies. Disclosure of strategies is another, more tentative, way to suggest action ideas.

Helpers also continue to use exploration skills throughout the action stage. Restatements and reflections of feelings are particularly useful for uncovering feelings related to change, demonstrating support, and ensuring that helpers accurately hear what clients are saying. When clients are stuck, insight skills such as challenge, interpretation, self-disclosure, and immediacy are used to uncover obstacles to action.

Skills in the action stage are not used as discretely as they are used in the exploration and insight stages. Rather, skills are used to accomplish the steps of working on four different types of action (relaxation, behavior change, behavioral rehearsal, decision making). Hence, in this section, I briefly present the skills that are used in the action stage. In Chapter 18, I discuss how the skills are integrated to work with the four types of action.

These action skills require more input on the part of the helper, so helpers have to be sure that clients are ready for these interventions (i.e., have explored enough). Helpers also need to be attentive to observing client reactions to see how they are responding and to make sure that clients are actively involved in the process.

OPEN QUESTIONS AND PROBES FOR ACTION

Open questions and probes for action are questions aimed specifically at helping clients explore action (see Exhibit 16.2). For example,

- What kinds of things have you tried?
- How did it work when you tried that?
- What ideas do you have about what to do in this situation?
- What might happen if you tried that?

Rationale for Using Open Questions and Probes for Action

Open questions and probes for action are particularly useful for gently guiding clients through the action stage. They are the primary tool through which helpers find out whether clients are ready to change, what they have tried before, what ideas they have for action, what barriers they see to change, and how they respond to action ideas. By using open questions and probes, the helper implicitly communicates that she or he is guiding or coaching the client to figure out about action rather than providing answers. Thus, helpers encourage clients to solve problems with their support, communicate respect that clients have self-healing capacity, and minimize the likelihood of imposing helpers' values on clients. By using open questions and probes, helpers can also teach clients a process of thinking through problems and possible solutions.

EXHIBIT 16.2

Overview of Open Questions and Probes for Action

Definition	*Open questions and probes for action* invite clients to explore action goals.
Example	"What have you tried before?" "What would be the benefits of changing?"
Typical intentions	To promote insight (see Web Form D).
Possible client reactions	Clear, feelings (see Web Form G). Recounting, affective exploration (see Web Form H).
Desired client behaviors	Convey empathy with your question. Make sure your questions are open instead of closed.
Helpful hints	Avoid asking multiple questions in a row. Focus on the client rather than on others. Observe client reactions to your questions.

Guidelines for Using Open Questions and Probes for Action

As discussed with open questions and probes for exploration and insight, open questions and probes for action should be done gently and with an air of curiosity. The helper is collaboratively inquiring and helping the client figure out about action. Helpers should be careful not to ask too many questions at one time, make sure to give clients time to respond, vary questions with other skills so that they do not sound repetitive, and make sure that questions are open rather than closed.

Examples of Open Questions and Probes for Action

The following shows a helper using open questions and probes for action (in italics) in a session:

> *Helper:* So you've talked quite a bit about these kids bullying you and kicking in your locker. *What are your thoughts about what you might do?*
>
> *Client:* I don't know.
>
> *Helper:* You sound a little anxious as you say that. What's going on inside?
>
> *Client:* I'm scared. There's four of them, and only one of me. They're a lot bigger.
>
> *Helper:* Yeah, I would be scared too. *What have they told you at school about this kind of bullying?*
>
> *Client:* They said that we should report it to the principal.
>
> *Helper:* *What would that be like for you?*
>
> *Client:* I don't know. I guess it feels like I would be grassing on them. They might get back at me. But the principal always says that bullying is not okay and that we should say something.
>
> *Helper:* *Would you like to try that?*
>
> *Client:* I think I would like to say something.

GIVING INFORMATION

Giving information can be defined as providing specific data, facts, resources, answers to questions, or opinions to clients (see Exhibit 16.3). There are several types of information:

- educating the client (e.g., "The rationale for asking you to develop your own ideas is for you to take responsibility for coming up with choices," "Role-playing involves practicing how you might respond differently when you talk to your mother," "Having a specific place to study allows students to concentrate better on their studies without distractions"),

---

EXHIBIT 16.3

Overview of Giving Information

Definition	*Giving information* refers to supplying data, facts, resources, answers to questions, or opinions.
Example	"Both the career center and counseling center have information about careers." "The test takes about 2 hours to complete."
Typical intentions	To give information, to promote change (see Web Form D).
Possible client reactions	Educated, new ways to behave, hopeful, no reaction (see Web Form G).
Desired client behaviors	Agreement, therapeutic changes (see Web Form H).
Helpful hints	Make sure the client needs the information. Remember to be empathic, gentle, and not authoritarian. Observe the client's reaction. Do not provide too much information at one time. Put crucial information in writing. Turn the focus back to the client after giving information.

- providing information about assessment or psychological tests (e.g., "The Strong Interest Inventory measures a person's interests and compares them with interests of people happily employed in a variety of occupations"), and
- educating the client about the world or psychological principles (e.g., "A moderate amount of stress is typically helpful to motivate a person, but too much or too little stress can be counterproductive"; "Many women become depressed after giving birth. There's even a term for it—it's called *postpartum depression*").

Rationale for Giving Information

In the action stage, helpers sometimes shift into a teacher's role to provide information. They occasionally act as educators, which is appropriate if the information is given in a caring manner when clients need information and are ready to listen. For example, a helper might educate a client about his mental condition or about what to expect in different situations. Or a helper might explain what happens during panic attacks as a way of teaching a client that the physical sensations she experiences (e.g., heart palpitations) are due to anxiety rather than a heart attack. Such information can lead to change when clients are open to learning.

Sometimes, however, helpers do not have information to give. Rather than assume that one must know everything before becoming a helper (obviously an impossible task), helpers can be aware of some basic information (e.g., referral sources) but then focus on helping clients figure out how to get the needed information themselves.

Information is not always the most appropriate intervention in a situation, however, even when the client requests this type of assistance and the helper knows the information. Sometimes clients need to explore how they feel about situations without being told what is "normal" or expected. Other clients need to seek out information themselves rather than having the investigative work done for them. Some clients need to be challenged to think about why they do not already have the desired information and to think about what motivates them to rely on others to give them information.

Guidelines for Giving Information

Before giving information, helpers may find it useful to ask what information or what misinformation clients possess (e.g., "What do you know about getting into graduate school?"). Thus, rather than assuming clients need information, helpers can assess clients' knowledge base. They can also ask clients what strategies they have used to gather information.

Examination of intentions is critical to ensure that information is delivered appropriately. Helpers should think carefully about their intentions. Helpers can ask themselves what is motivating them to want to give information at this particular point, and for whom (the client or helper) this information will be helpful. Helpers can ask themselves the following:

- Do I want to educate the client?
- Do I want to normalize the experience?
- Do I want to explain what is happening in the session?
- Does the client need this information?

If the answer to any of these questions is yes, if the issue is straightforward and not motivated by inappropriate needs, and if the helper has the requisite information, helpers can provide information. Sometimes helpers do have valuable information and can serve as resources for clients. When giving information, of course, helpers should be empathic, gentle, and sensitive to how clients are reacting. The goal of delivering information is not to lecture clients or act as an expert, but rather to educate clients when they are ready to learn and when it does not undermine clients' independence in searching out their own information.

If helpers determine that giving information is appropriate, they should not provide too much information at one time. In medical relationships, Meichenbaum and Turk (1987) found that patients remember very little of the information that doctors give them. Ironically, the more information given by doctors, the less patients remember. Similarly, when clients are anxious in helping situations, it is easy for them to forget information. Thus, helpers may just give a small amount of information and put crucial information (e.g., referral numbers, homework assignments) in writing to assist clients in accessing the information later.

As with disclosures, helpers turn the focus back to the client after providing information to see the client's reaction. For example, after describing his position on the use of prescription drugs for psychiatric illnesses, a helper might ask the client about her thoughts and reactions to using prescription drugs.

Sometimes when a client requests information, the helper is not sure that it is best to give the client information at this point. Helpers can ask themselves the following:

- Is the client trying to make me feel needed or like an expert?
- Is the client trying to avoid exploration or insight?
- Is the client resorting to familiar defenses of being dependent on others?
- Does giving information foster further dependency in the client?
- Does the client expect me to be like a medical doctor who asks questions about the problem and then gives a diagnosis and course of treatment?
- Is the client testing me or my credibility?

Rather than giving the information right away, the helper might may ask clients what is motivating them to ask for information, what they want to do with the information, or what they hope the helper will do for them (e.g., "I'd be happy to answer your question, but first let's talk about why you ask"). If the client is requesting information as a ploy in the interpersonal interaction (e.g., for dependency needs or to make the helper feel needed), the helper can use immediacy skills to address this issue (see Chapter 15). It is often better to find out what is beneath the request than to ignore it or engage in a power struggle over who controls the information.

Once the helper knows the motives behind the request for information, he or she can address these motives directly. For example, if the client expects the helper to make a diagnosis and dictate the course of treatment, the helper can either educate the client that she or he uses a different treatment strategy or refer the client to someone who is more likely to meet these expectations. Helpers need to think carefully about how to handle these situations (and, as always, talking the situation over with supervisors or trusted peers can aid helpers in dealing with such situations in the future).

On the other hand, there are times when it is good to avoid giving information. When helpers answer yes to any of the following questions, they might want to use other skills:

- Do I want to inappropriately minimize client anxiety?
- Do I want to show the client how much I know?

Examples of Giving Information

The following shows a helper giving information (in italics) in a session:

Client: So tell me all about your class. I think I want to take it next year.

Helper: It sounds like you would be interested in learning helping skills.

Client: Yeah, I've always had the idea that maybe I might want to be a social worker. But on the other hand, I'm not sure I would be very good at helping.

Helper: What concerns do you have about learning helping skills?

Client: I'm afraid of getting too involved with the clients. I feel so responsible for my friends when they talk about their problems. I feel like I have to solve all their problems and tell them exactly what to do.

Helper: So maybe you're worried that you won't be able to have any distance from clients in a helping setting.

Client: Yeah, do they talk about how to deal with that in the class?

Helper: Sounds like you really need some help with that.

Client: I do. I had a friend talk to me just yesterday, and I felt totally depressed when we were done because I felt like I had done nothing to help her. I'm afraid that she felt worse when we were done. It reminded me of my mother and father, who both want to talk to me ever since they divorced. Both want me to be on their side. Sometimes I feel split in half.

Helper: I can see why you'd be nervous about the helping situation after having to be a helper with your parents.

Client: Yeah. What was it like for you?

Helper: *I have had a good experience in the class. The professor has talked a lot about how we have to get personal issues dealt with in our own therapy or else it is difficult to help clients with their issues.* I wonder if you have ever explored the idea of getting into therapy?

Client: Not really. I don't know much about it.

Helper: *There's a counseling center right here on campus that offers 12 sessions of free therapy for students.*

Client: Really? I'll have to think about that. Maybe I'll check it out.

GIVING FEEDBACK ABOUT THE CLIENT

Giving feedback can be defined as the helper giving information to the client about his or her behaviors or impact on others (see Exhibit 16.4). It is a type of information (see previous section), but it is confined to information about the client specifically. Examples of feedback about the client include the following:

- You expressed yourself very clearly and concisely in the role-play.
- You are smiling a lot and seem more open to making changes.
- I noticed that you were tapping your foot during the relaxation exercise.

Rationale for Giving Feedback About the Client

Brammer and MacDonald (1996) suggested that effective feedback can increase clients' self-awareness, which can in turn lead to behavior change. For example, if the helper comments that Jennifer always ends her sentences with a question and thus sounds tentative when she speaks, this might lead Jennifer to become aware of how she talks and try to change her behavior. When she begins to make definite statements, other people might begin to take Jennifer more seriously.

EXHIBIT 16.4

Overview of Feedback About the Client

Definition	*Feedback* is giving information to the client about his or her behaviors or impact on others.
Example	"You maintained good eye contact during the role-play, but your voice sounded hesitant when you told your partner that you were leaving the relationship."
	"You did a good job of stating what is difficult about making a decision, but I wonder if you could give me an example."
Typical intentions	To give information, to promote change (see Web Form D).
Possible client reactions	New ways to behave, responsibility, misunderstood (see Web Form G).
Desired client behaviors	Cognitive–behavioral exploration, affective exploration, therapeutic changes (see Web Form H).
Helpful hints	Make sure you have a good relationship before you provide feedback. Give mostly positive feedback.
	Present positive feedback before negative feedback.
	Make sure to note that the feedback is your personal observation rather than "fact."
	Make the feedback descriptive and behavioral rather than evaluative. Observe the client's reactions.

Research shows that clients prefer positive feedback and think it is more accurate than negative feedback (Claiborn, Goodyear, & Horner, 2002). Positive feedback is good to use early on to establish the relationship and enhance credibility. In addition, if negative feedback must be given, it is best to precede it with positive feedback or to sandwich it between two pieces of positive feedback.

Feedback about the client (e.g., "You did a good job explaining your reasons") is similar to immediacy (e.g., "I feel good about our relationship") in that both involve something about the client. Feedback about the client is only about the client, whereas immediacy is about the interaction between helper and client in the therapeutic relationship. In addition, whereas immediacy is used in the insight stage to promote insight and deal with problems in the therapeutic relationship, feedback about the client is used in the action stage to assist clients in generating, implementing, and maintaining changes in thoughts, feelings, and behaviors.

It can be difficult for beginning helpers to provide feedback to clients because it is a different behavior than one usually uses in social interactions and can be met with resistance. Beginning helpers often become victims of the *mum effect*, a tendency to withhold bad news even if it is in the best interest of others to hear it (Egan, 1994). In ancient times, bearers of bad news were killed, which not too surprisingly led to some reluctance to be the one to bear bad news or give negative feedback.

Guidelines for Giving Feedback

Some guidelines to consider in giving feedback are the following:

- Give feedback about the client cautiously, with the clear understanding that the helper is offering his or her personal observations about the client's behavior.
- Make the statements descriptive (e.g., "You spoke very softly") rather than evaluative (e.g., "You aren't taking this role-play very seriously").
- Emphasize strengths (e.g., "You effectively articulated your feelings") before weaknesses (e.g., "but you didn't sound like you really believed it") to make it easier for clients to hear the feedback.
- Give feedback about things clients can change (e.g., nonverbal behaviors, actions) rather than about physical characteristics or life circumstances that cannot be changed (e.g., height, personality).
- Give feedback in close proximity in terms of time to the occurrence of the behavior (e.g., "You spoke with more assurance that time") rather than waiting for a long time and then trying to recreate the situation (e.g., "Last session you looked away from me and didn't say anything").

▪ As with the other action skills, give feedback with a lot of empathy and support. Negative feedback could damage the helping process if it is perceived as threatening or inaccurate, so helpers need to do it gently and tentatively after a good relationship is established.

Example of Feedback

The following shows a helper giving feedback (in italics) in a session:

Client:	I tried the homework you suggested about trying to make more friends.
Helper:	Fantastic. How did it go?
Client:	Well, I smiled more often and tried to look at people when I was crossing campus.
Helper:	That's great. How did that feel?
Client:	It was a little strange at first, but then it was nice to see people smiling back at me. No one came up to me, but it felt like a start.
Helper:	You were also going to try to initiate a conversation with someone in class. How did that go?
Client:	That didn't go so well. I picked Sally because she usually seems friendly. I sat near her as planned, but then I got scared at the last minute and didn't say anything to her.
Helper:	Let's role-play that so I can see how you did it. Let's pretend that I'm Sally.
Client:	I sat next to her but I didn't say anything, so there's nothing really to role-play.
Helper:	Okay, let's try it where I play you and you play Sally and see if we can come up with some ideas about how to do it. Would that be okay?
Client:	Sure, that would be great.
Helper:	Hi Sally, how's it going?
Client:	Oh hi, pretty good, except I'm stressed out about this test.
Helper:	Me too. Would you be interested in studying together?
Client:	Sure. Want to meet later for coffee and study?
Helper:	How did that feel? Do you think you'd be able to do that?
Client:	Yeah, I think I could. Let me try . . . Hi Sally. Umm, how's it going? Would you like to study for the exam together?
Helper:	*Great, you did it, you got it out, and you looked directly at me when you said it. That's a big improvement.*

Maybe next time you could slow down a bit when you are talking. Let's practice again, because it can really help to practice until you feel comfortable here.

PROCESS ADVISEMENT

With *process advisement,* helpers direct clients to do things *within* helping sessions (e.g., "Show me how you acted when your roommate asked to borrow your new dress," "Play the part of the man in your fantasy"). Process advisement is a type of advice or direct guidance (see the next section), but it is confined to directing what goes on in the session (see Exhibit 16.5).

Rationale for Giving Process Advisement

Helpers are experts on how to facilitate the helping process and, hence, often have suggestions about what clients can do in sessions to facilitate the change process. Clients, in contrast, are not experts in the helping process and consequently rely (within limits) on helpers for judgments about how to proceed in sessions. The primary use of process advisement in the action stage is through behavioral exercises such as behavioral rehearsal or role-playing (see Chapter 17).

EXHIBIT 16.5

Overview of Process Advisement

Definition	*Process advisement* refers to helper directives for what the client should do *within* the session.
Example	"Let's try a role-play to practice a new way of acting in that situation. You be yourself, and I'll be your boss. Try to use the assertive behaviors we practiced earlier."
Typical intention	To promote change (see Web Form D).
Possible client reactions	Educated, unstuck, new ways to behave, hopeful, confused, misunderstood, no reaction (see Web Form G).
Desired client behaviors	Agreement, therapeutic changes (see Web Form H).
Helpful hints	Give a credible rationale for using process advisement.
	Be clear and unapologetic about what you want the client to do.
	Observe how the client responds to process advisement and modify if needed to fit the client.
	Do not get involved in a control struggle over what to do; in such a situation, help the client explore the resistance or use immediacy to discuss the relationship.

Guidelines for Giving Process Advisement

Clients are generally agreeable to trying things in sessions that helpers deem appropriate if they trust the helper and are presented with a credible rationale for why the exercise might be helpful (e.g., "Let's try this role-play to help you learn how to be more assertive. It may feel silly at first, but it can be helpful"). So the idea is to present the idea in a clear, calm manner that transmits confidence that this exercise will help the client.

Helpers try to be attentive to signs that clients do not want to follow process advisements. Signs may range from passive resistance (e.g., hesitance, not responding, changing the topic) to more active resistance (saying "Yes, but . . . " or arguing). It may be that the helper has presented the process advisement poorly, and so the client is reluctant to try it. Or it could be the helpers present the process advisement in an apologetic manner (e.g., "I don't suppose you'd want to do this exercise that my supervisor suggested?"), which often defeats the possibility of gaining client cooperation. Or sometimes helpers are not clear about what they want the client to do. Furthermore, some helpers do not provide a clear rationale for why the activity is important or how it might help the client.

Some clients do not want to follow process advisement no matter how skillfully it is presented by the helper. At all times, helpers need to respect the client's decision not to participate in an exercise. Perhaps the worst thing to do with reluctant or resistant clients is to get into a control struggle with them because control struggles tend to escalate, sometimes leading to disastrous consequences, with both people feeling that they will lose "face" if they back down. If a control struggle starts, helpers can step back and use exploration skills to understand why clients are reluctant, or they can use immediacy to work with the therapeutic relationship.

Example of Process Advisement

The following shows a helper giving process advisement (in italics) in a session:

> *Helper:* You've talked a lot about your indecision about whether to put your mother in an assisted living home. *I wonder if you would be willing to try something here in the session?*
>
> *Client:* What?
>
> *Helper:* *What I'd like you to do is to pretend that your mother is over there in that chair and tell her how you're feeling.*
>
> *Client:* Yikes, that sounds a little scary.
>
> *Helper:* *Yeah, it might be at first. Would you be willing to try it?*
>
> *Client:* Sure, why not. So she's in that chair? (Helper nods.) Mom, I know you don't want to go, but I don't know what to do.

> *Helper:* *Take a deep breath.* (Pause while the client takes a deep breath) *Now think about what you would like to say.*
>
> *Client:* Okay, let me try again. Mom, I know you're scared of going to the assisted living place, and I am too, but I think it's time. I can't take care of you when I live 1,000 miles away, and it's not safe for you to be alone.
>
> *Helper:* Good. How did that feel?
>
> *Client:* It felt a lot better. I felt like I knew what I wanted to say.
>
> *Helper:* Yeah, you sounded good. *Now let's see how she might respond and how you could handle that . . .*

DIRECT GUIDANCE

Direct guidance can be defined as making suggestions, giving directives, or providing advice for what helpers think clients should do *outside* of helping sessions (see Exhibit 16.6). Examples include providing suggestions to parents who are exploring ways of dealing with bedtime for a young child, to a client about coping strategies after a hospitalization, or to a middle-aged person for dealing with an elderly parent with Alzheimer's disease.

EXHIBIT 16.6

Overview of Direct Guidance

Definition	*Direct guidance* refers to helper suggestions, directives, or advice for the client to implement *outside* the session.
Example	"When you have the nightmare the next time, wake yourself up and imagine a new ending where you get angry at the intruder and chase him out of the house."
Typical intention	To promote change (see Web Form D).
Possible client reactions	Educated, unstuck, new ways to behave, hopeful, confused, misunderstood, no reaction (see Web Form G).
Desired client behaviors	Agreement, therapeutic changes (see Web Form H).
Helpful hints	Make sure that you have thoroughly explored the problem.
	Collaborate with the client to figure out the best assignment.
	Choose a task that fits the problem, is not difficult to implement, and is based on the client's strengths.
	Give a credible rationale for the guidance.
	Be clear about what you want the client to do; write it down if necessary.
	Observe how the client responds to the direct guidance and modify if needed to fit the client.
	Do not get involved in a control struggle over what to do; in such a situation, help the client explore the resistance or use immediacy to discuss the relationship.

One form of direct guidance is homework assignments (a term commonly used in the behavioral literature, although I recognize that students often have negative reactions to this term). Helpers suggest that clients do homework (e.g., monitor exercise and eating behaviors, read a self-help book, seek information, practice being assertive, record dreams) so that clients can practice what they are learning in helping sessions. Homework can be a particularly useful way to keep clients involved in the change process in between sessions. In addition, homework can speed up the helping process because clients are actively involved in changing and bringing feedback about change efforts back to the session. Homework can also encourage clients to act on their own without the helper's immediate monitoring.

Of course, the manner in which homework is assigned can make a big difference in terms of client receptivity and willingness to implement the homework. Research suggests that clients are more likely to implement homework suggestions if therapists choose tasks that fit the problem, are not difficult to implement, and are based on clients' strengths (Conoley, Padula, Payton, & Daniels, 1994; Scheel, Seaman, Roach, Mullin, & Mahoney, 1999; Wonnell & Hill, 2002). In a study on homework, Conoley et al. (1994) gave an example in which a client was depressed and angry. During the session, the client said he wished he had written down instances in his journal when he felt badly the previous week so that he could remember them to talk about in the sessions. For homework, the helper followed up on what the client said and asked the client to write down instances when he felt badly, recording what he was thinking, doing, and feeling, and what the situation was so they could discuss the problem more specifically in the next session. The client responded favorably, saying he liked to write and that writing had helped him in the past. Thus, the recommendation was judged as not being difficult because it required only a small amount of time, was not anxiety producing, and was clear. In addition, it was based on the client's strengths, given that the client had indicated that he liked to write. Furthermore, it matched his problem because it facilitated the client in remembering situations in which he was depressed and angry. During the next session, the client indicated that he had implemented the recommendation. In contrast, the directive to write would not have been good for other clients who do not like to write.

It is important to note that helpers in some job settings (e.g., rehabilitation counseling, job placement) need to do more direct guidance than helpers do in other settings (e.g., college counseling centers). For example, clients in rehabilitation settings often need specific guidance for how they could handle their major life obstacles, whereas clients in university counseling centers may be able to solve their problems by talking with an interested helper. Similarly, clients from some cultures want more direct guidance. For example, in Asian cultures clients often want their helpers to give them specific advice, and they might think less of helpers who do not provide suggestions. They might not necessarily implement the advice, but advice is expected from experts in that culture.

Direct guidance is different from *information giving*. When helpers give information, they provide facts or data but do not suggest what clients should do. In contrast, direct guidance indicates what helpers think clients should do. For example, contrast the effects of "The counseling center is in the Shoemaker Building" (information) versus "You should go to the counseling center" (direct guidance). Information often has an implied directive about what the client ought to do (e.g., "In my opinion, students earn better grades when they get a full night of sleep before taking a test"), but it does not state directly that the client should take a particular action (e.g., "You should make sure you get 8 hours of sleep before taking the test").

Rationale for Giving Direct Guidance

Dear Abby, Ann Landers, Dr. Joyce Brothers, Dr. Phil, and others give advice to millions of people. Many people (including me) read the newspaper columns and listen to the radio shows, which have become immensely popular because they are so entertaining. Providing advice is probably as old as human speech, but what are the consequences? Do people follow the advice, and if so, is it helpful or harmful? Unfortunately, no one has the answers to these concerns, except perhaps anecdotally. My main concern about direct guidance given in these entertainment formats is that the advice is not preceded by thorough exploration; the wrong problem might be addressed, and the recipient might think that it is not necessary to explore all the angles of the problem. Furthermore, in such situations people might begin to rely on others to make their decisions rather than coming to trust their own instincts. Moreover, some people seek guidance from many people and then either become confused or consider only the opinions they want to hear. It can be valuable to gain input from many people, but it can then be difficult for people to determine what they want to do. In addition, people may follow direct guidance out of fear of hurting the feelings of the advice giver or out of fear of retribution rather than because of choosing freely.

Direct guidance, however, can occasionally be useful in helping situations, especially when given by a trusted helper whose opinions are based on solid knowledge and experience and are given after extensive client exploration and insight. Helpers can have good ideas about what might be helpful for clients to do. For example, Dorothy asked her helper for advice on negotiating her salary for her first job in an academic setting. This was an area her helper knew something about because she worked in an academic setting. They talked about the information Dorothy had gathered about the salary range of other recent hires, what her values were, and what she wanted. They then discussed how Dorothy could navigate the negotiation process. The helper suggested that Dorothy not name a specific salary but say that she was dissatisfied with what had been offered. They talked about that possibility, and Dorothy modified it to fit her style. The process was collaborative because the helper respected Dorothy's right and ability to make her own decisions. The helper was not invested in which strategy Dorothy chose but was interested in presenting alternatives that Dorothy might be able to implement. Although the strategy did not work exactly as planned when Dorothy tried it (which is typical in the real world), Dorothy was able to modify it during the negotiation. She accepted the job at a competitive salary and started her new job soon afterward.

Although most clients are able to make their own decisions, especially if they have input from others, an individual in a crisis situation may need more explicit guidance. When clients are suicidal, for example, they often have "tunnel vision" that prevents them from seeing options other than death. Helpers may need to intervene in such situations and try to ensure that clients do not harm themselves (refer to Chapter 19 for discussion about dealing with suicidal clients). It is important to emphasize that other than in extreme cases (e.g., child abuse, suicidal or homicidal risk), helpers typically do not take over and manage what clients do. Offering suggestions is quite different from demanding that clients do what you tell them to do.

Guidelines for Giving Direct Guidance

Before giving direct guidance, it is important for helpers to think about and become aware of their intentions. As with information, helpers should not give direct guidance until they have assessed clients' motivation (as well as their own). They should make sure they are using this skill for the client's benefit.

When giving direct guidance, it is helpful to remember that it is easier for clients to make small, specific changes than to change many big things all at once. Helpers are more likely to be helpful if they can be specific about which small steps could be done and when they could be done, and then they should reinforce approximations toward the desired behaviors. For example, rather than suggesting that an inactive client try to lose 5 pounds in the next week (which is not under the client's control), the helper might suggest that the client walk for 15 minutes three times in the next week, reinforce herself by taking a hot bath after each walk, and allow herself to read a novel (assuming the helper has discovered that the client enjoys doing these things).

I also suggest that helpers write down assignments to help clients remember them given that it is often difficult to remember everything that happens in sessions. Furthermore, clients are more likely to take written assignments seriously. Following up on assignments in subsequent sessions (e.g., asking clients about their experience in trying to implement the homework) is also important; otherwise, clients might feel that such assignments are frivolous and not to be taken seriously. And, as always, it is important to observe client reactions to see how they respond to such interventions.

When clients ask (or sometimes even beg) for direct guidance, helpers have to be particularly careful to distinguish between the honest and direct request for direct guidance and the expression of dependent feelings. When in doubt, it is probably best to deal first with the feelings involved (e.g., "You seem pretty desperate to get some advice. I wonder what's going on?") After such exploration, helpers have additional data to consider how to deal with the request. Helpers also have to assess their own motivation and ensure that their needs to take care of others do not interfere with allowing clients to make their own decisions.

Clients often have negative reactions if helpers ignore their requests for advice. Some clients want direct guidance and are angry when helpers refuse to tell them what to do. An example is a case presented in Hill (1989) in which an Asian woman wanted direct guidance about family issues in the early sessions, and the African American therapist did not give it to her because she wanted the client to work on insight. The client felt disregarded by the therapist and became less invested in the therapy thereafter. In cases such as this, it may be better to give advice if the helper genuinely feels he or she has useful advice, and then process with the client later about the origin of the desire for advice. In addition, openly addressing the client's feelings using immediacy skills may help repair breaches in relationships that occur when clients become angry at helpers for not providing any, enough, or the "right" direct guidance.

Cautions When Giving Direct Guidance

Helpers need to be aware that they can offer help but cannot force clients to take it. Helpers are not taking over for clients but are providing options for them to consider. Clients have the right to decide for themselves what to do, even in the most desperate of circumstances.

Furthermore, helpers have to know the limits of how much they can offer. Friedman (1990) recounted a fable about a rescuer who holds a rope over the rail of a bridge to save a drowning person. The drowning person grabs the rope but refuses to climb up. After a while, the rescuer holding the rope cannot hang on any longer because the drowning person is so heavy. The rescuer has to make a decision about letting go or falling from the bridge himself, which clearly would not help either the drowning person or the rescuer.

Another problem with direct guidance is that it can foster dependency by shifting the responsibility for solutions from clients to helpers. Clients can become passive and helpless if helpers insinuate that clients are not competent enough to solve their own problems. In addition, when helpers rather than clients are responsible for the guidance, clients often blame the helpers when things do not go so well. Moreover, when helpers use too much direct guidance, it can lead to tension, resistance, or rebellion if clients choose to ignore the advice. Hence, direct guidance can cause problems in therapeutic relationships if it is not done collaboratively, with helpers and clients together constructing the direct guidance.

Example of Direct Guidance

The following shows a helper giving direct guidance (in italics) in a session:

> *Client:* Our 3-year-old daughter has gotten into the habit of coming into our bedroom in the middle of the night and climbing in bed with us and wanting to stay until morning. At first it seemed okay because she seemed to need comforting, but it has gotten out of hand. We only have a double bed, and my husband takes up more than his half, so I end up being unable to sleep because I can't move. When I try to move her, she doesn't want to leave. So we've got to do something.
>
> *Helper:* You sound frustrated.
>
> *Client:* I am. We can't figure out what to do. I don't want to traumatize her if she needs comforting. She seems to really like sleeping with us.
>
> *Helper:* What have you tried so far?
>
> *Client:* Nothing really. It just started getting intolerable. So now I know we have to do something. Plus I think she's getting a little too old to be doing this.
>
> *Helper:* What is your goal?
>
> *Client:* When she wakes up and is upset, I'd like to comfort her and then have her go back to her bed. I don't want her to get into our bed. Once she gets in, it's hard to get her out.
>
> *Helper:* What are your usual strategies for dealing with problems with kids?
>
> *Client:* We talk things out ahead of time so the kids are prepared and are in on it.

> *Helper:* *Maybe that would work here if you talked with her ahead of time about what you are planning to do.* How would you do it?
>
> *Client:* Before bedtime, I could tell her that during the night when she wakes up, she can't come into our bed anymore. But I'm afraid there's nothing positive to replace it with.
>
> *Helper:* That's a good point. *What if you were to lie down next to her on her bed until she went back to sleep? Then you could go back to your own bed.*
>
> *Client:* That sounds like a good idea. So when she comes into our room, I would just take her back to her room, lay down with her for a while until she's asleep, and then go back to my bed. I think that would work, especially if I tell her about it ahead of time. I might miss some sleep but not as much as I am now.
>
> *Helper:* Sounds good. Do you see any problems?
>
> *Client:* Well, I might fall asleep on her bed, but probably not for long because it would be uncomfortable there too. I might also be groggy in the middle of the night and just let her in out of habit.
>
> *Helper:* *Well, it probably would only take three to five nights, so you could tell yourself that if you can just do it for that long, the habit will be broken.*
>
> *Client:* Good point. I'm going to do it. It fits with the way I like to do things, so I know it will work.

DISCLOSURE OF STRATEGIES

Helpers make suggestions through disclosing strategies that they personally have tried in the past (another form of disclosure). In effect, rather than telling clients what to do, helpers provide suggestions by disclosing what has worked for them previously if they think their strategy might work for the client (see Exhibit 16.7). Helpers then turn the focus back to the clients and ask for their reaction (e.g., "When I feel angry, I take a deep breath and count to 10. I wonder if that would work for you?").

Rationale for Disclosing Strategies

It is important to disclose only those strategies that seem like they might work for the client. The object is not to show off strategies that work for you but to help clients think about other possibilities.

Hearing what another person has done can provide specific ideas for new behaviors (e.g., "I brush my teeth as soon as I have finished eating so I don't forget or am too tired to do it") and can also encourage

---

EXHIBIT 16.7

Overview of Disclosure of Strategies

Definition	*Disclosure of strategies* refers to the helper's presentation of actions that he or she has used in the past to cope with problems.
Example	"When I have been in similar situations with my mother, I call her and ask to talk. I try to be as honest as possible and let her know that I messed up. Usually she is pretty understanding."
Typical intention	To promote change (see Web Form D).
Typical client reactions	Educated, unstuck, new ways to behave, hopeful, confused, misunderstood, no reaction (see Web Form G).
Desired client behaviors	Agreement, therapeutic changes (see Web Form H).
Helpful hints	Make sure that you have thoroughly explored the problem.
	Imagine a strategy you used that might benefit the client.
	Choose a strategy that fits the problem, is not difficult to implement, and is based on the client's strengths.
	Make the disclosure short; do not go into detail about what your problem was.
	Observe how the client responds to the disclosure. Shift the focus back to the client after the disclosure.

---

clients to think of novel action plans (e.g., "I treat myself to a cruise each year as a reward for working hard all year. I wonder what you could do?"). Disclosing what has worked for the helper is also somewhat disarming—rather than telling clients what to do, helpers communicate that they do not have the answers but are willing to share what has worked for them. By disclosing strategies, helpers provide ideas for clients without imposing the type of demands that may result from directives. Disclosing strategies is a more tentative way of giving information or direct guidance.

Guidelines for Using Disclosures Of Strategies

All of the suggestions related to other types of disclosures apply here (e.g., disclose about concerns that are resolved and do not make you feel too vulnerable). It is especially important to turn the focus back to the client after giving the disclosure. For example, the helper might say,

> When I'm reading a textbook, I make myself read a chapter, and then I reward myself by doing something I like—I might get a soda, make a phone call, or play a video game, although I limit any of those activities to 10 minutes. Would that work for you?

Helpers should be aware that a client might be unduly influenced to do exactly what the helper does. For this reason, the helpers might provide the option tentatively, indicate that it might or might not work for the client, and then turn the focus back to the client for her or his reaction. In addition, helpers need to be careful not to disclose strategies in a way that would shift the focus from the client to the helper (e.g., "Let me tell you all about what I did because it's so fascinating and interesting").

Example of Disclosing Strategies

The following shows a helper disclosing strategies (in italics) in a session:

> *Client:* I know that I need to exercise, but I can never seem to find anything I like to do.
>
> *Helper:* *One thing that works for me is to go for a half-hour walk every morning with my husband. I get exercise and get to spend some time with my husband at the beginning of the day.* I wonder if something like that would work for you?
>
> *Client:* Well, that kind of appeals to me, but I'm really out of shape.
>
> *Helper:* *I started out walking 10 minutes a day and worked my way up over several years. Now I hate to miss my morning walk.* Would 10 minutes be easier for you?
>
> *Client:* Yeah, but how would I get my husband involved?
>
> *Helper:* What thoughts do you have about that?

What Do You Think?

- Clients often ask for information. How would you decide when to give clients the requested information and when to probe them for their ideas?
- How can you determine whether clients really want or need direct guidance?
- Argue for or against the opinion that direct guidance should generally be given tentatively and only after thorough exploration and insight.
- What would it be like for you to tell clients that you do not know the answer to their questions? How might not knowing an answer influence the client's perception of the helper?
- How do you feel about receiving information from other people? What feelings do you have when you seek information or when people ask you for information?
- Debate the pros and cons related to radio talk-show psychologists giving direct guidance after having spoken only briefly with callers.

RESEARCH SUMMARY

Is the Action Stage Necessary?

Citation: Wonnell, T. L., & Hill, C. E. (2000). Effects of including the action stage in dream interpretation. *Journal of Counseling Psychology, 47*, 372–379. doi:10.1037/0022-0167.47.3.372

Rationale: Hill (1996, 2004) postulated a three-stage model of dream work that is similar to the helping skills model proposed in this book. Wonnell and Hill wondered whether the action stage of the dream model is necessary to help clients gain insight and make changes in their lives. They also wondered about therapists' perspectives on what makes it easy or difficult to do the action stage.

Method: Volunteer clients (undergraduate students) were randomly assigned to one of two conditions for a single session with a trained doctoral student therapist: (1) dream sessions conducted using the full model (exploration, insight, and action) and (2) dream sessions conducted without the action stage (just exploration and insight). Therapists adhered closely to the Hill (1996, 2004) dream model in all sessions, and sessions in the two conditions were about the same length. After sessions, therapists rated how easy it was to conduct the session, and then indicated what made the session easy or difficult.

Interesting Findings:
▪ Conditions did not differ in terms of session quality or client insight.
▪ Clients who went through the action stage gained more in terms of action (i.e., self-ratings of how much action they gained, self-ratings of how much they gained in terms of problem definition and problem-solving, and judge-rated quality of action plans devised as a result of the session) than did clients who did not go through the action stage.
▪ Therapists thought that it was easiest to conduct the action stage when they felt confident in their own action stage skills, and when they were working with clients who were motivated to understand their dreams, involved in the process, psychologically minded, had explored their dreams thoroughly and gained insight before the action stage, and presented dreams that were relatively recent.

Conclusions:
▪ The action stage is not needed if clients only wish to attain insight into their dreams.
▪ The action stage is needed if clients are to make changes based on what they have learned about their dreams. Focusing on exploration and insight does not lead to as much action as does focusing on action after exploration and insight.
▪ It is easier to work with clients who are motivated to understand their dreams and who get involved in the therapeutic process.

Implications for Therapy:
▪ Therapists need to focus on action if they want clients to make changes. Therapists also need to be skilled in using the action stage.
▪ Clients need to be motivated to work on their dreams.

BONUS MATERIALS Practice exercises, labs, and other resources for students and teachers are available on the companion website: http://pubs.apa.org/books/supp/hill4.

Steps for Working With Four Action Tasks 17

Vision without action is a daydream. Action without vision is a nightmare.

—*Japanese proverb*

A helper at a homeless shelter listened to Debi talk about her rage, feelings of powerlessness, and sense of humiliation at being evicted from her home. The helper challenged Debi's irrational thoughts that she was worthless and a social outcast. The helper disclosed about her own experiences with poverty and losing her job and how she had been forced to figure out what she wanted to do with her life. Debi felt better after expressing her feelings and gaining insights about how she had gotten to this situation, but she also wanted to learn skills so she would never be homeless again. The helper asked for more details about how she had come to lose her job and home. Debi said that she had been fired because of downsizing and had become discouraged about getting another job after being turned down by 15 employers. The helper gave Debi some tests to figure out her interests, helped her write a resume, and then did role-playing with her about how to do a job interview. Debi applied for several jobs while living at the shelter and was offered one that she liked. The helper then worked with Debi to help her develop the skills she would need to do the job well (being on time, dressing appropriately, not using the telephone for personal calls). Debi was still in her job at a 6-month follow-up.

http://dx.doi.org/10.1037/14345-017
Helping Skills: Facilitating Exploration, Insight, and Action, Fourth Edition, by C. E. Hill

R ather than learning and practicing single skills as we did in the exploration and insight stages, we combine the skills (open questions and probes for action, information, feedback about the client, process advisement, direct guidance, and disclosure of strategies) into a series of steps for four action tasks: (a) relaxation, (b) behavior change, (c) behavior rehearsal, and (d) decision making. Thus, we practice the steps for each of these tasks rather than focusing as specifically on the individual skills.

These steps are not presented as rigid requirements for how to do these four action tasks. Rather, I try to present them as clearly as possible so that trainees can have an idea of how to implement them. Helpers will want to modify the steps to fit their own styles and to meet the needs of individual clients.

Action work is creative and rarely follows a clear set of steps. For example, some clients might be ready to start changing and will not need to spend as much time exploring action; other clients might not have tried to change their behavior in the past, so steps about assessing past change attempts can be skipped. When clients have strong reactions to any of the steps, helpers can step back, help clients process their reactions, and possibly alter their strategies. So I encourage readers to try to follow what is presented here to familiarize themselves with the concepts and then modify the steps as needed.

Relaxation

Relaxation is particularly important for clients who have problems with stress and anxiety. An extensive amount of data shows that relaxing one's muscles reduces anxiety (Jacobson, 1929; Lang, Melamed, & Hart, 1970; Paul, 1969) and that it is useful to teach clients to relax when they get anxious (Bernstein & Borkovec, 1973; Goldfried & Trier, 1974). When people are relaxed, they are more open and able to handle information, so relaxation is a good thing for helpers to teach before trying to implement other behavioral interventions.

Examples of markers for helpers to do relaxation are when clients have a fear of flying, are extremely anxious about taking tests or speaking in public, have anxiety in social situations, or seem especially tense during the session. In contrast, helpers should be cautious about offering to do relaxation with clients who are paranoid, fear losing control, or have delusions. See Exhibit 17.1 for the steps for relaxation. Essentially, the helper is first going to teach relaxation and then help the client figure out how to implement it outside of the session.

EXHIBIT 17.1

Steps for Relaxation

Steps	Skills (and examples)
1. Identify and describe specific situations of stress/anxiety	Open questions and probes ("How are you feeling?") Process advisement ("Let's try a relaxation exercise.")
2. Teach relaxation	Process advisement (get comfortable, relax, repeat a phrase when breathing out, let all thoughts go, return to phrase)
3. Imagine applying relaxation in a specific situation	Direct guidance ("Imagine yourself going in to take a test. Now practice your breathing.")
4. Assign relaxation practice	Direct guidance ("Could you try doing a relaxation exercise at least 5 minutes a day?")
5. Follow-up	Open questions and probes "How was it when you tried to do the relaxation?" "What might make it more likely for you to be able to use the relaxation in your daily life?")

STEP 1: IDENTIFY AND DESCRIBE SPECIFIC SITUATIONS OF STRESS AND ANXIETY

Through exploration, clients often identify stress and anxiety as a major problem. Helpers can also observe when clients seem particularly tense (e.g., they might speak rapidly, act fidgety, or panic). Helpers may then ask whether the client would like to learn relaxation techniques to calm down in the immediate moment and to be able to calm themselves down outside of sessions in times of stress. The explanation is that if a person is physiologically relaxed, this state is incompatible with anxiety, and relaxation is a good coping strategy.

If the client agrees to learn relaxation, the helper can ask for description of a specific example of a time when the client experienced stress and anxiety. It is important to ask for a lot of details, involving all the different senses (e.g., touch, smell, sight, taste) involved in the experience of the situation.

STEP 2: TEACH RELAXATION

Benson's (1975) extensive research has found two main components of effective relaxation: (a) the repetition of any word, sound, prayer, thought, phrase, or muscular activity and (b) the passive return to repeating when other thoughts intrude. Following Benson's suggestions (modified somewhat here), helpers can teach clients to relax by going through the following steps, using a calm voice and speaking slowly:

1. "Get as comfortable as possible in your seat. Remove everything from your lap and put your feet firmly on the floor. Close your eyes. Imagine sand being poured into your head and filling your body so that your whole body begins to feel heavy."
2. "Relax your body starting from your toes up through your head. Shrug your shoulders and release the tension. Now focus on your breath. Breathe in . . . breathe out. As you breathe in, imagine taking in fresh, clean, restoring air. As you breathe out, imagine getting rid of bad air."
3. "Pick a word (e.g., *one, peace*), sound (e.g., *om*), prayer (e.g., the Lord's Prayer), thought, or phrase (e.g., *the river runs through it*). Pick something that fits with your beliefs and feels comfortable to you. Repeat that phrase each time you breathe out."
4. "Let all your other thoughts go. When you find yourself thinking about something else, don't worry, just passively let it go and return to repeating."
5. "Do this for 3 to 5 minutes and then sit quietly for a minute."

Another method is deep muscle relaxation (Jacobson, 1929), wherein the helper teaches the client to systematically concentrate on one muscle at a time and tense it for 30 seconds and then relax. The helper goes systematically through the major muscle groups of the body, perhaps starting at the feet and tensing and then relaxing opposing muscles (e.g., bend feet toward self, bend feet away from self). Going through the whole body takes 20 to 30 minutes. After practicing relaxation systematically several times, many people can begin to induce it when needed.

Another relaxation method is *mindfulness,* which Kabat-Zinn (2003) defined as the awareness that comes from attending nonjudgmentally to one's experience in the moment. The idea behind mindfulness is to become aware of (i.e., mindful) about emotions and reactions, take them out and observe them, and then let them go (Segal, Williams, & Teasdale, 2002). A good example of mindfulness involves eating. When eating mindfully, one pays full attention to eating, savoring every bite, tasting each flavor, and smelling each aroma rather than gobbling down the food while doing something else. To practice mindfulness, the helper can ask the client to take a raisin and first examine it carefully, looking at it, smelling it, and feeling it. After carefully studying the raisin, the client can put the raisin in his or her mouth and let it sit there and feel it, and then slowly bite it and let the flavor ooze out. One thus becomes mindful in the present moment of experience and then tries to generalize this experience outside the session.

Because doing a relaxation exercise during a session could be difficult or scary for some clients (e.g., they might feel worried about whether they are doing it "right," they might feel vulnerable sitting with their eyes closed), helpers can ask clients about thoughts and feelings before, during, and after the exercise. Helpers can thus help clients talk about the experience.

STEP 3: IMAGINE APPLYING RELAXATION IN A SPECIFIC SITUATION

If the relaxation was used because the client was anxious talking about something outside of the session, the helper can now help the client imagine the situation while staying relaxed (using a method similar to guided imagery or systematic desensitization). The helper can ask the client to close her or his eyes and then gently lead her or him through the steps of the situation described in Step 1. For example, the helper might say to Ralf,

> Now imagine that you are getting into your car to go to work. Focus on your breathing as you start the car and feel the sense of relaxation come over you. (pause) Now picture yourself getting onto the ramp to go onto the highway. Focus on your breathing. Breathe in. Breathe out. (pause) You are on the ramp and you start to worry about whether the cars will let you in. Keep focusing on your breathing. (pause) You keep up a steady speed and look each way as you get up to the highway. Breathe in. Breathe out. (pause) You maintain your speed and notice that you can move over into the lane easily. You wave to the driver and breathe deeply. Cars are zooming by but you find that you can focus on just being where you are. You feel comfortable. Focus again on your breathing.

If the relaxation was used because the client was anxious in the session, the helper can gently introduce what the client was talking about and ask the client to talk about the topic while keeping track of breathing. If the helper observes the client starting to get anxious again, he or she can gently remind the client to focus on his or her breathing and relax. By teaching the client to manage anxiety in the moment, the helper can teach a valuable skill that the client can then employ outside the session.

STEP 4: ASSIGN RELAXATION PRACTICE

If it seems useful, helpers can suggest that clients practice deep breathing, relaxation, or mindfulness 5 to 10 minutes, once or twice a day (e.g., in morning before breakfast and in the late afternoon) in a quiet place with no distraction. A good explanation for practicing is that the client will then be able to induce relaxation in new situations more quickly.

STEP 5: FOLLOW-UP

In subsequent sessions, helpers can ask about the client's experience practicing the relaxation. If the client was able to easily do the exercise, the helper could encourage the client to continue practicing. They could also talk about and rehearse trying to implement relaxation during difficult situations (e.g., flying, examinations).

If the client was not able to or chose not to do the relaxation exercises, the helper can nonjudgmentally ask about what was going on. The helper and client can then work to modify the exercise or might choose to drop the idea of this exercise.

Behavior Change

Sam wants to have more meaningful relationships. How might you help him? After reading this section, check the example at the end of the section to see if your ideas fit with this model.

During the exploration and insight stages, many clients identify specific behaviors that need to be changed. They might report doing too much of some behaviors (e.g., eating too much, drinking too much alcohol or coffee, nail biting, playing too many computer games), not enough of other behaviors (e.g., exercise, teeth brushing, keeping the apartment clean), and inappropriate or unconstructive behaviors (e.g., poor social skills, poor study skills, procrastination). The foci in earlier stages were on exploring the context more generally with brief mention of the specific problem, whereas in the action stage our attention turns to a clearer, fuller description of the problem in and of itself. This model of behavior change is ideal for problems that are intrapersonal and under the person's control (e.g., procrastination, exercise); interpersonal problems (e.g., assertiveness) are more appropriate for behavioral rehearsal.

Our goals are to clearly identify the problem, assess the environment, determine specific changes, search for reinforcers, and monitor the changes. See Exhibit 17.2 for the steps for behavior change. Essentially, the helper works with the client to explore the problem, the idea of changing, and previous change attempts, all leading to clarifying the problem and goals. Then the helper works with the client to generate options and figure out how to implement the chosen options.

STEP 1: CLARIFY THE SPECIFIC PROBLEM

In this step, we need to make sure that we understand the problem and that it is specific enough to work with behaviorally. It is important to choose a specific, observable problem (e.g., studying more) rather than

EXHIBIT 17.2

Steps for Behavior Change

Steps	Skills (and examples)
1. Clarify the specific problem	Open questions and probes ("Describe the last time you drank too much." "What happened before the drinking started?" "What happened during the event?" "What were the consequences?")
2. Explore the idea of action for this problem	Open questions and probes ("What would it be like to change?" "What would it be like to stay the same?" "What are the benefits of changing?" "What are the barriers to changing?") Restatements and reflections of feelings ("You sound scared about changing." "You have talked a lot about how you would like to change.")
3. Assess previous change attempts and resources	Open questions and probes ("What have you tried that worked?" "What have you tried that didn't work?" "What kind of support do you have from your wife?" Restatements and reflections of feelings ("You have done a lot of different things." "You sound pleased that you were able to speak up.")
4. Clarify problem and goals	Open questions and probes ("We've talked extensively about your drinking, and I'm wondering what you now think is your problem?" "What are your goals related to drinking?")
5. Generate options together	Open questions and probes ("What ideas do you have?") Direct guidance ("Maybe you could make one comment at the beginning of class.") Disclosure of strategies ("When I am in that situation, I try to work early in the morning.")
6. Choose an option	Open questions and probes ("Which option fits best for you?" What are the positive things about this first option?")
7. Determine reinforcers	Open questions and probes ("If you were able to do what we suggested, what would be reinforcing for you?")
8. Problem solve about implementing actions	Open questions and probes ("How would you do this?" "What do you expect would happen if you did this?")
9. Assign homework	Direct guidance ("How about if you try to drink one less cup of coffee each day this week and see how it feels? "What problems do you see coming up if you try to do this assignment?")
10. Check on progress and modify assignments	Open questions and probes ("What happened when you asked for a raise?") Feedback ("You did a really good job of speaking firmly when you told your son to behave.")

something nonbehavioral, vague, or amorphous (e.g., feeling better). In addition, it is best to focus on one problem at a time because dealing with several problems simultaneously can be confusing and diffuse change efforts. If the client has multiple problems, the helper could work with the client to list all the problems, order them, and then choose the most important one, making sure that it is one that can probably be dealt with using a behavioral approach.

Because it is much easier to deal with a specific episode rather than talking generally about the problem, the helper might ask for a specific example (along with details) of the time the behavior occurred: "Tell me about the last time you got angry. Describe the situation as fully as possible." The helper can then probe for the ABCs of the event: first asking about the antecedents, then inquiring about the behaviors during the event, and finally asking about the consequences of the event:

- Antecedents: "What was going on before you got angry?"
- Behaviors: "Describe exactly what happened when you got angry."
- Consequences: "What happened as a consequence of your anger?"

If the client is vague or unsure about the details or is not a good observer, the helper might ask the client to monitor his or her behavior over the course of 1 to 2 weeks to gather specific information about the ABCs. For example, if Joetta wants to reduce her overeating, her helper might ask her to write down all the food she eats, where she eats, who she is with when she eats, and how she feels before and after eating. Clients often learn that their behavior differs dramatically from what they reported earlier to helpers. For example, an overweight man who claims that he never snacks might learn that he consistently nibbles on snacks while working or watching television. A person who feels lonely might discover that she never looks people in the eye or says hello.

By the end of this step, the helper should know the details about a specific behavior in a specific situation that the client wants to address (e.g., wanting to drink less coffee, wanting to brush teeth more often, wanting to exercise more). The helper should also know what happened before, during, and after the specific instance (e.g., details of the last time the client procrastinated).

STEP 2: EXPLORE THE IDEA OF ACTION FOR THIS PROBLEM

Rather than assume clients are eager to change, it is important to allow them to explore the idea of changing. Although clients might be unhappy with the way things are, they are often scared by what things might be like if they change (e.g., it is better to live with the misery you know than to risk the unknown).

Furthermore, not every client is ready to change. As described in Chapter 2, there are five stages of clients' readiness for change: pre-contemplation, contemplation, preparation, action, and maintenance (Prochaska, DiClemente, & Norcross, 1992). Assessing the client's current stage is important before proceeding to the action stage. In the precontemplation and contemplation stages, clients typically require much time to explore their feelings and develop insights before making a commitment to change; homework might involve listing the benefits of change and obstacles to change. Clients in the preparation and action stages are often more ready to move directly to action. Clients in the maintenance stage probably are more interested in stabilizing the changes they already have made.

If helpers plunge too quickly into action with clients who are not ready, they typically hear "Yes, but . . . ." Clients who are not ready will have many reasons why action is not possible. Alternatively, some clients may simply listen politely but have no intention of following through on the action.

Furthermore, helpers should not be invested in whether clients choose to change. Rather than perceiving that their success as a helper is based on clients making changes, helpers need to view their success as based on helping clients decide what is best for them. After all, how can helpers possibly know what is ultimately best for clients?

The key is to provide a good-enough climate so that clients feel comfortable talking about and then making decisions about changing. Helpers can encourage clients to express their thoughts and feelings about action and examine the benefits and drawbacks of changing or not changing by using open questions and probes about action:

- "What are the benefits of changing?"
- "What are the benefits of not changing?"
- "How would changing make you feel?"
- "What keeps you from changing?"
- "What feelings are you having when you contemplate making changes in your life?"

The helper also can support clients and facilitate exploration of change through restatements and reflection of feelings, such as:

- "It's exciting for you to think about doing something new."
- "You sound like you want to change."

The primary skills used in this step are open questions and probes about action, restatements, and reflections of feelings. Open questions and probes are often used to begin the discussion, which helpers can then facilitate by restating and reflecting feelings, thereby drawing clients into a discussion of values, needs, and problems related to change.

If the client is clearly conflicted about changing, it might be helpful to challenge the client about the discrepancies (see Chapter 12). Alternatively, the helper might use a two-chair technique (see Chapter 12) to allow the client to experience and express both sides of the conflict. Resolution of the conflict is typically easier after both sides of the conflict are brought into awareness. For this technique, the helper uses process advisement. For example,

Helper:	Be the side of you that says you should quit biting your fingernails. Pretend that you're talking to that part of you sitting in the chair over there.
Client (to empty chair):	It's disgusting when you do that. You look awful. Just stop it.
Helper:	Can you say it a little louder, like your father might have said it to you when you were 12 years old?
Client (to empty chair):	Yeah, (louder) just stop it. You look ugly when you chew your fingernails. What's wrong with you, anyway? Stop it right now.
Helper:	Now go over to the other chair and be the 12-year-old side of you who wants to chew her fingernails. What would you have wanted to say back to your father?
Client (from other chair to empty chair):	I'll chew my fingernails if I want. You can't stop me. I don't care what you think. All you want is for me to be perfect, so I'll look good for you. (Role-play continues for a while.)
Helper:	How did that feel to you going through that? Did you learn something new about why you might chew your fingernails?
Client:	I sure did. I can see that I wanted to get back at my father. It was a small way that I could have some control over my life.
Helper:	When you think about it that way, what do you think about being ready to change your fingernail biting now?
Client:	I think I'm ready to quit biting my fingernails. I'm pretty disgusted by it too at this

> point. But I do want to come back after
> that to try to understand more about my
> relationship with my father.
>
> *Helper:* Okay, then. Let's spend some time working
> on the fingernails first and then go back to
> the issue with your father.

After weighing the benefits and drawbacks to change, some clients might choose not to change because the costs of changing are not worth the benefits. Sometimes change is too painful, and sometimes clients discover that their current life is not so bad. Choosing not to change can be just as valid a choice as deciding to change. For example, Sandra told her helper that she wanted to quit playing computer games. After they explored for a while and discussed the benefits and barriers to quitting, Sandra realized that she did not actually want to quit. Although she felt guilty and embarrassed admitting she played games, playing the games helped her relax and center herself after a day of work. The helper, who was able to listen nonjudgmentally and not have an opinion about whether Sandra should or should not play video games, suggested that they go back and try to explore more about the guilt and "shoulds."

By the end of this step, the client should have made a decision about whether to go forward with the change process. Clients are rarely 100% in favor of change, but the advantages should clearly outweigh the disadvantages. If the client is reluctant, the helper can return to exploration and insight to process the feelings.

STEP 3: ASSESS PREVIOUS CHANGE ATTEMPTS AND RESOURCES

When the helper has established that the client wants to change, she or he can work with the client to assess what attempts, if any, the client has already made. Finding out about previous attempts can avoid encouraging actions that have not worked in the past, indicate that the helper respects the client's change efforts, and lets the client know the helper is aware that the client has been attempting to solve problems. After all, clients have usually had lengthy experiences with their problems and have undoubtedly tried, and have many feelings about, various alternatives. Instead of being the experts, helpers thus act as consultants, collaboratively working with clients to determine what they have tried and how these strategies have worked.

In this step, then, helpers assess what worked and what did not work in the previous attempts. In effect, the helper is assessing the forces facilitating change as well as the forces inhibiting change.

Helpers can focus on both internal (e.g., motivation, anxiety, insecurity, self-confidence) and external factors (resources that clients have available in their environment to support them when they make changes, social support, obstacles such as discrimination and social injustice) that facilitate and hinder change.

One particular external factor that is typically important to assess is the client's support system. Breier and Strauss (1984) noted that the benefits of a social support system include a forum for ventilation, reality testing, support and approval, integration into the community, problem solving, and constancy. Positive support can provide encouragement and reinforcement (e.g., having a supportive, nonjudgmental partner can enable one to stick to a diet). In contrast, negative support can undermine the person's resolve (e.g., if a woman decides to go on a diet and her partner says that she was more attractive before or can't stay on a diet, it will be difficult for that woman to continue the diet). In addition, helpers can discuss with clients how change will influence their social network.

It is good to know as much as possible about the factors influencing the change process from the outset so that the same problems are not repeated. It is important to realize that clients may not be aware of all the influencing factors, but it is good to get as many as possible out in the open. Helpers use open questions and probes to assess the facilitating and restraining influences:

- "What worked that you have tried before?"
- "What didn't work?"
- "What problems did you encounter that made it difficult the last time?"
- "When you tried the last time, what things made it easier for you?"
- "How do others respond to you about this problem?"
- "How would others react if you changed?"

It is important for helpers to remember to support client exploration of change attempts because it is often quite threatening to discuss. Using restatements and reflections of feelings can also demonstrate to clients that helpers are listening. For example:

- "Sounds like you've tried lots of things to help you overcome your depression."
- "You sound frustrated that, after all your efforts, nothing happened."

Using approval-reassurance can let clients know that helpers are aware of their hard work in exploring and that helpers value what clients are saying. For example,

- "You've done a great job working so hard to get information about services available in the community. You've been very resourceful."

By the end of this step, the helper should have a fairly good idea about what the client has tried before, effective and ineffective strategies, and facilitating and restraining forces. The helper integrates this new information with data gathered during the exploration and insight stage to begin to conceptualize the strengths and obstacles the client will have in terms of making changes (e.g., having positive values vs. resistance to authority figures telling client to change).

STEP 4: CLARIFY OR RECONCEPTUALIZE THE PROBLEM

Now that the client has explored the problem thoroughly, the helper might ask the client how she or he now feels about the original problem or goal. The client may well change the problem description. For example, rather than wanting to slow down her eating all the time, Chris decided she wanted to eat more slowly during Saturday night dinners with her husband.

STEP 5: GENERATE OPTIONS TOGETHER

One of the biggest benefits for clients of working with helpers is that they can come up with options together for working on change. Through collaboration, two people (or even better, a group) can usually generate more ideas than can one person alone. The goal in this step is to generate as many ideas as possible to enable clients to see that there are many alternatives. Reality can come later when deciding among the possibilities, but the ideas must first be generated. One strategy is to set a specific time limit, such as 2 minutes, for this process. It is also important for clients to lift restrictions on themselves while generating ideas and to suspend judgment about what is possible so they do not censor any possibilities. Although I usually recommend that helpers not take notes, it often helps during this step to write down the ideas so helpers can refer back to them in the next step.

To aid in the process of generating ideas and options, helpers can use open questions and probes to ask clients to think of all the actions that come to mind, no matter how unlikely or silly these might initially sound:

- "If money or time were not an issue, how would you try to change this problem?"
- "What would you suggest to someone else in this situation?"

Helpers can also make suggestions because it can open clients up to new ideas they might not have considered. Of course, it is important for helpers not to get invested in their ideas but just to offer possibilities to give clients more options. Helpers can also think about Grandma's rule ("Eat vegetables before dessert") in thinking of strategies, so they might suggest doing the new behavior (e.g., studying) before something fun (e.g., watching television). Alternatively, helpers could use Premack's principle, which involves pairing a low-frequency behavior (e.g., teeth brushing) with a high-frequency behavior (e.g., surfing the Internet).

- "What about talking to your boss?"
- "Maybe you could . . . "

Helpers can also disclose about strategies they have tried in similar situations. By disclosing, helpers admit that they too have had problems and thus might help the client feel less disturbed. But it is always important to remember that what works for one person may not work for another, and that the disclosure is being used just to generate more options:

- "When I have trouble remembering all the things I have to do, I make a list."
- "I try to keep a routine and brush my teeth right after my shower."

By the end of this step, a list of possibilities for the client to try has been developed. No order of preference is expected at this point, but hopefully many ideas have been generated.

STEP 6: CHOOSE AN OPTION OR OPTIONS

Once a number of options have been generated, the task for the helper is to help the client think through the options systematically. Clients need to select ideas that are specific, realistic, within the realm of possibility, and consistent with their values. It might be easiest to start by asking the client to cross off any options that are totally bad (from the list that the helper wrote). Alternatively, helpers can ask the client to choose the three or four most likely options and then work with the client to evaluate the good and bad aspects of each of these options. Helpers can also ask about clients' values to determine whether any of the options violate these values. For example, even though a quick way to obtain money might be to rob a bank, one hopes that clients have values against theft. It is also important to note that clients should choose options that involve changing themselves rather than trying to change other people (except for behavior change with children). It is not only difficult to change others, but it presents ethical problems. For example, rather than trying to get a partner to exercise more, the helper may want to help the client change something about his or her own behavior (e.g., reduce nagging, get a hobby). The following are examples of open questions and probes that helpers might use to help a client choose the options:

- "What do you like about the first option?"
- "What do you dislike about the first option?"
- "What are your values related to the first option?"
- "Using a 5-point scale (5 = high), rate the likely effectiveness of this option."
- "What would be the obstacles related to the first option?"

After going through the top options, clients will hopefully have a few possibilities that might work for them and can choose which ones she or he wants to implement. This step may be quite short if the client immediately jumps into the problem solving that takes place in Step 6. The client may be quite reluctant, however, which can alert the helper to problems that must be addressed by cycling back to the exploration and insight stages. Finally, some clients may have gotten enough out of action at this stage and not need to go further (e.g., the client may have a clear idea about what to change and not need further help).

The helper needs to make sure that the client goals are realistic. For example, if an overweight person wants to lose 50 pounds in 1 month, the helper can work with the client to choose a more realistic goal. Instead of encouraging the overweight client to begin a severely restricted diet of 800 calories per day, the helper might encourage the client to walk 20 minutes a day in addition to eating more moderately (e.g., 1,500 calories per day) to facilitate gradual weight loss, which is more likely to be maintained.

STEP 7: DETERMINE REINFORCERS

In this step, if reinforcers have not come up naturally, helpers work with clients to identify realistic reinforcers, things that they can use to reward themselves for changing, given that change is more likely to happen with reinforcers. Importantly, reinforcers are individual, such that what works for one person (e.g., the helper) might not work for another (e.g., the client). For example, one client might find it reinforcing to look forward to going on a vacation to a Caribbean island if she exercises 30 minutes 5 days a week for 3 months. Another client might need the more immediate reinforcement of being able to call a friend after he studies for 1 hour. To determine reinforcers, helpers can ask:

- "If you were able to do the things you mentioned what might be rewarding for you?"
- "What things are generally reinforcing for you?"

The client may need some help identifying reinforcers. The helper (and the group) might generate options as they did earlier in Step 5.

STEP 8: PROBLEM SOLVE ABOUT IMPLEMENTING ACTIONS

Once the target behavior is identified, baseline information has been gathered, realistic goals set, options generated and chosen, and reinforcers identified, the helper works with the client to figure out how to implement the changes: how and when the client will try the new behavior, what they expect will happen, and how they will cope with adversities that inevitably arise. Essentially, they work together to do problem solving. For example, if the client wants to increase the amount of exercising by the client going to the gym more often, the helper and client might work together to identify when the client could go to the gym. They might also identify potential barriers and figure out how to solve them.

This process is creative because each client is different. Some principles are the following:

- It is generally preferable to look for ways to increase positive behavior (e.g., increase smiling) than to decrease negative behaviors (e.g., reduce amount of time spent alone) because it is easier to change in the positive direction.
- The chosen behaviors must be observable, behavioral, culturally appropriate, and specific (e.g., smiling at strangers) rather than broad and vague (e.g., becoming more friendly) because specific behaviors are easier to work on and monitor for changes.
- Helpers target specific behaviors to change (e.g., a certain amount of homework) rather than trying to change the outcome (e.g., the final grade) because specific behaviors are within one's control, whereas the outcome is not (e.g., one never knows how instructors will grade).
- The principle of "baby steps" is also important here. Rather than expecting the client to make huge changes immediately, small changes are more likely to be attainable. It can also be useful to inform clients that actually incorporating behavior change into one's repertoire takes a long time. It generally takes 21 days of daily implementation before the new behavior begins to feel like a habit. By being aware of this, clients can pace themselves a bit better and not expect to make changes overnight.

By the end of this step, the helper and client should have a good idea of how the client can change. If the client is eager and cooperative and seems to enjoy doing the behavioral work, the helper can proceed to

Step 9. If the client has not gotten involved in this step, the helper could work with the client to understand the resistance, whether it relates to issues in the therapeutic relationship (e.g., not liking the helper telling the client what to do) or whether it relates to dynamic issues within the client (e.g., not being ready to give up anger at a parent).

STEP 9: ASSIGN HOMEWORK

Helpers often assign homework so that the client can implement tasks that they have collaboratively developed in the session. For example, after discussing study skills, a helper might make a contract with a client to study at least 30 minutes a night at his desk (where he does nothing else but study), after which he can reinforce himself by getting a soda and calling his girlfriend.

Helpers might also warn clients to "go slow" to prevent too much enthusiastic initial behavior that often results in not being able to sustain the change. Many people enthusiastically say they will make an extreme change (e.g., exercise 3 hours a day) but then get discouraged when they discover how difficult it is to carry out this change. It is better to take too small a step than to overestimate what one can do.

To assign tasks, helpers use direct guidance. For example, the helper might say,

> Based on what we've talked about in the session, I'd like to suggest a couple of things. First, keep a journal for the next week. When you catch yourself chewing your nails, write down what you are feeling so we can try to figure out what's going on there. Also, put a quarter in a jar for each time you're able to stop biting your fingernails and save up for something special that you'd like. What do you think of those two suggestions?

In addition, it is not good for helpers to be too "bossy" when assigning homework. Several studies have shown that clients become resistant and uncooperative if helpers become too directive (Bischoff & Tracey, 1995; Gillespie, 1951; Mahalik, 1994; Patterson & Forgatch, 1985), so helpers need to remember to be collaborative in developing homework assignments with clients. One way to do this is to follow up direct guidance with open questions and probes to see how the client reacts to the direct guidance.

- "What I'd like you to try over the next week is to say hello to one new person each day when you're walking on campus. How would that be for you?"
- "How about writing in a journal at least 5 minutes a night. Would that work for you?"

Helpers also need to work with clients to identify potential facilitating and restraining forces in implementing the tasks to avoid failure to complete the assignment. For example, a man thinking about beginning an exercise program in which he walks for 15 minutes each day might identify the restraining forces as the time commitment and weather and the facilitating forces as eventual weight loss and increased self-efficacy. Furthermore, if the client does not discuss social support as a facilitating or restraining force, it is a good idea to ask specifically about this because other people can be powerful helping and hindering forces. The idea here is to play out the behavior change and see what the roadblocks are to successful implementation. To assess the facilitating and restraining forces, the helper can use open questions and probes:

- "What things would help you in doing the homework?"
- "What things would prevent you from doing the homework?"
- "What kind of social support do you have to help you do the homework?"

Then, helpers can work with the client to figure out ways to manage the restraining forces. For example, the helper can work with the client to help him or her figure out how to arrange his schedule to allow for 15 minutes of exercise and what to do when the weather is bad.

An example of how this step might be implemented involves Charlene, a 30-year-old homemaker, who was depressed, overweight, and out of shape. Through the exploration and insight stages, the helper discovered that Charlene was frustrated about staying home but felt that it was her duty to take care of the children full time. She came to the insight that she thought she should be a stay-at-home mom because she believed that was the only way her husband would love her. She recounted memories of her parents having an awful relationship and her dad resenting her mom for having a successful career. Through helping, she came to understand that she could achieve in a career without destroying her husband. At this point, however, she realized that she had been unemployed outside the home for so long that she did not know how to cope with the world of work. The helper worked with Charlene to devise a plan to get her back in shape physically to gain some confidence. Her homework for the first week was to take a 30-minute walk at least three times with her husband (to lose weight and have some private time with her husband) and to monitor her caloric intake.

By the end of this step, the client has chosen some task that he or she can practice outside the session. Of course, some clients might not need outside tasks because it is not appropriate for their problems or because they are not ready to take this step.

STEP 10: CHECK ON PROGRESS
AND MODIFY ASSIGNMENTS

Problems almost always arise when clients try to implement actions outside sessions. Changing is often more difficult than anticipated and includes unanticipated obstacles. On the basis of experiences clients have had trying out homework in the real world, helpers can work with clients in subsequent sessions to modify homework assignments.

Helpers need to determine what did and did not work for the client in trying to implement the tasks, without judging clients for their efforts, so that modifications can be made to the tasks. If helpers think of themselves as uninvested observers or scientists, they can help clients modify the plans to make them more effective. Rather than becoming angry with clients for not implementing the homework perfectly, helpers might try to view modifications as a natural part of the process. Often clients are not aware of all the barriers in their environment until they try to change, so modifications are often needed. Helpers can use open questions and probes, such as "How did it go last week when you tried to talk to your mother?"

Developing effective homework is a process of trial and error. The helper uses open questions and probes and direct guidance to figure out how to help the client modify the task:

- ■ "Last week we discussed whether you could study 30 minutes before you took a break, but that seemed like it was too long. What would you think about trying to study for 15 minutes and stopping as soon as you have a hard time concentrating?"
- ■ "So it seems that it did not work so well when you tried to confront your roommate when you were really angry about their leaving the dishes unwashed. I wonder if it would be a little easier to talk with her at a time that you're not angry and maybe just say that you want to talk about how to keep the apartment clean?"

Clients can become discouraged with relapses. Brownell, Marlatt, Lichenstein, and Wilson (1986) advocated that a slip or lapse need not lead to a relapse. Helpers can suggest that clients forgive themselves for lapses and learn from them. For example, when Frank drinks too much at a party after having been sober for 6 months, he might learn that he cannot drink even in moderation. This learning might lead him to take steps to determine how to handle parties in the future. In contrast, if Frank beats himself up too much for the relapse, he will probably feel worse about himself and will not be able to cope productively with the problem, which might lead him right back to the problematic drinking.

Throughout this step, helpers can also give clients feedback about their progress. Reinforcement for what they are doing well provides support and encouragement for clients. Given how hard it is to make changes, it helps to get support. All feedback should be given in a caring manner, be brief and to the point, focus on client behavior rather than personality characteristics, be given in moderate doses so as not to overwhelm the client, and have a balance between positive and negative feedback (Egan, 1994).

- "You did a really good job recording how many times you yell at your daughter and what provokes you to yell. Now let's try to figure out other ways to behave when you get angry."
- "Congratulations on being able to keep organized this week."
- "It seems that you had some trouble keeping up your end of the bargain about getting home before curfew several times this week."

By the end of this step, the client should have had some success implementing the change process for one particular problem. The helper and client will then have to decide if helping is over or if they want to go back and tackle another problem. In either event, it is a good time for the helper and client to evaluate how they feel about what has gone on so far.

EXAMPLE OF STEPS FOR BEHAVIOR CHANGE

In this example, the helper has already explored with Sam his feelings about his recent diagnosis of terminal cancer. They have come to the insight that his depression over the diagnosis is due to feelings that he has not yet lived fully. They have traced his passivity back to his having controlling parents who told him how to live his life. Sam now recognizes that no matter what his childhood was like, he is the one responsible for the rest of his life and he cannot blame anyone else.

Readers should note that this example is meant to illustrate how the steps can work. Of course, each situation is different, and it will not always go so smoothly for each helper who tries this out. In addition, sometimes there is not enough time to go through all the steps in one session, so this process gets divided into several sessions.

Helper: So what specifically would you like to work on changing? (Step 1)

Client: I want to change my lifestyle, but I am not certain how to do that.

Helper: What do you mean by that?

Client: I want to change my priorities in terms of how I spend my time.

Helper: You've been talking about how you would like the remainder of your life to be different. What would it mean for you to make changes at this time? (Step 2)

Client: It would be scary because I've been resistant and angry and blaming my parents for so long, but I want to try.

Helper: You sound sure about wanting to change.

Client: Yeah, I am, even though it's going to be tough. Maybe if I take it slowly, it will be easier. But I don't have much time left, so I want to get started.

Helper: Okay, well, let's take the issues one at a time. First, you indicated that you want to have more meaningful relationships. What have you tried in the past? (Step 3)

Client: Well, I'm shy, and it's not easy for me to make friends. I never joined groups or clubs. I guess I hoped that people would come to me. My parents always pushed people on me, so I never took an active role in making friends. I don't need a lot of friends. I would be more interested in having two or three close friends—people I could really count on. (Step 4)

Helper: You sound like you know yourself pretty well.

Client: Yeah, I've thought a lot about myself and these issues.

Helper: Okay, let's brainstorm how you might go about making some new friends. What ideas do you have? (Step 5)

Client: I thought about joining a cancer support group. There would be people there who are going through the same thing I am and would understand me. Also, my neighbor suggested that there's a poker game starting with a bunch of guys in the building. It's only once a month, but I like playing poker. I always wanted to do something like that, but I thought I should be working. Oh, I just remembered that a person who I used to be friends with in college moved back to town. Maybe I could get together with him.

Helper: Those sound like terrific ideas. Which ones are most appealing? (Step 6)

Client: Actually, I think I could easily do them all. The cancer support group is once a week, and it's not far away. The poker game is only once a month. And I've been meaning to call my friend, so that doesn't seem like too much at all. I definitely want to do all those things.

Helper: I like your enthusiasm. Let's just pick one right now to talk about in depth.

Client: Okay, we can focus on the cancer support group first.

Helper: So tell me about it.

Client: The group is at a local hospital. I think there are eight to 10 people in it, and all of them have terminal cancer.

Helper: What would be the most difficult part about going?

Client: I won't know anyone.

Helper: What might you say to yourself to help you with that?

Client: I might say that they don't have to become my best friends. I just need to talk to some people who are experiencing the same things as I am.

Helper: Would that help?

Client: A little bit, but I think I might still have some trouble making myself go to it.

Helper: Can you think of what you might do to reinforce yourself for going? (Step 7)

Client: Maybe if I go to the group, I could stop afterward and get a coffee.

Helper: Would that be a good motivator?

Client: Yeah, I think it would.

Helper: Could we set it up where you go to the support group next week? (Step 9)

Client: I think this would be reasonable. I'm kind of looking forward to it.

(Next session)

Helper: How did it go when you went to the cancer support group? (Step 10)

Client: I went, and it was okay, but I didn't really feel comfortable. Everyone was a lot younger than me.

Helper: That's too bad because you were looking forward to it.

Client: Yeah, I'm a little disappointed. But I heard about a different group that's supposed to have more older people. I think I might try that.

Helper: How was it telling yourself that these people don't have to be your best friends?

Client: That worked pretty well. I also told myself that I didn't have to go back if I didn't like it, and that helped. But what really helped was getting myself the coffee afterward. In fact, I went into the coffee shop and met up with a person I had gone to college

with and we had a good talk. So that turned out
really well.

Helper: Okay, so what can you take out of this with you?

Client: I think I've just got to get out there and try different
things. I'm definitely going to try this other support
group. And maybe I'll hang out at the coffee shop
too—they have an Internet connection so maybe
I could just spend some time there and see what
happens.

Behavioral Rehearsal

Behavioral rehearsal is used to teach clients skills for responding in
more adaptive ways to specific life situations (Goldfried & Davison,
1994). Helpers teach clients new behaviors through role-playing how
they could behave differently in specific situations. Although behavioral rehearsal can be used for many concerns (e.g., rehearsing for a
job interview, practicing for a public speech), I focus here on problems
with *assertiveness* (i.e., standing up for oneself) because these are so
prevalent.

According to Alberti and Emmons (2001), the goal of assertiveness training is to teach clients to stand up for their rights without
infringing on the rights of others. The assumption here is that open
and direct communication is most likely to lead to good relationships
(admittedly a Western value). Unassertive people let others walk all
over them, whereas aggressive people walk all over other people.
Both unassertive and aggressive people can be taught to express positive and negative feelings more appropriately, although one cannot
guarantee that clients will get their way when they assert themselves.
In fact, aggressive people who are used to getting their way are not
likely to respond favorably to a previously unassertive person acting assertively. Hence, helpers also assist clients in thinking not only
of how to present an initial, empathic, assertive statement but also
then of how to respond assertively to escalated aggressiveness or to
change goals.

I assume here that assertiveness problems (or the need to practice
how to respond in an interpersonal situation) have been revealed in the
exploration and insight stages. At this point, then, helpers ask whether
clients would like to learn some skills for how to respond differently.
If the client agrees, the helper proceeds slowly through the following

steps for behavioral rehearsal (summarized in Exhibit 17.3). I encourage helpers not to rush through the steps because it is usually helpful for clients to explore thoroughly in each step.

STEP 1: ASSESS THE BEHAVIOR IN A SPECIFIC SITUATION

The helper asks the client to describe a specific example of when the lack of assertiveness occurred (e.g., a client did not tell a roommate that she did not like her borrowing her clothes without asking, a client got angry and blew up at a colleague for not doing his share of the work). It is best to ask the client to choose a specific example (e.g., the last time it happened) because behavioral rehearsal works best with specific situations. For example, if the client presents a problem of extreme awkwardness and unassertiveness in interactions with interesting men, the helper might ask for detailed information about the last time this happened, covering the ABCs (antecedents, behaviors and feelings in the specific situation, and consequences).

Once the client has provided enough information so that the helper has an idea how the other person in the situation behaved, the helper can ask the client to role-play the situation with the helper playing the part of the other person. The helper should try to make the role-play as realistic as possible, modifying it as the client provides additional details.

During the role-play, the helper carefully observes the client's behavior (e.g., eye contact, voice volume, statement of needs, attitude) to get an idea of how the client actually behaves, although the helper does not comment on the behaviors at this point. After the initial role-play, helpers can ask clients for self-evaluations to help clients focus on their behavior and their experience of the situation.

STEP 2: DETERMINE BEHAVIORAL GOALS

Helpers work with clients to determine specific, realistic goals for how they would like to behave differently (e.g., make one comment during class discussion, calmly tell son to take out the garbage, ask neighbor to turn down the music) given that clients are more likely to make changes when they have clear, doable goals. To construct goals, helpers and clients can generate different possible behaviors and determine which behaviors would feel comfortable to clients.

There is no "right" way to be assertive, so this step is crucial in devising goals that clients can embrace. For example, one female client might want to learn how to ask an interesting man to go out for a date, whereas another would not find this action desirable.

EXHIBIT 17.3

Steps for Behavioral Rehearsal

Steps	Skills (and examples)
1. Assess the behavior in a specific situation	Open questions and probes ("Tell me about the last time you asked for a raise.") Process advisement ("Let's do a role-play of that situation. I'll be your boss and you be you.")
2. Determine behavioral goals	Open questions and probes ("What would you like to accomplish?" "What would you like to see happen?" "How would you like to be?") Restatements and reflections of feelings ("You sound scared about changing." "You have talked a lot about how you would like to change.")
3. Generate and evaluate possibilities	Open questions and probes ("What are some ideas of what you might try?" "Of the various things we've suggested, which ones might fit for you?")
4. Provide a model	Process advisement ("Let's try the role-play again, but this time I'd like to be you and give an example of how you might respond. You be the boss. Would that be okay?") Open questions and probes ("What did you like and dislike about what I did? How would you modify it?"
5. Role-play and provide feedback and coaching	Process advisement ("Let's try the role-play again, but this time you be you and I'll be your boss.") Feedback ("You did a really good job of saying exactly what you wanted without being either too whiny or too aggressive. One thing you could work on is giving a little more eye contact when you say it.")
6. Assign homework	Direct guidance ("How about if you try to talk to your boss tomorrow and try out some of the things we practiced?" "What problems do you see coming up if you try to do this assignment?")
7. Check on progress and modify assignments	Open questions and probes ("What happened when you talked with your boss?") Feedback ("You did a really good job of speaking firmly, and you said what we practiced. You waffled a little bit at the end though. . . . I wonder what was going on there?")

During this step, it is helpful to talk about values that might influence goals (e.g., a woman may not feel comfortable approaching a man for a date because she holds a strong value that men should initiate contact, a man might not want to ask his parents for money because he has a value that he should be independent, a student may not want to ask the professor for help because of not wanting to appear stupid). It also can be helpful to talk about rights (e.g., to privacy, to self-determination), which are of course influenced by values and culture. In addition, it is important to help clients explore their feelings about the different goals and the possible consequences of their goals (e.g., they might get their way but lose a friend).

STEP 3: GENERATE AND EVALUATE POSSIBILITIES

Similar to the step in behavior change, the goal here is to generate various possible ways of dealing with the situation, trying to help the client think creatively about options (e.g., what have others tried in the past, what might work?). This step involves problem solving given the specific situation. Once several options have been generated, the helper can work with the client to explore the feasibility and desirability of the different options, hopefully leading the client to choose the best options.

STEP 4: PROVIDE A MODEL

Once the target behavior is determined, helpers can provide a model of how clients could implement the new behaviors by playing the part of the client. For example, the helper could ask the client to be the instructor, and then the helper would show how she would ask an instructor for an extension of a deadline because of a documented illness. Several principles may prove helpful when thinking about assertiveness:

- Helpers should start with relatively easy behaviors first (e.g., questioning a clerk in a store) rather than major behaviors (e.g., asking for a raise) to maximize the possibility of success. The client might first work on initiating a conversation with a man in class and work up to asking him out on a date.
- Helpers can encourage clients to be empathic with the other person. By thinking about the other person's feelings, clients are more likely to present themselves more compellingly (e.g., "I know you would really like to talk with me right now, but I can't do it now. Can we set up a time to talk tomorrow?").
- It is often better not to provide a lengthy explanation following an apology because this can invite the other person to find solutions. Hence, rather than saying, "I'm so sorry that I can't go to lunch right now because I've got to run errands and do a million things but maybe another time," the person might say, "I'm sorry that I won't be able to go to lunch right now."
- A helpful technique is to be a "broken record" and keep repeating yourself when the other person does not listen. For example, if you are saving a seat for someone in a theater and another person

tries to take the seat, you might say, "I'm sorry, but this seat is saved." When they try to debate with you, you continue saying, "I'm sorry, this seat is saved."

Once the role-play is done, the helper can ask the client what parts the client liked and did not like and how it would be for the client to do what the helper did. If it seems as if it would be useful, the helper can try role-playing again to provide a better model.

STEP 5: ROLE-PLAY AND PROVIDE FEEDBACK AND COACHING

Helpers then can ask clients to be themselves again, with the helper being the other person, and try the chosen behavior in a role-play of the problematic situation. During the role-play, the helper again observes the client's behavior carefully and provides honest positive feedback after the role-play ("You did a really good job of using eye contact and of stating your needs"). Even if the positive feedback is about something minor, clients need to feel that they are doing something well and making some progress. Helpers then can give corrective feedback about one or two specific things (it is important not to overwhelm the client with too much feedback at one point).

Helpers ask clients to do additional role-plays until the client feels confident that she or he can perform the desired behaviors. Before each role-play, the helper provides coaching about what clients could try differently in the next role-play (e.g., "Okay, say it louder and with more conviction this time"). During the role-plays, helpers may also discover that they need to do relaxation training or cognitive restructuring with clients to overcome obstacles to change.

STEPS 6 AND 7: ASSIGN HOMEWORK AND MODIFY ON THE BASIS OF EXPERIENCES

These steps are the same as in the previous section in this chapter on behavior change.

EXAMPLE OF STEPS FOR BEHAVIORAL REHEARSAL

This example is a continuation of the helping session with Sam, the client we met in the last section on behavior change. The following dialogue occurred after the helper and Sam talked about his progress with joining the cancer support group:

Client: One other thing, though. I would like to have a good relationship with a woman before I die. I wonder, you know, I've been thinking a lot about my ex-wife lately. I think that a lot of the problems in our marriage were due to my passivity and never having resolved things with my parents. Now that I have some understanding of my relationship with my parents, I think I could be different with my ex-wife. I realize now that she is not my mother. She does have some quirks, but I do still care for her.

Helper: How would you feel about checking whether she's still interested? (Step 1)

Client: I know that she's not with anybody because of what my daughter says. If I got back together with my ex-wife, I could also spend more time with my daughter, which is something I really want to do.

Helper: It sounds like that might work. But I need to caution you that things might not be so smooth given all the past history that you and she had. You were very passive and might still have a tendency to fall into those behaviors. Perhaps we could work on some assertiveness training to help you stand up to her better and say what's on your mind.

Client: That would be helpful. Could we begin today?

Helper: Sure, give me an example of a recent situation with your ex-wife in which you were passive and you wished that you had behaved differently.

Client: She might say something like she thinks I ought to be spending more time with our daughter. She gets mad that I don't take more responsibility. She has her ideas of exactly what I should be doing and doesn't mince words. Yesterday she called and wanted to know exactly what I planned to do about the babysitting situation. I just said I didn't know, I hadn't really thought about it, and I was really busy right then. I felt irritated that she was bringing it up and was so bossy that I shut down and wouldn't give her any satisfaction.

Helper: Okay, let's role-play to get a clear idea of what happened. I'll be your ex-wife, and you be you. I want you first to role-play exactly what you did in the situation. So, I'm your ex-wife. (as ex-wife) Sam, I want you to take more responsibility for our daughter. I just can't handle it all. I'm working full time, and I can't be the one to take off for everything. I'm going to lose my job if I keep taking off every time she gets sick or needs to go to the doctor. You know that the day-care center won't let her come if she has even the slightest sniffle. Plus, she needs to see her father more. She needs to have you around.

Client: (whines) Well, I just can't do more right now. I'm so busy at school.

Helper: Okay, let's stop there. What are you aware of feeling?

Client: I felt resentful. She's bossing me around again, and I don't like it. She's right, of course, that I ought to spend more time taking my share of the burden, but as soon as she starts up, I just don't want to do anything. I hear my mother's voice nagging me, and I shut down.

Helper: That's great, you can really identify what's going on inside you. And did you notice your tone of voice?

Client: Not really. I didn't notice anything.

Helper: You sounded totally different from before. You actually started whining. Before, in talking with me, you were talking like an adult, but as soon as you role-played talking with your ex-wife, you sounded like a whiny child (illustrates).

Client: Wow, that's incredible. That's exactly what I do with my mother. I can't believe that it came out so quickly without my awareness. And you played it exactly the way my ex-wife does—so bossy and controlling. I hate it when we get into these power struggles. Neither of us wins. But I can see how she feels that she has no choice but to get bossy and controlling when I get so passive and withdrawn.

Helper: Now what would you like to say to her instead? (Step 2)

Client: I would like to say that she's right and that we need to work out a schedule because I really want to do my part. I want to spend more time with my daughter—that's really not a chore. But I wish she wouldn't treat me like a child. Perhaps if we could work on this like two equal adults, we could resolve this problem. I recognize my side of it, but she's got to see what she's doing too.

Helper: That sounds great. Let's try it out here. Say this to her. (Step 4—note that Step 3 was skipped because the client did not seem to need a model.)

Client: (to ex-wife) I really want to make this work. Could we set up a schedule?

Helper: (as ex-wife) Well, I don't know if I trust you.

Client: (to ex-wife) I've done a lot of work, and I'm beginning to see my side of the problem. I can't promise that I will be perfect, but I do want to try.

Helper: (as ex-wife) OK, let's try, but I'm cautious about how this is going to work.

Client: (to ex-wife) I'm cautious too, but I think it's worth it to try. Perhaps we could go for some couples counseling to get some help?

Helper: (as ex-wife) Sounds like a really good idea. (as helper) How was that for you?

Client: Good. I liked how it went. Thank you.

Helper: You were terrific when you said you wanted to set up a schedule. You sounded firm but not nasty. You weren't whiny. You sounded more in control of the situation, and I believed that you wanted to work it out with her. I think if I were your ex-wife, I would be willing to talk with you rationally. Do you think that you could do this with her?

Client: I think I could. I would have to overcome a lot of past experiences with her. But I think I could do that. I want to because I want things to change.

Helper: Well, you were able to do it here, so I have confidence that you could be assertive with her. One thing that might help is if you took a deep breath before you say anything to her. Think about what you want to say, what you want to accomplish. Remind yourself that you are an adult and that she's not your mother.

Client: Yeah, I think that would work. If I told her ahead of time what I was trying to do, she would be very understanding. She often has said that we get tangled up in these situations that we can't seem to resolve. I think she knows that she gets bossy and doesn't want to but just feels really frustrated with the situation.

Helper: Let's role-play it one more time to make sure you have it down. Again, I'm your ex-wife. (as ex-wife) Sam, I want you to take more responsibility for our daughter. I want you to spend more time with her and help me out more when she needs to go to the doctor. I can't keep taking off work every time she needs to be taken out of day care (pause). (as helper) Now remember to take a deep breath, Sam, and think about what you want to say to her.

Client: You know, you're absolutely right to be angry at me. I haven't done my share in the past, and I want to start doing my share now. But we need to step back and talk about how you and I are going to handle this situation. I want to quit acting like the bad child and forcing you to play the nagging mother to increase my involvement with our daughter. I'd like us to work on this like equal adults because I want us to have a better relationship.

Helper: That's great. You didn't have any whine in your voice. You assertively told her what you would like to happen rather than blaming her.

Client: Thanks, it felt good. I might have to practice it a couple more times, but I liked how it felt. I think it would work with her too.

Helper: Unfortunately, we are almost out of time for today. But I wanted to check in with you about how you felt about the ideas we came up with for you to make some changes.

Client: I am really excited because I think this is something I can try. I feel hopeful about being able to have a better relationship with her.

Helper: So you think you'll be able to try this out with your wife? (Step 5)

Client: Yes, I definitely will.

Helper: Great. Try it out and let's talk next week about how it went. We can see if we need to make any changes in the plan then after we see how it goes.

(Next session)

Helper: So how did it go this last week when you tried to talk with your ex-wife? (Step 6)

Client: Well, some good, some bad. The part that worked was I did say that I wanted to set up a schedule. And I was clear and didn't whine.

Helper: Terrific. Way to go.

Client: But the part that didn't go so good was that she didn't respond positively, and then I slipped back into the same old, whiny pattern.

Helper: That often happens. So let's do some problem solving. What might you do when she doesn't respond well? (continues, and does another role-play with how the ex-wife responded)

Decision Making

Clients often have major life decisions to make: which job to take, whether to go to graduate school, whether it is best to buy a house or rent an apartment, or whether or not to get married to a specific person. In decision making, helpers work with clients to help them articulate their options, explore their values, and evaluate the options according to their values (Carkhuff, 1973; Hill, 1975).

I should note that students have varying reactions to this exercise. Some love the clear, specific steps, whereas others feel that the process is too mechanistic. Whether or not students like the task probably depends on personality, but I suggest that trainees try it out and see if there is anything valuable that can be taken from it.

As they do with the other three behavioral tasks, clients reveal during the exploration and insight stages that they need to make a decision about something (e.g., choosing between graduate programs, deciding where to go on vacation, deciding between two people for a dating partner, choosing between three nursery schools for a child). Sometimes clients easily make the decision by exploring, and sometimes they are able to make a decision after simply listing the pros and cons of each possibility, but other times clients still feel blocked. At this point, the helper can ask if the client would like to try an exercise to help make the decision. The steps for decision making are summarized in Exhibit 17.4.

STEP 1: ARTICULATE THE OPTIONS

The helper first asks the client to describe and explore various options. This step often involves work on generating options (similar to steps in behavior change and behavioral rehearsal). It sometimes takes a fair amount of exploration for all the options to emerge, and clients sometimes add or modify options as they go through the steps so helpers may need to go back and add to this list.

EXHIBIT 17.4

Steps for Decision Making

Steps	Skills (and examples)
1. Articulate the options	Open questions and probes ("Tell me the various options that you have thought about.")
2. Values clarification	Open questions and probes ("What values do you have that might be related to what you decide to do?")
3. Weight the relative importance of the values	Process advisement ("Now I would like you to give a number that describes the importance you place on each value. You can give a rating of 1 to 10, but no two values should get the same weighting.")
4. Rate the options	Process advisement ("Now I would like you to rate each option based on your values. Use a scale of −3 to +3, where −3 indicates that you would be very unlikely to do this option, and +3 means that you would do this option. I'd also like to hear your reasoning for each rating.")
5. Evaluate the results and revise the weightings	Open questions and probes ("How do these results fit for you?" "What was surprising?" "How would you like to modify it?" "How was this process for you?")
6. Follow-up	Open questions and probes ("What thoughts did you have about the decision we came up with last week?" "What do you need to modify about it?")

As an example, let us consider that the helper is working with a middle-aged teacher, Bess, who is trying to plan her future. Bess states that she has several options she has been considering: She and her husband could retire at 55, sell their house, and travel around the country in a recreational vehicle; she could wait until 65 to retire and then get involved in volunteer activities; she could keep teaching indefinitely since there is no mandatory retirement age in her job. As Bess is talking, the helper makes a grid and records the options along the top with one option in each column (see Exhibit 17.5).

EXHIBIT 17.5

Example of Bess's Decision-Making Chart: Articulating the Options

Value	Option		
	Retire at 55 and tour country	Retire at 65 and volunteer	Stay at same job indefinitely

STEP 2: VALUES CLARIFICATION

Next, the helper asks the client to generate no more than 10 relevant values, desires, needs, or things that influence the choice and are relevant to making the decision. Once again, the client may need help in generating values because these are often not things we are aware of.

Through considerable exploration, Bess says that the important considerations for her are that she wants to travel, she likes to be intellectually stimulated, she wants to spend time with her husband, she wants more time to be with friends, she wants to have enough money to be comfortable, she wants to feel that she is doing something meaningful with her life, and she wants to be near her children, especially when they have grandchildren. The helper writes these values in the rows of the grid (see Exhibit 17.6).

STEP 3: WEIGHT THE RELATIVE IMPORTANCE OF THE VALUES

The helper then asks the client to weight the importance of each value, desire, and need (1 = *not important,* 10 = *extremely important*). Each weight is used only once so that the client is forced to figure out priorities, and it helps to suggest that the least important receives a weighting of 1 and the most important a weighting of 10, with some numbers left unused if fewer than 10 values are listed. Bess says that intellectual stimulation is her most important value and gives it a weight of 9, whereas she ranks having time to spend with friends at the bottom of her list and gives it a weight of 2 (see Exhibit 17.7).

EXHIBIT 17.6

Example of Bess's Decision-Making Chart: Articulating the Values

	Option		
Value	Retire at 55 and tour country	Retire at 65 and volunteer	Stay at same job indefinitely
Travel			
Intellectual stimulation			
Time with spouse			
Friends			
Money			
Being near children			
Meaning in life			

EXHIBIT 17.7

Example of Bess's Decision-Making Chart: With Weighted Values

	Option		
Value	**Retire at 55 and tour country**	**Retire at 65 and volunteer**	**Stay at same job indefinitely**
Travel (5)			
Intellectual stimulation (9)			
Time with spouse (7)			
Friends (2)			
Money (5)			
Being near children (1)			
Meaning of life (8)			

STEP 4: RATE THE OPTIONS

The goal in this step is to evaluate all the options based on the values. Using a scale of −3 to +3 (−3, −2, −1, 0, +1, +2, +3), the helper asks the client to rate the various options on each of the values and also to discuss the reasons for the ratings. Thus, for each option and value, the helper asks, "If you were to do this option, rate the result based on this specific value."

For example, Bess says that retiring at 55 would get a +3 on travel because they would be touring the country, but she rates retirement at 55 a −3 on intellectual stimulation because she would not be teaching any longer and probably would not be doing as much reading and talking with others about ideas (see Exhibit 17.8).

The next step is to multiply the rating for the option by the weight for the value and then add up the scores for each option. For Bess, the options of retiring at 65 and working indefinitely both received the highest total scores, indicating that she preferred these two options to the other option. The process of putting numbers on feelings helped Bess sort through her feelings (see Exhibit 17.9).

STEP 5: EVALUATE THE RESULTS AND REVISE THE WEIGHTINGS

The goal here is to look at the results and see how they fit for the client. A key is to pay attention to the client's reaction upon learning the results. If the client is happy, the task is done. But if the client seems

EXHIBIT 17.8

Example of Bess's Decision-Making Chart: With Ratings of Options

	Option		
Value	Retire at 55 and tour country	Retire at 65 and volunteer	Stay at same job indefinitely
Travel (5)	+3	+1	−2
Intellectual stimulation (9)	−3	+1	+3
Time with spouse (7)	2	+1	−2
Friends (2)	+1	+1	−1
Money (5)	−3	+1	+3
Being near children (1)	−2	+2	+2
Meaning of life (8)	0	+1	+2

EXHIBIT 17.9

Example of Bess's Decision-Making Chart

	Option		
Value	Retire at 55 and tour country	Retire at 65 and volunteer	Stay at same job indefinitely
Travel (5)	+3 (15)	+1 (5)	−2 (−10)
Intellectual stimulation (9)	−3 (−27)	+1 (9)	+3 (27)
Time with spouse (7)	2 (14)	+1 (7)	−2 (−14)
Friends (2)	+1 (2)	+1 (2)	−1 (−2)
Money (5)	−3 (−15)	+1 (5)	+3 (15)
Being near children (1)	−2 (−2)	+2 (2)	+2 (2)
Meaning of life (8)	0 (0)	+1 (8)	+2 (16)
Total	−13	38	34

Note. The number in parentheses after each of the values is the weighting of that value (range is 1 to 10, where 10 = the greatest weighting). The numbers in the columns are the ratings of each option on the particular value (range from −3 to +3, where +3 = the highest rating). The number in the parentheses after the rating for each option is the multiplicative value of the rating by the weighting of the value (e.g., +3 × 5 for the option of retiring at 55 for the value of traveling).

disappointed, this indicates that something is wrong in the grid and we want to discover the problem. It might be necessary to modify the options or add more options, to revise the values, or to change the ratings, all based on extensive exploration. It might also be helpful to use behavioral rehearsal or a two-chair technique to help the client think through the various options and obstacles.

Thus, the helper asked Bess what she thought about these results. When Bess looked at the total scores for each option, she realized that the scores were not reflective of what she truly wanted. In fact, she realized that traveling and having free time were less important than she had initially thought because she could think of ways to travel and get free time while still working, but that being near children was more important because she did not want to miss out on seeing her grandchildren grow up, so she revised these ratings (see Exhibit 17.10).

STEP 6: FOLLOW-UP

It is important for helpers to come back in subsequent sessions and check in with clients about their feelings. In the case of Bess, the helper asked her reactions during the next session. Bess replied that she had

EXHIBIT 17.10

Example of Bess's Decision-Making Chart: Revised

Value	Option		
	Retire at 55 and tour country	Retire at 65 and volunteer	Stay at same job indefinitely
Travel (4)	+3 (12)	+1 (4)	−1 (−4)
Intellectual stimulation (9)	−3 (−27)	+1 (9)	+3 (27)
Time with spouse (7)	2 (14)	+1 (7)	−1 (−7)
Friends (2)	+1 (2)	+1 (2)	−1 (−2)
Money (3)	−3 (−9)	+1 (3)	+3 (9)
Being near children (5)	−2 (−10)	+2 (10)	+2 (10)
Meaning of life (8)	0 (0)	+1 (8)	+2 (16)
Total	−18	43	49

Note. The number in parentheses after each of the values is the weighting of that value (range is 1 to 10, where 10 = the greatest weighting). The numbers in the columns are the ratings of each option on the particular value (range from −3 to +3, where +3 = the highest rating). The number in the parentheses after the rating for each option is the multiplicative value of the rating by the weighting of the value (e.g., +3 × 5 for the option of retiring at 55 for the value of traveling).

gone home and talked with her husband. She realized that she and her husband had different values related to retirement, and talking about the decision-making grid helped them clarify these differences. They decided they needed a few sessions of marital counseling to resolve their differences.

What Do You Think?

- Debate the merits of working on specific types of action versus just allowing the client to do action on his or her own after attaining insight.
- How do you know when to move from one action step to another? How do you know when you have spent enough time in each of the steps?
- How should helpers decide which action possibilities to pursue for clients?
- What do you think is going on when clients say "Yes, but . . . " frequently?
- How can you tell the difference between client resistance to change and the helper's lack of competence in progressing through the action steps?

RESEARCH SUMMARY

Directives in China

Citation: Duan, C., Hill, C. E., Jiang, G., Hu, B., Chui, H., Hui, K., . . . Yu, L. (2012). Therapist directives: Use and outcomes in China. *Psychotherapy Research, 22*, 442–457. doi: 10.1080/ 10503307.2012.664292

Rationale: Asians are commonly thought to view therapy as much like going to a medical doctor, with the expectation that therapists will quickly diagnose and fix problems by giving directives (i.e., homework, advice, suggestions, and recommendations). Hence, we would expect that Asians (in this study, Chinese) would prefer to work more in the action stage than in the exploration and insight stages. The empirical literature on directives, which has been conducted in the United States, has shown that directives are used quite often, especially by cognitive-behavioral therapists. Furthermore, Scheel, Seaman, Roach, Mullin, and Mahoney (1999) found that clients were more likely to implement homework assignments when they perceived the therapist to have influence, and when the homework assignment was not difficult to complete. Duan et al. wondered if these results would generalize to clients in China.

Method: Ninety-six Chinese college students who sought counseling at a university counseling center in mid-China were seen by 43 therapists who mostly had a client-centered orientation. After every session, clients and therapists separately wrote all the directives that therapists provided during sessions, rated the quality of the primary recommendation, and rated the quality of the working alliance. Starting with the second session, clients indicated how much they had implemented the primary recommendation and rated their psychological functioning.

Interesting Findings:
- Clients indicated that therapists had provided about two directives per session, whereas therapists indicated they had provided about one directive per session.
- Both therapists and clients reported that directives typically focused on cognitive or behavioral changes rather than emotional changes.
- Clients typically reported in the second session that they had implemented the primary directive given in the first session, particularly if it was easy.
- Client implementation of directives was not related to treatment outcome.
- The more therapists reported having given directives, the higher the clients rated the working alliance and the outcome of therapy.

Conclusions:
- Directives seem to influence counseling outcomes differently in China than in the United States. In the United States, when therapists use their influence and give easy-to-implement directives, clients implement these directives and feel better (Scheel, Hanson, & Razzhavaikina, 2004). In contrast, Chinese therapists use directives to strengthen therapeutic relationships. Directives seem to make Chinese clients feel that the therapist is an expert who cares about them and invests in helping them by giving directives, which creates a strong alliance with the therapist, in turn leading to a positive outcome.
- We cannot assume that interventions operate in the same manner cross-culturally.

(continued)

RESEARCH SUMMARY (*Continued*)

Implications:
With Chinese clients, helpers might consider offering one or two directives for cognitive or behavioral changes per session so that clients feel that helpers are experts who care about them. But because directives may work more through building the relationship than through implementation, helpers should not expect that Chinese clients will necessarily implement the directives. Remember that this study was conducted in China, so results may not generalize to clients of Chinese origin in the United States (refer back to Chapter 5 about the importance of not assuming that everyone from a given culture will have the same reactions or need the same interventions).

BONUS MATERIALS

Practice exercises, labs, and other resources for students and teachers are available on the companion website: http://pubs.apa.org/books/supp/hill4.

Integrating the Skills of the Action Stage

18

Ideal teachers are those who use themselves as bridges over which they invite their students to cross, then having facilitated their crossing, joyfully collapse, encouraging them to create bridges of their own.

—*Leo Buscaglia*

Tako came into therapy feeling vague dissatisfaction in his marriage and work. He worked long hours and felt that he was not very connected with his wife. Working with his helper, he explored his desire to change his lifestyle. In the insight stage, he came to understand that he worked too much because of cultural demands about providing for his family and achieving. In the action stage, Tako decided that he wanted to have a better relationship with his wife. He and his helper brainstormed several ways that Tako could make changes.

I n initial sessions, helpers may focus completely on exploration and insight, with only minimal attention to action (depending on client needs). If action is approached in initial sessions, it is usually brief and focused on exploring the possibility of changing, helping clients think about whether and what they want to change or if they want to return for another session. In later sessions, the focus of the action stage moves to discussing and choosing specific action plans, evaluating the positive

http://dx.doi.org/10.1037/14345-018
Helping Skills: Facilitating Exploration, Insight, and Action, Fourth Edition, by C. E. Hill

and negative consequences of changes the client has tried to make, making modifications in action plans, and planning for termination of the helping relationship.

The action stage is often challenging for beginning helpers, who tend either to avoid action in favor of being empathic and insightful or become overly directive and authoritarian while neglecting their empathic skills. Leaving enough time for action can also be difficult for beginning helpers who have trouble with time management in sessions.

Action is also difficult for many clients. Demoralization and hopelessness are major hurdles that clients must overcome before they can change (Frank & Frank, 1991). Clients often feel discouraged or defeated about their ability to change because of negative experiences with past attempts. Accordingly, helpers might encourage clients to take "baby steps" (i.e., make small changes such as 15 minutes of walking) and explore the idea of change first, while recognizing how hard it is to change.

Although the action stage presents many challenges for both helpers and clients, helpers should not neglect helping clients make changes in their lives. They do, however, need to approach the action stage with appropriate caution, self-awareness, and empathy for their clients.

Implementing the Action Skills

It is difficult to make changes, so clients need empathy, support, and encouragement from helpers throughout the entire action stage, even if they decide not to change or have only accomplished one small step toward their goals. Clients need to feel that helpers are on their side. In addition, clients appreciate knowing that their helpers are benevolent coaches or guides rather than harsh parents or dictators.

NEED FOR FLEXIBILITY

Flexibility and creativity are critical in the action stage. I presented the steps for the four types of action in a clear-cut linear manner in the previous chapter so students can learn them easily. But in practice, these steps are rarely implemented in such a straightforward manner, and the four types are not so easily distinguished. Helpers need to learn the steps for all four types and then modify them to fit the needs of the client.

If one intervention does not work, helpers need to try something else. If several interventions are unsuccessful or the client continually says, "Yes, but . . . " in response to interventions, helpers might explore how clients feel about the therapeutic relationship or the process of change. Helpers also can use insight skills to help clients understand their resistance to change.

Furthermore, when clients implement changes in the real world, things rarely go as planned. Clients need to be prepared for disappointment or for others not responding well to their changes. It can be useful for helpers to prepare clients for such disappointment.

NEED TO REMAIN HUMBLE ABOUT THE DIFFICULTIES IN CHANGING

Changing is hard, and people are complicated. Helpers need to remember that carrying out action ideas is not easy. If it were easy, clients would have already implemented the ideas. All of us sometimes have a fantasy about the wizard who will be able to tell us what to do, but taking over for clients has the potential of undermining their efficacy and self-healing potential.

It can also be useful for helpers to recall that the problems clients bring in are real and that their suggestions can have major consequences. For example, if a client is asking for help about whether she should tell her father about dating someone of another race or religion, the helper needs to be sensitive that advice to be open and honest might have adverse consequences (e.g., the client being disowned). This concern speaks to the helper being cautious about exploring carefully the full context before rushing to action.

Remembering how difficult it is to make changes in our own lives can assist helpers in being empathic with clients who are struggling with changing. Helpers also need to remember that clients' problems developed over many years; changing ingrained patterns is difficult.

CULTURAL CONSIDERATIONS

Some clients want and expect a lot of action and direction from their helpers, whom they perceive as authorities or wise people (Pedersen, Draguns, Lonner, & Trimble, 2002). If a helper does not focus on action, these clients might lose respect for the helper and the helping process. Such clients may get frustrated if helpers do not tell them what to do.

Another cultural consideration is that helpers may need to incorporate spirituality into the action stage (e.g., using prayer as an action strategy) for clients for whom spirituality and religion are important issues (Fukuyama & Sevig, 2002). If helpers are not responsive to such needs, clients may feel disrespected and may devalue the helping process. But because spirituality is a sensitive topic, helpers might wait to pick up clues from clients as to whether they would like a focus on spirituality. And of course helpers should only work with spirituality if they feel that they can do so authentically.

Finally, helpers need to be aware of barriers to action faced by clients from other cultures. For example, clients who are poor may not have transportation, child care, or access to public services. Clients who are immigrants often face discrimination and language problems. Clients who are elderly and infirm may not be able to leave their houses. Asian clients may not want to go outside the family for help or may not know how to change in a way that respects and incorporates the family's needs. Helpers need to be aware of such cultural considerations, ask clients about possible barriers, and be sensitive to different needs.

As I mentioned at the end of the insight stage, it may be difficult for a majority group client (e.g., a middle-aged White male) to engage in the action stage with a minority individual (e.g., a younger biracial female) because it upsets the normative power differential in society. This older male client may feel a need to assert his dominance and feel uncomfortable receiving guidance from a younger woman.

Difficulties Helpers Might Experience in the Action Stage

MOVING TOO QUICKLY TO ACTION

Some helpers rush to action before they have established a firm enough foundation of exploration and insight. They might feel impatient with the long process of exploration and insight; they might feel that they "know" what the client should do; they might feel compelled to "do" something for the client. Unfortunately, when helpers move too quickly to action, clients often are resistant, not attuned with the helper, unable to take responsibility for their changes, or unmotivated to make changes. Helpers need to remember to spend the majority of their time in exploration to establish the foundation for insight and action.

If information or advice is provided before clients are ready for it, clients might not be able to use it. For example, some volunteers in battered women's shelters provide information to the women about how to make it on their own when the women first come in. At this point, the women more often need to explore their feelings about being in an abusive relationship. They are not ready yet to use information, no matter how helpful or well intentioned it is.

Some helpers move to action before they know enough about the client's situation. They might jump quickly to a solution before exploring the complexity of the situation. It can appear disparaging to clients for helpers to jump to quick solutions and imply that they were inept for not knowing how to solve such simple problems. If problems were so simple, clients would have solved them on their own.

NEEDING TO BE THE EXPERT

Providing information and giving advice gratify some helpers' needs to be viewed as the expert. Some helpers like being perceived as "knowing it all" and enjoy having clients admire them. These helpers might be trying to look like the experts at the expense of encouraging clients to seek out their own information and make their own decisions. Other helpers might embrace the role of expert because they want to assist clients, and they believe that helpers should provide all the answers and give lots of helpful information to clients. Both types of helpers do a disservice in neglecting the client's role in the information-generating process. Although helpers might know more about helping than their clients do, they do not know more than clients about clients' inner experiences or what actions clients should implement.

TOO MUCH INVESTMENT IN THE CLIENT CHANGING

Perhaps the major clinical issue that arises in the action stage is the helper becoming too invested in the client changing. Some helpers feel so responsible for developing action plans that they try to make decisions for the client. They feel that things would be much easier if clients just did what they were told to do. However, taking over for clients is typically counterproductive (except in extreme cases of suicidal or homicidal ideation or intent) because clients become dependent and do not develop the skills needed to make changes in the future. In addition, what might work for the helper might not work for the client. Furthermore, if helpers become too invested in what they think clients should do, it is difficult for helpers to listen supportively and objectively to clients. Hence, helpers generally need to be uninvested (but not uncaring) in what action the client chooses (or does not choose). Helpers must allow clients to make their own decisions and should serve as guides and supporters rather than as bosses.

IMPOSING ONE'S VALUES ON CLIENTS

Sometimes helpers lose sight of trying to help clients uncover their values and instead impose their own beliefs and values on clients. It can be difficult for helpers to accept that clients have different values, especially when the values differ significantly from the helper's cherished beliefs. For example, a client dying of a terminal illness might want to talk about the possibility of suicide. If helpers are rigid about the value of life, they might not allow clients to explore the possibility of suicide, thus limiting the client's ability to contemplate all the options thoroughly and make an informed decision. In another example, a helper might tell a client to smile more because he wants all women to appear happy. Helpers always need to be attentive to their own issues and needs and try to minimize their effect on clients.

NOT BEING BOLD ENOUGH IN ENCOURAGING CLIENTS TO MAKE CHANGES

Helpers may not challenge clients enough to make changes. Some helpers are worried about intruding on their clients and thus do not encourage them to change. They believe it is not their place to challenge. Although clients need to be the ones who choose to change, helpers can encourage and challenge clients when they are stuck and struggling. In addition, helpers are sometimes nervous about challenging clients because they are not sure what to do to help.

NOT BEING SUPPORTIVE ENOUGH

Sometimes helpers become so involved in developing the action plan during this stage that they forget to be supportive. Encouragement and reinforcement are crucial for both actual change and efforts to change. I suspect that when helpers remember aspects of their lives that are difficult to change, they may be more sympathetic to clients who have difficulty changing.

GETTING STUCK ON ONE ACTION IDEA

Helpers often remain committed to action ideas that they have developed, even when it is clear that these ideas are inappropriate and clients cannot or will not follow them. Perhaps these helpers have spent a lot of time thinking about what their clients should do and have become invested in the action plans. However, helpers need to realize that helping requires flexibility and that action ideas often require adjustment because helpers and clients are not aware of all the problems that can arise. They need to select and keep the parts of the action plans that work and revise the parts that do not.

ADHERING TOO RIGIDLY TO THE STEPS

Helpers who follow the action steps in Chapter 17 precisely will probably feel frustrated because the exact sequence of steps will not apply to every client. These steps are provided so that students can see a structure of how to proceed through the action stage. Helpers will need to learn and practice the steps as presented but then use their creativity and flexibility to modify the procedures for themselves and the individual client. This stage allows for incredible flexibility as helpers try to creatively work with individual clients to help them.

Strategies for Overcoming the Difficulties

There are a number of strategies that helpers can use to manage the difficulties.

SELF-REFLECTION

When helpers get trapped in any of the pitfalls (moving too quickly to action, becoming too invested in clients' changing, imposing their values on clients, not being challenging enough, not being supportive enough, or getting stuck on one plan), they might spend some time reflecting and hypothesizing about what caused them to have problems. If helpers discover that they get overly invested or use a lot of direct guidance across several clients and clients are reacting with resistance, helpers need to look inward to understand themselves so that they do not harm clients. Consulting with peers, seeking personal therapy, and receiving supervision are all helpful methods for learning more about oneself. In addition, helpers can go back and use the management strategies suggested in Chapters 10 and 17 for dealing with anxiety (e.g., relaxation, imagery, positive self-talk, focus on the client).

USE EXPLORATION SKILLS

When an impasse or problem arises in the action stage, it is often helpful to return to cultivating an empathic attitude and using the exploration skills (open questions and probes, restatement, and reflection). The helper needs to try to understand what is going on with the client at this particular time. When clients feel misunderstood, helpers also need to rebuild trust and reassure clients that helpers can listen to and collaborate with them.

DEAL WITH PROBLEMS IN THE THERAPEUTIC RELATIONSHIP

Helpers can ask clients how they are feeling about what is going on in the helping relationship, particularly when they have reached an impasse, defined by Elkind (1992) as a deadlock or stalemate that causes helping to become so difficult that progress is not possible. Using immediacy to deal with the relationship and resolve problems is particularly crucial (see Chapter 14). Helpers need to listen for feedback from clients and be willing to hear how they might improve their work with their clients. If appropriate for the helping situation, helpers can talk about their own immediate feelings (without burdening clients with their personal problems). Acknowledging their part in the problems in helping relationships (e.g., apologizing if they have made a mistake) can be therapeutically beneficial. Helpers also can thank clients for sharing their feelings and working hard to make positive changes in their lives.

What Do You Think?

- Which of the following obstacles do you anticipate that you are most likely to experience in using the action skills?

  _____ Moving too quickly to action
  _____ Needing to be the expert
  _____ Being too invested in clients' changes
  _____ Imposing one's values on clients
  _____ Not encouraging enough change
  _____ Not being supportive
  _____ Getting stuck on one action idea
  _____ Adhering too rigidly to the steps

- Which strategies would work to help you cope with the obstacles in the action stage?

  _____ Self-reflection
  _____ Address issues related to the therapeutic relationship
  _____ Consultation with supervisors, peers, or teachers
  _____ Return to exploration skills

RESEARCH SUMMARY

Encouraging Clients to Do Homework

Citation: Mahrer, A. R., Gagnon, R., Fairweather, D. R., Boulet, D. B., & Herring, C. B. (1994). Client commitment and resolve to carry out postsession behaviors. *Journal of Counseling Psychology, 41,* 407–414. doi:10.1037/0022-0167.41.3.407

Rationale: Mahrer et al. noted that many therapists, especially those who have a behavioral orientation, assign homework. But they contended that therapists do not just assign homework; rather, they also use certain interventions to encourage clients to commit themselves to carrying out the homework. Given that ultimately clients are the ones who have to go out and implement the homework, it seems important to figure out how to motivate clients to want to implement it. Furthermore, they speculated that different kinds of homework may require different types of motivational strategies.

Method: The authors found 241 published transcripts from a wide variety of therapists and individual adult clients. Judges read transcripts and identified all instances in which clients explicitly and manifestly expressed a commitment, resolution, intention, readiness, willingness, and determination to carry out some postsession behavior. These events were grouped into two categories of different types of postsession behaviors (problem reduction and new ways of being and behaving). Judges then went back through the transcripts and identified all the therapist methods used to encourage clients to carry out these postsession behaviors.

Interesting Findings:
- Of the 241 transcripts, only 22 (9%) included clear explicit client statements of commitment and resolve to carry out postsession behaviors. The therapists in these 22 cases were disproportionately often cognitive–behavioral in orientation and disproportionately less often psychodynamic or humanistic or client-centered in orientation.
- Half of the client statements were of a commitment to reduce a specific behavior, whereas the other half were of a commitment to increase some particular behavior.
- Sixteen therapist methods were identified as occurring before clients stated a commitment to carrying out homework assignments (about five methods were used per instance).
- A method commonly used for both types of problems was concrete specificity (the therapist being specific about defining the exact behavior to be implemented, the context in which it might occur, the other people who might be involved, and when and how to carry out the behavior).
- In addition, to help clients reduce some behavior, therapists often
  - justified the rationale (argued for how and why the change should be implemented),
  - encouraged or pressured (pushed the client to carry out the behavior), and/or
  - assigned specific homework (requested that the client carry out the homework).
- In addition, to help clients increase some behavior, therapists often
  - encouraged client initiation (allowed the client to come up with the specific postsession behavior without blocking or getting in the client's way),
  - asserted or asked about client readiness and willingness to carry out the behavior,
  - did behavior-context clarification (clarified the behavior and situation in which the change would take place), and/or
  - did in-session role-plays with clients to help them practice new behaviors).

(continued)

RESEARCH SUMMARY *(Continued)*

Conclusions:

- Therapists had many methods for helping clients develop a resolve to carry out postsession changes.
- The most typical methods involved encouraging the client to come up with his or her own ideas for changes.
- Therapists often persisted using several methods until client resolve and commitment was obtained. It appeared that clients and therapists were working together collaboratively to develop change strategies.

Implications for Therapy:

- It is often a good idea to let clients initiate the change process.
- Therapists may need to use a number of methods to encourage clients to make changes, but it is important to collaborate with clients in this process.

BONUS MATERIALS

Practice exercises, labs, and other resources for students and teachers are available on the companion website: http://pubs.apa.org/books/supp/hill4.

INTEGRATION | V

Putting It All Together
Working With Clients in the Three-Stage Model

19

*And the time came when the risk to remain tight in a bud was
more painful than the risk it took to blossom.*

—*Anaïs Nin*

In this final chapter, I discuss putting all the helping skills
detailed in previous chapters together to work in sessions
with clients. As I have said before, it is important to learn the
individual skills to make sure you have the ability to use each
one, and practicing the individual skills is crucial. But once
you have the basic ability to use the skills, you then need to
integrate them for use with specific clients. Thus, once you
learn the individual skills, they recede into the background,
and session management and case conceptualization become
more salient.

There is no "right" way to implement the helping model.
Each helper has a different style, and each client has different
needs and unique reactions. Furthermore, because there are
a myriad of settings with different policies and procedures, it
is not possible to provide an exact road map or cookbook for
helpers for everything that they need to know.

http://dx.doi.org/10.1037/14345-019
Helping Skills: Facilitating Exploration, Insight, and Action, Fourth Edition,
by C. E. Hill

In this chapter, I focus on some general issues that cross approaches and settings, but I recognize that these will not fit perfectly for any given setting. A caveat before starting, however, is that I do not focus here on issues such as matching helpers and clients or on client and therapist characteristics that predict outcome, although obviously these are important for the helping process (see Lambert, 2013, for excellent reviews of these literatures). In addition, the guidelines presented here focus on helping provided in an open-ended manner using the exploration–insight–action skills rather than manual-driven therapeutic approaches (e.g., manualized cognitive–behavior therapy).

Session Management

The first big task for helpers is to figure out what to do during sessions with clients. I focus on goals and tasks for intakes with new clients, between sessions, supervision, subsequent sessions with clients, and termination.

INTAKES

Many mental health clinics use initial intake sessions with potential clients to formulate a diagnosis, assess for risk, and determine the best treatment. The actual intake protocol depends on the agency, but it is usually based on a clinical interview. Whiston (2005) noted that a good intake usually involves gathering information about the following:

- Client demographics (e.g., name, age, sex, address, ethnicity, education and work history, previous counseling experiences).
- Presenting concerns (e.g., specific problems, urgency of request): Gather information about each problem from affective, cognitive, and relational perspectives; gather details about each problem (when the problem began, its history, what was going on in the client's life at the time of the problem, how others contribute to the problem, intensity of the problem, changeability of the problem, methods used to solve the problem).
- Client background information or psychosocial history: Obtain a brief overview of the client's background as it relates to the presenting problem (e.g., family of origin, current family and relationships, employment and school status, living situation).
- Health and medical history: This information is needed to understand the client holistically and usually includes current health issues, medications, substance use or abuse, caffeine intake, sleep, eating patterns, and exercise patterns.

- Risk factors: Assess for danger to self and others and alcohol and substance abuse.
- Expectations for therapy: Assess what the client expects related to the process (i.e., what goes on during sessions) and outcome (i.e., what changes as a result) of helping.

Although the purpose of the intake is to gather information and thus calls for the helper to be more directive and to use more closed questions than she or he normally would in helping sessions, it is important for helpers to use attending and exploration skills (e.g., reflections of feelings, restatements, summaries) to help the client feel at ease and explore. Without good attending and helping skills, helpers will not get much information from clients.

At the end of the intake, helpers ask clients if they want to commit to becoming involved in the helping process. If clients are uncertain about whether they want to commit to helping, helpers might suggest that they meet for three to six sessions and then reevaluate.

FIRST SESSION

For the purposes of this chapter, I am assuming that the actual helping is conducted by a different person than the one who conducted the intake. Research shows that it is better for the same person to conduct the intake and therapy (Nielsen et al., 2009), but I present them separately here to distinguish between their different purposes and because they are often conducted by different people.

Before the first session, helpers review the intake record to see what to expect but remain open to making their own assessments of clients. In terms of the session itself, helpers start the session, establish goals, clarify expectations, develop a focus, check in about continuing, and end the session.

Beginning the Session

Helpers begin the initial session by informing clients whether they will be recorded, observed live, or supervised (e.g., "I will be recording this session, and my supervisor is watching through that one-way mirror") and about the disposition of any such tape recordings ("All recordings will be erased as soon as my supervisor listens to them"). Helpers also clarify issues of confidentiality. They say something like,

> Everything you say will be kept in strict confidence, with a couple of exceptions: If you reveal anything about abuse or intent to harm yourself or others, or if a child or older person is suspected of being abused in some way, I will need to break confidentiality.

Note that such statements about the limits of confidentiality are not just good therapeutic practice, they are also legally required. Although it is crucial to provide relevant information about confidentiality at this point, clients do not usually need a lot of detail because they are more interested in moving on to talk about what brought them to helping.

Helpers should also inform clients at the beginning of the session about the helping process. First, the helper explains the process (e.g., "We are going to be spending 30 minutes together, and our goal is to help you explore whatever topic you would like to address"). Helpers can also briefly self-disclose about facts or credentials to educate clients about their background as helpers (e.g., "I am a beginning helper"), especially if clients ask for such information.

In addition, helpers often tell clients about some of the rules (e.g., length of sessions, cost) at the beginning of the initial session. They inform clients about other rules in later sessions as the need arises (e.g., when clients ask for information that is too personal, the helper might explain why he or she chooses not to divulge such information; when a client repeatedly asks for hugs, the helper might explain why that is not a good idea). Providing information about the process of helping educates clients about what to expect given that they are more likely to be full partners in the helping process if they know what is expected.

Helpers can then ask clients whether they have any questions about what to expect from the process (e.g., "Is there anything you want to know about the process?"). After answering questions, helpers turn the focus onto clients by using an open question or probe, such as "What would you like to talk about?" or "What's on your mind?" to encourage clients to share their concerns. It is sometimes an awkward transition from providing information to turning the focus over to the client, so helpers might take a deep breath and explain that the focus is shifting.

If a client does not respond right away to the opening probe, or if she or he responds by saying "I don't have anything to talk about," the helper might pause (empathically of course) to give the client a chance to think and talk. It is important not to rush clients but to give them the message that it is their turn to talk. When helpers listen patiently and empathically, clients often begin talking within a few minutes. If the client still does not talk, the helper might reflect possible feelings (e.g., discomfort, uncertainty) to allow the client to focus on feelings. Some clients are anxious about whether what they have to say is important enough to be discussed in the session and need reassurance that the helper is listening and thinks what they are talking about is important. If the client still does not talk, the helper might ask an open-ended question, such as "Can you tell me more about the problems that brought you here?"

The most important thing helpers do at this point in the session is to listen empathically to encourage the client to begin talking and exploring.

Throughout the exploration stage, helpers listen carefully to what clients are saying and use appropriate attending behaviors to provide a warm presence and encourage clients to explore. They also carefully observe clients' responses and modify attending behaviors accordingly (e.g., if clients draw away from eye contact, helpers should not look at them intensely). In addition, helpers offer approval and reassurance (e.g., "That's tough," "You're doing a good job talking about the problem") if the client seems to need encouragement. Most important, when clients are talking productively about their concerns, helpers sit quietly and listen attentively and empathically.

Establish Goals and Clarify Expectations

An important task of the first session is to determine why the client sought out a helping experience at this particular time and what the client's goals are for counseling. It is helpful to know what motivated the client to seek help at a given time because this tells the helper something about what is going on with the client. Many people have experienced distress for a long period, but something tips them over the edge to seek help at a particular time.

In addition, it is important to learn what the client expects and wants from the helping experience ("What do you want to accomplish?"). If expectations are unrealistic, the helper can clarify what helping can realistically provide. If the number of sessions is limited, helpers and clients need to have realistic expectations for what can be accomplished. With more sessions, helpers can help clients with more deeply rooted personality problems (e.g., working through childhood sexual abuse, engrained interpersonal deficits). The helper and the client must agree that the goals are reasonable and possible to attain.

Throughout this process of establishing goals, the helper may come to realize that he or she is not the best helper for this client (e.g., the client has an active eating disorder, and the helper has no expertise in eating disorders; the client needs medication, and the helper cannot prescribe; the client wants a cognitive–behavioral approach, and the helper uses a psychodynamic approach; the helper has strong negative countertransference reactions to the client). The most ethical thing to do in this situation is to gently and nonjudgmentally refer the client to a more qualified service provider.

Establish a Relationship

The ultimate goal in the first session is to establish rapport and let clients know that the helper is interested in them and their experiences. If a client is able to talk and explore, the helper would use exploration skills, perhaps especially focusing on reflections of feelings to see how much the client can engage with feelings. If a client just wants to just talk without reflecting deeply, if the client is silent and has a hard time engaging, if a client gets embarrassed and seems anxious with the helper, of if a client seems especially avoidant, the helper might want to be incredibly gentle and use more open questions and probes about thoughts and feelings. Of course, the helper would notice all these observations and reflect about them after the session, but during the first session, the helper would primarily want to be patient and try to understand the client's experiential world.

Check in About Continuing

Near the end of the first session, helpers can use immediacy to ask clients how they felt about the session and the work that was done. This processing of sessions is important so that helpers can become aware of how clients reacted to various interventions. For helpers to be able to plan the next sessions, they need to know what worked and what was not effective. As discussed in Chapter 2, clients often do not reveal their feelings about the helper and the helping process unless asked explicitly. Helpers should not, however, ask only for clients' reactions to elicit platitudes about their skills. In fact, they should be suspicious if clients talk only about how wonderful helpers were. Instead, they should be genuinely interested in hearing both the positive and negative reactions from clients.

Ending the First Session

Helpers need to be aware of the time in sessions. Five to 10 minutes before the end of the session, helpers might mention that the session is almost over. Mentioning the approaching end of the session sets the boundary that time is important and gives clients time to prepare for leaving the session and to reflect on what they have accomplished. Some clients wait until a couple of minutes before the end of session to bring up important feelings. They could be ambivalent about discussing the topic, anxious about the helper's reaction, or hoping to manipulate the helper into extending the session.

HELPERS' WORK BETWEEN SESSIONS

Helpers need to think about their clients between sessions to try to conceptualize their problems. Specifically, they need to think about the origins of clients' problems, the underlying themes in the problems, and appropriate interventions.

One way to facilitate this conceptualization process is for helpers to listen to the audiotapes or, even better, to watch the videotapes of their sessions. Observing sessions enables helpers to recreate what they were thinking and feeling and to observe clients' reactions to their interventions. Watching sessions can also provide a powerful self-confrontation about one's use of attending and helping skills.

I suggest that helpers write process notes (see Web Form F for an example form) after each session to facilitate their recall of the salient issues that were covered during the session. In the process notes, which are best completed immediately after sessions, helpers can use their experience and perceptions to write about the following areas:

- manifest content (what the client talked about),
- underlying content (unspoken meanings in what the client said),
- defenses and barriers to change (how the client avoids anxiety),
- client distortions (ways in which the client responds to you as she or he has to other significant persons in her or his life, i.e., transference),
- countertransference (ways in which your emotional, attitudinal, and behavioral responses may have been stimulated by the process), and
- personal assessment (your evaluation of your interventions; what you would do differently and why).

Helpers should look for underlying themes and recurring patterns across all the problems that clients raise. For example, is the client always the passive victim in every encounter, does the client idealize everyone, or is the client always angry? These themes provide important clues for the underlying problems that need attention in therapy.

Thorough exploration allows helpers to develop hypotheses about clients that lay the foundation for choosing interventions. They should pay close attention to each client's personality and verbal and nonverbal behaviors. How does the client respond to interventions? How does the client's way of interacting influence the helping process?

Helpers can make observations about clients and develop hypotheses about what factors led clients to come to their current state. After thinking about a client, helpers should be able to answer several questions:

- How serious is the problem?
- How is the client behaving?
- How much does the client disclose or withhold about the problem?
- Are there discrepancies in what the client is saying?
- What is the client's role in the creation and maintenance of the problem?

Helpers also need to educate themselves about theories and research to obtain a framework with which to understand client dynamics (i.e., what causes and maintains problems). Helpers need to select a theoretical framework and read current research so they can think carefully about their interventions with clients. Furthermore, if a client is from a different culture or has a problem with which the helper is not familiar, the helper should read about the issue and consult with supervisors between sessions to ensure that she or he is giving the best available services to the client.

SUPERVISION

In addition to reflecting on their own about clients, beginning helpers meet with supervisors for assistance in conceptualizing clients. Supervisors can aid helpers in thinking about various hypotheses about what caused and maintained problems as well as possible interventions to help clients. They can also provide a different perspective to aid helpers when they become stuck in their perceptions and countertransferences.

SUBSEQUENT SESSIONS

Subsequent sessions differ slightly from intake and initial sessions. Helpers need to be prepared to shift gears a bit.

Beginning the Session

At the beginning of subsequent sessions, helpers might sit quietly and wait for clients to talk about what is on their minds, although they might need to educate clients that they are expected to bring in material to begin the session if clients seem confused about why the helper is not taking the initiative. Alternatively, helpers might summarize what took place in the former session, start by asking how the client felt about the previous session, or simply ask what the client would like to talk about during the session. All are appropriate, but which helpers choose to use depends on the client and the helper. The helper might personally like more or less structure or assess that the client needs more or less structure.

Helpers cannot assume that clients will continue talking about what they discussed the previous session or that clients have the same feelings that they had during the previous session. Many beginning helpers spend a great deal of time debriefing after sessions and approach subsequent sessions with an agenda about what to do to help clients with problems raised in the previous session. Helpers are often surprised, however, when clients are not concerned with or interested in talking about the same issues. When clients leave the therapy setting, many things happen that change the way they feel. They may have spent time thinking about the issues and resolved them, or they may want to discuss other issues that might have become more salient in the interim. Thus, helpers have to be prepared to respond to clients in the moment. Being prepared, yet flexible, is one of the biggest challenges for beginning helpers.

Develop a Focus

It is best for helpers to focus on one problem at a time; otherwise, there is a danger of becoming so diffuse that nothing gets accomplished. A clear focus typically involves a specific incident or behavior, such as a fight with a roommate, procrastination over completing assignments, or concern over how to communicate with a partner. The focus should be neither too vague nor too diffuse. To develop a focus, helpers typically ask clients what is troubling them *now*. It may take a while, however, to determine the most pressing issue because clients often start with one concern, although another issue is actually more critical. For example, Michael initially said that he was concerned about his grandmother's imminent death. After talking for a few minutes, it emerged that Michael was actually more concerned about the end of a relationship with a woman whom he had been dating for 4 years. Thus, the helper shifted to focus on Michael's feelings about the breakup for the rest of the session. If it is not possible to get the client to focus, the lack of focus in itself becomes the important issue for the session that the helper needs to talk about with the client.

Helpers must respect the client's decisions about the focus of the sessions. For example, Moira wanted to work on existential issues such as the meaning of life, whereas the helper was much more concerned with the high likelihood that Moira was about to flunk out of school and lose her job. Although the helper needs to keep the holistic picture of the client in mind (and perhaps later challenge the client about the discrepancies), it is important especially in the initial session for the helper to not impose his or her wishes on the client (unless the client is in imminent danger). Of course, helpers can reflect about whether their perceptions of client needs are motivated by their own needs.

Helpers also need to maintain the focus on a specific concern (even though each specific concern has many parts). Many beginning helpers let clients jump from topic to topic (e.g., academic concerns, interpersonal relationships, spirituality), so that by the end of a session, clients have covered a lot of things superficially but have not explored anything in depth. Focusing on a specific issue is important to making progress, especially in brief treatments. Helpers can use a combination of skills to assist clients in focusing on one issue in depth. Specifically, they can observe clients to determine which issue has the most salience for them (e.g., where is the most intense affect?). After identifying the most important issue, helpers can reflect the feelings clients are experiencing about that issue. Helpers can branch off to explore aspects of the central focus. Although the focus stays on the problem, helpers also facilitate client exploration of how the concern is affected by, and influences, other parts of the person's past, current, and future life. For example, if the helper determines that academic concerns are the central focus for Sam, the helper might ask him to explore parental expectations for academic performance and to explore thoughts about his future occupational preferences, then encourage him to talk about study skills. In this way, the helper is sticking to the central topic of academic concerns but is helping Sam explore many aspects of it.

In addition, helpers need to remember to keep the focus on the client, even when the client talks primarily about others. For example, if a client says, "My mother is really awful," the helper can say, "You are really irritated with your mother," thereby changing the focus from the mother to the client's reaction to her or his mother. The guiding principle is that it is easier and more efficient (and more ethical) to help a client change than to attempt to help the client change another person.

The Working Phase

The goal during subsequent sessions is to respond to issues that clients bring up in each session. Essentially, the helper cycles through exploration, insight, and action with many problems to help the client begin to be able to do this process independently. Essentially, the goal is for helpers to work themselves out of a job so that clients can function on their own with good support systems in place.

There are often many phases in the work with clients, but these vary considerably based on the individual client. Some clients just want symptom relief, and so the work with them is often brief (e.g., 12 to 20 sessions) and primarily involves a clear focus on specific problems (e.g., anxiety about public speaking, fear of flying). Other clients want more focus on interpersonal problems and may need longer term work gaining insight into maladaptive patterns and coming up with more adaptive behaviors. Still other clients are more interested in longer term work to understand more deep-rooted problems that require considerable exploration (e.g., personality problems, dealing with troubling family issues, resolving grief or trauma, exploring the meaning of life). Still others who are quite disturbed might need supportive maintenance throughout life.

During longer term therapy, in addition to working on clients' presenting problems, there is also often a focus on the therapeutic relationship using immediacy skills. Conflicts inevitably arise in every relationship; if these conflicts can be dealt with in a different way than the clients are accustomed to, clients can have a corrective experience (Castonguay & Hill, 2012; Hill & Knox, 2009). Furthermore, if clients can learn to behave differently in the therapeutic relationship, they might learn new behaviors that they can use in outside relationships.

Ending Sessions

Because it is important to set clear boundaries, helpers need to begin and end sessions on time. If clients are late, helpers typically end sessions at the appointed time. Helpers might say something like, "Our time is up for today." Helpers might also want to reinforce clients for what they have accomplished in the session and encourage them to think about carrying these changes over to their lives outside the sessions.

TERMINATION

Therapy does not continue forever (even in long-term psychoanalytic therapy), so separation is inevitable. After helpers and clients have accomplished as much as they can within the confines of their contracted relationship, it is time to end the therapy relationship. The helper and client might have gone through several cycles of exploration–insight–action, dealing with several different problems, with the client gradually taking more responsibility until he or she feels ready to manage his or her life independently. One goal of therapy is to prepare clients to leave therapy and become self-reliant. Just as parents raise children to grow up and leave home, helpers teach and encourage clients to cope without the helper.

When to Terminate

Sometimes the end of helping is imposed by external time limits (e.g., beginning helpers often are only allowed to provide one to three sessions with volunteer clients; some counseling centers on university campuses allow only six sessions, although others allow 12 sessions). Other times, the client or therapist moves or the client can no longer afford treatment, and treatment ends. In such cases, helpers have to be ready to terminate with clients and refer them if needed (information about referrals is given later in the chapter).

In contrast, in open-ended, long-term therapy, helpers and clients together decide when they are ready to terminate the relationship. Rarely is there such a thing as a "cure," because cure implies a static state rather than the continual changes and challenges involved in living. Most often, clients decide they are tired, have reached a plateau and are ready for a break, do not have anything else pressing to talk about, or have accomplished as much as they can or want to with a particular helper. Sometimes clients directly tell helpers that they are ready to terminate. At other times, helpers have to suggest to clients that they think they are ready to terminate. According to the "Ethical Principles of Psychologists and Code of Conduct" (American Psychological Association, 2010), helpers should terminate with clients when they feel they are no longer working productively. Helpers need to be mindful of continuing therapy sessions only when clients are benefiting from it, although this can be hard to determine and there can certainly be plateaus. I suggest that it is crucial for helpers to have frequent discussions with clients about what they are getting out of treatment and how they feel about continuing.

Budman and Gurman (1988) proposed that helpers adopt a model such as that of family doctors. Just as one would never expect that antibiotics would inoculate patients against infections for the rest of their lives, they argued that helpers should not assume that one course of therapy could cure a client for life. It makes more sense for helpers to see clients until the current issues or crises are resolved and then see them again when other crises or life transitions arise. With such a model, termination is not typically as difficult because clients know that they can return to their helpers if they need further help (if that helper is still available).

How to Terminate

Mann (1973) considered termination of therapy to be an important task because loss is an existential fact of life; everyone must cope with loss. He recommended that helpers spend considerable time in planning and preparing for termination in both short- and long-term therapy.

Clients sometimes think that helpers are exaggerating the concerns about termination because they cannot anticipate how they will feel when they leave the therapy relationship. Once they have terminated, they have an understanding of the feelings involved, but then it is too late for helpers to process the feelings of abandonment and loss with clients. Hence, before termination, helpers must assess whether clients might have strong feelings about ending the relationship so that these feelings can be addressed adequately.

There are three main steps to effective termination of therapy relationships: (a) looking back, (b) looking forward, and (c) saying goodbye (Dewald, 1971; Marx & Gelso, 1987; Ward, 1984).

In looking back, helpers review with clients what they have learned and how they have changed. Clients can also provide feedback about the most and least helpful aspects of the therapy process. Reviewing the process can help clients consolidate their changes and feel a sense of accomplishment and can aid helpers in gaining a sense of what skills they need to improve for future clients.

In looking forward, helpers and clients discuss future plans, and consider the client's need for possible additional counseling. Helpers review with clients the issues they still want to address, given that no therapy process is ever complete. We keep changing (for better or worse) for the rest of our lives. The task for helpers is to assist clients in identifying the ongoing issues, determining how they will address these issues, and clarifying how they can find support in their lives for making changes. If such plans are not realistic, helpers can gently confront clients so they do not set themselves up for failure.

Finally, in saying goodbye, both helpers and clients share their feelings about ending and say their farewells.

Termination is often challenging for both helpers and clients. Once two people have spoken about many deep and personal issues, it is frequently difficult for them to think about not seeing each other again. Thus, termination often brings up issues of loss for both helpers and clients. Some evidence shows that helpers and clients who have the most trouble with termination are those who have a history of painful losses (Boyer & Hoffman, 1993; Marx & Gelso, 1987). If loss has been painful in the past, it can be difficult to go through another loss. Other clients may not experience intense sadness but may struggle with how to thank the helper and show appreciation for the helper's role in their process of change. Other clients may be disappointed about not having received the "magic cure" and feel upset that they still have unresolved problems. Yet other clients have such a difficult time thinking about termination that they quit prematurely to avoid having to process the loss.

Helpers need to talk openly with clients about the separation. Furthermore, they need to make sure that they have time to deal with the clients' feelings that might arise from ending the relationship (and deal with their own loss issues in therapy or supervision).

Making Referrals or Transfers

Clients' needs are sometimes beyond what helpers are qualified to address or capable of delivering. For example, a client might have an eating disorder, substance abuse problem, or serious mental illness, and the helper might lack expertise in that area. Sometimes the helper and client have accomplished as much as they can together, and the client needs a different kind of help. For example, a referral may be needed because a client needs marital or family therapy, but the helper is trained only in individual therapy (note that family treatment is typically more beneficial than individual treatment if clients are having difficulties with family members; Haley, 1987; Minuchin, 1974; Nichols & Schwartz,

1991; Satir, 1988). In addition, clients might need referrals for medication, long-term therapy, assessment of learning disabilities, financial assistance, housing information, spiritual guidance, or legal advice.

With a referral, the helper provides the name of another provider but leaves it up to the client to follow through. In contrast, with a transfer, the helper facilitates the client's process of switching to someone else for treatment. For example, in the clinic in our department, when a doctoral student therapist leaves for internship, she or he often discusses with ongoing clients whether they would like to be transferred to another therapist within the clinic. Some clients are eager to continue their work with another therapist, although others do not want to see another therapist. If the client wishes to be transferred, the helper introduces the client to the new helper and tries to facilitate the process of the transfer.

The helper needs to explain the reason for the referral or transfer to the client. Otherwise, clients could easily feel that they are hopeless, need endless treatment, or are "bad clients." If helpers do a thorough job of the three steps of termination discussed earlier, clients are less likely to have negative feelings about being referred or transferred.

Dealing With Difficult Clients and Clinical Situations

Even helpers who are generally talented in using the helping skills have difficulties with some clients. Sometimes they try to get such clients to quit or try to refer them to other treatment. Knowledge of different types of clients, along with good supervision, can assist helpers in dealing with difficult clients. In this section, I discuss some of the most challenging situations that helpers face.

RELUCTANT AND RESISTANT CLIENTS

Most clients (and indeed most people) have at least some reluctance to change. Some possible roots of reluctance are lack of trust, fear of falling apart, shame, fear of change, and lack of motivation to change (Egan, 1994; Young, 2001). For many clients, it is easier to stick with known misery than to face the unknown of what life might be like after changing. Signs of reluctance are varied and often covert. Reluctant clients might talk only about safe subjects, seem unsure of what they want from therapy, act overly cooperative, set unrealistic goals and then give up on them, not work very hard at changing, blame others for their problems, criticize the helper, come late to sessions, fail to keep appointments, forget to pay fees, intellectualize, terminate prematurely, use humor, ask for personal favors, present irrelevant material, engage in small talk, or disclose important things on the way out the door.

Whereas reluctance is relatively passive, resistance (i.e., feeling coerced and wanting to fight back) is more active (Egan, 1994). Resistant clients often present themselves as not needing help and as feeling misused. They show minimal willingness to form a relationship and often try to manipulate the helper. They might be resentful, try to sabotage the therapy process, terminate as quickly as possible, and act abusively or belligerently to the helper. Clients who come to therapy because they are forced to do so (e.g., are ordered by the court to participate in therapy) are often resistant. For example, one male client who was ordered by a judge to participate in 12 therapy sessions because he had urinated on public property was resistant about being there and got very little out of the experience (he even asked the helper for a date!).

Egan (1994) suggested that resistance can come from seeing no reason for therapy, resenting being referred for help, feeling awkward about participating in therapy, or having a history of rebelliousness. Other reasons for resistance are having values or expectations that are inconsistent with the help being offered, having negative attitudes about therapy, feeling that going for therapy is admitting weakness and inadequacy, feeling a lack of trust, or disliking the helper. Reluctant and resistant clients are typically at the precontemplation stage in terms of readiness to change (refer back to Chapter 2).

When faced with clients who are reluctant or resistant, helpers often become confused, panicked, angry, guilty, or depressed (Egan, 1994). They might try to placate the client, become impatient with or hostile to the client, become passive, or lower their expectations and do a halfhearted job. Alternatively, helpers might become warmer and more accepting to win over the client, engage in a power struggle with the client, allow themselves to be abused or bullied, or try to terminate the therapy process. The source of the stress is not only the client's behavior but also the helper's self-defeating attitudes and assumptions. Helpers might be saying things to themselves like, "All clients should be committed to change," "Every client must like and trust me," "Every client can be helped," "No unwilling client can be helped," "I am responsible for what happens to the client," "I must succeed with every client," or "I am a rotten helper if I cannot help this client." Becoming aware of these self-defeating attitudes and assumptions can enable helpers to reduce their influence on the therapy process.

Helpers need to deal with reluctance and resistance, and they also should avoid reinforcing these processes in clients (Egan, 1994). Goldfried and Davison (1994) suggested that the role of the helper is to make the reluctant or resistant client ready for change; hence, the challenge for helpers is to find creative ways to deal with reluctance and resistance. Here are several suggestions for dealing with reluctance and resistance (Egan, 1994; Pipes & Davenport, 1999; van Wormer, 1996; Young, 2001):

- Learn to see reluctance and resistance as normal.
- Recognize that reluctance and resistance are sometimes a form of avoidance and are not necessarily due to ill will toward the helper.
- Explore your own reluctance and resistance to changing problematic aspects of your life. Once helpers figure out how they cope with their own reluctance and resistance, they probably are more able to help clients with theirs. An awareness of their own foibles can make helpers more empathic and less impatient.
- Examine the quality of your interventions. Helpers might be provoking resistance by being too directive or too passive or by disliking the client.
- Consider whether you would be willing to do what you're asking the client to do.
- Be empathic; try to understand what it is like to be the client. It is hard to fight with someone who is being empathic, accepting, not threatening, and not wanting to fight. In effect, you join with the client rather than resisting the client.
- Do not use labels, jargon, or bureaucratic language with hostile clients.
- Work directly with the client's reluctance and resistance rather than ignoring it, being intimidated by it, or being angry at the clients for his or her behaviors.
- Help clients explore feelings about their reluctance or resistance to therapy.
- Be realistic about what you can accomplish with a client.
- Establish a relationship on the basis of mutual trust and shared planning rather than trying to assume all the power.
- Work with the client to search for incentives for changing.
- Draw attention to the behavior and invite the client to explore it.
- Listen carefully to what the client says and agree with part of it but then show that you are doing something different; this can provide some reassurance and enhance your credibility.
- Do not give up.

CLIENTS WHO ARE ANGRY

For most helpers, it is extremely stressful when clients are angry at them and express that anger in a direct and hostile way (Deutsch, 1984; Farber, 1983; Hill, Kellems, et al., 2003; Matsakis, 1998; Plutchik, Conte,

& Karasu, 1994). In fact, in one study, more than 80% of helpers said that they felt afraid or angry when clients were verbally abusive toward them (Pope & Tabachnick, 1993). Matsakis (1998) noted that client anger often disrupts the therapy process, especially when helpers feel angry, confused, hurt, guilty, anxious, or incompetent, instead of being able to remain empathic and objective and talk about the client's anger.

To avert the negative consequences associated with inappropriately managing client anger, several authors have suggested that helpers respond to client anger as they would to any other emotion by encouraging clients to talk openly about it (Adler, 1984; Burns & Auerbach, 1996; Cahill, 1981; Hill, Kellems, et al., 2003; Joines, 1995; Kaplan, Brooks, McComb, Shapiro, & Sodano, 1983; Lynch, 1975; Matsakis, 1998; Newman, 1997; Ormont, 1984). These authors also recommended that helpers work with clients to help them uncover underlying feelings, express anger verbally instead of acting it out physically, and decide what to do about the anger. To achieve these goals, they suggested that helpers need to listen nonjudgmentally and nondefensively when clients are angry and try to understand the anger.

Furthermore, if clients are justified in their anger at the helpers, helpers can apologize and alter their inappropriate or unhelpful behaviors. Clients often have valuable feedback for helpers, and helpers are wise to attend to this feedback. If clients are not justified in their anger at helpers, helpers can listen carefully and try to understand the client's feelings. Consultation with supervisors can be helpful in such difficult situations to try to understand what is happening.

OVERLY TALKATIVE CLIENTS

Some clients talk nonstop about things that are not related to therapeutic goals (although helpers have to be careful about making judgments about what is worth discussing in therapy). In the Client Behavior System (see Chapter 2 and Web Form H), this type of client behavior is considered recounting rather than affective or cognitive–behavioral exploration. Talkativeness is often a defense on the part of clients, in that it is an attempt to keep others at a distance. In situations in which the client's talking is not productive, the helper needs to intervene cautiously after several minutes and interrupt the talking, saying something such as, "Sorry to interrupt, but I'm not going to be able to help you unless I can add a few things here and there. Let me see if I understand what you're saying right now . . . ." Subsequently, helpers could hold up a hand or make a T-sign to indicate a timeout, and say, "Excuse me again, but I want to make sure I am hearing you correctly." Thus, helpers let clients know that they are interrupting to assist (not because of boredom or irritation).

Interruptions done in a hostile manner ("Whoa, hold on there, you're talking too much") could hinder the therapeutic relationship and make the client feel that she or he had done something bad. If interruptions are done appropriately, gently, and respectfully, however, clients could feel relieved that their helpers interrupted them to help them overcome their defenses and learn how to interact more appropriately.

Rather than getting angry at a client for monopolizing the conversation, the helper can empathize with the client's difficulty in communicating. The helper can also hypothesize about why the client uses talking as a defense, recognizing that it keeps the client from forming close relationships. Such conceptualization can lead to the development of better interventions.

Helpers can also use their immediacy skills with overly talkative clients if they judge that the client can handle the interpersonal challenge. Helpers can talk about how they feel when clients do not let them have a chance to talk and ask about clients' experiences when talking.

OVERLY QUIET CLIENTS

Clients are sometimes shy and do not talk much anywhere. Other times clients are quiet because they are anxious or have difficulty expressing themselves; they may fear being in interpersonal situations because of poor interactions with significant others in the past. At yet other times, clients are resistant and hostile and may defiantly challenge the helper to break through and get them to talk. It is important for the helper to try to assess why the client is being quiet. Being aware of the likely reason for the quietness can enable the helper to think about what to do. Helpers will want to use a different strategy with the client who is introverted and shy than with the hostile, defiantly silent client.

First and foremost, the helper can try to adjust to the client's pace and let her or him open up gradually. Open questions and probes can be quite helpful with quiet clients because they clearly specify what the helper wants the client to talk about. But I would emphasize that often helpers fill silence because of their own anxiety rather than respecting clients' needs to go slowly. Again, it can help to talk about this issue with clients.

CLIENTS WITH SUICIDAL IDEATION

When a client mentions suicide or appears to be depressed and considering suicide, the helper needs to take the suicide gestures seriously. Suicide is a leading cause of death (the 11th leading cause of death across all age groups, the third leading cause of death among youth ages 15 to 24) and is often viewed by clients as the only way out of problems. The helper needs to actively and directly assess the seriousness of the suicide risk rather than ignoring or minimizing it (Berman, Jobes, & Silverman, 2006; Rudd, Joiner, Jobes, & King, 1999). Helpers can assume clients are asking for help when they bring up the topic of suicide.

There are a series of steps that helpers can follow with suicidal clients. First, a general assessment of suicidal risk usually involves asking directly about suicidal potential. Helpers might ask the following questions:

- "Are you thinking about suicide?"
- "Do you have a plan for attempting suicide?"
- "Do you have the means to carry out the plan?"
- "Have you attempted suicide in the past?"
- "Do you use (or plan on using) alcohol or drugs?"
- "Have you been withdrawn and isolated lately?"
- "Have you been focused on death (e.g., giving away prized possessions or planning your funeral)?"
- "Are you feeling helpless or worthless?"
- "Do you have plans for the future?"
- "Who knows about your suicidal feelings?"
- "How do you think others would feel if they knew you committed suicide?"

If a client indicates a clear intent to commit suicide, has a clear viable plan, and has the means to carry out the plan (e.g., a client plans on killing himself or herself in the immediate future and has obtained the means necessary to accomplish this plan), the client is at a high risk of suicide. In such a case, the helper needs to take steps to ensure the client's safety (Frankish, 1994). Given that procedures will vary depending on the setting, helpers should acquaint themselves with the procedures before seeing clients. The following are general suggestions.

Ideally, the beginning helper would consult with a colleague or supervisor to determine the best steps to take. In some cases, helpers (in consultation with supervisors) might decide that suicidal clients need to be hospitalized to protect themselves from self-injury. Some clients realize the danger and agree to be hospitalized to receive intensive psychiatric and psychological treatment. In other cases, helpers may have to admit clients to the hospital against their will. In yet other cases, helpers (in consultation with supervisors) may ascertain that hospitalization is not necessary and instead can develop a written behavioral contract with the client that involves the client agreeing not to hurt himself or herself and promising to contact the helper or a crisis line for assistance if thoughts of suicide occur (this should be done only if there is a good relationship with the client and the helper has help from a supervisor). In these cases, it may be useful for helpers to notify the client's family, close friends, or significant others about the client's suicidal ideation. Note that when clients threaten to harm themselves, confidentiality no longer applies. Hence, helpers can perform the necessary steps to ensure the safety of suicidal clients (still, of course, being empathic rather than authoritarian and demanding).

Helpers can provide the numbers of 24-hour crisis lines and assist the client in identifying a support system to help the client. Additional sessions can be suggested, or the helper can offer to talk to the client by phone between sessions to provide extra support. Helpers can also refer clients for additional treatment (e.g., group therapy). If a suicidal client does not show up for treatment, the helper might consider (after consultation with the supervisor) calling the client. For legal purposes, helpers should document in writing the procedures that were followed to assess and assist suicidal clients, including the questions that were asked, consultations that occurred, the decision-making process, and interventions that were made.

As helpers who have provided crisis counseling know, dealing with someone who is contemplating suicide can be challenging and frightening. Beginning helpers often fear that asking about suicidal feelings encourages clients to think about or commit suicide. In fact, the opposite is typically true—by talking about suicidal feelings, clients can bring their worst fears into the open and feel like someone listens and understands them. Clients often appreciate that helpers view their problems as serious. If helpers are not willing to discuss suicidal feelings, clients often feel even more alone, ashamed, strange, or crazy. Perhaps the worst thing to do is to diminish or negate the feelings (e.g., "You'll feel better tomorrow"), point out positive aspects of their lives (e.g., "You have so much to live for"), or give false reassurance (e.g., "Everything will be okay"). These responses often result in clients feeling not only depressed and suicidal but also desperate because they cannot get help, hopeless that they are beyond help, misunderstood, and worried that their suicidal feelings are unacceptable or too frightening to others. But it is also important that helpers not feel that they have to become the only lifeline for the suicidal client, or else the helper will burn out and not be of help to anyone; mobilizing other resources is crucial.

One of the most difficult issues any mental health professional can face is dealing with the aftermath of a client's suicide. Many helpers agonize, feel guilty, and spend a lot of time second-guessing whether there was something else they could have done to prevent the suicide. A certain amount of introspection is important and may enable helpers to handle similar situations better in the future, but helpers should not unnecessarily take on too much responsibility. It is often wise for helpers to seek supervision and therapy after such a difficult situation to help them cope and understand their feelings (Knox, Burkard, Jackson, Schaak, & Hess, 2006).

SEXUAL ATTRACTION

Sexual attraction toward clients is a common occurrence in therapeutic relationships. Approximately 87% of surveyed helpers reported that they have been sexually attracted to a client at some point in their careers, and many of these helpers felt guilty, anxious, and confused about the attraction (Pope, Keith-Spiegel, & Tabachnick, 1986; Pope & Tabachnick, 1993). Feeling attracted is not unethical, but acting on the attraction (e.g., socializing with the client, having a sexual relationship) is considered unethical because it can harm clients.

As a beginning helper, you may find yourself sexually attracted to someone you are trying to help. Although discussing this attraction with a supervisor could be uncomfortable (some helpers might feel ashamed or guilty for having these feelings), a supervisor can assist you in working through these feelings in a healthy, rather than destructive, manner (Ladany et al., 1997; Pope, Sonne, & Holroyd, 1993; The research summary at the end of the chapter further explores Ladany et al.'s research). It is important to talk about the attraction with a supervisor to reduce the likelihood of acting out in sessions with clients. For example, Sally found herself attracted to a client who communicated admiration, respect, and even awe for the assistance she provided for him. Although Sally had a good relationship with her partner, she enjoyed the positive feedback from the client and began thinking about him in a romantic way. Fortunately, she talked with her supervisor, who helped her sort out her feelings and come to understand that they related at least partially to the intimacy of the helping situation. Sally benefited from coming to understand how these feelings developed and how they could negatively influence the therapy process. The supervisor also normalized the helper's feelings by letting the helper know that many helpers (including the supervisor) become attracted to clients during their career.

Yet another difficult situation is when the client expresses sexual attraction to the helper, especially given that it is often gratifying for the helper to feel attractive. The helper needs to strike a balance between allowing the client to express his or her feelings and not actively encouraging the attraction. Of course, any sexual contact is unethical, as is becoming involved with clients outside of sessions. Consultation with a supervisor and self-reflection about one's motivations are important here.

Example of an Extended Interaction

An example of a therapeutic interaction is presented here to illustrate working through all three stages (exploration, insight, and action). For ease of presentation, this example presents the three stages in a single session, although working through all three stages for a given problem often requires more than a single session. The process is condensed considerably to allow for illustration of all three stages.

The example involves a first session with a young woman, Maria, who sought assistance because she could not decide on a major. Career concerns are common issues that many people struggle with throughout the life cycle (Brown & Brooks, 1991; Zunker, 1994). However, career difficulties are not as simplistic as psychologists once thought. It is not simply a matter of deciding on one's talents, interests, and skills. Our career identities are intertwined with our personal lives (Blustein, 1987; Brown, 1985; Hackett, 1993; Herr, 1989; Richardson, 1993; Savickas, 1994; Spokane, 1989) and hence both must be addressed in the helping process.

EXPLORATION STAGE

Helper: Tell me a little about yourself and why you came for helping today. (The helper uses an open question or probe to start the interaction and to allow Maria to communicate her most pressing concerns.)

Client: I'm a junior at the university. I should have declared a major already, but I just cannot decide what I want to do. I feel stuck, and they're trying to force me to declare something in the next couple of weeks. I don't want to just put something down and then have to shift after a semester or two. But I just don't have anything that I'm particularly good at. You know, in high school when everyone else was in plays or orchestra or dancing or sports, I wasn't really doing anything. I don't have any major talents. I seem to be mediocre in everything.

Helper: You sound anxious about having to declare a major so quickly. (The helper wants to focus Maria on her feelings about the urgency of the situation.)

Client: I am really anxious. You wouldn't believe how anxious I am. I haven't been able to sleep at night.

I just keep trying to figure out what I want to do with my life. I guess I have never had any major ambitions.

Helper: I wonder if you have feelings about trying to figure out who you are? (The helper wants to determine how much of Maria's life is influenced by this issue.)

Client: I have been feeling out of sorts. But I guess it's really hard to tell how much of it is because of trying to choose a major and not knowing who I am or where I'm going, and how much of it is due to feeling badly that I have never had a boyfriend and also feeling under stress that my parents are going through a divorce.

Helper: Wow! Sounds like you have a lot of difficult things going on right now. (The helper wants to support Maria.)

Client: Yeah, it's been a rough semester. I just found out my parents were going to get a divorce over the holidays. They said that they stayed together until my younger sister went to college. I'm not sure that their staying together was actually so good for us because they were always fighting. Each of my parents has always talked to me about how horrible the other one was. I feel like I've always been the mediator, trying to help each of them understand the other.

Helper: How was it for you being the one in the middle? (The helper wants to allow Maria to explore her feelings more deeply.)

Client: Part of me liked it because they both needed me. But it was also pretty bad because I felt like they both depended on me too much and I couldn't live my own life. I was glad to get away to college, but then I felt guilty about leaving. I go home a lot. I also feel like I have to take care of my little sister and shield her from the pain. I don't want her to end up feeling as badly about herself as I do about myself.

Helper: It sounds like you feel pretty overwhelmed right now. (The helper wants to help Maria become aware of her feelings.)

Client: I do. I feel about 20 years older than the other kids here. They are always talking about parties and drinking. It all seems so trivial.

Helper: You mentioned that you have to choose a major soon. You also said that there's nothing you're particularly good in. Tell me more about that. (The helper wants to guide Maria back to exploring her problem in choosing a major.)

Client: Well, I think I'm an average student. I get *B*s in most of my courses. I probably don't put as much time in as I could, but I just can't get into studying.

Helper: Tell me something about the courses that you have enjoyed. (The helper wants to help Maria explore specific interests.)

Client: Well, I'm rotten at math and science. I almost flunked biology last semester. I guess the classes I have enjoyed most are my psychology courses. I like trying to figure people out. You know, I'm always the person whom people talk to about their problems. I'm taking this class in helping skills and am excited about it. I think I'm pretty good at helping. At least I enjoy being a helper.

INSIGHT STAGE

Helper: What do you think got you so excited about learning helping skills? (The helper wants to assist Maria in thinking about her motives.)

Client: Everyone has always come to me with their problems, and I feel like I'm good at listening. And I was able to help my sister when she got so upset.

Helper: I wonder if operating as a helper in your family helped you become interested in the helping field? (The helper tries an interpretation to see whether Maria can engage in the interpretive process.)

Client: You know, you may be right. Maybe helping my sister and mediating my parents' arguments helped me develop effective helping skills. It's funny that I've never really thought about majoring in psychology before. I guess my parents have always looked down on psychology. They would never go to a helper because they have always said people should solve their own problems. Well, they didn't do too good a job on their own. But I don't know, what do you think I should do? Why did you choose psychology?

Helper: I really liked to help other people with their problems. I also found that all my friends turned to me to talk about their problems. (The helper uses disclosure to reassure Maria that her feelings are normal.)

Client: That's interesting. Do you like the field?

Helper: Yes, I like it a lot. Tell me more about your thoughts about psychology. (The helper wants to turn the focus back to Maria.)

Client: Well, I think I might like to do it, but I don't know if I'm smart enough for it. I've heard an awful lot about how you have to be really smart to get into graduate school in psychology. I might not be able to make it.

Helper: You know, you say you're not really smart, but I haven't heard much evidence for that. (The helper challenges Maria about her lack of self-efficacy.)

Client: Well, I haven't gotten very good grades in college. I did get pretty good grades in high school though, and my SAT scores were pretty high. In fact, I was close to the top of my class.

Helper: So something has happened during college to make you lose your confidence and not do as well in your classes. What might have contributed to your inability to study? (The helper wants to facilitate Maria to think about insight and so restates and then asks an open question.)

Client: I'm not sure. Perhaps it has to do with my family, but I'm not sure how.

Helper: Perhaps your concern about your parents and leaving home has distracted you from your ability to study. (The helper works with Maria to stimulate insight. Maria had a glimmer that her difficulties were related to her family, so the helper gives an interpretation that goes just beyond what Maria has stated.)

Client: Hmm, I had never thought about that, but you're probably right. I've been so concerned about everyone else that I haven't had time to take care of myself. It's not really fair that my parents messed up my life just because they can't get their act together.

Helper: Yeah, you seem angry at them. (Maria has responded well to the interpretation, so the helper wants to help her explore her feelings about her discoveries.)

Client: I am. I have been so worried about leaving my sister at home and not being able to calm my parents during their horrible arguments. These are supposed to be the best years of my life. And all I'm concerned about is them. When do I get my chance?

Helper: I wonder if your parents really need you as much as you think they do? (The helper challenges Maria about her assumed need to be in the middle.)

Client: Maybe they don't. In fact, maybe if I quit interfering, they would be able to make a decision about what they need to do. And, you know, my sister is not a kid anymore. She's 18 years old. I mean, I love them, but maybe I've been doing too much, going home all the time.

ACTION STAGE

Helper: So what would you like to do differently? (The helper wants to move Maria into thinking about how to make changes in her life.)

Client: Well, I think I'm going to tell my parents that I am going to stop listening to each of their problems. I am going to suggest that they go to a helper. It's been so helpful talking to you. That's what I think they need to do. If they don't do it, that's their problem, but I've got to get out from the middle.

Helper: What feelings might come up for you in telling your parents your decision not to be in the middle? (The helper wants to have Maria explore her feelings about this change.)

Client: I'm pretty fed up right now, so I think I could do it. The difficult part will come when my mom calls late at night crying and says I'm the only one who really understands her. You wouldn't believe how many times she's done that right before a major exam.

Helper: What could you do when that happens? (The helper wants to guide Maria into problem solving what to do in the specific situation.)

Client: Well, I could go to the library to study when I really need to focus on my work. Then my mom couldn't reach me. I really study better at the library anyway because the residence hall is so noisy.

Helper: That's a great idea. (The helper reinforces Maria's feelings.)

Client: Yeah, I don't know why I didn't think of that sooner. I guess I was just stuck in thinking I was the only one who could help my mom. You know, maybe I even kept her from going to a helper because she could always talk to me. In fact, maybe I wanted her to talk to me because it made me feel so important and helpful.

Helper: Yeah, that might be hard to give up. You feel pretty special when you believe that you're the one who can make everyone feel better. (The helper wants to warn Maria that it might be hard to change.)

Client: Yeah, it could be hard. But I think it's time to start living my own life instead of living in their world.

Helper: What could you do to make the transition easier? (Again, the helper wants to prepare Maria for the difficulties involved in changing.)

Client: Well, I would like to continue to talk with you. Would that be possible? I think if I had your support, it would be easier to change.

Helper: Sure, we could arrange for eight sessions. That's the limit of the number of sessions I can offer to you through the counseling center. (The helper wants to let Maria know the limits of her availability.)

Client: That would be great. Thanks.

Helper: Now back to the major. What are your thoughts about what you would like to do about that at this point? (The helper wants to bring some closure to the topic about the major since that was Maria's presenting concern.)

Client: I'm leaning toward psychology. I get excited about some of the psychology courses I've had, particularly the ones that involve personality and helping people. But I'm also interested in English. I've always liked to write. I've kept a journal for years. I have a fantasy of some day writing a novel or working on a newspaper.

Helper: Perhaps you can do some more thinking about your likes and dislikes before the next session. It would also be a good idea to gather some information about majors and careers. There's some excellent information in the career center on campus. Perhaps you could go there before our next session. (The helper wants to give Maria specific guidance about how to proceed with this issue but does not want to seem too pushy.)

Client: Terrific. Sounds like a great idea. Where do I take the tests?

Helper: I'll take you down and show you where to sign up after the session. How are you feeling about

what we've done today? (The helper wants to give
Maria specific information about how to find the
tests and also wants to assess how Maria felt about
the session.)

Client: I feel better than I've felt for so long. I actually have
energy. I can't wait to take the tests. I can't wait to
talk to my parents. I think they are going to understand that I need to do this for myself. They've been
worried about me. It's not like me to be as upset
as I've been. I can see some light at the end of the
tunnel. It's very exciting.

Helper: Good for you. So let's plan on meeting next week at the
same time?

Although this example may seem a little too easy, it is fairly typical of sessions with motivated undergraduate psychology majors at
my university. Again, as I noted earlier, every session is different, but
this example provides some idea of how a beginning session might go.

Concluding Comments

I hope this book has provided you with the essential tools to begin
your journey toward becoming a helper. I would encourage you to
complete the Counselor Self-Efficacy Measure (Web Form K) so you
can make a self-assessment of your therapy skills, your skills in managing sessions, and your skills in terms of handling difficult clinical
situations. You can complete the measure for how you feel right now,
as well as retrospectively for how you think you were before reading
this book and practicing the skills. This assessment might give you
some ideas about what you have learned as well as areas that still
need work.

As a result of learning about helping skills, many of you may have
decided that you would like to pursue a career that involves extensive
use of these skills; others may have decided not to pursue such a career.
Regardless of the path you have chosen, these helping skills can be used
to enhance your personal and professional functioning. I encourage
each of you to set specific goals on how to continue to develop these
skills, given that this text and these practice exercises provide only a
foundation on which your skills can be cultivated. Many sites are available for advanced training in therapy skills (e.g., graduate programs in
counseling and clinical psychology, social work, counseling, psychiatry,

psychiatric nursing). Volunteering at nonprofit agencies also provides a useful setting for obtaining additional practice for your skills while assisting people with pressing concerns. Whatever your path, I hope that it involves continued exploration of your feelings, increased self-awareness and insight, and positive changes that enable you to fulfill your potential and succeed in your interpersonal relationships and in your career.

I would appreciate any feedback (using the form at the end of the book) that you might have about this text. I continue to revise this book to make it responsive to student needs, and hearing about your experiences helps me do that.

Thank you for joining me on this journey of learning helping skills. I wish you the best in your continued endeavors.

What Do You Think?

- What do you think would be the effects of discussing confidentiality for the therapeutic relationship?
- How would you know when you have explored enough?
- Discuss other possible ways that helpers could manage sessions (e.g., begin sessions, develop a focus, end sessions).
- Debate whether clients should ever be forced to go for helping.
- Describe the personality characteristics a helper could have that might influence her or his ability to respond effectively to reluctant or resistant clients, overly talkative clients, suicidal clients, or angry clients.
- What would you do if you felt sexual attraction for a client?
- What steps might you take if you were a helper dealing with a suicidal client?
- What do you think about the suggestions regarding termination?
- Who should decide that it is an appropriate time to terminate, and what marker should help them decide that termination is appropriate?
- What do you think the ideal length of a therapy relationship is?
- Debate the issue of whether time limits are beneficial for the therapeutic process.
- What theoretical orientation is emerging for you? Describe your goals for learning more about this theoretical orientation.
- What goals do you have for the continued development of your therapy skills?

RESEARCH SUMMARY

Sexual Attraction

Citation: Ladany, N., O'Brien, K. M., Hill, C. E., Melincoff, D. S., Knox, S., & Petersen, D. A. (1997). Sexual attraction toward clients, use of supervision, and prior training: A qualitative study of predoctoral psychology interns. *Journal of Counseling Psychology, 44,* 413–424. doi:10.1037/0022-0167.44.4.413

Rationale: Researchers (Gabbard, 1994, 1995; Pope, Keith-Spiegel, & Tabachnik, 1986) have found that more than 84% of therapists have been sexually attracted to a client at some point during their practice of psychotherapy. Such feelings are generally thought to be both reality-based but also evidence of countertransference and clearly need to be dealt with because sexual contact between therapists and clients is expressly considered unethical. Ladany et al. wondered about the experience of being attracted to a client, how the attraction develops, what client and therapist factors are associated with the attraction, the impact of the attraction on the therapy, and how the attraction was managed.

Method: Thirteen psychology interns (students at the end of their doctoral training) were interviewed about one case in which they felt sexual attraction. Interviews were analyzed using qualitative research methods.

Interesting Findings:
- Sexual attraction typically emerged as the relationship grew closer.
- Therapists typically felt scared and guilty about feeling attracted to a client.
- Therapists typically described clients to whom they became attracted as physically attractive and good therapy clients (e.g., brilliant, sophisticated, articulate).
- Therapists did not think that clients were aware of their attraction.
- Therapists typically believed that they were more involved, invested, caring, and attentive than usual when they felt attracted to the client, but they also believed that the attraction created tension or distance and they had trouble terminating with the client.
- Therapists typically believed that their sexual attraction did not influence therapy outcome, and they reported that their feelings were resolved by the end of therapy.
- Therapists typically reported that they tried to manage the attraction by spending time thinking about it (self-supervision). Only half of therapists disclosed their attraction to their supervisors; those who did talk to their supervisors about it found it to be helpful because supervisors normalized, validated, and supported them.

Conclusions:
- Attraction can play a major role for therapists in the process of working with clients.
- Therapists often feel guilty and anxious about being sexually attracted to their clients. Therapists may be especially vulnerable when clients are particularly engaging.

Implications for Therapy:
- Therapists need to be aware of their feelings about clients, and try to understand where these feelings come from.
- Discussing both positive and negative feelings about clients with a trusted supervisor can be helpful.
- Supervisors should be alert to the possibilities of both positive and negative feelings about clients and should ask supervisees about such feelings.

BONUS MATERIALS   Practice exercises, labs, and other resources for students and teachers are available on the companion website: http://pubs.apa.org/books/supp/hill4.

Glossary

Acculturation: adapting to the norms of the dominant culture.

Action: making changes in one's thoughts, emotions, or behaviors.

Action stage: helpers collaborate with clients to explore the idea of change, explore options for change, and help them figure out how to make changes.

Adaptors: habitual nonverbal acts that are often outside awareness and have no communicative purpose (e.g., head scratching, licking one's lips, playing with a pen).

Anal stage: the second stage of development from a psychoanalytic perspective; babies obtain their gratification from anal (toileting) activities.

Approval–reassurance: provides emotional support, reassurance, encouragement, and reinforcement.

Assertiveness training: teaching clients to stand up for their rights in a nonaggressive and nonpassive way that does not infringe on the rights of others.

Attachment theory: explains the behavioral and emotional responses that keep young children in close proximity to caregivers. With secure attachment, people feel connected with a significant person as a secure base and feel safe to explore; with insecure attachment, the person worries about whether she or he can rely on others, deal with emotions, or is worthy of care. If the caretaker repeatedly withdraws when the child seeks proximity, the child learns to not rely on others for help when threatened. If the attachment figure is unpredictable, the child typically tries even harder to get a response from the caregiver.

Attending: helpers orienting themselves physically toward clients so that they can listen.

Autonomy: an ethical principle that refers to the right (of both the consumer and the provider) to make choices and take actions, provided the results do not adversely affect others.

Awareness: recognition of feelings or thoughts but not of the underlying motivations for these feelings or thoughts.

Baby steps: small changes.

Behavior change: increasing desired behaviors or decreasing undesired behaviors.

Behavioral rehearsal: teaching skills for responding in more adaptive ways to specific life situations.

Behavioral theory: an approach that focuses on behavior; the assumption is that behavior is learned and can be modified.

Beneficence: an ethical principle that refers to the intent "to do good" by helping and promoting growth in others.

Blank screen: when the helper is neutral and reveals as little about himself or herself as possible so that the client can project his or her own issues onto the helper.

Body posture: orienting one's body (typically forward or back), to communicate listening to the other person.

Boundaries: the ground rules and limits of the helping relationship, typically about the structure of helping (e.g., length, fees, policies about touching and violence, confidentiality) or the interpersonal nature of the relationship (e.g., not having sex with client, having boundaries on friendships with clients).

Brief therapy: helping is limited to a few sessions.

Burnout: being emotionally or physically exhausted from caring for others.

Case conceptualization: hypotheses about the client's functioning and dynamics, typically based on theoretical orientation and observation of the client.

Chair work: exercises that help the client work on conflicts between two opposing sides in oneself (e.g., "I wish I could, but I'm scared" or "I'd like to, but I stop myself"; two-chair technique) or conflicts with significant others (empty-chair technique).

Challenges: point out maladaptive beliefs and thoughts, discrepancies, or contradictions of which the client is unaware or unwilling to change.

Client: the person receiving support.

Client-centered theory: a theory based on humanistic assumptions that people are oriented toward self-actualization and that clients are active agents engaged in a self-healing process.

Closed question: inquiries that request a one- or two-word answer ("yes," "no," confirmation) and is used to gather data or information.

Cognitive theory: helps clients restructure their thinking and make it more rational.

Collaboration: working jointly with clients to explore, gain insight, and move to action, rather than giving clients answers.

Collectivism: the relative importance placed on the group as opposed to the individual. Collectivist cultures tend to focus more on the family and view people as interdependent.

Compassion: feeling aware of and open to another person's suffering without judgment. Compassion goes beyond empathy and understanding by genuinely allowing oneself to feel the pain and suffering and desire to relieve it. Another way to think of compassion is loving kindness, of genuinely caring about the other person because of who they are, not because they deserve it or not.

Confidentiality: the ethical principle of not divulging information shared in the helping session, except in limited circumstances (intent to harm self or other, abuse, need for supervision).

Consciousness: mental activity that is readily available to awareness.

Contemplation: thinking about change.

Core conflictual relationship theme: describes how people engage in typical interpersonal patterns, composed of wishes or needs, expected responses from others, and subsequent responses from the self.

Countertransference: the helper's reactions to the client that originate in the unresolved issues of the helper.

Cultural competence: being culturally sensitive, particularly in terms of striving to understand culture and how it influences work with clients; striving to understand how culture influences beliefs about helping; honestly confronting biases, prejudices, and discriminatory behaviors and working to keep them out of the helping process; having a wide range of helping skills and using them flexibly to fit the needs of clients from different cultures; being knowledgeable about the cultures of clients; understanding the extent to which discrimination and oppression influence clients' lives and contribute to their problems; acknowledging and addressing cultural differences while still communicating willingness to help, seeking supervision or referring when necessary.

Culture: the customs, values, attitudes, beliefs, characteristics, and behaviors shared by a group of people at a particular time in history, or any group of people who identify or associate with one another on the basis of some common purpose, need, or similarity of background. Culture includes race/ethnicity, gender, age, ideology, religion, socioeconomic status, sexual orientation, disability status, occupation, and dietary preferences.

Decision making: helping clients articulate their options, explore their values, evaluate the options according to their values, and then make choices.

Defenses/Defense mechanisms: unconscious methods for dealing with anxiety through denial or distortion of reality.

Denial: actively rejecting painful affect.

Direct guidance: making suggestions, giving directives, or providing advice for what helpers think clients should do outside of helping sessions.

Disclosure of fact: reveals information about the helper.

Disclosure of feelings: reveals personal nonimmediate information about the helper's feelings to provide a model and help the client explore feelings.

Disclosure of insight: reveals an understanding the helper has learned about himself or herself and is used to facilitate the client's understanding of his or her thoughts, feelings, behaviors, and issues.

Disclosure of similarities: reveals personal nonimmediate information about ways in which helpers and clients are similar; used to encourage clients to think about their personality.

Disclosure of strategies: helpers reveal strategies they personally have used in the past to provide ideas for clients and help clients feel less alone or different.

Displacement: shifting uncomfortable feelings toward someone who is less powerful and less threatening than the individual from whom the feelings originated.

Dual relationships: when someone in power (e.g., a helper, professor, supervisor) adds another role to his or her interaction with a less powerful individual (e.g., a client, student, supervisee). Dual relationships may lead to the harm or exploitation of the less powerful person.

Ego: an internal mechanism that develops to help the child delay gratification and negotiate with the outside world.

Electra conflict: a psychoanalytic construct suggesting that girls develop an attraction for their fathers; resolution occurs when girls identify with their mothers.

Emblems: nonverbal substitutes for words (e.g., a wave is a universal greeting).

Emotion-focused therapy: an approach that assumes that emotions are at the core of both unhealthy and healthy functioning and thus need to be the focus of intervention.

Empathy: understanding clients at both a cognitive level (their thoughts and expressions) and an affective level (their feelings). Empathy also includes genuinely caring about the client, nonjudgmentally accepting the client, being able to predict the client's reactions, and communicating one's experience to the client in a sensitive and accurate manner. Empathy is not a specific response type or skill; rather, it is an attitude or manner of responding with genuine caring and a lack of judgment. Empathy involves a deep respect for clients and for the clients' willingness and courage to explore their problems, gain insights, and make changes.

Enculturation: refers to retaining the norms of one's indigenous culture.

Ethics: principles and standards that ensure that professionals provide quality services and are respectful of the rights of the people with whom they work.

Existential psychotherapy: an approach that focuses on helping clients examine existential issues such as meaning of life, death anxiety, isolation, and freedom.

Exploration: talking in depth about thoughts and feelings related to the clients' problems.

Exploration stage: helpers work with clients to enable them to establish a relationship, tell their stories, talk about problems, and express related feelings.

Extinction: reduces the probability of a behavior occurring by withholding reinforcers after the behavior is established.

Eye contact: looking directly into another person's eyes.

Facial expression: communicating thoughts and feelings through eyes, mouth, and facial muscles.

Fidelity: an ethical principle related to keeping promises and being trustworthy in relationships with others.

Focus: working on one problem at a time.

Focusing: a method for helping the client experience feelings at a deeper level.

Free association: saying whatever thoughts come to mind without censure.

Gaze avoidance: avoiding looking directly at another person.

Generalization: the transfer of learning from one situation to similar situations.

Gestures: arm movements that often communicate meaning, especially when used in conjunction with verbal activity.

Giving feedback: giving information to the client about his or her behaviors or impact on others.

Giving information: providing specific data, facts, resources, answers to questions, or opinions.

Grammatical style: the way language is used.

Head nods: moving one's head up and down to indicate listening to another person and encouraging him or her to continue talking.

Helper: an individual providing assistance to another person.

Helping: one person assisting another in exploring feelings, gaining insight, and making changes.

Homework assignments: a type of direct guidance; given to help clients practice what they learned in session.

Hot buttons: biases that get triggered or set off in the helping setting.

Id: primitive urges that seek immediate gratification.

Identification: emulating characteristics in others.

Illustrators: nonverbal behaviors that accompany speech (e.g., measuring the size of a fish with the hands).

Immediacy: helper's disclosure of immediate feelings about the client, himself or herself in relation to the client, or the therapeutic relationship.

Individualism: the relative importance placed on the individual as opposed to the group, such that people are viewed as independent and autonomous.

Information about the helping process: educates clients about what to expect during helping.

Informed consent: agreement to the contract involved in the helping process, typically related to such things as length of treatment, fees, confidentiality, and limits on confidentiality.

Insight: seeing things from a new perspective, making connections between things, or having an understanding of why things happen as they do. Intellectual insight refers to having a cognitive understanding or explanation, whereas emotional insight refers to having connected affect to intellect such that there is a sense of personal involvement and responsibility for the understanding.

Insight stage: helpers work with clients to assist them in gaining awareness and insight.

Intakes: an initial session with clients in which helpers get background information, formulate a diagnosis, assess for risk, and determine the best treatment.

Intellectualization: avoiding painful feelings by focusing on ideas.

Intentions: conscious and unconscious goals or plans for what the helper would like to accomplish in sessions in working with clients.

Internal representations: images clients form of their helpers to help them cope between sessions.

Internal working models: mental representations of self, others, and relationships.

Interpersonal psychotherapy: an approach that helps clients work on interpersonal relationships, with a major emphasis on examining the therapeutic relationship.

Interpretations: interventions that go beyond what a client has overtly stated or recognized and present a new meaning, reason, or explanation for behaviors, thoughts, or feelings so clients can see problems in a new way.

Interruption: cutting off the other person's speech.

Justice: an ethical principle of fairness or equality of opportunities and resources for all people.

Kinesics: the relationship of bodily movements (arm and leg movements, head nods) and communication.

Listening: trying to hear and understand the messages that clients communicate at both verbal and nonverbal levels.

Marker: indicators of readiness for the implementation of a particular skill.

Metacommunication: communication about communication; helpers disclose to clients about their perceptions of and reactions to client actions.

Mindfulness: attending to each aspect of experience as it unfolds in the present moment.

Minimal encouragers: nonlanguage sounds, nonwords, and simple words such as "um-hmm," "yeah," and "wow" that encourage others to continue talking.

Modeling or observational learning: occurs when a person observes another person (a model) perform a behavior and receive consequences.

Narrative therapy: an approach that helps clients tell their stories and then rewrite their stories in more adaptive ways.

Narratives: stories or accounts of events or experiences.

Nonmaleficence: an ethical principle that refers to helpers ensuring that their interventions and actions do not inadvertently harm their clients.

Observing: paying attention to what is going on overtly with clients in terms of nonverbal behaviors and mannerisms, trying to pick up on the behavioral cues of the client and how the client is coming across.

Oedipal conflict: a psychoanalytic construct suggesting that boys develop an attraction for their mothers; resolution occurs when boys identify with their fathers.

Open-ended therapy: a structure such that an ending is not initially planned but occurs naturally.

Open questions about the relationship/process statements: the helper invites the client to share feelings about the therapeutic relationship. These inquiries are probes into the client's reactions to the relationship and address what is going on in the immediate moment.

Open questions and probes for action: questions aimed specifically at helping clients explore making changes.

Open questions and probes for feelings: ask clients to clarify or explore feelings but do not request specific information or purposely limit the nature of the client response.

Open questions and probes for insight: questions that invite clients to think about deeper meanings for their thoughts, feelings, or behaviors.

Open questions and probes for thoughts: ask clients to clarify or explore thoughts in general but do not request specific information or purposely limit the nature of the client response.

Operant conditioning: behaviors are controlled by their consequences.

Oral stage: The first stage of development from psychoanalytic theory in which babies obtain their gratification from oral (eating, biting) activities.

Outcome: changes that occur as a result of what goes on during helping sessions.

Preconscious: thoughts and experiences that can be accessed if one attends to it.

Precontemplation: not thinking about change; not being ready to change.

Process: what goes on during helping sessions.

Process advisement: directing clients to do things *within* helping sessions; a type of advice or direct guidance that is confined to directing what goes on in the session.

Process notes: written summaries of what occurred in sessions.

Projection: perceiving that others have the characteristics that are unconsciously disliked in one's self.

Proxemics: how space is used in interactions.

Psychodynamic/psychoanalytic theory: a complex, rich description of the development of personality and treatment, based on examining the inner and often unconscious dynamics (underlying processes such as feelings, ideas, impulses, drives) of people.

Punishment: occurs after a behavior and reduces the probability that the behavior will occur again.

Racial identity: refers to how individuals identify with their racial or ethnic culture.

Rationalization: making excuses for an anxiety-producing thought or behavior.

Reaction formation: acting in a manner that is opposite to what one is feeling.

Reactions: conscious and unconscious responses to the other's interventions or behaviors.

Real relationship: the genuine, nondistorted connection between the helper and client.

Referral: giving a recommendation for another service provider. The helper provides the name of another provider but leaves it up to the client to follow through.

Reflections of feelings: statements that repeat or paraphrase the client's statements, including an explicit emphasis on the client's feelings.

Regression: engaging in behaviors from an earlier stage of development at times when one is anxious.

Regulators: nonverbal behaviors (e.g., head nods, postural shifts) that monitor the flow of conversation.

Reinforcement: anything that follows a behavior and increases the probability that the behavior will occur again. An event, behavior, privilege, or material object whose addition increases the likelihood of a behavior occurring again is a positive reinforcer. Primary reinforcers (e.g., food, water, sex) are biological necessities, whereas secondary reinforcers (e.g., praise, money) gain their reinforcing properties through association with primary reinforcers.

Relaxation: a bodily state of being nonanxious, at ease, at peace, relieved of pressure, low tension, or absence of arousal.

Reluctance: being passively unwilling to change, perhaps because of lack of trust, fear of falling apart, shame, fear of change, or lack of motivation to change.

Repression: not allowing painful material into one's conscious thought.

Resistance: active unwillingness to change because of feeling coerced and wanting to fight back.

Restatements: a repeating or paraphrasing of the content or meaning of what a client has said; typically contain fewer but similar words as the client's and are more concrete and clear than the client's statement.

Schemas: clusters of related thoughts, feelings, actions, and images.

Self-awareness: a stable characteristic (i.e., self-knowledge or self-insight) or a state of heightened self-focus (i.e., sensitivity in the here-and-now).

Self-care: taking care of oneself.

Self-compassion: having compassion for yourself or loving yourself as you truly are.

Self-reflection: thinking about oneself and one's motivations.

Session management: organizing one's time, goals, and tasks in helping sessions.

Sexual attraction: feeling physically or emotionally drawn to another person.

Shaping: the gradual training of a complex response by reinforcing closer and closer approximations to the desired behavior.

Silence: a pause during which neither helper nor client is speaking.

Social support: having a network of family and friends on whom one can count for emotional or instrumental help.

Skills: verbal interventions that helpers use to intervene with clients.

Sublimation: changing unacceptable impulses into socially appropriate actions.

Suicide ideation: considering killing oneself.

Summaries: ties together several ideas or picks out the highlights and general themes of the content expressed by the client. Summaries do not go beyond what the client has said or delve into the reasons for feelings or behaviors but consolidate what has been said.

Superego: an internalization of society's morals and values; develops through resolution of the Oedipal/Electra conflict.

Supervision: a more experienced helper consulting with or working with a less experienced helper to help the less experienced person become a better helper.

Termination: ending the helping relationship.

Theoretical orientation: beliefs about how people develop and how to help people change.

Therapeutic relationship: the feelings and attitudes that counseling participants have toward one another and the manner in which those are expressed.

Time-limited therapy: helping is limited by a certain number of sessions.

Tone of voice: the modulation of the voice to communicate different emotions.

Topdog: one's controlling and dominant voice that engages in criticism ("shoulds").

Transfer: giving a recommendation for another service provider and facilitating the process of switching to someone else for treatment.

Transference: client distortions of the helper based on past experiences. The client places on the therapist characteristics that belong to other people with whom one has unresolved issues.

Unconditional positive regard: caring about, understanding, and appreciating clients for who they are, regardless of how they behave.

Unconscious: mental activity that is not available to immediate awareness.

Underdog: one's passive voice that often whines and acts helpless.

Undoing: behaving in a ritualistic manner to take away or make amends for unacceptable behaviors.

Values clarification: helping people become aware of and clarify what their lives are for and what is worth working for.

Veracity: the ethical principle of telling the truth.

Virtuous manner: the ethical principle of behaving in a virtuous manner. Virtues are not as concerned with laws and rules as much as much as with striving to be a person of positive moral character.

Working (or therapeutic) alliance: the part of the relationship focused on the therapeutic work. The alliance consists of the bond (i.e., the connection between the helper and client), an agreement on goals (a consensus about changes the client needs to make), and an agreement on tasks (a consensus about what is to take place during the helping process to meet the goals).

References

Adler, G. (1984). Special problems for the therapist. *International Journal of Psychiatry in Medicine, 14,* 91–98.

Ainsworth, M. D. S. (1989). Attachments beyond infancy. *American Psychologist, 44,* 709–716. doi:10.1037/0003-066X.44.4.709

Ainsworth, M. D. S., Blehar, M. C., Waters, E., & Wall, S. (1978). *Patterns of attachment: A psychological study of the Strange Situation.* Hillsdale, NJ: Erlbaum.

Alberti, R. E., & Emmons, M. L. (2001). *Your perfect right: Assertiveness and equality in your life and relationships* (8th ed.). Atascadero, CA: Impact.

American Association for Marriage and Family Therapy. (2002). *AAMFT code of ethics.* Alexandria, VA: Author.

American Psychological Association. (2003). Guidelines for multicultural education, training, research, practice, and organizational change for psychologists. *American Psychologist, 58,* 377–402

American Psychological Association. (2010). *Ethical principles of psychologists and code of conduct (2002, Amended June 1, 2010).* Retrieved from http://www.apa.org/ethics/code/index.aspx

American Psychological Association, with Hill, C. E. (2013). *Dream work in practice* [DVD]. Washington, DC: American Psychological Association.

Andersen, B., & Anderson, W. (1985). Client perceptions of counselors using positive and negative self-involving statements. *Journal of Counseling Psychology, 32,* 462–465. doi:10.1037/0022-0167.32.3.462

Archer, D., & Akert, R. M. (1977). Words and everything else: Verbal and nonverbal cues in social interpretation. *Journal of Personality and Social Psychology, 35,* 443–449. doi:10.1037/0022-3514.35.6.443

Arlow, J. A. (1995). Psychoanalysis. In R. J. Corsini & D. Wedding (Eds.), *Current psychotherapies* (5th ed., pp. 15–50). Itasca, IL: F. E. Peacock.

Arredondo, P., Toporek, R., Brown, S. P., Jones, J., Locke, D. C., Sanchez, J., & Stadler, H. (1996). Operationalization of the multicultural competencies. *Journal of Multicultural Counseling and Development, 24,* 42–78. doi:10.1002/j.2161-1912.1996.tb00288.x

Atkinson, A. P., Dittrick, W. H., Gemmell, A. J., & Young, A. W. (2004). Emotion perception from dynamic and static body expressions in point-light and full-light displays. *Perception, 33,* 717–746. doi:10.1068/p5096

Atkinson, D. R., & Hackett, G. (1998). *Counseling diverse populations* (2nd ed.). Boston, MA: McGraw-Hill.

Atkinson, D. R., Morten, G., & Sue, D. W. (1998). *Counseling American minorities: A cross-cultural perspective* (5th ed.). Boston, MA: McGraw-Hill.

Axelson, J. A. (1999). *Counseling and development in a multicultural society* (3rd ed.). Pacific Grove, CA: Brooks/Cole.

Ayoko, O. B., & Hartel, C. E. J. (2003). The role of space as both a conflict trigger and a conflict control mechanism in heterogeneous workgroups. *Applied Psychology: An International Review, 52,* 383–412. doi:10.1111/1464-0597.00141

Bachelor, A. (1995). Clients' perception of the therapeutic alliance: A qualitative analysis. *Journal of Counseling Psychology, 42,* 323–337. doi:10.1037/0022-0167.42.3.323

Bandura, A. (1965). Influence of models' reinforcement contingencies on the acquisition of imitative responses. *Journal of Personality and Social Psychology, 1,* 589–595. doi:10.1037/h0022070

Bandura, A. (1969). *Principles of behavior modification.* New York, NY: Holt, Rinehart & Winston.

Bandura, A. (1977). *Social learning theory.* Englewood Cliffs, NJ: Prentice Hall.

Barkham, M., & Shapiro, D. A. (1986). Counselor verbal response modes and experienced empathy. *Journal of Counseling Psychology, 33,* 3–10. doi:10.1037/0022-0167.33.1.3

Basch, M. F. (1980). *Doing psychotherapy.* New York, NY: Basic Books.

Basescu, S. (1990). Tools of the trade: The use of self in psychotherapy. *Group, 14,* 157–165. doi:10.1007/BF01459151

Beattie, G., & Shovelton, H. (2005). Why the spontaneous images created by the hands during talk can help make TV advertisements more effective. *British Journal of Psychology, 96*, 21–37. doi:10.1348/000712605X103500

Beauchamp, T. L., & Childress, J. F. (1994). *Principles of biomedical ethics* (4th ed.). New York, NY: Oxford University Press.

Beck, A. T. (1976). *Cognitive therapy and the emotional disorders.* New York, NY: International Universities Press.

Beck, A. T., & Emery, G. (1985). *Anxiety disorders and phobias: A cognitive perspective.* New York, NY: Basic Books.

Beck, A. T., & Freeman, A. (1990). *Cognitive therapy of the personality disorders.* New York, NY: Guilford Press.

Beck, A. T., Rush, A. J., Shaw, B. R., & Emery, G. (1979). *Cognitive therapy of depression.* New York, NY: Guilford Press.

Beck, J. S. (1995). *Cognitive therapy: Basics and beyond.* New York, NY: Guilford Press.

Benson, H. (1975). *The relaxation response.* New York, NY: Morrow.

Berman, A. L., Jobes, D. A., & Silverman, M. M. (2006). *Adolescent suicide: Assessment and intervention* (2nd ed.). Washington, DC: American Psychological Association. doi:10.1037/11285-000

Bernstein, D. A., & Borkovec, T. D. (1973). *Progressive relaxation training.* Champaign, IL: Research Press.

Berry, J., & Sam, D. (1996). Acculturation and adaptation. In J. Berry, M. Segall, & C. Kagitcibasi (Eds.), *Handbook of cross-cultural psychology: Social behavior and applications* (Vol. 3, pp. 291–325). Boston, MA: Allyn & Bacon.

Beutler, L. E., & Bergan, J. (1991). Value change in counseling and psychotherapy: A search for scientific credibility. *Journal of Counseling Psychology, 38*, 16–24. doi:10.1037/0022-0167.38.1.16

Bibring, E. (1954). Psychoanalysis and the dynamic psychotherapies. *Journal of the American Psychoanalytic Association, 2*, 745–770. doi:10.1177/000306515400200412

Bischoff, M. M., & Tracey, T. J. G. (1995). Client resistance as predicted by therapist behavior: A study of sequential dependence. *Journal of Counseling Psychology, 42*, 487–495. doi:10.1037/0022-0167.42.4.487

Blanck, G. (1966). Some technical implications of ego psychology. *The International Journal of Psychoanalysis, 47*, 6–13.

Blustein, D. L. (1987). Integrating career counseling and psychotherapy: A comprehensive treatment strategy. *Psychotherapy: Theory, Research, Practice, Training, 24*, 794–799. doi:10.1037/h0085781

Bohart, A. C., Elliott, R., Greenberg, L. S., & Watson, J. C. (2002). Empathy. In J. C. Norcross (Ed.), *Psychotherapy relationships that work: Therapist contributions and responsiveness to patients* (pp. 89–108). New York, NY: Oxford University Press.

Book, H. E. (1998). *How to practice brief psychodynamic psychotherapy: The core conflictual relationship theme method.* Washington, DC: American Psychological Association. doi:10.1037/10251-000

Borys, D. S., & Pope, K. S. (1989). Dual relationships between therapist and client: A national survey of psychologists, psychiatrists, and social workers. *Professional Psychology: Research and Practice, 20,* 283–293. doi:10.1037/0735-7028.20.5.283

Bowlby, J. (1969). *Attachment and loss: Vol. 1. Attachment.* New York, NY: Basic Books.

Bowlby, J. (1988). *A secure base.* New York, NY: Basic Books.

Boyer, S. P., & Hoffman, M. A. (1993). Counselor affective reactions to termination: Impact of counselor loss history and perceived client sensitivity to loss. *Journal of Counseling Psychology, 40,* 271–277. doi:10.1037/0022-0167.40.3.271

Brainerd, C. J., & Reyna, V. F. (1998). When things that never happened are easier to "remember" than things that did. *Psychological Science, 9,* 484–489. doi:10.1111/1467-9280.00089

Brammer, L. M., & MacDonald, G. (1996). *The helping relationship: Process and skills* (6th ed.). Boston, MA: Allyn & Bacon.

Breier, A., & Strauss, J. S. (1984). The role of social relationships in the recovery from psychotic disorders. *The American Journal of Psychiatry, 141,* 949–955.

Brown, D. (1985). Career counseling: Before, after, or instead of personal counseling. *Vocational Guidance Quarterly, 33,* 197–201. doi:10.1002/j.2164-585X.1985.tb01310.x

Brown, D., & Brooks, L. (1991). *Career counseling techniques.* Boston, MA: Allyn & Bacon.

Brownell, K. D., Marlatt, G. A., Lichenstein, E., & Wilson, G. T. (1986). Understanding and preventing relapse. *American Psychologist, 41,* 765–782. doi:10.1037/0003-066X.41.7.765

Budman, S. H., & Gurman, A. S. (1988). *Theory and practice of brief therapy.* New York, NY: Guilford Press.

Bugental, J. T. (1965). *The search for authenticity.* New York, NY: Holt, Rinehart & Winston.

Burns, D. D. (1999). *The feeling good handbook* (rev. ed.). New York, NY: Plume/Penguin Books.

Burns, D. D., & Auerbach, A. (1996). Therapeutic empathy in cognitive-behavioral therapy: Does it really make a difference? In P. M. Salkovskis (Ed.), *Frontiers of cognitive therapy* (pp. 135–164). New York, NY: Guilford Press.

Cahill, A. J. (1981). Aggression revisited: The value of anger in therapy and other close relationships. *Adolescent Psychiatry, 9,* 539–549.

Carkhuff, R. R. (1969). *Human and helping relations* (Vols. 1 and 2). New York, NY: Holt, Rinehart & Winston.

Carkhuff, R. R. (1973). *The art of problem-solving.* Amherst, MA: Human Resource Development.

Carkhuff, R. R., & Anthony, W. A. (1979). *The skills of helping: An introduction to counseling skills.* Amherst, MA: Human Resources Development.

Carkhuff, R. R., & Berenson, B. G. (1967). *Beyond counseling and psychotherapy.* New York, NY: Holt, Rinehart & Winston.

Carroll, L. (1962). *Alice's adventures in wonderland.* Harmondsworth, England: Penguin Books. (Original work published 1865)

Cashdan, S. (1988). *Object relations therapy.* New York, NY: Norton.

Cassidy, J., & Shaver, P. R. (Eds.). (2008). *Handbook of attachment: Theory, research, and clinical application* (2nd ed.). New York, NY: Guilford Press.

Castonguay, L., & Hill, C. E. (Eds.). (2007). *Insight in psychotherapy.* Washington, DC: American Psychological Association. doi:10.1037/11532-000

Castonguay, L. & Hill, C. E. (Eds.) (2012). *Transformation in psychotherapy: Corrective experiences across cognitive behavioral, humanistic, and psychodynamic approaches.* Washington, DC: American Psychological Association.

Chui, H., Hill, C. E., Ain, S., Ericson, S., Del Pino, H. G., Hummel, A., . . . & Spangler, P. T. (2013). *Training undergraduate students to use challenges: Changes in self-efficacy and written challenges, helpfulness of training components, and predictors of the effects of training.* Manuscript in preparation.

Claiborn, C. D., Goodyear, R. K., & Horner, P. A. (2002). Feedback. In J. C. Norcross (Ed.), *Psychotherapy relationships that work: Therapist contributions and responsiveness to patients* (pp. 217–233). New York, NY: Oxford University Press.

Cobb, S. (1976). Social support as a moderator of life stress. *Psychosomatic Medicine, 38,* 300–314.

Conoley, C. W., Padula, M. A., Payton, D. S., & Daniels, J. A. (1994). Predictors of client implementation of counselor recommendations: Match with problem, difficulty level, and building on client strengths. *Journal of Counseling Psychology, 41,* 3–7. doi:10.1037/0022-0167.41.1.3

Conte, H. R., Plutchik, R., Picard, S., & Karasu, T. B. (1989). Ethics in the practice of psychotherapy: A survey. *American Journal of Psychotherapy, 43,* 32–42.

Cornett, C. (1991). The "risky" intervention: Twinship self-object impasses and therapist self-disclosure in psychodynamic psychotherapy. *Clinical Social Work Journal, 19,* 49–61.

Cournoyer, R. J., & Mahalik, J. R. (1995). Cross-sectional study of gender role conflict examining college-aged and middle-aged men. *Journal of Counseling Psychology, 42,* 11–19. doi:10.1037/0022-0167.42.1.11

Crits-Christoph, P., Barber, J. P., & Kurcias, J. S. (1991). Introduction and historical background. In P. Crits-Christoph & J. P. Barber (Eds.),

Handbook of short-term dynamic psychotherapy (pp. 1–16). New York, NY: Basic Books.

Crits-Christoph, P., Cooper, A., & Luborsky, L. (1988). The accuracy of therapists' interpretations and the outcome of dynamic psychotherapy. *Journal of Consulting and Clinical Psychology, 56,* 490–495. doi:10.1037/0022-006X.56.4.490

Crits-Christoph, P., & Gibbons, M. B. C. (2002). Relational interpretations. In J. C. Norcross (Ed.), *Psychotherapy relationships that work: Therapist contributions and responsiveness to patients* (pp. 285–300). New York, NY: Oxford University Press.

Cunha, C., Goncalves, M. M., Hill, C. E., Mendes, I., Ribiero, A. P., Sousa, I., Angus, L., & Greenberg, L. S. (2012). Therapist interventions and client innovative moments in emotion-focused therapy for depression. *Psychotherapy, 49,* 536–548.

Curtis, J. M. (1981). Indications and contraindications in the use of therapist's self-disclosure. *Psychological Reports, 49,* 499–507. doi:10.2466/pr0.1981.49.2.499

Curtis, J. M. (1982). Principles and techniques of non-disclosure by the therapist during psychotherapy. *Psychological Reports, 51,* 907–914. doi:10.2466/pr0.1982.51.3.907

Darwin, C. R. (1872). *The expression of the emotions in man and animals* (1st ed.). London, England: John Murray. doi:10.1037/10001-000

Delaney, D. J., & Heimann, R. A. (1966). Effectiveness of sensitivity training on the perception of non-verbal communications. *Journal of Counseling Psychology, 13,* 436–440. doi:10.1037/h0023975

Deutsch, C. J. (1984). Self-reported sources of stress among psychotherapists. *Professional Psychology: Research and Practice, 15,* 833–845. doi:10.1037/0735-7028.15.6.833

Dewald, P. A. (1971). *Psychotherapy: A dynamic approach.* New York, NY: Basic Books.

Duan, C., & Hill, C. E. (1996). Theoretical confusions in the construct of empathy: A review of the literature. *Journal of Counseling Psychology, 43,* 261–274. doi:10.1037/0022-0167.43.3.261

Duan, C., Hill, C. E., Jiang, G., Hu, B., Chui, H., Hui, K., Liu, J., & Yu, L. (2012). Therapist directives: Use and outcomes in China. *Psychotherapy Research, 22,* 442–457.

Duan, C., Hill, C. E. Jiang, G., Hu, B., Lei, Y., Chen, J., & Yu, L. (2013). *The use of directives in counseling in China: The counselor perspective.* Manuscript submitted for publication.

Eells, T. D. (2007). *Handbook of psychotherapy case formulation* (2nd ed.). New York, NY: Guilford Press.

Egan, G. (1994). *The skilled helper* (5th ed.). Monterey, CA: Brooks/Cole.

Eibl-Eibesfeldt, I. (1971). *Love and hate: The natural history of behavior patterns.* New York, NY: Holt, Rinehart & Winston.

Ekman, P. (1993). Facial expression and emotion. *American Psychologist, 48,* 384–392. doi:10.1037/0003-066X.48.4.384

Ekman, P., & Friesen, W. V. (1969). Non-verbal leakage and clues to deception. *Psychiatry: Journal for the Study of Interpersonal Processes, 32,* 88–106.

Ekman, P., & Friesen, W. V. (1984). *Unmasking the face* (reprint ed.). Palo Alto, CA: Consulting Psychologists Press.

Elkind, S. N. (1992). *Resolving impasses in therapeutic relationships.* New York, NY: Guilford Press.

Elliott, R. (1985). Helpful and nonhelpful events in brief counseling interviews: An empirical taxonomy. *Journal of Counseling Psychology, 32,* 307–322. doi:10.1037/0022-0167.32.3.307

Elliott, R., Barker, C. B., Caskey, N., & Pistrang, N. (1982). Differential helpfulness of counselor verbal response modes. *Journal of Counseling Psychology, 29,* 354–361. doi:10.1037/0022-0167.29.4.354

Elliott, R., Greenberg, L. S., Watson, J., Timulak, L., & Freire, E. (2013). Research on humanistic-experiential psychotherapies. In M. J. Lambert (Ed.), *Bergin and Garfield's handbook of psychotherapy and behavior change* (6th ed., pp. 495–538). New York, NY: Wiley.

Elliott, R., Shapiro, D. A., Firth-Cozens, J., Stiles, W. B., Hardy, G. E., Llewelyn, S. P., & Margison, F. R. (1994). Comprehensive process analysis of insight events in cognitive–behavioral and psychodynamic–interpersonal psychotherapies. *Journal of Counseling Psychology, 41,* 449–463. doi:10.1037/0022-0167.41.4.449

Elliott, R., Watson, J. C., Goldman, R. N., & Greenberg, L. S. (2004). *Learning emotion-focused therapy: The process–experiential approach to change.* Washington, DC: American Psychological Association. doi:10.1037/10725-000

Ellis, A. (1962). *Reason and emotion in psychotherapy.* New York, NY: Lyle Stuart.

Ellis, A. (1995). Rational emotive behavior therapy. In R. Corsini & D. Wedding (Eds.), *Current psychotherapies* (5th ed., pp. 161–196). Itasca, IL: R. E. Peacock.

Epstein, R. S., Simon, R. I., & Kay, G. G. (1992). Assessing boundary violations in psychotherapy: Survey results with the exploitation index. *Bulletin of the Menninger Clinic, 56,* 150–166.

Erikson, E. H. (1963). *Childhood and society* (2nd ed.). New York, NY: Norton.

Etkin, A., Pittenger, C., Polam, H. J., & Kandel, E. R. (2005). Toward a neurobiology of psychotherapy: Basic science and clinical applications. *The Journal of Neuropsychiatry and Clinical Neurosciences, 17,* 145–158. doi:10.1176/appi.neuropsych.17.2.145

Falk, D., & Hill, C. E. (1992). Counselor interventions preceding client laughter in brief therapy. *Journal of Counseling Psychology, 39,* 39–45. doi:10.1037/0022-0167.39.1.39

Farber, B. A. (1983). Psychotherapists' perceptions of stressful patient behavior. *Professional Psychology: Research and Practice, 14,* 697–705. doi:10.1037/0735-7028.14.5.697

Farber, B. A., & Doolin, E. M. (2011). Positive regard and affirmation. In J. C. Norcross (Ed.), *Psychotherapy relationships that work: Evidence-based responsiveness* (2nd ed., pp. 168–186). New York, NY: Oxford University Press.

Farber, B. A., & Geller, J. D. (1994). Gender and representation in psychotherapy. *Psychotherapy: Theory, Research, Practice, Training, 31,* 318–326. doi:10.1037/h0090216

Fitzpatrick, M. R., Stalikas, A., & Iwakabe, S. (2001). Examining counselor interventions and client progress in the context of the therapeutic alliance. *Psychotherapy: Theory, Research, Practice, Training, 38,* 160–170. doi:10.1037/0033-3204.38.2.160

Fonagy, P., Gergely, G., & Target, M. (2008). Psychoanalytic constructs and attachment theory and research. In J. Cassidy & P. Shaver (Eds.), *Handbook of attachment* (2nd ed., pp. 783–810). New York, NY: Guilford Press.

Fouad, N. A., & Brown, M. T. (2000). Role of race and social class in development: Implications for counseling psychology. In S. D. Brown & R. W. Lent (Eds.), *Handbook of counseling psychology* (3rd ed., pp. 379–408). New York, NY: Wiley.

Frank, J. D., & Frank, J. B. (1991). *Persuasion and healing: A comparative study of psychotherapy* (3rd ed.). Baltimore, MD: Johns Hopkins University Press.

Frankish, C. J. (1994). Crisis centers and their role in treatment: Suicide prevention versus health promotion. *Death Studies, 18,* 327–339. doi:10.1080/07481189408252681

Frankl, V. (1959). *Man's search for meaning.* New York, NY: Simon & Schuster.

Freud, S. (1958). Recommendations to physicians practicing psychoanalysis. In J. Strachey (Ed. and Trans.), *The standard edition of the complete psychological works of Sigmund Freud* (Vol. 12, pp. 109–120). London, England: Hogarth Press. (Original work published 1912)

Freud, S. (1933). *New introductory lectures on psychoanalysis* (J. H. Sprott, Trans.). New York, NY: Norton.

Freud, S. (1943). *A general introduction to psychoanalysis* (J. Riviere, Trans.). New York, NY: Garden City. (Original work published 1920)

Freud, S. (1949). *An outline of psychoanalysis* (J. Strachey, Trans.). New York, NY: Norton. (Original work published 1940)

Freud, S. (1953a). Fragment of an analysis of a case of hysteria. In J. Strachey (Ed.), *Standard edition of the complete psychological works of Sigmund Freud* (Vol. 7, pp. 15–122). London, England: Hogarth. (Original work published 1905)

Freud, S. (1953b). Remembering, repeating, and working through. In J. Strachey (Ed.), *Standard edition of the complete psychological works of Sigmund Freud* (Vol. 12, pp. 147–156). London, England: Hogarth. (Original work published 1914)

Freud, S. (1959). The dynamics of transference. In E. Jones (Ed.), J. Riviere (Trans.), *Collected papers* (pp. 312–322). New York, NY: Basic Books. (Original work published 1912)

Freud, S. (1961). The ego and the id. In J. Strachey (Trans. & Ed.) *The standard edition of the complete psychological works of Sigmund Freud* (Vol. 19, pp. 3–66). London, England: Hogarth. (Original work published 1923)

Freud, S. (1963). *Character and culture.* Oxford, England: Crowell-Collier. (Original work published 1923)

Friedman, E. H. (1990). *Friedman's fables.* New York, NY: Guilford Press.

Fromm-Reichmann, F. (1950). *Principles of intensive psychotherapy.* Chicago, IL: University of Chicago Press.

Fukuyama, M. A., & Sevig, T. D. (2002). Spirituality in counseling across cultures: Many rivers to the sea. In P. B. Pedersen, J. G. Draguns, W. J. Lonner, & J. E. Trimble (Eds.), *Counseling across cultures* (5th ed., pp. 273–296). Thousand Oaks, CA: Sage.

Fuller, F., & Hill, C. E. (1985). Counselor and helpee perceptions of counselor intentions in relationship to outcome in a single counseling session. *Journal of Counseling Psychology, 32,* 329–338. doi:10.1037/0022-0167.32.3.329

Gabbard, G. O. (1994). Sexual excitement and countertransference love in the analyst. *Journal of the American Psychoanalytic Association, 42,* 1083–1106.

Gabbard, G. O. (1995. The early history of boundary violations in psychoanalysis. *Journal of the American Psychoanalytic Association, 43,* 1115–1136.

Geller, J. D. (2003). Self-disclosure in psychoanalytic and existential therapy. *Journal of Clinical Psychology, 59,* 541–554. doi:10.1002/jclp.10158

Geller, J. D., Cooley, R. S., & Hartley, D. (1981). Images of the psychotherapist: A theoretical and methodological perspective. *Imagination, Cognition and Personality, 1,* 123–146. doi:10.2190/64EY-QLW8-765A-K0KH

Geller, J. D., & Farber, B. A. (1993). Factors influencing the process of internalization in psychotherapy. *Psychotherapy Research, 3,* 166–180. doi:10.1080/10503309312331333769

Gelso, C. J., & Carter, J. A. (1985). The relationship in counseling and psychotherapy. *The Counseling Psychologist, 13,* 155–243. doi:10.1177/0011000085132001

Gelso, C. J., & Carter, J. A. (1994). Components of the psychotherapy relationship: Their interaction and unfolding during treatment. *Journal of Counseling Psychology, 41,* 296–306. doi:10.1037/0022-0167.41.3.296

Gelso, C. J., & Fretz, B. R. (2001). *Counseling psychology* (2nd ed.). Belmont, CA: Thomson-Wadsworth.

Gelso, C. J., & Hayes, J. A. (1998). *The psychotherapy relationship: Theory, research, and practice.* New York, NY: Wiley.

Gelso, C. J., & Hayes, J. A. (2007). *Countertransference and the therapist's inner experience: Perils and possibilities.* Mahwah, NJ: Erlbaum.

Gelso, C. J., Hill, C. E., Mohr, J., Rochlen, A., & Zack, J. (1999). Describing the face of transference: Psychodynamic therapists' recollections about transference in cases of successful long-term therapy. *Journal of Counseling Psychology, 46,* 257–267. doi:10.1037/0022-0167.46.2.257

Gendlin, E. T. (1981). *Focusing* (2nd ed.). New York, NY: Bantam Books.

Gendlin, E. T. (1996). *Focusing-oriented psychotherapy: A manual of the experiential method.* New York, NY: Guilford Press.

Gillespie, J. F., Jr. (1951). Verbal signs of resistance in client-centered therapy. *Dissertation Abstracts International, 5*(01), 454B. (University Microfilms No. AAI000305)

Glass, A. L., & Holyoak, L. J. (1986). *Cognition* (2nd ed.). New York, NY: Random House.

Goates-Jones, M. K., Hill, C. E., Stahl, J., & Doschek, E. (2009). Therapist response modes in the exploration stage: Timing and effectiveness. *Counselling Psychology Quarterly, 22,* 221–231. doi:10.1080/09515070903185256

Goldfried, M. R. (2012). The corrective experience: A core principle for therapeutic change. In L. G. Castonguay & C. E. Hill (Eds.), *Transformation in psychotherapy: Corrective experiences across cognitive behavioral, humanistic, and psychodynamic approaches* (pp. 13–30). Washington DC: American Psychological Association.

Goldfried, M. R., Burckell, L. A., & Eubanks-Carter, C. (2003). Therapist self-disclosure in cognitive–behavior therapy. *Journal of Clinical Psychology, 59,* 555–568. doi:10.1002/jclp.10159

Goldfried, M. R., & Davison, G. C. (1994). *Clinical behavior therapy* (expanded ed.). Oxford, England: Wiley.

Goldfried, M. R., & Trier, C. S. (1974). Effectiveness of relaxation as an active coping skill. *Journal of Abnormal Psychology, 83,* 348–355. doi:10.1037/h0036923

Good, G. E., Robertson, J. M., O'Neil, J. M., Fitzgerald, L. E., Stevens, M., DeBrod, K. A., . . . Braverman, D. G. (1995). Male gender role conflict: Psychometric issues and relations to psychological distress. *Journal of Counseling Psychology, 42,* 3–10. doi:10.1037/0022-0167.42.1.3

Gourash, N. (1978). Help-seeking: A review of the literature. *American Journal of Community Psychology, 6,* 413–423. doi:10.1007/BF00941418

Grace, M., Kivlighan, D. M., & Kunce, J. (1995). The effect of nonverbal skills training on counselor trainee nonverbal sensitivity and responsiveness and on session impact and working alliance ratings. *Journal of*

Counseling & Development, 73, 547–552. doi:10.1002/j.1556-6676.1995.
tb01792.x

Greenberg, L. S. (2002). *Emotion-focused therapy.* New York, NY: Guilford
Press.

Greenberg, L. S. (2011). *Emotion-focused therapy.* Washington, DC:
American Psychological Association.

Greenberg, L. S., Rice, L. N., & Elliott, R. (1993). *Facilitating emotional
change.* New York, NY: Guilford Press.

Greenson, R. R. (1967). *The technique and practice of psychoanalysis*
(Vol. 1). Madison, CT: International Universities Press.

Grissom, G. R., Lyons, J. S., & Lutz, W. (2002). Standing on the shoulders of a giant: Development of an outcome management system
based on the dose model and phase model of psychotherapy. *Psychotherapy Research, 12,* 397–412. doi:10.1093/ptr/12.4.397

Gross, A. E., & McMullen, P. A. (1983). Models of the help-seeking process. In B. DePaulo, A. Nadler, & J. D. Fisher (Eds.), *New directions in
helping* (Vol. 2, pp. 45–70). New York, NY: Academic Press.

Haase, R. F., & Tepper, D. T., Jr. (1972). Nonverbal components of
empathic communication. *Journal of Counseling Psychology, 19,* 417–424.
doi:10.1037/h0033188

Hackett, G. (1993). Career counseling and psychotherapy: False dichot-
omies and recommended remedies. *Journal of Career Assessment, 1,*
105–117. doi:10.1177/106907279300100201

Haldeman, D. C. (2002). Gay rights, patient rights: The implications of
sexual orientation conversion therapy. *Professional Psychology: Research
and Practice, 33,* 260–264. doi:10.1037/0735-7028.33.3.260

Haley, J. (1987). *Problem-solving therapy.* San Francisco. CA: Jossey-Bass.

Hall, E. T. (1963). A system for the notation of proxemic behavior. *American Anthropologist, 65,* 1003–1026. doi:10.1525/aa.1963.65.5.02a00020

Hall, E. T. (1968). Proxemics. *Current Anthropology, 9,* 83–108. doi:10.1086/
200975

Hanna, F. J., & Ritchie, M. H. (1995). Seeking the active ingredients of
psychotherapeutic change: Within and outside the context of therapy.
Professional Psychology: Research and Practice, 26, 176–183. doi:10.1037/
0735-7028.26.2.176

Harper, R. G., Wiens, A. N., & Matarazzo, J. D. (1978). *Nonverbal communication: The state of the art.* New York, NY: Wiley.

Hays, P. A. (2001). *Addressing cultural competencies in practice: A framework
for clinicians and counselors.* Washington, DC: American Psychological
Association. doi:10.1037/10411-000

Helms, J. E. (1990). *Black and White racial identity: Theory, research, and
practice.* Westport, CT: Greenwood.

Helms, J. E., & Cook, D. A. (1999). *Using race and culture in counseling
and psychotherapy: Theory and practice.* Needham, MA: Allyn & Bacon.

Herr, E. L. (1989). Career development and mental health. *Journal of Career Development, 16,* 5–18.

Highlen, P. S., & Hill, C. E. (1984). Factors affecting client change in individual counseling: Current status and theoretical speculations. In S. D. Brown & R. W. Lent (Eds.), *Handbook of counseling psychology* (pp. 334–398). New York, NY: Wiley.

Hill, C. E. (1975). A process approach to establishing counseling goals and outcomes. *The Personnel & Guidance Journal, 53,* 571–576. doi:10.1002/j.2164-4918.1975.tb04586.x

Hill, C. E. (1978). Development of a counselor verbal response category system. *Journal of Counseling Psychology, 25,* 461–468. doi:10.1037/0022-0167.25.5.461

Hill, C. E. (1989). *Therapist techniques and client outcomes: Eight cases of brief psychotherapy.* Newbury Park, CA: Sage.

Hill, C. E. (1992). An overview of four measures developed to test the Hill process model: Therapist intentions, therapist response modes, client reactions, and client behaviors. *Journal of Counseling & Development, 70,* 728–739. doi:10.1002/j.1556-6676.1992.tb02156.x

Hill, C. E. (Ed.). (2004). *Dream work in therapy: Facilitating exploration, insight, and action.* Washington, DC: American Psychological Association. doi:10.1037/10624-000

Hill, C. E. (2005a). The role of individual and marital therapy in my development. In J. D. Geller, J. C. Norcross, & D. E. Orlinsky (Eds.), *The psychotherapist's own psychotherapy: Patient and clinician perspectives* (pp. 129–144). New York, NY: Oxford University Press.

Hill, C. E. (2005b). Therapist techniques, client involvement, and the therapeutic relationship: Inextricably intertwined in the therapy process. *Psychotherapy: Theory, Research, & Practice, 42,* 431–442. doi:10.1037/0033-3204.42.4.431

Hill, C. E. (2007). My personal reactions to Rogers (1957): The facilitative but neither necessary nor sufficient conditions of therapeutic personality change. *Psychotherapy: Theory, Research, Practice, Training, 44,* 260–264. doi:10.1037/0033-3204.44.3.260

Hill, C. E., Carter, J. A., & O'Farrell, M. K. (1983). A case study of the process and outcome of time-limited counseling. *Journal of Counseling Psychology, 30,* 3–18. doi:10.1037/0022-0167.30.1.3

Hill, C. E., & Gormally, J. (1977). Effects of reflection, restatement, probe, and nonverbal behavior on client affect. *Journal of Counseling Psychology, 24,* 92–97. doi:10.1037/0022-0167.24.2.92

Hill, C. E., Helms, J. E., Spiegel, S. B., & Tichenor, V. (1988). Development of a system for categorizing client reactions to therapist interventions. *Journal of Counseling Psychology, 35,* 27–36. doi:10.1037/0022-0167.35.1.27

Hill, C. E., Helms, J. E., Tichenor, V., Spiegel, S. B., O'Grady, K. E., & Perry, E. S. (1988). The effects of therapist response modes in brief psychotherapy. *Journal of Counseling Psychology, 35,* 222–233. doi:10.1037/0022-0167.35.3.222

Hill, C. E., Kellems, I. S., Kolchakian, M. R., Wonnell, T. L., Davis, T. L., & Nakayama, E. Y. (2003). The therapist experience of being the target of hostile versus suspected-unasserted client anger: Factors associated with resolution. *Psychotherapy Research, 13,* 475–491. doi:10.1093/ptr/kpg040

Hill, C. E., & Knox, S. (2002). Therapist self-disclosure. In J. C. Norcross (Ed.), *Psychotherapy relationships that work: Therapist contributions and responsiveness to patients* (pp. 255–265). Oxford, England: Oxford University Press.

Hill, C. E., & Knox, S. (2008). Facilitating insight in counseling and psychotherapy. In S. D. Brown & R. W. Lent (Eds.), *Handbook of counseling psychology* (4th ed., pp. 284–302). New York, NY: Wiley.

Hill, C. E., & Knox, S. (2009). Processing the therapeutic relationship. *Psychotherapy Research, 19,* 13–29.

Hill, C. E., Knox, S., Hess, S., Crook-Lyon, R., Goates-Jones, M., & Sim, W. (2007). The attainment of insight in the Hill dream model: A single case study. In L. G. Castonguay & C. E. Hill (Eds.), *Insight in psychotherapy* (pp. 207–230). Washington, DC: American Psychological Association. doi:10.1037/11532-010

Hill, C. E., & Lambert, M. J. (2004). Methodological issues in studying psychotherapy processes and outcomes. In M. J. Lambert (Ed.), *Handbook of psychotherapy and behavior change* (5th ed., pp. 84–136). New York, NY: Wiley.

Hill, C. E., & Lent, R. W. (2006). A narrative and meta-analytic review of helping skills training: Time to revive a dormant area of inquiry. *Psychotherapy: Theory, Research, Practice, Training, 43,* 154–172. doi:10.1037/0033-3204.43.2.154

Hill, C. E., Lystrup, A., Kline, K., Gebru, N. M., Birchler, J., Palmer, G., . . . Pinto-Coelho, K. (2013). Aspiring to become a therapist: Personal strengths and challenges, influences, motivations, and expectations of future therapists. *Counselling Psychology Quarterly, 26,* 267–293.

Hill, C. E., Nutt-Williams, E., Heaton, K. J., Thompson, B. J., & Rhodes, R. H. (1996). Therapist retrospective recall of impasses in long-term psychotherapy: A qualitative analysis. *Journal of Counseling Psychology, 43,* 207–217. doi:10.1037/0022-0167.43.2.207

Hill, C. E., & O'Grady, K. E. (1985). List of therapist intentions illustrated in a case study and with therapists of varying theoretical orientations. *Journal of Counseling Psychology, 32,* 3–22. doi:10.1037/0022-0167.32.1.3

Hill, C. E., Roffman, M., Stahl, J., Friedman, S., Hummel, A., & Wallace, C. (2008). Helping skills training for undergraduates: Outcomes and predictors of outcomes. *Journal of Counseling Psychology, 55,* 359–370. doi:10.1037/0022-0167.55.3.359

Hill, C. E., Satterwhite, D. B., Larrimore, M. L., Mann, A. R., Johnson, V. C., Simon, R., . . . Knox, S. (2012). Attitudes about psychotherapy: A qualitative study of introductory psychology students who have never been in psychotherapy and the influence of attachment style. *Counselling & Psychotherapy Research, 12,* 13–24. doi:10.1080/1473314 5.2011.629732

Hill, C. E., Siegelman, L., Gronsky, B., Sturniolo, R., & Fretz, B. R. (1981). Nonverbal communication and counseling outcome. *Journal of Counseling Psychology, 28,* 203–212. doi:10.1037/0022-0167.28.3.203

Hill, C. E., Sim, W., Spangler, P., Stahl, J., Sullivan, C., & Teyber, E. (2008). Therapist immediacy in brief psychotherapy therapy: Case Study II. *Psychotherapy: Theory, Research, Practice, Training, 45,* 298–315. doi:10.1037/a0013306

Hill, C. E., Sullivan, C., Knox, S., & Schlosser, L. (2007). Becoming psychotherapists: Experiences of novice therapists in a beginning graduate class. *Psychotherapy: Theory, Research, Practice, Training, 44,* 434–449. doi:10.1037/0033-3204.44.4.434

Hill, C. E., Thompson, B. J., Cogar, M. M., & Denman, D. W. (1993). Beneath the surface of long-term therapy: Client and therapist report of their own and each other's covert processes. *Journal of Counseling Psychology, 40,* 278–287. doi:10.1037/0022-0167.40.3.278

Hill, C. E., Thompson, B. J., & Corbett, M. M. (1992). The impact of therapist ability to perceive displayed and hidden client reactions on immediate outcome in first sessions of brief therapy. *Psychotherapy Research, 2,* 143–155. doi:10.1080/10503309212331332914

Hill, C. E., Thompson, B. J., & Ladany, N. (2003). Therapist use of silence in therapy: A survey. *Journal of Clinical Psychology, 59,* 513–524. doi:10.1002/jclp.10155

Hill, C. E., Thompson, B. J., & Mahalik, J. R. (1989). Therapist interpretation. In C. E. Hill (Ed.), *Therapist techniques and client outcomes: Eight cases of brief psychotherapy* (pp. 284–310). Newbury Park, CA: Sage.

Holroyd, J. C., & Brodsky, A. (1977). Psychologists' attitudes and practices regarding erotic and nonerotic physical contact with patients. *American Psychologist, 32,* 843–849. doi:10.1037/0003-066X.32.10.843

Honos-Webb, L., & Stiles, W. B. (1998). Reformulation of assimilation analysis in terms of voices. *Psychotherapy: Theory, Research, Practice, Training, 35,* 23–33. doi:10.1037/h0087682

Horvath, A. O., & Bedi, R. P. (2002). The alliance. In J. C. Norcross (Ed.), *Psychotherapy relationships that work: Therapist contributions and responsiveness to patients* (pp. 37–70). New York, NY: Oxford University Press.

Horvath, A. O., Del Re, A. C., Flückiger, C., & Symonds, D. (2011). Alliance in individual psychotherapy. In J. C. Norcross (Ed.), *Psychotherapy relationships that work: Evidence-based responsiveness* (2nd ed., pp. 25–69). New York, NY: Oxford University Press.

Howard, K. I., Lueger, R. J., Maling, M. S., & Martinovich, Z. (1993). A phase model of psychotherapy outcome: Causal mediation of change. *Journal of Consulting and Clinical Psychology, 61,* 678–685.

Hunter, M., & Struve, J. (1998). *The ethical use of touch in psychotherapy.* Thousand Oaks, CA: Sage. doi:10.1080/10720169808400156

Israel, T., Gorcheva, R., Burnes, T. R., & Walther, W. A. (2008). Helpful and unhelpful therapy experiences of LGBT clients. *Psychotherapy Research, 18,* 294–305.

Ito, T. A., & Batholow, B. D. (2009). The neural correlates of race. Trends in Cognitive. *Neuroscience, 13,* 524–531.

Ivey, A. E. (1994). *Intentional interviewing and counseling: Facilitating client development in a multicultural society* (3rd ed.). Pacific Grove, CA: Brooks/Cole.

Izard, C. E. (1977). *Human emotions.* New York, NY: Plenum.

Jackson, J., Hill, C. E., Spangler, P. T., Ericson, S., Merson, E., Liu, J., . . . & Reen, G. (2013). *Training undergraduate students to use interpretation: Changes in self-efficacy and interpretation use, helpfulness of training components, and predictors of the effects of training.* Manuscript in preparation.

Jacobson, E. (1929). *Progressive relaxation.* Chicago, IL: University of Chicago Press.

Joines, V. S. (1995). A developmental approach to anger. *Transactional Analysis Journal, 25,* 112–118.

Jourard, S. M. (1971). *The transparent self.* New York, NY: Van Nostrand Reinhold.

Jung, C. G. (1984). *Dream analysis.* Princeton, NJ: Princeton University Press.

Kabat-Zinn, J. (2003). Mindfulness-based interventions in context: Past, present, and future. *Clinical Psychology: Science and Practice, 10,* 144–156. doi:10.1093/clipsy.bpg016

Kaplan, A., Brooks, B., McComb, A. L., Shapiro, E. R., & Sodano, A. (1983). Women and anger in psychotherapy. *Women & Therapy, 2,* 29–40. doi:10.1300/J015v02n02_04

Kazdin, A. E. (2013). *Behavior modification in applied settings* (7th ed.). Long Grove, IL: Waveland Press.

Kendon, A. (1967). Some functions of gaze-direction in social interaction. *Acta Psychologica, 26,* 22–63. doi:10.1016/0001-6918(67)90005-4

Kertay, L., & Reviere, S. L. (1998). Touch in context. In E. W. Smith, P. R. Clance, & S. Imes (Eds.), *Touch in psychotherapy: Theory, research, and practice* (pp. 16–35). New York, NY: Guilford Press.

Kestenbaum, R. (1992). Feeling happy versus feeling good: The processing of discrete and global categories of emotional expressions by children and adults. *Developmental Psychology, 28,* 1132–1142. doi:10.1037/0012-1649.28.6.1132

Kiesler, D. J. (1988). *Therapeutic metacommunication: Therapist impact disclosure as feedback in psychotherapy*. Palo Alto, CA: Consulting Psychologists Press.

Kiesler, D. J. (1996). *Contemporary interpersonal theory and research: Personality, psychopathology, and psychotherapy*. Oxford, England: Wiley.

Kim, B. S. K., & Abreu, J. M. (2001). Acculturation measurement: Theory, current instruments, and future directions. In J. G. Ponterotto, J. M. Casas, L. A. Suzuki, & C. M. Alexander (Eds.), *Handbook of multicultural counseling* (2nd ed., pp. 394–424). Thousand Oaks, CA: Sage.

Kim, B. S. K., Atkinson, D. R., & Umemoto, D. (2001). Asian cultural values and the counseling process: Current knowledge and directions for future research. *The Counseling Psychologist, 29*, 570–603. doi:10.1177/0011000001294006

Kim, B. S. K., Atkinson, D. R., & Yang, P. H. (1999). The Asian Values Scale: Development, factor analysis, validation, and reliability. *Journal of Counseling Psychology, 46*, 342–352. doi:10.1037/0022-0167.46.3.342

Kitchener, K. S. (1984). Intuition, critical evaluation and ethical principles: The foundation for ethical decisions for counseling psychology. *The Counseling Psychologist, 12*, 43–55. doi:10.1177/0011000084123005

Kitson, C., & Sperlinger, D. (2007). Dual relationships between clinical psychologists and their clients: A survey of UK clinical psychologists' attitudes. *Psychology and Psychotherapy: Theory, Research, and Practice, 80*, 279–295.

Kleinke, C. L. (1986). Gaze and eye contact: A research review. *Psychological Bulletin, 100*, 78–100. doi:10.1037/0033-2909.100.1.78

Knox, S., Burkard, A. W., Jackson, J. A., Schaak, A. M., & Hess, S. (2006). Therapists-in-training who experience a client suicide: Implications for supervision. *Professional Psychology: Research and Practice, 37*, 547–557. doi:10.1037/0735-7028.37.5.547

Knox, S., Goldberg, J. L., Woodhouse, S., & Hill, C. E. (1999). Clients' internal representations of their therapists. *Journal of Counseling Psychology, 46*, 244–256. doi:10.1037/0022-0167.46.2.244

Knox, S., Hess, S. A., Petersen, D. A., & Hill, C. E. (1997). A qualitative investigation of client perceptions of the effects of helpful therapist self-disclosure in long-term therapy. *Journal of Counseling Psychology, 44*, 274–283.

Kolden, G. G., Klein, M. H., Wang, C., & Austin, S. B. (2011). Congruence/genuineness. In J. C. Norcross (Ed.), *Psychotherapy relationships that work: Evidence-based responsiveness* (2nd ed., pp. 187–202). New York, NY: Oxford University Press.

Kopta, S. M., Howard, K. I., Lowry, J. L., & Beutler, L. E. (1994). Patterns of symptomatic recovery in psychotherapy. *Journal of Consulting and Clinical Psychology, 62*, 1009–1016. doi:10.1037/0022-006X.62.5.1009

Kraft, H. S. (2007). *Rule number two: Lessons I learned in a combat hospital.* New York, NY: Little, Brown.

Ladany, N., Hill, C. E., Thompson, B. J., & O'Brien, K. M. (2004). Therapist perspectives on using silence in therapy: A qualitative study. *Counselling & Psychotherapy Research, 4,* 80–89. doi:10.1080/14733140412331384088

Ladany, N., O'Brien, K. M., Hill, C. E., Melincoff, D. S., Knox, S., & Petersen, D. A. (1997). Sexual attraction toward clients, use of supervision, and prior training: A qualitative study of psychotherapy predoctoral interns. *Journal of Counseling Psychology, 44,* 413–424. doi:10.1037/0022-0167.44.4.413

Laing, R. D., & Esterson, A. (1970). *Sanity, madness, and the family.* Middlesex, England: Penguin.

Lambert, M. J. (2013). The efficacy and effectiveness of psychotherapy. In M. J. Lambert (Ed.), *Handbook of psychotherapy and behavior change* (6th ed., pp. 169–209). New York, NY: Wiley.

Lang, P. J., Melamed, B. G., & Hart, J. (1970). A psychophysiological analysis of fear modification using an automated desensitization procedure. *Journal of Abnormal Psychology, 76,* 220–234. doi:10.1037/h0029875

Lauver, P., & Harvey, D. R. (1997). *The practical counselor: Elements of effective helping.* Pacific Grove, CA: Brooks/Cole.

Levy, L. H. (1963). *Psychological interpretation.* New York, NY: Holt, Rinehart & Winston.

Lieberman, M. D., Eisenberger, N. I., Crockett, M. J., Tom, S. M., Pfeifer, J. H., & Way, B. M. (2007). Putting feelings into words: Affect labeling disrupts amygdala activity in response to affective stimuli. *Psychological Science, 18,* 421–428. doi:10.1111/j.1467-9280.2007.01916.x

Liu, X., Ramirez, S., Pang, P. T., Puryear, C. B., Govindarajan, A., Deisseroth, K., & Tonegawa, S. (2012). Optogenetic stimulation of a hippocampal engram activates fear memory recall. *Nature, 484,* 381–385.

Loftus, E. (1988). *Memory.* New York, NY: Ardsley House.

Luborsky, L., & Crits-Christoph, P. (1990). *Understanding transference: The CCRT method.* New York, NY: Basic Books.

Lynch, C. (1975). The freedom to get mad: Impediments to expressing anger and how to deal with them. *Family Therapy, 2,* 101–122.

Madigan, S. (2011). *Narrative therapy.* Washington, DC: American Psychological Association.

Mahalik, J. R. (1994). Development of the Client Resistance Scale. *Journal of Counseling Psychology, 41,* 58–68. doi:10.1037/0022-0167.41.1.58

Mahler, M. S. (1968). *On human symbiosis of the vicissitudes of individuation.* New York, NY: International Universities Press.

Mahrer, A. R., Gagnon, R., Fairweather, D. R., Boulet, D. B., & Herring, C. B. (1994). Client commitment and resolve to carry out post session behaviors. *Journal of Counseling Psychology, 41,* 407–414.

Maki, M. T., & Kitano, H. H. L. (2002). Counseling Asian Americans. In P. B. Pedersen, J. G. Draguns, W. J. Lonner, & J. E. Trimble (Eds.), *Counseling across cultures* (5th ed., pp. 109–131). Thousand Oaks, CA: Sage.

Malan, D. H. (1976a). *The frontier of brief psychotherapy.* New York, NY: Plenum. doi:10.1007/978-1-4684-2220-7

Malan, D. H. (1976b). *Toward a validation of dynamic psychotherapy: A replication.* New York, NY: Plenum. doi:10.1007/978-1-4615-8753-8

Mallinckrodt, B. (2000). Attachment, social competencies, social support, and interpersonal process in psychotherapy. *Psychotherapy Research, 10,* 239–266. doi:10.1093/ptr/10.3.239

Mann, J. (1973). *Time-limited psychotherapy.* Cambridge, MA: Harvard University Press.

Markus, H., & Kitayama, S. (1991). Culture and the self: Implications for cognition, emotion, and motivation. *Psychological Review, 98,* 224–253. doi:10.1037/0033-295X.98.2.224

Maroda, K. J. (2010). *Psychodynamic techniques: Working with emotion in the therapeutic relationship.* New York, NY: Guilford Press.

Martin, J., Martin, W., & Slemon, A. G. (1989). Cognitive–mediational models of action–act sequences in counseling. *Journal of Counseling Psychology, 36,* 8–16. doi:10.1037/0022-0167.36.1.8

Marx, J. A., & Gelso, C. J. (1987). Termination of individual counseling in a university counseling center. *Journal of Counseling Psychology, 34,* 3–9. doi:10.1037/0022-0167.34.1.3

Maslow, A. (1970). *Motivation and personality* (rev. ed.). New York, NY: Harper & Row.

Matarazzo, R. G., Phillips, J. S., Wiens, A. N., & Saslow, G. (1965). Learning the art of interviewing: A study of what beginning students do and their pattern of change. *Psychotherapy: Theory, Research & Practice, 2,* 49–60. doi:10.1037/h0088611

Matsakis, A. (1998). *Managing client anger: What to do when a client is angry at you.* Oakland, CA: New Harbinger.

Matsumoto, D., Kudoh, T., Sherer, K., & Wallbott, H. (1988). Antecedents of and reactions to emotions in the United States and Japan. *Journal of Cross-Cultural Psychology, 19,* 267–286. doi:10.1177/0022022188193001

McCullough, L., Kuhn, N., Andrews, S., Kaplan, A., Wolf, J., & Hurley, C. L. (2003). *Treating affect phobia: A manual for short-term dynamic psychotherapy.* New York, NY: Guilford.

McGoldrick, M. (Ed.). (1998). *Re-visioning family therapy: Race, culture, and gender in clinical practice.* New York, NY: Guilford Press.

McGoldrick, M., Giordano, J., & Garcia-Preto, N. (Eds.). (2005). *Ethnicity and family therapy* (3rd ed.). New York, NY: Guilford Press.

McGough, E. (1975). *Understanding body talk.* New York, NY: Scholastic Book Service.

McLeod, J., & McLeod, J. (2011). *Counselling skills: A practical guide for counselors and helping professionals* (2nd ed.). Berkshire, England: McGraw-Hill Open University Press.

McWhirter, E. H. (1994). *Counseling for empowerment*. Alexandria, VA: American Counseling Association.

McWilliams, N. (2004). *Psychoanalytic psychotherapy: A practitioner's guide*. New York, NY: Guilford Press.

Meador, B. D., & Rogers, C. R. (1973). Client-centered therapy. In R. Corsini (Ed.), *Current psychotherapies* (pp. 119–166). Itasca, IL: F. E. Peacock.

Meara, N. M., Schmidt, L. D., & Day, J. D. (1996). Principles and virtues: A foundation for ethical decisions, policies, and character. *The Counseling Psychologist, 24,* 4–77. doi:10.1177/0011000096241002

Medin, D. L., & Ross, B. H. (1992). *Cognitive psychology*. New York, NY: Harcourt Brace Jovanovich.

Meichenbaum, D., & Turk, D. C. (1987). *Facilitating treatment adherence: A practitioner's handbook*. New York, NY: Plenum. doi:10.1007/978-1-4684-5359-1

Mendel, W. M. (1964). The phenomenon of interpretation. *The American Journal of Psychoanalysis, 24,* 184–189. doi:10.1007/BF01872049

Meyer, B., & Pilkonis, P. A. (2002). Attachment style. In J. C. Norcross (Ed.), *Psychotherapy relationships that work: Therapist contributions and responsiveness to patients* (pp. 367–382). Oxford, England: Oxford University Press.

Mickelson, D., & Stevic, R. (1971). Differential effects of facilitative and nonfacilitative behavioral counselors. *Journal of Counseling Psychology, 18,* 314–319. doi:10.1037/h0031231

Mikulincer, M., & Shaver, P. R. (2007). *Attachment in adulthood: Structure, dynamics, and change*. New York, NY: Guilford Press.

Miller, J. B. (1976). *Toward a new psychology of women*. Boston, MA: Beacon.

Miller, W. R., Benefield, R. G., & Tonigan, J. S. (1993). Enhancing motivation for change in problem drinking: A controlled comparison of two therapist styles. *Journal of Consulting and Clinical Psychology, 61,* 455–461. doi:10.1037/0022-006X.61.3.455

Minuchin, S. (1974). *Families and family therapy*. Cambridge, MA: Harvard University Press.

Mitchell, S. A. (1993). *Hope and dread in psychoanalysis*. New York, NY: Basic Books.

Montagu, A. (Ed.). (1971). *Touching: The significance of the human skin*. New York, NY: Columbia University Press.

Muran, J. C. (Ed.). (2007). *Dialogues on difference: Studies of diversity in the therapeutic relationship*. Washington, DC: American Psychological Association. doi:10.1037/11500-000

Natterson, J. M. (1993). Dreams: The gateway to consciousness. In G. Delaney (Ed.), *New directions in dream interpretation* (pp. 41–76). Albany: State University of New York Press.

Neff, K. (2011). *Self-compassion: Stop beating yourself up and leave insecurity behind*. New York, NY: HarperCollins.

Newman, C. R. (1997). Maintaining professionalism in the face of emotional abuse from clients. *Cognitive and Behavioral Practice, 4*, 1–29. doi:10.1016/S1077-7229(97)80010-7

Nichols, M., & Schwartz, R. (1991). *Family therapy: Concepts and methods* (2nd ed.). Boston, MA: Allyn & Bacon.

Nielsen, S. L., Okiishi, J., Nielsen, D. L., Hawkins, E. J., Harmon, S. C., Pedersen, T., . . . Jackson, A. P. (2009). Termination, appointment use, and outcome patterns associated with intake therapist discontinuity. *Professional Psychology: Research and Practice, 40*, 272–278. doi:10.1037/a0013286

Nirenberg, G. I., & Calero, H. H. (1971). *How to read a person like a book*. New York, NY: Hawthorn Books.

Nisbett, R. E., & Wilson, T. D. (1977). Telling more than we can know. *Psychological Review, 84*, 231–259. doi:10.1037/0033-295X.84.3.231

Norman, S. L. (1982). Nonverbal communication: Implications for and use by counselors. *Individual Psychology: Journal of Adlerian Theory and Research, 38*, 353–359.

Nutt-Williams, E., & Hill, C. E. (1996). The relationship between therapist self-talk and counseling process variables for novice therapists. *Journal of Counseling Psychology, 43*, 170–177. doi:10.1037/0022-0167.43.2.170

O'Neil, J. M. (1981). Male sex-role conflicts, sexism, and masculinity: Psychological implications for men, women, and the counseling psychologist. *The Counseling Psychologist, 9*, 61–81. doi:10.1177/001100008100900213

Orlinsky, D. E., & Geller, J. D. (1993). Patients' representations of their therapists and therapy: New measures. In N. E. Miller, L. Luborsky, J. P. Barber, & J. P. Docherty (Eds.), *Psychodynamic treatment research: A handbook for psychodynamic research* (pp. 423–466). New York, NY: Basic Books.

Orlinsky, D. E., & Ronnestad, M. H. (2005). *How psychotherapists develop: A study of therapeutic work and professional growth*. Washington, DC: American Psychological Association. doi:10.1037/11157-000

Ormont, L. R. (1984). The leader's role in dealing with aggression in groups. *International Journal of Group Psychotherapy, 34*, 553–572.

Patterson, G. R., & Forgatch, M. S. (1985). Therapist behavior as a determinant for client noncompliance: A paradox for the behavior modifier. *Journal of Consulting and Clinical Psychology, 53*, 846–851. doi:10.1037/0022-006X.53.6.846

Paul, G. L. (1969). Outcome of systematic desensitization: II. Controlled investigations of individual treatment, technique variations, and current status. In C. M. Franks (Ed.), *Behavior therapy: Appraisal and status* (pp. 105–159). New York, NY: McGraw-Hill.

Pedersen, P. B. (1991). Multiculturalism as a generic approach to counseling. *Journal of Counseling & Development, 70,* 6–12. doi:10.1002/j.1556-6676.1991.tb01555.x

Pedersen, P. B. (1997). *Culture-centered counseling interventions: Striving for accuracy.* Thousand Oaks, CA: Sage.

Pedersen, P. B., Draguns, J. G., Lonner, W. J., & Trimble, J. E. (Eds.). (2002). *Counseling across cultures* (5th ed.). Thousand Oaks, CA: Sage.

Pedersen, P. B., & Ivey, A. (1993). *Culture-centered counseling and interviewing skills: A practical guide.* Westport, CT: Praeger.

Perls, F. S. (1969). *Gestalt therapy verbatim.* Moab, UT: Real People Press.

Perls, F. S., Hefferline, R. F., & Goodman, P. (1951). *Gestalt therapy.* New York, NY: Julian Press.

Piper, W. E. (2008). Underutilization of short-term group therapy: Enigmatic or understandable? *Psychotherapy Research, 18,* 127–138. doi:10.1080/10503300701867512

Pipes, R., & Davenport, D. (1999). *Introduction to psychotherapy: Common clinical wisdom* (2nd ed.). Needham Heights, MA: Allyn & Bacon.

Plutchik, R., Conte, H. R., & Karasu, T. B. (1994). Critical incidents in psychotherapy. *American Journal of Psychotherapy, 48,* 75–84.

Poortinga, Y. H. (1990). Toward a conceptualization of culture for psychology. *Cross-Cultural Psychology Bulletin, 24,* 2–10.

Pope, K. S. (1994). *Sexual involvement with therapists: Patient assessment, subsequent therapy, forensics.* Washington, DC: American Psychological Association. doi:10.1037/10154-000

Pope, K. S., Keith-Spiegel, P., & Tabachnick, B. (1986). Sexual attraction to clients: The human therapist and the (sometimes) inhuman training system. *American Psychologist, 41,* 147–158. doi:10.1037/0003-066X.41.2.147

Pope, K. S., Sonne, J. L., & Holroyd, J. (1993). *Sexual feelings in psychotherapy: Explorations for therapists and therapists-in-training.* Washington, DC: American Psychological Association. doi:10.1037/10124-000

Pope, K. S., & Tabachnick, B. (1993). Therapists' anger, hate, fear, and sexual feelings: National survey of therapists' responses, client characteristics, critical events, formal complaints, and training. *Professional Psychology: Research and Practice, 24,* 142–152. doi:10.1037/0735-7028.24.2.142

Prochaska, J. O., DiClemente, C. C., & Norcross, J. C. (1992). In search of how people change: Applications to addictive behavior. *American Psychologist, 47,* 1102–1114. doi:10.1037/0003-066X.47.9.1102

Prochaska, J. O., Norcross, J. C., & DiClemente, C. C. (1994). *Changing for good.* New York, NY: Guilford Press.

Prochaska, J. O., Norcross, J. C., & DiClemente, C. C. (2005). Stages of change: Prescriptive guidelines. In G. P. Koocher, J. C. Norcross, & S. S. Hill (Eds.), *Psychologists' desk reference* (2nd ed., pp. 226–231). New York, NY: Oxford University Press.

Regan, A. M., & Hill, C. E. (1992). Investigation of what clients and counselors do not say in brief therapy. *Journal of Counseling Psychology, 39*, 168–174. doi:10.1037/0022-0167.39.2.168

Reid, J. R., & Finesinger, J. E. (1952). The role of insight in psychotherapy. *The American Journal of Psychiatry, 108*, 726–734.

Reik, T. (1935). *Surprise and the psychoanalyst.* London, England: Routledge.

Reik, T. (1948). *Listening with the third ear.* New York, NY: Grove.

Rennie, D. L. (1994). Clients' deference in psychotherapy. *Journal of Counseling Psychology, 41*, 427–437. doi:10.1037/0022-0167.41.4.427

Rhodes, R. H., Hill, C. E., Thompson, B. J., & Elliott, R. (1994). Client retrospective recall of resolved and unresolved misunderstanding events. *Journal of Counseling Psychology, 41*, 473–483. doi:10.1037/0022-0167.41.4.473

Richardson, M. S. (1993). Work in people's lives: A location for counseling psychologists. *Journal of Counseling Psychology, 40*, 425–433. doi:10.1037/0022-0167.40.4.425

Rimm, D. C., & Masters, J. C. (1979). *Behavior therapy: Techniques and empirical findings.* New York, NY: Academic Press.

Robitschek, C. G., & McCarthy, P. R. (1991). Prevalence of counselor self-reference in the therapeutic dyad. *Journal of Counseling & Development, 69*, 218–221. doi:10.1002/j.1556-6676.1991.tb01490.x

Rogers, C. R. (1942). *Counseling and psychotherapy.* Boston, MA: Houghton Mifflin.

Rogers, C. R. (1951). *Client-centered therapy: Its current practice, implications, and theory.* Boston, MA: Houghton Mifflin.

Rogers, C. R. (1957). The necessary and sufficient conditions of therapeutic personality change. *Journal of Consulting Psychology, 21*, 95–103. doi:10.1037/h0045357

Rogers, C. R. (1959). A theory of therapy, personality, and interpersonal relationships, as developed in the client-centered framework. In S. Koch (Ed.), *Psychology: A study of a science: Vol. 3. Formulations of the person and the social context* (pp. 184–256). New York, NY: McGraw-Hill.

Rogers, C. R. (Ed.). (1967). *The therapeutic relationship and its impact: A study of psychotherapy with schizophrenics.* Madison: University of Wisconsin Press.

Rogers, C. R. (1980). *A way of being.* Boston, MA: Houghton Mifflin.

Rogers, C. R., & Dymond, R. (1954). *Psychotherapy and personality change.* Chicago, IL: University of Chicago Press.

Rose, A. J., Carlson, W., & Waller, E. M. (2007). Prospective associations of co-rumination with friendship and emotional adjustment: Considering the socio-emotional trade-offs of co-rumination. *Developmental Psychology, 43*, 1019–1031. doi:10.1037/0012-1649.43.4.1019

Rosenthal, R., Hall, J. A., DiMatteo, M. R., Rogers, P. L., & Archer, D. (1979). *Sensitivity to nonverbal communication: The PONS test.* Baltimore, MD: Johns Hopkins University Press.

Rudd, M. D., Joiner, T. E., Jobes, D. A., & King, C. A. (1999). The outpatient treatment of suicidality: An integration of science and recognition of its limitations. *Professional Psychology: Research and Practice, 30,* 437–446. doi:10.1037/0735-7028.30.5.437

Safran, J. D., & Muran, J. C. (2000). *Negotiating the therapeutic alliance: A relational treatment guide.* New York, NY: Guilford Press.

Safran, J. D., Muran, J. C., Samstag, L. W., & Stevens, C. (2002). Repairing alliance ruptures. In J. C. Norcross (Ed.), *Psychotherapy relationships that work: Therapist contributions and responsiveness to patients* (pp. 235–254). Oxford, England: Oxford University Press.

Satir, V. M. (1988). *The new peoplemaking.* Palo Alto, CA: Science and Behavior Books.

Savickas, M. L. (1994). Vocational psychology in the postmodern era: Comment on Richardson (1993). *Journal of Counseling Psychology, 41,* 105–107. doi:10.1037/0022-0167.41.1.105

Scheel, M. J., Hanson, W. E., & Razzhavaikina, T. I. (2004). The process of recommending homework in psychotherapy: A review of therapist delivery methods, client acceptability, and factors that affect compliance. *Psychotherapy: Theory, Research, Practice, Training, 41,* 38–55.

Scheel, M. J., Seaman, S., Roach, K., Mullin, T., & Mahoney, K. B. (1999). Client implementation of therapist recommendations predicted by client perception of fit, difficulty of implementation, and therapist influence. *Journal of Counseling Psychology, 46,* 308–316. doi:10.1037/0022-0167.46.3.308

Segal, Z. V., Williams, J. M. G., & Teasdale, J. D. (2002). *Mindfulness-based cognitive therapy for depression.* New York, NY: Guilford Press.

Segall, M. H. (1979). *Cross-cultural psychology.* Monterey, CA: Brooks-Cole.

Shakespeare, W. (1980). *Macbeth.* New York, NY: Bantam. (Original work published 1623)

Shapiro, E. G. (1984). Help-seeking: Why people don't. *Research in the Sociology of Organizations, 3,* 213–236.

Sileo, R. J., & Kopala, M. (1993). An A-B-C-D-E worksheet for promoting beneficence when considering ethical values. *Counseling and Values, 37,* 89–95. doi:10.1002/j.2161-007X.1993.tb00800.x

Simon, J. C. (1988). Criteria for therapist self-disclosure. *American Journal of Psychotherapy, 42,* 404–415.

Singer, E. (1970). *New concepts in psychotherapy.* New York, NY: Basic Books.

Skinner, B. F. (1953). *Science and human behavior.* New York, NY: Macmillan.

Skovholt, T. M., & Jennings, L. (2004). *Master therapists: Exploring expertise in therapy and counseling.* New York, NY: Pearson/Allyn & Bacon.

Skovholt, T. M., & Rivers, D. A. (2003). *Skills and procedures of helping.* Denver, CO: Love.

Smith, E. W. L. (1998). A taxonomy and ethics of touch. In E. W. Smith, P. R. Clance, & S. Imes (Eds.), *Touch in psychotherapy: Theory, research, and practice* (pp. 36–51). New York, NY: Guilford Press.

Smith, M. L., Glass, G. V., & Miller, T. J. (1980). *The benefits of psychotherapy.* Baltimore, MD: Johns Hopkins University Press.

Snyder, J. F., Hill, C. E., & Derksen, T. P. (1972). Why some students do not use university counseling facilities. *Journal of Counseling Psychology, 19,* 263–268. doi:10.1037/h0033075

Spangler, P. Hill, C. E., Dunn, M. G., Hummel, A., Walden, T., Liu, J., . . . Salahuddin, N. (2013). *Training undergraduate students to use immediacy: Changes in self-efficacy, helpfulness of training components, and predictors of the effects of training.* Manuscript in preparation.

Spangler, P., Hill, C. E., Mettus, C., Guo, A. H., & Heymsfield, L. (2009). Therapist perspectives on the dreams about clients: A qualitative investigation. *Psychotherapy Research, 19,* 81–95. doi:10.1080/10503300802430665

Speisman, J. C. (1959). Depth of interpretation and verbal resistance in psychotherapy. *Journal of Consulting Psychology, 23,* 93–99. doi:10.1037/h0047679

Spence, D. P., Dahl, H., & Jones, E. E. (1993). Impact of interpretation on associative freedom. *Journal of Consulting and Clinical Psychology, 61,* 395–402. doi:10.1037/0022-006X.61.3.395

Spokane, A. R. (1989). Are there psychological and mental health consequences of difficult career decisions? *Journal of Career Development, 16,* 19–23.

Stadter, M. (1996). *Object relations brief therapy: The therapeutic relationship in short-term work.* Northvale, NJ: Jason Aronson.

Stahl, J., & Hill, C. E. (2008). A comparison of four methods for assessing natural helpers. *Journal of Community Psychology, 36,* 289–298. doi:10.1002/jcop.20195

Stenzel, C. L., & Rupert, P. A. (2004). Psychologists' use of touch in individual psychotherapy. *Psychotherapy: Theory, Research, & Practice, 41,* 332–345. doi:10.1037/0033-3204.41.3.332

Strong, S. R., & Claiborn, C. D. (1982). *Change through interaction: Social psychological processes of counseling and psychotherapy.* New York, NY: Wiley.

Strupp, H. H., & Binder, J. L. (1984). *Psychotherapy in a new key: A guide to time-limited dynamic psychotherapy.* New York, NY: Basic Books.

Strupp, H. H., & Hadley, S. W. (1977). A tripartite model of mental health and therapeutic outcomes: With special reference to negative effects in psychotherapy. *American Psychologist, 32,* 187–196. doi:10.1037/0003-066X.32.3.187

Sue, D., Sue, D. W., & Sue, S. (1994). *Understanding abnormal behavior* (4th ed.). Princeton, NJ: Houghton Mifflin.

Sue, D. W., & Sue, D. (1999). *Counseling the culturally different: Theory and practice* (3rd ed.). New York, NY: Wiley.

Suinn, R. M. (1985). Imagery rehearsal applications to performance enhancement. *The Behavior Therapist, 8,* 155–159.

Summers, R. F., & Barber, J. P. (2010). *Psychodynamic therapy: A guide to evidence-based practice.* New York, NY: Guilford Press.

Sweeney, M. A., & Cottle, W. C. (1976). Nonverbal acuity: A comparison of counselors and noncounselors. *Journal of Counseling Psychology, 23,* 394–397. doi:10.1037/0022-0167.23.4.394

Teyber, E. (2006). *Interpersonal process in psychotherapy: A relational approach* (5th ed.). Pacific Grove, CA: Brooks/Cole.

Thompson, B., & Hill, C. E. (1991). Therapist perceptions of client reactions. *Journal of Counseling and Development, 69,* 261–265.

Tinsley, H. E. A., de St. Aubin, T. M., & Brown, M. T. (1982). College students' help-seeking preferences. *Journal of Counseling Psychology, 29,* 523–533. doi:10.1037/0022-0167.29.5.523

Truax, C. B. (1966). Reinforcement and nonreinforcement in Rogerian psychotherapy. *Journal of Abnormal Psychology, 71,* 1–9. doi:10.1037/h0022912

Truax, C. B., & Carkhuff, R. R. (1967). *Toward effective counseling and psychotherapy.* Chicago, IL: Aldine.

Van den Stock, J., Righart, R., & de Gelder, B. (2007). Body expressions influence recognition of emotions in the face and voice. *Emotion, 7,* 487–494. doi:10.1037/1528-3542.7.3.487

van Wormer, L. (1996). Teaching/learning the language of therapy: Guidelines for teacher and student. *Issues in Social Work Education, 16,* 28–45.

Vivino, B., Thompson, B., Hill, C. E., & Ladany, N. (2009). Compassion in psychotherapy: The perspective of psychotherapists nominated as compassionate. *Psychotherapy Research, 19,* 157–171. doi:10.1080/10503300802430681

Wachtel, P. L. (2008). *Relational theory and the practice of psychotherapy.* New York, NY: Guilford Press.

Wadlinger, H. A., & Isaacowitz, D. M. (2011). Fixing our focus: Training attention to regulate emotion. *Personality and Social Psychology Review, 15,* 75–102. doi:10.1177/1088868310365565

Wampold, B. E. (2001). *The great psychotherapy debate: Models, methods, and findings.* Mahwah, NJ: Erlbaum.

Wampold, B. E., Mondin, G. W., Moody, M., Stich, P., Benson, K., & Ann, H. (1997). A metaanalysis of outcome studies comparing bona fide psychotherapies: Empirically "all must have prizes." *Psychological Bulletin, 122,* 203–215. doi:10.1037/0033-2909.122.3.203

Ward, D. E. (1984). Termination of individual counseling: Concepts and strategies. *Journal of Counseling and Development, 63,* 21–25. doi:10.1002/j.1556-6676.1984.tb02673.x

Waters, D. B., & Lawrence, E. C. (1993). *Competence, courage, and change: An approach to family therapy.* New York, NY: Norton.

Watson, D. L., & Tharp, R. G. (2006). *Self-directed behavior: Self-modification for personal adjustment* (9th ed.). Florence, KY: Cengage Learning.

Watzlawick, P., Weakland, J. H., & Fisch, R. (1974). *Change: Principles of problem formation and problem resolution.* New York, NY: Norton.

Webster, D. W., & Fretz, B. R. (1978). Asian-American, Black and White college students' preference for help-giving sources. *Journal of Counseling Psychology, 25,* 124–130. doi:10.1037/0022-0167.25.2.124

Weiss, J., Sampson, H., & the Mount Zion Psychotherapy Research Group. (1986). *The psychoanalytic process: Theory, clinical observations, and empirical research.* New York, NY: Guilford Press.

Whiston, S. C. (2005). *Principles and applications of assessment in counseling.* Belmont, CA: Thomson, Brooks/Cole.

White, M. (2007). *Maps of narrative practice.* New York, NY: Norton.

Williams, E. N., Hayes, J. A., & Fauth, J. (2008). Therapist self-awareness: Interdisciplinary connections and future directions. *Handbook of counseling psychology* (4th ed., pp. 303–319). New York, NY: Wiley.

Williams, E. N., Hurley, K., O'Brien, K., & DeGregorio, A. (2003). Development and validation of the Self-Awareness and Management Strategies (SAMS) Scales for therapists. *Psychotherapy: Theory, Research, Practice, Training, 40,* 278–288. doi:10.1037/0033-3204.40.4.278

Williams, E. N., Judge, A., Hill, C. E., & Hoffman, M. A. (1997). Experiences of novice therapists in prepracticum: Trainees', clients', and supervisees' perceptions of therapists' personal reactions and management strategies. *Journal of Counseling Psychology, 44,* 390–399. doi:10.1037/0022-0167.44.4.390

Wolfe, B. E. (2005). *Understanding and treating anxiety disorders.* Washington, DC: American Psychological Association.

Wonnell, T. L., & Hill, C. E. (2000). Effects of including the action stage in dream interpretation. *Journal of Counseling Psychology, 47,* 372–379.

Wonnell, T. L., & Hill, C. E. (2002, June). *The action stage and predictors of action in dream interpretation.* Paper presented at the annual meeting of the Society for Psychotherapy Research, Santa Barbara, CA.

Yalom, I. D. (1980). *Existential psychotherapy.* New York, NY: Basic Books.

Yalom, I. D. (1995). *Theory and practice of group psychotherapy* (4th ed.). New York, NY: Basic Books.

Young, M. E. (2001). *Learning the art of helping: Building blocks and techniques.* Upper Saddle River, NJ: Prentice-Hall.

Zunker, V. G. (1994). *Career counseling: Applied concepts and life planning* (4th ed.). Pacific Grove, CA: Brooks/Cole.

Index

About the Author

Clara E. Hill, PhD, earned her doctorate at Southern Illinois University in 1974. She started her career that year as an assistant professor in the Department of Psychology, University of Maryland, and is currently still there as a professor. She has been president of the Society for Psychotherapy Research, editor of the *Journal of Counseling Psychology*, and co-editor of *Psychotherapy Research*. Awards include the Leona Tyler Award (Society of Counseling Psychology), the Distinguished Psychologist Award (Division 29 of the American Psychological Association), the Distinguished Research Career Award (Society for Psychotherapy Research), and the Outstanding Lifetime Achievement Award (Section on Counseling and Psychotherapy Process and Outcome Research, Society for Counseling Psychology). Her major research interests are helping skills, psychotherapy process and outcome, training therapists, dream work, and qualitative research. She has published 187 journal articles, 67 chapters in books, and 11 books (including *Helping Skills, Dream Work in Therapy, Insight in Psychotherapy, Transformation in Psychotherapy,* and *Consensual Qualitative Research*). She is married with two children and one grandchild.

Feedback Form

To the reader of this book:

    I hope that *Helping Skills: Facilitating Exploration, Insight, and Action* (4th ed.), has been useful to you in learning the helping skills. I would like to hear your feedback so that we can improve future editions of the book. Please complete this sheet and send it to me.

Thank you for your help.

Name (optional): _____

School and address: _____

_____

Department: _____

Instructor's name: _____

Name of course for which this book was used: _____

_____

1. What did you like most about this book?

2. What did you like least about this book?

3. In the space below or on a separate sheet of paper, please write specific suggestions for improving this book and anything else that you would like to write about your experience using this book and trying to learn the helping skills.

4. What is the most important or surprising thing you learned about helping skills from reading this book?

Please return this form to:

Clara Hill, PhD
Department of Psychology
University of Maryland, College Park
College Park, MD 20474
Fax: (301) 314-9566
e-mail: cehill@umd.edu